Tijuana Dreaming

TIJUANA DREAMING

Life and Art at the Global Border

EDITED BY JOSH KUN AND FIAMMA MONTEZEMOLO

WITH A FOREWORD BY IAIN CHAMBERS

DUKE UNIVERSITY PRESS
Durham & London 2012

Library of Congress Cataloging-in-Publication Data appear
on the last printed page of this book.

Duke University Press gratefully acknowledges the support of the
Duke University Center for International Studies' Globalization
and the Artist Project, which provided funds toward the
production of this book.

---➤ CONTENTS

We would like to thank all of the contributors for sharing their work with this collection and for their patience and diligence in helping us make it a reality.

All translations were done by John Pluecker, except for "The Line," which was translated by Cecilia Bastida, and "Counterculture, Rockers, Punks, New Romantics, and Mods in Tijuana," which was translated by John Farrell.

Special thanks are due to Inna Arzumanova of the USC Annenberg School for Communication and Journalism for overseeing the chief organizational and administrative tasks required in preparing the volume for publication.

Fiamma Montezemolo wishes to thank the Transart Foundation for the grant that allowed her to complete her conversation with Néstor García Canclini in Chapter 5.

Because this volume collects new and previously published work into a single collection for the first time, a number of these essays have had previous lives elsewhere and are reprinted here by permission: Fiamma Montezemolo, "Tijuana: Hybridity and Beyond: A Conversation with Néstor García Canclini," in *Third Text* 23:6 (2009), 733–50; Guillermo Fadanelli, "La Cancion de Tijuana," in *Revista Nexos* no. 359 (Mexico City, November 2007); Ejival, "Counterculture, Rocks, Punks, New Romantics, and Mods in Tijuana," in *Strange New World: Art and Design from Tijuana / Extrano Nuevo Mundo: Arte y Diseno Desde Tijuana*, ed. Rachel Teagle (Museum of Contemporary Art San Diego, 2006); Jennifer Insley, "Redefining Sodom: A Latter-Day Vision of Tijuana," in *Mexican Studies / Estudios Mexicanos* 20:1 (Berkeley: University of California Press, 2004), 99–121; Jesse Lerner, "Borderline Archeology," in *Cabinet: A Quarterly of Art and Culture* 13 (New York: Immaterial Incorporated, 2004), 33–35; Santiago Vaquera, "Postcards from the Border: In Tijuana, Revolución Is an Avenue," in *Border Transits: Literature and Culture across the Line*, ed. Ana M. Manzanas (Amsterdam: Rodopi Press, 2007); Kathryn Kopinak, "Globalization in Tijuana Maquiladoras: Using Historical Antecedents and Migration to Test Globalization Models," in *Papeles de Población* 9:37 (Centro de Investigación y Estudios Avanzados de la Población [CIEAP], at the Universidad

Autónoma del Estado de México, Toluca, 2003), 219–42; Michelle Téllez, "Community of Struggle: Gender, Violence, and Resistance on the US-Mexico Border," in *Gender and Society* 22 (October 2008); and Luis Humberto Crosthwaite, "La Línea," in *Instrucciones Para Cruzar La Frontera* (Joaquin Mortiz, 2003).

The following were first published in Spanish and have been translated for this volume by permission of the authors: Heriberto Yépez, *Tijuanologías* (Mexico: Umbral-Universidad Autonoma de Baja California Press, 2006); Roberto Castillo Udiarte, *Elamoroso guaguaguá* (Tijuana: UIA/El Día Ediciones, 2002); Tito Alegría Olazábal, "¿Existen las metrópolis transfronterizas? El caso de Tijuana/San Diego," in *Ciudades en la frontera*, ed. Haroldo Dilla (Santo Domingo: Editorial Manatí, 2008), 127–65; and Rafa Saavedra, "Crossfader Playlist."

A Line in the Sand

> For the phenomena that interest me are precisely those that blur these bound-
> aries, cross them, and make their historical artifice appear, also their violence,
> meaning the relations of force that are concentrated there and actually capi-
> talize themselves there interminably. —JACQUES DERRIDA, *Monolingualism*
> *of the Other; or, The Prosthesis of Origin*

Back in the days of modern nation building and the accompanying outreach of empire, many lines were drawn in the sand. Invariably straight as a die, oblivious of the social and natural ecologies on the ground, frontiers, borders, and distinctions were drawn up on maps in the Foreign Offices and State Departments of London, Paris, Berlin, and Washington. Much of today's world is witness to the physical and cultural violence of these abstract divisions unilaterally established in distant metropoles. Look at the map. Once out of Europe and the Northern Hemisphere, the modern invention of nation and border is mirrored in straight lines running all over Africa and the Middle East (in Asia older inheritances often deviated that logic). This, too, was the case with the frontier established in Southern California drawn between the United States and Mexico. It runs between the confluence of the Gila and Colorado rivers and the Pacific, and was established after Mexico's defeat and the subsequent treaty of Guadalupe Hidalgo in 1848. The treaty registered the appropriation of 1.36 million square kilometers of territory by the aggressive northern, slave-owning, imperial neighbor. While the U.S. Army occupied Mexico City, La Intervención Norteamericana led to the incorporation of what is today the southwestern United States: New Mexico, Colorado, Arizona, Nevada, Utah, Wyoming, California.

Acts of violence, invariably sanctified by "law," establish a place, give it a name, and sanctify its authority. In all of these cases, the colonial cut has produced a postcolonial wound. While the Euro-American "winners" who wrote the history of these events (Walter Benjamin) remain self-assured in their political and cultural authority to define and explain subsequent developments, the "losers," the defeated, the subaltern, find themselves invariably operating within spaces and languages they had rarely chosen. If, according to Heidegger, space acquires significance only when it is transformed into a particular place, both space and place, as Henri Lefebvre argued, are never given but always socially produced. So if from high above the Southern California coastline from Los Angeles to Tijuana seemingly represents a unified urban sprawl, oblivious to border legislation and national confines, close-up we inevitably encounter a very different story.

Here we discover the power of architecture to carve and articulate the land in a multiplicity of borders and confines. The power of architecture to mold, modify, and morph a territory reveals the architecture of power: it is never merely a technical, neutral, or "scientific" language.

In border zones, such as that between Israel and the Occupied Territories, it promotes a set of social and historical practices that lead to what Eyal Weizman calls a "laboratory of the extreme" and a "dynamic morphology of the frontier." The territory, Weizman continues, is never as flat as a map, but striated beneath our feet (aquifers, land rights) and above our heads (air corridors, electromagnetic waves full of radio signals, cellular phone networks, GPS positioning, wide-band computer communications). The situation in the Occupied Territories is exemplary rather than exceptional. Similar procedures scan the Mediterranean, just as they patrol the U.S.-Mexico border. Maps are multiple, simultaneously vertical and horizontal: a three-dimensional matrix. They produce flexible, mobile frontiers that sustain invisible lines and shifting configurations of material and immaterial territory. So frontiers are not only physical, but also mobile and flexible instances of authority. The classical colonial modality of impositions from the center on the periphery through the direct imposition of a singular power and authority now gives way to an altogether more diffuse appropriation. This promotes a new conceptual landscape that invites us to consider how the order of power is inscribed, articulated, and becomes in multidimensional space.

Borders are violently imposed, are signs of power, but they are also critically and culturally productive. The border is a framing device that gives shape and sense to what it contains, what it seeks to include and exclude. If the border ushers in an instance of the exceptional state—each and every one finds his or her biographical status and citizenship temporally suspended before being reconfirmed (or challenged)—it reveals, in the very intensity of its biopolitics, the underlying protocols that define and confine its own domestic population. Borders force us to reconsider the historical, political, and cultural configurations that gave rise to their necessity. They bring back into the picture what they were previously designed to exclude: the defeated, the subaltern, the other; other histories, other territories of belonging and becoming, push up against this seemingly impassable framing. If legally rigid, borders are historically fluid and socially complex: for some they represent simply stamps on a passport, for others an apparently impossible barrier, yet every day they continue to be crossed, and hence simultaneously challenged and confirmed, in both legal and illegal fashion.

In 2000 the Chilean artist Alfredo Jaar staged a forty-five-minute event on the Mexican-U.S. border at Valle Del Matador (Tijuana–San Diego) titled "The Cloud." The cloud, composed of hundreds of white balloons, was released to float high up over the fence, impervious to the 3,000 U.S. Border Patrol agents along the sixty-six-mile frontier in San Diego County, as a tribute to the thousands who have lost their lives trying to cross this line in the desert. Music was played both sides of the border, poetry read, and a moment of silence observed. Despite the massive investment in militarized personnel and sophisticated surveillance devices in this war zone, the frontier was evoked, mourned, and temporarily punctured. For the frontier, both to those who seek at all costs to maintain it and to those who seek to overcome and subvert its arbitrary division, has many dimensions. The blind rigidity of its bureaucracy is increasingly accompanied by a fluidity and flexibility in its application.

To leave familiar territory and cross the frontier is somehow to enter a shadow land where familiar rules come undone. Moving among the unknown, confronting one's fears and exposure, the frontier crossing is not only that characterized in the northern imagination by existential uncertainties and a "touch of evil" south of the border; for the vast majority migrating into the north of the world, border crossings are a zone of potential death and subsequently of guaranteed exploitation. If much study and critical writing on border zones has concentrated on these inhuman conditions, it has rarely sought to examine the premises and privileges of its own world in the cruel light of this structural reality that represents an undeclared war on the poor of the planet. The disciplinary imperative has been precisely that: disciplinary. The desire has been to render the unknown transparent to one's intellectual and cultural will. To explain has somehow meant to annul a potential disturbance and bring it all home, rationally reduced to domestic reason and subordinated to one's view of the world. Yet borders, beyond the obvious installation of authority, surveillance, and control, exist only in the act of being crossed. Borders are brought to life, and acquire their performative power, only when they are traversed, transgressed, and trespassed; in other words, they are not simply the sites of the hegemonic power imposing the reach of its law, but also of other, subaltern, subversive, and subterranean powers constantly pushing up against the fence, and sometimes crossing over.

If so many of today's borders represent postcolonial wounds, *una herida abierta* (Gloria Anzaldúa) bleeds into the accounting of time and place both sides of the cut. There persists proximity, even communality, often denied, negated, and repressed by those who feel their history is the unique narrative, which proposes an unsuspected cartography for traveling into border zones. The sociological, anthropological, and political mapping of such confines invariably fails to chart the full significance of this unauthorized space and associated practices. Beyond political reasoning, there is a poetics of sound and vision, of music, literature, and the visual arts, that proposes modalities of narrating a multiple modernity irreducible to the homogeneous attention of border control. The inscription of these other languages on the metropolitan body of modernity propels us into considering the disquieting annihilation of distance—both physical and metaphysical—between worlds once considered different and apart, but now suspended and sustained in a shared planetary matrix. These are also critical proximities. Such borders do not merely propose casting our attention to the previously abandoned margins of a modernity unilaterally conceived, those distant confines out there in the periphery far from the centers of our concern, but rather, and altogether more radically, invest our very understanding of modernity. Once-separated worlds—the first and the third, the north and the south of the planet, the rich and the poor—now exceed their confines.

Moving in circuits that simultaneously lie below and beyond the national frame—those of the visual arts, of local acts that travel in transnational literary and visual languages or in sound—connections and communities are formed. Modernity is blogged, temporarily caught in a snapshot, faded in and out and pasted together; it is translated and transformed in the transit of local coordinates and conditions. Subsequent versions also travel elsewhere. Despite the unequal and unjust access to the means of cultural reproduction, each and every take leaves a trace, produces a fold, creates an unsuspected intensity, forms a friction, in a modernity that is not only ours to manage and define. The once-background "noise" of the "outside" world here becomes an altogether more insistent sound. It acquires sense and shape in a modernity that branches out in a heterogeneous assemblage. Orchestrated by power, certainly, but those powers are not only those of existing planetary hegemony. The previously silenced, excluded, negated, and ignored also inhabit this space, proposing their sense of place.

Meanwhile, in Tijuana, on the border, in a city of at least 1.5 million souls, such abstract concerns acquire life and directions, and with them deviation and drift. The processes are not prescriptive; they refer to practices and potential. The violence of modern state formation, the rough justice of border settlements, and the multiple currents and eddies of a hybridizing modernity are obviously condensed in the configurations of this frontier city. Of course, but daily textures, the issues and tissues of both politics and poetics, the criss-crossing of global capital, crime and the corruption of power, not only draw Tijuana close to Los Angeles, London, and Tokyo, but transform its presumed "border" condition into an unsuspected critical space that casts its own particular light into the heart of modernity itself.

In this altogether more fluid reality where presumed peripheries and margins propose an urgent centrality, the border itself reveals its unnerving duplicity. Whose border is it? Each side of the confine claims it. While El Norte reinforces its authority on this space with a multimillion-dollar industry in surveillance and policing, it is nevertheless still unable to fully contain it or suppress its disquieting phantoms. Not only do drugs and undocumented labor continue to cross its confines, but both southern traffic and border disturbance continually interrogate the cage that simultaneously seeks to keep the South out and the North in. The frontier not only creates the figure of the foreigner who is excluded, it also constitutes, limits, and defines the very nature of what exists inside the frontier, what lies repressed in the domestic scene. In this ambivalence, all the premises—from patrolling the border to those disciplines that pretend to explain its histories and contemporary conditions—are exposed to unauthorized questioning.

From considerations of Tijuana as a border city we are pushed into thinking the whole world as a multiplicity of border zones, traversed by legislation, enforcement, and bureaucracy, and then complicated by the unaccounted histories and cultures embodied in the migrancy of unauthorized bodies and cultures. If, most obviously, we encounter this situation and its arbitrary violence in the southwestern desert of the United States, along the northern edges of the Sahara and on the waters of the Mediterranean Sea, on both sides of the English Channel, in the ambivalent territories of Palestine and Kurdistan, between Asia and Australia in the Timor Sea, it is too easy to forget that these borders also run through the streets, tongues, arrangements, and divisions of first-world cities. The multiethnic populations of Los Angeles, London, and Paris are also researched, profiled, and policed, for even if these populations are certainly resident in the nation they are frequently considered to be not fully part of the nation. The externally exercised biopolitics of yesterday's colonial administration has not so much disappeared as transmuted into the techno-logically sustained, and hence hypothetically altogether more flexible, man-agement of the modern political body of the occidental metropolis.

At the same time, ongoing attempts to legislate and control space, to maintain the distinction between inside and outside, is constructed on a mo-bile terrain where categories and definitions continually slip into sites of contestation: space is never empty, it is invariably peopled and folded into multiple and multilateral processes of social becoming. The desire for trans-parency and rational control—by both government authorities and academic disciplines—is always destined to be thwarted, no matter what are the terri-ble short-time consequences in terms of lives and suffering.

There exist unregistered tempos and spaces that deviate and befuddle the accountable logic of linear time, of progress and its ideology of accumulative productivity. In the drift across the border of rational management and over the categorical divide, beyond the conceptual limits of prescribed histories, cultures, and identities, there exists a fiesta of multiplicity that challenges the homogeneous accounting of time and space.

What is being entertained here is the undoing and dispersal—not the can-cellation—of an earlier configuration of knowledge, leading, in turn, to the unwinding of the legislative authority of the Northern Hemisphere (the West) as the unique Subject of History. This is to propel thinking into uncharted territory. To borrow a metaphor from urban geography, it suggests a vast and indefinite area—like the sprawling urban slums and shantytowns of Tijuana, Rio, Lagos, Cairo, or Istanbul, peopled by a complex, anonymous, marginal-ized underclass neither recognized as urban nor as rural—which lies between disciplinary definitions and other modalities of knowledge. If the former present themselves in terms of an epistemic configuration that pretends to impose itself universally and hence unilaterally, the latter, as a heterogeneous and unsystematic interrogation of that configuration, sets a limit, proposing an insistent border that provokes a transit, a transformation, an interrogative elsewhere. In this, Tijuana is profoundly global. While caught in the net of a political economy that sprawls across continents and seas, where labor is not national but transnational and always shadowed and disciplined by a reserve army of "illegal" immigrants, the net, as the Italian philosopher Gianni Vat-timo once pointed out, is also full of holes.

Caught in a global calculus, Tijuana also brings to the equation unknown factors. Halting the idea of rhizomatic and intercultural patterns for a mo-ment, we can witness how heterogeneous elements, processes, and flows co-alesce in a precise critical instance like Walter Benjamin's dialectical image that flares up in a moment of danger: there to register the unanswered questions, the questions that perhaps will never be answered but which continue to haunt our language and understanding. Here it is language itself that provokes a further opening in the net. Torn away from the empirical medium of transparent communication imposed by the Anglophone world, language swells with signification, and border cities, where seemingly different historical blocs and cultural configurations push up against each other, become overloaded paradigms of an excess of sense. Here the explosion of ethnographic detail is decanted into aesthetic inscription.

For it is poetics, as the custodian of the excess of language (literary, visual, sonorial, performative), that most profoundly registers the inscription of time and place. Following the sound, listening to the prose, the poetry, and the poetical, caught in the visual frame, we are pushed into another space, another "Tijuana," that is irreducible to sociological statistics, historical explanation, and political management. The cultural dimension is not here an adjunct or accessory to the sociohistorical matrix, but is rather a critical apparatus in its own right. In its reassembling practices and procedures, art proposes new conditions for receiving the "social," the "historical," and the "political." The reassembling, as Walter Benjamin pointed out, referring to the task of translation as piecing together the fragments of language, does not arrive at constituting a new totality. The fragments are freed from their previous unity, and are left to find another arrangement.

This is the unsuspected power of language whatever its provenance. It proposes a potentiality: not only a way of being in the world, but also one of becoming. It is precisely on this cusp that art seeds a political inheritance with a poetical interruption, drawing out of the folds of time and memory, other, unsuspected patterns and paths. This is to suggest that we respond and locate ourselves in the arts in terms of a critical configuration that exceeds the prescribed social location as "art," "aesthetics," or "entertainment." A slash across the continuity of common sense is affected. For we are invariably taught to consider the text, the printed page, the performance, particularly of subaltern cultural formations, as the social and cultural mirror of reality (however complicated the reflection), and hence as a relatively stable object of study and attention. Yet language as literature, as a transformative poetics, as sound, is itself a reality that invests us with the imperative to reconsider and review the very terms of aesthetical and ethical sense; that is, to rethink the very conditions of "reality." This, to propose a Deleuzian figure, is a "line of flight" that permits the escape of postcolonial art and literature from the perpetual cycle of cultural representation, repression, and resistance. It is to transform the noted Bhabhian concept of a "third space" into a dynamic, unfolding vector in which the very terms of inherited understanding are exposed to a questioning they have neither foreseen nor authorized. At this point, the literary, the poetical, the artistic provide the cardinal points of a new critical compass: one that promotes a diverse navigation of a planetary, but differentiated, modernity.

Here the city, its form, function, and future, is split open, exposed to unsuspected winds. Fragmented, cut up, translated, sampled, and remixed, the solidity of the city as social and historical edifice cracks under the heterogeneous requests of its own multiplying archive. Domestic elements migrate into new configurations of sense, become strangers to themselves. They propose the undisciplined extension of practices and analyses that breach the boundaries of the existing authorization of knowledge, evacuating local, national, and disciplinary grounds. This suggests that in order to explain the "logic" of contemporary Tijuana in a cross-disciplinary and intercultural manner, that is, to respond to its mobile textures, grammar, and unfolding languages, we need to veer away from habitual referents toward a more experimental series of ethnographies that emerge in the interstices of new cultural configurations. In order to look at the city, rather than merely see it, there are many roads that can be taken. Some are subject to dense cultural traffic; others propose isolated, but perhaps exemplary, encounters. We are often forced to slow down, get out and observe close up, other times to catch distant profiles in the mirror. The trip is always incomplete and inconclusive: it is a critical journey. What, in the performative instances of multiple metropolitan languages, is forcibly brought home is that the old imperial distances of center and periphery have evaporated. There may well be other, altogether more flexible, discriminatory practices and economies that have replaced that stern logic, but there is now also a significant proximity and communality sustained in an urban global grammar that seeds both differences and interdependence. In this sense, a border city like Tijuana, just like the Pakistani city of Peshawar on the North-West Frontier (its three million population swelled with Pashtun Afghan refugees), is saturated with its own variations of the signs and sounds of planetary modernity, and brimming with the violent economies of illegal migration and frontier life. Such cities suggestively replace Walter Benjamin's Paris to propose themselves as the new paradigmatic "capitals" of the twentieth-first century.

The violence of the line, the brutality of borders, and the fetishization of frontiers is obviously a deeply reductive framing of social and historical space. An ecodynamics would of course situate such limits and teach us something different. An eagle hovering in the hot air currents over the Iranian desert near the Pakistan border, like its cousin, along with the coyote, the whale, and the butterfly in northern Mexico and the southwestern United States are all humanistically appropriated but ultimately unredeemed by their diverse linguistic and national denominations. A similar fluidity lies in the unlicensed journeys of the artwork. It is this precise edge, where poetics suggests another politics, which provokes an often-unsuspected critical language. Here artistic practices are not simply modalities of historical witnessing and testimony, but rather, in proposing configurations of time and space, establish the places of another critical cartography. The realities of Tijuana come to be mapped, surveyed, visited, and lived differently, diversely, anew. An inheritance is reworked, an archive remixed, a city rendered mobile by maps it had not previously recognized nor certified. In this sense, Tijuana proposes a model of the unsettled becoming of a modernity that invests not only its own particular body and borders but also the multiple reach of the planetary languages in which it is suspended and sustained.

In this there lies the postcolonial return of the repressed as every metropolis becomes a potential migrant zone, crossed and cut up by a multiple series of borders. The previously excluded now reemerges within to reconfigure the economical, social, and cultural profile of the modern city. There is, as Michel de Certeau observed some time ago, no "outside." Modernity itself is not a quality to be controlled, defended, and defined, but rather an ongoing urban grammar that worlds the world, collaging differences and communalities. Here in the complex prism of individual places, we encounter a modernity that no longer merely mirrors a single reasoning, but rather proposes variants in which local syntax exists and persists as a critical challenge and an ongoing interrogation. In the coeval, but unequal and unjust, mix of planetary modernity, it now becomes impossible to chart a simple hierarchy of development and "progress." Here the classical distinction between tradition and modernity dissolves into another space; an assumed linearity breaks up in an altogether more fluid series of dynamics in which tradition and locality, as sites of translation and transformation, live on and engage with the surrounding world from within modernity itself: the faith healer with the cell phone. This suggests that it is crucial to unbind both critical and poetical narratives from linear time. Development in the non-European world is also always, as it has been for five hundred years, about planetary locations and their possibilities. The so-called south of the world is always already within modernity.

Such a change in perspective retrieves subjects and societies from the seemingly impossible race of modernity: not yet there, almost there, hopelessly behind. It emerges in the wake of the theoretical leap proposed by the Sardinian intellectual Antonio Gramsci, and more recently reproposed by the Palestinian critic Edward Said. For both thinkers, the political, cultural, and historical struggle lies not between modernity and tradition, but rather between hegemony and the subaltern. From this 180-degree shift in cultural coordinates there emerges a radical revaluation of the dynamic and always inconclusive sense of culture. Recognizing in resistance, deviance, and drift the conditions of critique, it becomes possible to register the powers that seek both to configure and to contest the "common sense" of hegemony. On the cusp of this scenario, Tijuana lies both at the "third-world" end of Latin America and at the beginning of the "American Dream." In terms of its positionality and as a contemporary metropolitan proposition, contemporary Tijuana continues to rehearse Frantz Fanon's provocative reassembling of worldly relationships when in *The Wretched of the Earth* he declared that the first world was literally the creation of the third world. The dream, power, wealth, freedom, and hegemony are structurally sustained by what they exclude, negate, and repress. We now clearly find ourselves moving in dimensions that exceed contemporary cosmopolitanism, tapping complex asymmetries of power that break the boundaries of comfortable definitions, abstract securities, and the reassuring logic of transparent representation.

In the montage of the metropolis yet to come, sounds and signs betray simple mapping. They propose not so much "authentic" views of the "real" Tijuana as the altogether more disquieting deflection of inherited languages and definitions as they come to be folded into the unsuspected materialities of life. A further take, another combination, an unplanned idiom, wrenches modernity out of its abstract state (and hegemonic universalism) and decants its possibilities into the idiolectical realization of a particular configuration of place. What comes from elsewhere, from south of the border, potentially disrupts and ultimately reworks a modernity that if now worldly no longer depends only on a privileged part of the planet for its legitimacy. Over the border, across the line, in the "unconscious," lies the challenge of the opaque, the unseen, and the unrecognized: not the irrational but further "reasons" that are irreducible to a single, however powerful, rationality.

This is the crack in the wall, the hole in the fence, which both betrays and exposes the arrogant pretensions of believing that your (or rather my) culture and history has the unique right to legislate the world. If all of this continues to occur "under Western eyes" (Joseph Conrad), it is certainly no longer only authorized by the West. If the terms are clearly of European provenance (*literature, art, aesthetics, nation*), they are at the same time subjected to the transformative practices of "deterritorialization" and "reterritorialization." In their local accents and flexible cadences the transit and translation of such terms expose a planetary promise and potential that denies their points of "origin." Further, it leads to the uncomfortable realization that "my" culture and history is not only mine. Despite the barriers, the controls, the surveillance, and the disciplinary protocols, my space has been invaded, contaminated, creolized, translated, and transformed into a planetary syntax that provides a home for a thousand dialects, a million idioms. This leads to emerging languages formed in the inconclusive transit of time, on the threshold of place, in the mobility induced by a worldly becoming.

At this point, in Tijuana, on the border, neither the reconfiguration of existing critical dispositions nor the reconfirmation of the logics of a planetary political economy provides sufficient explanation. There is now the necessity of a critical and cultural disengagement from the existing lexicon of sense. The latter, as hegemonic reality, as institutional power and disciplinary language, is not, however, simply canceled; rather, it comes to be exposed to interrogations it has never authorized. That particular occidental inheritance, and the universalist pretensions of its archive, now spills out into a critical field that is also inhabited by others. Those who were once the "objects" of an anthropological, sociological, literary, historical, and aesthetic gaze are now "subjects" who refuse to inhabit those categories passively. Here, crossing the border, cutting the conceptual fence and exiting from the disciplinary frame, the work in this volume may begin to teach us how to begin to live, to work, to think and become in a world that does not simply mirror our passage. It is precisely here, contrasting the inventive fluidity of lived responses to the abstract rigidity of occidental classification that an intercultural critique is rendered possible. Historical, cultural, and political sense is not a category but, evoking a lineage that runs from Ibn Khaldûn through Giambattista Vico to Marx and Gramsci, a shifting constellation of practices. These, as they are here enacted in the unfolding complexities of contemporary Tijuana, force the world into an opening that cannot be reduced to a single version pretending universal validity.

Josh Kun and Fiamma Montezemolo

The Factory of Dreams

> Tijuana is an industrial park on the outskirts of Minneapolis. Tijuana is a colony of Tokyo. Tijuana is a Taiwanese sweatshop. —RICHARD RODRIGUEZ, *Days of Obligation*

> My city is not only a street full of stupid gringos living an endless summer and two-colored Indians who sell paper flowers, of striped donkeys and suitcases full of cheap jewelry, of broken sad eyes with a Sony videocamera, of terraces full of motherfuckers who take poppers and kiss the ground looking for a Mexican señorita. . . . My city is a cage of illusions full of mirrors, wise poets and wannabe pop stars. Poverty is in the suburbs and God is in every church, in the digital spots of the TV.—RAFA SAAVEDRA, *Buten Smileys*

> There are many Tijuanas. Each one of them is half myth, half temporarily out of service. —HERIBERTO YÉPEZ, A.B.U.R.T.O.

There were dancers in matching red-and-yellow mechanic suits balancing on rusting steel railings. There were DJs tweaking mixing boards, blasting cavernous dub from hollowed-out Volkswagen vans. Abandoned auto parts became makeshift sculptures. Spray-paint stencils of wrenches and demolished cars covered four stories of towering cement walls. There were television monitors to watch. There were T-shirts to buy.

This was Tijuana in the fall of 2002, at the Nuevo Ferrari *yonke*, or junkyard, on boulevard Díaz Ordaz, where a local artist collective inspired by junkyard aesthetics of rescue and recycling, YONKEart, had organized the Yonke Life party—a multimedia art happening that fell somewhere between a rave and a gallery installation featuring some of the turn-of-the-twenty-first-century Tijuana art and music scene's more familiar names, the street artist Acamonchi and house music specialist Tolo among them. Up on the junkyard roof, beneath the burned-out Ferrari sign and in front of stacks of crushed car frames, an audience of bundled-up young *tijuanenses* sat in upholstered car seats salvaged from Ford Rangers and watched a locally made indie film that ended with a kid telling his father he wants to be a rapper, not a mariachi singer. Off in the distance, Tijuana was a swelling ocean of flickering hillside lights, spilling out in bejeweled waves that seemed to go on forever.

In many ways, YONKEart was a kind of sequel to a similar event held a year earlier, only then the site was not a still-active junkyard, but a no-longer-active jai alai stadium in the heart of the city's main tourist artery, Avenida Revolución. Billed as Maquiladora de Sueños, or Factory of Dreams, it was a party/art show wrapped around a high concept: instead of a maquiladora factory that assembled foreign parts into products for export and foreign consumption, this factory would assemble art and culture for local consumption. The notion was literalized in an installation of grainy photo portraits of women workers from Tijuana's thousands of maquiladora factories accompanied by audio recordings of their self-testimonies of everyday factory life, in a collection of found objects culled from factory floors, and in a live "dream-sweatshop" performance where young women dressed as maquiladora workers assembled packets of wishes and dreams out of spare wires, memory chips, power boards, and PC parts. They were joined by a range of projects that blurred art and life: small-scale architecture models of Tijuana colonias; border checkpoint tourist kitsch made of old computer parts; custom border-transit pants designed by the local art and design company Torolab to accommodate visas, permits, and passports; and a line of "cyber-norteño" clothing that featured high-tech ponchos, Day-Glo mesh serapes, and parachute dresses with vaquero stitching. The artist Jaime Ruiz Otis scavenged maquiladora dumpsters for polyethylene bags and rubber gloves, filled them with foam, and then hung the new creations from the ceiling of the jai alai so they swung above the dance floor like deindustrial pendulums—humble chandeliers of high-finance manufacturing. For Ruiz, the suspended bags were meant to be reminders of labor, hours of brutal, tedious assembly-line work looming over the pleasures of a party.

The event was the brainchild of Pedro Beas, a member of the Nortec Collective, then a six-member group of electronic musicians, producers, and DJs who were rising to local and international fame for their clever merger of electronic dance music with the accordions, tambora, and tuba-laced brass of Mexican norteño and banda sinaloense. After forming in 1999, Nortec's musical and cultural mash had rapidly made them the poster boys for both millennial Tijuana and the city's millennial generation, the software-generated and digitally compressed soundtrack—where traditional and acoustic regional Mexican styles bled into newly minted global club cultures—to a sprawling and combusting border city that was then, as it is now, facing massive challenges in the age of free trade and economic globalization.[1]

Maquiladora de Sueños and Yonke Life were both products of global Tijuana and vibrant, grassroots expressions of it, and they both aspired to translate (and grapple with) the impact of asymmetrical global economics, uneven international information networks, and ravenous neoliberal trade and fiscal policy into locally conceived cultural events and performances. The mergers they represent—between culture and economics, art and politics, the analog and the digital, the infinitely virtual and finitely material, the promise of the global and the pain of the global—are the mergers that helped inspire the impetus for this book. Both events engaged Tijuana as a city of both assemblage and deassemblage, a city of internationally bankrolled industrial parks and three-story, binational chop shops where stripped luxury scrap parts are given new life in the automotive Frankensteins (German-Italian mechanical mutts) that swerve across Tijuana's rotary circles.

Tijuana Dreaming is our attempt to explore the many dimensions of this globally impacted Tijuana, from the mid-sixties up through the futurist digital urbanisms that the Tijuana writer and blogger Rafa Saavedra has called TJ2020.html (we include a "mixtape" of some of Saavedra's self-chosen "greatest hits" here). While scholarship and press on Tijuana has tended to favor either highly utopian ("City of Postmodern Tomorrow," "Artistic Mecca") or highly dystopian ("Global Junkyard," "Slum of Empire") views, we have been inspired by cultural events like Maquiladora de Sueños and Yonke Life in that they live somewhere in the middle and reveal a city that is actively shaping its identity on the rocky ground between culture as global critique and culture as global capital, and between globalization's perils and its tempting, taunting promises.

Tijuana, Reassembled

In recent years, Tijuana has been the subject of numerous battles over definition. "This is Tijuana," one anthology declared, while another insisted that, no, "Here is Tijuana." As Humberto Félix Berumen, a leading Tijuana scholar, shows in his essay that we include here, Tijuana is a city of multiple discourses and archetypes that only relatively recently emerged as a "narratable city," a city of legible narratives and comprehensible ideas. Trendy and appealing for some, horrific and frightening for others, Tijuana has invariably been described, in both print and new media, as "hybrid," "not Mexico," "the End of Latin America and the beginning of the American Dream," "the happiest place on earth," "a laboratory of postmodernity," "a third space," "a porous border," "a Walled City," a "drug capital" on the U.S. travel advisory list.

Historically often a city of passage and increasingly a city of immigrant destination, narco networking, and Homeland Security intensity in post-9/11 geopolitics, contemporary Tijuana is a city of superlatives: Tijuana the most-
crossed space in the world, Tijuana the ugliest city in the world, Tijuana the
most violent, Tijuana the most creative, Tijuana the most dangerous. These
are all, as Heriberto Yépez explains in his contribution here, "Tijuanologies,"
academic theories, cultural myths, and pop culture hyperboles that have
come to be more visible than any of the city's own social realities.

Tijuana lives on multiple maps. Situated at the edge of the Mexican postrevolutionary nationalist imaginary, Tijuana is a waiting room for undocumented migrants from Latin America and continental Mexico and a passage-
way (for anything) to the other side. Situated at the edge of the U.S. national
imaginary, Tijuana has historically been a pleasure playground for the U.S.
tourist in search of cheap, nearby thrills and a financial playground for the
global CEO looking to maximize Pacific Rim profits with cheap nonunion
labor. Or as Santiago Vaquera-Vásquez puts it in his essay here, "Tijuana can
be read as an outpost in the middle world between the first and the third." As
such, it has a vexed relation to any one particular national formation and harbors a singular confluence of cultural differences that nonetheless elude, or
even reject, contemporary notions of cosmopolitanism. Tijuana has emerged
as a unique site for contemplating the drastic and devastating asymmetries
and inequities—the "negative globalization" that is increasingly synonymous
with globalization itself—that characterize the global experience. "Today's
globalization is radically different from its predecessors on one essential
point," Daniel Cohen writes. "It is difficult to be an actor but easy to be a
spectator. . . . The new global economy creates an unprecedented rupture between the expectations to which it gives birth and the reality it brings about."[2]

This collection approaches Tijuana from its coordinates on the map of this
new global economy where liquid flows are put into action only through the
proliferation of immobile partitions, control mechanisms, and security environments (the Tijuana novelist and writer Luis Humberto Crosthwaite gives us
border crossing as border immobility, border flows as border waiting, in his
short story included here). These essays are all aware of Tijuana's place along
what Thomas P. M. Barnett, a former secretary of defense strategist, has
dubbed "the political equator," the dividing line between the world's "func-
tioning core" and its "non-integrating gap" that is guaranteeing that globalization is not actually a global phenomenon.[3] The geographer Harm de Blij
similarly contends that the global map is divided between a global core and a
global periphery, and what keeps the two sectors apart is "the Western Wall

around the global core," a series of borders that keep the inequities and asymmetries of globalization in place.[4] Of the eleven control sites he and other economic geographers have identified (southern Spain–northern Africa, North Korea–South Korea, and Israel–West Bank, among them), the U.S.-Mexico border at its Pacific edge—the home turf of Tijuana—is number one on the list.

Tijuana Dreaming investigates Tijuana's place on this global map of flows and partitions, actors and spectators, winners and losers, by approaching the city's history according to two distinct, though intertwined periods. First, *the age of tourism* (1889–1965), which begins with the city's founding as a small, family-owned cattle *rancheria* in 1889 and extends through its Prohibition-era development into a tourist outpost and "city of sin" vice magnet for U.S. pleasure seekers heavily financed by Alta California entertainment entrepreneurs, media tycoons, and railroad barons. Though Tijuana's tourist heyday began to dwindle in the late 1960s, in some sense the city remains forever locked in the sombreros and curio shops of tourist postcards, in a black-and-white 1920s-tinted image of itself as a Las Vegas–Old Mexico hybrid of tequila hangovers, casino smoke, and cheap, dirty sex where the mythic Donkey Show still has some gravitational pull. In her essay for this collection, Jennifer Insley-Pruitt shows how this history of myth and black legend has been transformed by some of Tijuana's leading contemporary literary figures, and Berumen, Vaquera-Vásquez, and the Mexico City writer Guillermo Fadanelli all return to Tijuana's tourist haunts and nightclub utopias in order to make sense of the city in the present tense.

But the essays in this volume are born mostly from this second historical period, *the age of globalization* (1965–present), which begins in earnest with the transformation of Tijuana into a city of export-oriented assembly with the passage of the Border Industrialization Program (BIP) in 1965, a proposed Mexican remedy to the end of the U.S. Bracero Program that rescinded the labor invitations that had brought so many Mexicans north beginning in the 1940s. The BIP, aimed at generating employment and economic development along the border, was a monumental piece of legislation that would radically alter Tijuana's social and economic landscape by removing international tariff barriers, opening Tijuana (as well as other border cities) up to the arrival of foreign maquiladora assembly plants, and setting the stage for the passage of the North American Free Trade Agreement nearly thirty years later.[5] Indeed, as the sociologist Leslie Sklair has argued, the BIP did far more than simply create new border jobs. It aimed to redefine the border region into a "development zone" and "dynamic growth pole" whose very essence and identity were rooted in its value as an economic resource for northern Mexico's entrance into the global economy.[6] Early Tijuana maquiladora assembly plants like Litton Industries and Fairchild, for example, shipped their memory boards and electrical transformers from Baja California to Alta California and were instrumental in the growth of Silicon Valley's multibillion-dollar global tech industry.

The 1965 BIP legislation—which had early roots in 1930s drives to cast Baja California as a "free perimeter" or "free zone" for industrial imports—was preceded four years earlier by the Programa Nacional Fronterizo, or PRONAF, Mexico's first internally driven attempt to pump money and investment into the consumer and industrial markets of its northern border, urging Mexican nationals to "buy Mexican" and reframing the border as a consumer zone, "Mexico's show window." PRONAF and the BIP both paved the way for the free trade policies and economic border deregulation of NAFTA in the 1990s, and taken together all three powerfully shaped Tijuana's entrance into the global economy. And all three powerfully impacted the city's own identity as an emergent hub of globalized urbanism characterized by chronic population explosions, fragile urban infrastructures and emergency architectures, booming industrial parks and fading tourist industries, and a massive community of working poor that grows alongside both an ascendant middle class and an ascendant narco culture of quick wealth, ephemeral bling, urban terror, and fragile human life.

It is this Tijuana that emerges in Josh Kun's contribution here, a beleaguered and militarized city marred by sadness and beset by kidnappings and drug violence, where so much can be lost in the desperate hunt for power and wealth. If, as the pioneering Tijuana journalist Jesús Blancornelas once wrote, "corruption is the mother of drug trafficking," then uneven economic globalization is at least one mother of that corruption.[7] The post-1965 economic transformation of Tijuana helped turn the city into fertile soil for the economic desperation and social instability that drug cartels thrive on, and with the arrival of the Arellano-Felix cartel in the early 1990s, Tijuana's pivotal position as a drug route between the United States and South America was secured. While drug violence had been a part of Tijuana's urban profile since the early nineties, it was in the following decade that the violence spilled out beyond the world of narcos, politicians, and millionaires. When Tijuana's murder rate reached its all-time high in 2008, the city seemed as if it were under siege. Innocent people were dying, kindergartners were caught in shoot-outs, military tanks hovered over thoroughfares, and the killings got more and more grisly. The *encobijados*, or bodies wrapped in blankets, of the nineties had become the three hundred bodies dissolved in acid by El Pozolero in 2009. The wealthy fled north to San Diego, the middle classes bulletproofed their windows, and the city's working poor, including so many thousands of maquiladora workers who still left their colonias every morning at dawn for the assembly plants, were more vulnerable than ever before.

If the capital of tourist Tijuana is the infamous downtown main drag of Avenida Revolución—the fabled multiblock strip of clubs, bars, curio shops, and pharmacies that is usually the first, and often only, stop on the itinerary of the Tijuana tourist—then the capital of this vulnerable global Tijuana is the zone known as the 5 y 10. Named for a former five-and-dime store, the 5 y 10 cluster of shops, malls, markets, and pedestrian bridges lies at the heart of the eastern La Mesa district and is the chief commercial center and transportation hub for Tijuana's working classes. Over the river from the city's central bus terminal and a short distance from both the La Mesa prison and some of the city's maquiladoras and maquiladora housing colonias, it's an overcrowded and exhaust-choked crossroads that's the bustling epicenter of global Tijuana's everyday hustle. While many of these essays are shadowed by Tijuana's tourist past and informed by its tourist myths, we see them all in dialogue in some way with the city that is reborn daily at the 5 y 10. It's here where investments in border industry cross paths with divestments in border ecology, health, and economic justice; it's here where low-wage workers employed by global corporations do their daily consuming before returning to homes without sewage and clean water (an estimated 40 percent of the city lacks proper sewage and water). It's precisely this world that is documented in *Maquilapolis*, the 2006 film by Vicky Funari and Sergio de la Torre about this "city of factories," which figures centrally in Tarek Elhaik's piece for this collection.

Beginning in 1965, Tijuana became one of many international cities that felt the brunt of widespread deindustrialization campaigns and drives toward outsourced manufacturing. David Harvey has argued that it was in the post-1965 period that "the production of geographical difference" begins to become a hallmark of globalization.[8] By focusing on Tijuana in this historical period, this collection examines the impact of capitalism's "uneven geographical development" on one city, a further reminder that the most intense dramas of globalization continue to occur not on global stages, but on local and regional ones. Tijuana is an ideal site to follow through on Saskia Sassen's important urgings that globalization does not minimize the role of nations and cities, but that globalization actually exists through nations and cities which function as "enablers" and "enactors" of the global.[9] The essays in this collection look nothing like a world made flat, its national differences evened out by globalization's helping hand, but instead show us—whether in

Tito Alegría's debunking of cultural integration myths or Teddy Cruz's attention to ecological and infrastructural disjunctures or even Luis Humberto Crosthwaite's meditation on the border-crossing line itself—how the economic changes that swept through Tijuana in the late 1960s still require national differences to maintain the very exploitations and inequalities that successful economic globalization requires.

They also remind us of the connections that Alejandro Lugo has recently insisted upon in his own study of the impact of assemblage economies on border lives: the globalization of border cities is not born of a historical vacuum but is "a socio-historical product of the politics of conquest of two global empires—the Spanish empire (1521–1810) and the American empire (1848–present)."[10] Tijuana is a global city, then, not only because it has been made to play a contemporary role in free trade's reorganization of North America and neoliberalism's reimagining of social life, sovereignty, and subjectivity, but because it inherits two imperial lineages, both of which set the stage for the domination and administration of the Mexican working classes that the current era of assembly and manufacturing still depends upon. For Sassen, a global city is characterized by two central traits: it is a site "of the overvalorization of corporate capital and the further devalorization of disadvantaged economic actors" on the one hand, and on the other, it is a "strategic site for disempowered actors because it enables them to gain presence, to emerge as subjects, even when they do not gain direct power."[11] The essays gathered here reflect on both of these traits as they've emerged in Tijuana, where since 1965 intense corporate investment and economic development have been coupled with both local struggles for economic parity (through both formal and informal, legal and illegal, industries) and struggles for social and cultural visibility.

Yet one area where some of the more foundational scholarly accounts of global cities—or "world cities" and "international cities"—have shed less light is culture. The sociologist Kathryn Kopinak, whose overview of Tijuana's relationship to economic globalization is included here, has written at length on what she calls "the social costs of industrial growth" in the Tijuana region, but the essays gathered here also force us to consider the cultural costs and the cultural results of industrial growth, how Tijuana's "urban imaginaries" are expressed and articulated through cultural performance and cultural production.[12] The pieces we've included from Ejival, Jesse Lerner, René Peralta, and Tarek Elhaik explore these "urban imaginaries" by looking at Tijuana's musical countercultures, its architectural ruins and ghosts, and its contemporary cinematic archives. Even in his primarily historical and economic 1993 study of maquiladoras, Sklair made it clear that the border's economic restructuring has distinctive cultural impacts. "The concrete manifestations of the globalization of capital are apparent on the export oriented assembly zones," he wrote. "But their effects are being felt more widely in politics and culture."[13] Indeed, as Margath Walker has shown, culture has played a central role not only in the imaginaries of young grassroots artists, musicians, writers, designers, and other creatives hoping to make sense of Tijuana, but in the policies and planning of the city of Tijuana itself where, to borrow George Yúdice's phrase, culture becomes expedient, an economic resource of global visibility and global policy. One of Yúdice's key case studies in this area is inSITE, the internationally recognized art triennial that since 1992 has been staging large-scale art installations and performances that focus on the San Diego–Tijuana region. While Yúdice applauds inSITE's role in fostering artistic growth in the border region and putting Tijuana on a global map of artistic interest, he also sees it as a kind of artistic corollary of NAFTA's free-trade economic policies, only here it's culture that is assembled with foreign money by local workers, it's culture that acts as capital, and it's culture that is imbued with economic value for global investors and consumers. He goes so far as to dub inSITE "an artistic maquiladora whose executives (the directors of the art event) contract with managers (the curators) to map out the agenda for flexible workers-for-hire (artists) who in turn produce or extract (cultural) capital by processing a range of materials."[14] The extent to which Tijuana's city officials themselves seem to be embracing a free-trade approach to cultural capital and investment can be seen in the 2005–2007 city municipal plan, which contained over twenty references to fostering cultural development in Tijuana. For Walker, this is an attempt to "embed Tijuana deeply and successfully in the global economy by situating its culture for economic gain."[15] Or in the words of Tijuana's municipal planners: "Our border position has converted our city into an open space of stimulating innovation and tolerance whose economic vitality and cultural creativity has projected to the international scale."[16] A similar language and developmental logic was at the core of 2010's Tijuana Innovadora, a privately funded $5 million two-week conference and image makeover held at CECUT, the city's leading cultural institution, designed to showcase Tijuana as a center of innovations in technology, science, and culture. Aimed at hundreds of elite global attendees (Al Gore and a cofounder of Wikipedia among them), the event, in the words of the conference's official video promo, was designed to showcase Tijuana as the capital of "the intelligent frontier" and in language that echoed PRONAF and BIP in the sixties, thereby "generate national investment that will expand the region's economy."

"It's Time for Tijuana": Global Myths, Global Realities

With over two million people, Tijuana is the second largest city on North America's Pacific Coast (smaller than Los Angeles, bigger than Seattle and San Francisco). When paired with San Diego to the north, the two cities are responsible for an estimated $6 billion a year in exports and an estimated $8 billion in cross-border trade. The Web site for the nonprofit Tijuana Economic Development Corporation—available in English, Japanese, and Chinese—announces to potential corporate clients that "It's time for Tijuana," advertising the city's rich, seemingly endless resources of "human capital" and promoting its prime Pacific Rim import-export real estate—"globally strategic, yet very near-shore." As the site puts it, "Having your business in Tijuana not only means you'll be in a great city next to US markets—it also means you get access to Mexico's globally-oriented menu of free trade agreements."[17]

Since the launch of the BIP in 1965, the lure of this regional wealth and the strength of this regional industry has made Tijuana a destination not only for companies looking for tariff-free trade corridors, but for all that "human capital," those millions of migrants from the south looking to find work on the factory floors of the city's thousands of maquiladoras (which, it's estimated, on average employ a million workers at a time). As Berumen reminds us in his essay, others, of course, begin by simply seeing Tijuana as a *ciudad de paso*, a city there to be crossed and passed by on the way into the United States, a necessary gateway to the world that beckons on the other side of the rusting border wall. While many make it across, more do not, and for them, the maquiladoras are always waiting. The hillsides with views of San Diego and the shantytowns out beyond the official Tijuana city grid are waiting too, and before long migrants become residents, the ciudad de paso becomes a hometown where families are raised, where generations pass.[18]

These processes are at the core of Lawrence Herzog's many writings on globalization's impact on the social and ecological infrastructures of Tijuana. For Herzog, Tijuana is an "an ideal laboratory for understanding how globalization is shaping a new kind of urbanism," this city that sits at the most-crossed land border in the world and cradles the U.S.-Mexico border's largest port of entry.[19] Yet while the essays in this collection have much in common with Herzog's portrait of "global Tijuana"—which he outlines according to a taxonomy of various ecologies of trade, consumerism, and community—they stop short of celebrating it as a completed global project, an imaginary border utopia free of disjunctures and economic injustices, where global factories and free-trade policies simply generate new kinds of freely participating border consumers who become "global citizens" of a new cross-border global order.

Instead, we see Tijuana as a global city precisely because of the uneven, precarious, and often destructive nature of globalization itself, which might produce new markets and new consumers as neoliberal victories, but also produce a border citizenship that is unstable and fragile and a combustive urban infrastructure defined by informal, or "shadow," economies (including drug and human trafficking) as much as by the formal flows of global industry. Instead of a city of "global citizens" participating equally in globalization, tijuanenses are more frequently part of what Josiah Heyman has called the border's "consumer proletariat," people alienated from both the means of production and the means of consumption.[20] As Harvey has reminded us, globalization indeed moves across national spaces, but does so unevenly; some sites and spaces are more resource rich for globalization's abundances, others more resource rich for globalization's scarcities.[21] Tijuana falls into the latter category; part of what makes it global is its scarcity in the service of affluence.

It is, after all, a city born from not just any geopolitical border, but from the only one in the world that divides one of the world's poorest nations from the world's richest, which, as Alexis McCrossen has shown, makes it highly attractive to markets, which are by definition attracted to the kind of "accumulation of asymmetries in such close proximity" that has become a primary characteristic of Tijuana's urban profile.[22] Or as Andreas Huyssen has written of cities in the age of globalization, "Rather than producing connectivities and flows equally between all regions of the planet, globalization functions in horizontal clusters through and among which global, local, and regional dimensions are ricocheting with varying intensities and breadth."[23] Tijuana is a ricochet city, a cluster of connectivities and flows that can be as smooth as they are rough. Things cross and things are detained. There's traffic and there's waiting. Flows become inspections. Tijuana constantly reminds: the global is also gridlock.

In much recent U.S. scholarship on Tijuana, that gridlock, while always present, is frequently overshadowed by theories of transnational traffic, cross-border networks, and transnational urban planning. A 2000 study by a former city architect of San Diego, Michael Stepner, and a San Diego city planner, Paul Fiske, for example, included Tijuana–San Diego in the world's most important "global city regions," with Tijuana as one half of a rich binational pairing that ought to attract investors and urban planners alike (it was an idea previously explored in 1974 by Kevin Lynch and Donald Appleyard, who had tempered their binational visions by wondering if the region was a "temporary paradise").[24] Three years earlier, Herzog had already begun developing this idea when he wrote of the Tijuana–San Diego region as a "transfrontier metropolis" that was a "prototype of global urban space." Like Stepner and Fiske, Herzog focused on the shared traffic: combined population numbers, binational commuters, binational consumers, cross-border tourists, global factories, cross-border bedroom communities, shared infrastructures, shared fates of urban design. "The age of land warfare is past," he wrote. "Global markets and free trade are the new dominant realities, and property at the edges of nations is attracting investors, businesses, and governments. Industrial parks, highways, rail systems, and airports that once bypassed international frontiers are relocating there."[25] We worry about just how close a "transfrontier metropolis" is to the "Tijuana–San Diego megaregion" promoted by the maquiladora industry, which uses Tijuana's human capital and tariff-free industrial parks as incentive for future global investment that, contrary to any vision of cross-border parity, will only increase the economic divide between San Diego and Baja California. We have included the work of San Diego–based architect and planner Teddy Cruz in the collection precisely to address these contradictions and these innovations in regional planning as he represents one of the leading contemporary voices in reimagining the infrastructures and public spaces of the cross-border landscape.

The increasingly popular view of the border megacity, where national edges function more as market openings and less as state partitions, reappeared in the influential 2003 collection *Postborder City*, from Michael Dear and Gustavo LeClerc. The volume shed much-needed light on the history of Baja California and on Tijuana's central role in the inter-California region, but did so by anchoring Tijuana in a transnational geography the authors named "Bajalta California," a Southern California–northern Mexico zone of trade, culture, and community where the geopolitical border takes a backseat to the idea of a "postborder" where flows of ideas, culture, and finance shape a porous Bajalta border region.[26] While the essays in *Tijuana Dreaming* certainly participate in and contribute to a transnational body of ideas and culture, and while they certainly understand Tijuana's key coordinates on the Southern California–northern Mexico map, their approach to the city begins on the southern side of a border partition that keeps San Diego's gross domestic product roughly eleven times that of Tijuana. Viewed from Los Angeles or San Diego, the Tijuana–San Ysidro border may be a zone of free trade and free-flowing economic traffic with edges ripe for investment and planning, but viewed from Tijuana it is first and foremost a barrier and partition between core and periphery, a surveilled zone of Homeland Security policing and economic unevenness, a key example of what Ruth Wilson Gilmore means by a "fatal power-difference coupling."[27] Like the prisons Gilmore writes about, the national edges of the new global economy are also mechanisms and icons of domestic militarism, "geographical solutions to social and economic crises, politically organized by a racial state that is itself in crisis." Especially since the vicious 1994 legislative tag team of NAFTA (opening the border to free movement of goods and parts) and Operation Gatekeeper (closing the border to the free movement of people), Tijuana has been a key site for witnessing what Heyman has described as the border's "mobilities-enclosures continuum"—where some are allowed to move ("kinetic elites"), while others remain detained. The border becomes a risk-management hub, a filter for "safe" travelers and against "risky" travelers that produces "differential mobility effects."[28]

Alejandro Lugo has gone one step further and argued against the alleged common sense of borders as places of crossing, insisting instead that borders are primarily places of inspection characterized by the "pervasive pattern of cultural surveillance." To speak only of the crossings themselves masks the inspections that take place before and after crossing (if crossing is even permitted). For Lugo, then, national borders are far from being the romanticized zones of flux, hybridity, and postmodern deterritoriality that became the familiar subject of so much cultural theory in the 1990s; rather, borders can be redefined as "ethnographic objects that are mainly characterized by supervision and scrutiny."[29]

As you might expect, theories of Tijuana's role in a cross-border global megacity have had less currency in Tijuana itself, where scholars and critics are typically more focused on local asymmetry, not inter-California regional prosperity, and have tended to approach globalization not in terms of transnational flows and transnational geographies but in terms of how shifts in global economics have impacted highly localized struggles around culture and politics and local struggles around social equality and civic health. Leading the way has been the Tijuana scholar Tito Alegría (we include a sample of his recent work here), whose 2009 study *Metrópolis transfronteriza* offers a passionate and thorough refutation of the "transfrontier metropolis" and "megacity" ideas. He argues that Herzog, Dear, and Leclerc confuse interaction with integration. "The flows [between Tijuana and San Diego] are the means of a relationship," he writes. "But they are not sufficient for an integration."[30] There is no doubt that Tijuana is the product of more than a century's worth of cross-border influence (indeed, one cannot imagine the birth of modern Tijuana itself without the Prohibition-era investments of U.S. capital) but Alegría contends that there has been no integration of Tijuana into the north-of-the-border economy that fuels cities like Los Angeles and San Diego. Alegría names three "brakes" that slow transfrontier integration: the increase of impediments to south-to-north migrations, the increasing disparities between U.S. and Mexican salaries and prices, and the increasing difficulty for tijuanenses to cross the border north into San Diego County with everyday frequency (he estimates that less than half of the city can do so legally). As a result, where others see U.S.-Mexico transnationalism, Alegría sees structural differences between the United States and Mexico. If there is "interurban binational flux," he says, it exists precisely because of structural disparities and inequalities.

These disparities became particularly acute as part of a broader post-9/11 condition, which cemented the border's role less as an instigator of interaction and more as a consolidator of difference. Two key exceptionalities developed. First, an Agambian state of exception was increasingly applied to the border as a zone that was almost constantly alarmingly "orange," dangerous, and fertile ground for terrorist invasion. Second, a cultural exceptionality developed that, as the curator Lucía Sanromán and the photographer Ingrid Hernández demonstrate in their pieces here, emerged from within by leading Tijuana filmmakers, anthropologists, architects, and artists eager to interpret and represent their globalizing city through a new generational lens, and from without by curators, cultural critics, and arts journalists who enthusiastically characterized the city as a cultural and artistic hot spot. Or as the New York Times put it (in a piece they headlined "It's Hot. It's Hip. It's Tijuana?"), "Its fabled lawlessness has become a kind of freedom and license for social mobility and entrepreneurship that has attracted artists and musicians, chefs and restaurateurs, and professionals from Mexico and elsewhere." Tijuana's sudden hipness took on particular force in the art world with Tijuana's art scene landing on the radar of international curators and journalists, suddenly making it the trendiest art city in Mexico between 2003 and 2006. Between 2005 and 2006 alone, three major exhibitions showcased Tijuana-specific art: 2005's Tijuana Sessions (for ARCO in Madrid, Spain) and Tercera Nación (Tijuana), and 2006's Strange New World (MCASD, San Diego).[31] This recent art boom has at least a few roots in the successes and global recognition of inSITE, which has long been perhaps the most vocal and consistent proponent of Tijuana as both a site for art (a destination for artists, curators, and critics not from the Tijuana–San Diego region) and a site of artists (the artistic home base of artists living and working in Tijuana). While many celebrated this new attention on Tijuana as a place for something other than violence and vice, others worried that art that was critical of the onslaught of globalization became an (perhaps inadvertent) advertisement for it. Dubbing Tijuana's art boom "arte NAFTA" that was spun by curators into a "pop optimism" about the border, Heriberto Yépez wrote that "border art is being manipulated to invent a favorable image of Mexico's cultural integration with the U.S."[32]

As Yépez's own critique made clear, the international attention given Tijuana's art scene was often paired with the common characterization of Tijuana as the ultimate postmodern city of the third world, the archetypal "third space" of liminality and in-betweenness once theorized by Homi Bhabha. Tijuana's role as a kind of theorist's darling begins in 1990 with the publication of Néstor García Canclini's watershed book, *Culturas híbridas: Estrategias para entrar y salir de la modernidad*. "During the two periods in which I studied the intercultural conflicts at the Mexican side of the border, in Tijuana, in 1985 and 1988," he wrote in a passage now famous among borderlands scholars, "it occurred to me at more than one time that this city is, along with New York, one of the greatest laboratories of postmodernity."[33] For García Canclini, Tijuana's bilingualism, its continuous cultural mixtures of North and South, its meetings of first and third worlds, made it an exquisitely hybrid city. His characterization gradually helped make Tijuana synonymous with global hybridity and postmodern urbanism, a notion that spread through the popular press, academia, and the art world (Heriberto Yépez's essay in this collection offers a critique of this trend).[34] Yet in an interview included here, García Canclini revisits his earlier claims with a more critical eye toward hybridity and the uncritical reappropriations and use of his writing on Tijuana by fellow critics.

As Diana Palaversich and Eduardo Barrera have both noted, García Canclini's characterization of Tijuana as a postmodern capital was undoubtedly influenced by the 1980s and 1990s performance art work of Guillermo Gómez-Peña and the Border Arts Workshop.[35] Their important performance interventions into discourses of cultural nationalism and cultural purity—launched from the San Diego–Tijuana border—frequently portrayed Tijuana as an ideal site for thinking about binational cultural flows, polyglot tongues, and improvisational borderlands identities that move across the border's "gap between worlds."[36] While acutely aware of this tradition (and in some cases, overtly grappling with it), the essays in *Tijuana Dreaming* do not extend this theoretical current and instead go behind the often too-easy romance of Tijuana postmodernism and hybridity to explore the city's culture and identity through critical lenses that we believe are more generative for understanding the city so that it is not wholly defined by, or synonymous with, the borderline itself. The conflation of *Tijuana* with *border* has helped enable, to borrow a phrase from Palaversich, Tijuana's "international blessing as one of the first examples of the brave new postmodern world," which has tended to distract many scholars and critics outside of the city from examining the social, political, and economic fractures that continue to shape it from within.[37]

Tijuana may be the Mexican city most visited by U.S. tourists and one of the Mexican cities most referenced when media talk turns to the "crisis" of contemporary border life, yet scholarship and critical writing about Tijuana available in English is scarce. Only one of Tijuana's contemporary novelists (Luis Humberto Crosthwaite) has had work translated, and not one of the city's contemporary generation of scholars and critics has seen their long-form work available in English for students, faculty, and interested readers north of the line. As a result, Tijuana is much talked about, but little heard. Courses on border issues tend to rely on the scant, and often very dated, pieces of writing available. Tijuana has been, historically, a city defined by its misrepresentation in myth and fantasy, synonymous with a kind of critical ventriloquism that leaves its own critical and intellectual and artistic voices all too silent in transnational conversations.

This anthology aims to correct that imbalance by including a number of essential articles by leading scholars from Tijuana and greater Mexico in translation for the very first time. The essays explore Tijuana's cultural life through four central prisms: *panoramas* that view the city in its broadest cultural, historical, and discursive terms and position contemporary cultural life in Tijuana in the context of the city's representational history; the new *urbanisms* that have energized urban planning in Tijuana, new theories of social and civic life and domestic innovation that respond to the city's unique infrastructural, demographic, and environmental pressures; the *cultural developments* in visual art, literature, and music that have taken Tijuana's artistic life beyond conventional discourses of "border art" as they have been deployed in the art world and the academy alike; and *globalisms*, views of the challenges facing Tijuana in the global age, the ghosts of its cinematic past that cloud its future, the violence and fear that have begun to reshape the city's sense of itself.

Yet even in the face of this violence and fear, in the face of so many asymmetries and ruptures, the essays in this collection all seem to come back to a love of the city that borders on obsession and is fueled by a critical passion. "In my lifetime," Yépez writes, "I have not felt a love as profound as the confusing passion that I feel for Tijuana, an obsession that does not preclude criticism and which more accurately provokes sudden repudiation. Tijuana elicits a crazy love, a narcotic love. Tijuana is addictive." *Tijuana Dreaming* is our attempt to pay tribute to that love in all of its diversity, to take those addictions seriously by creating a collection that will help enrich conversations about Tijuana's role in the current global landscape. Or, to paraphrase something Teddy Cruz once told the *New York Times* when he was asked why he has focused so much of his work on Tijuana, we assembled this collection because we believe that to study Tijuana is, quite simply, "to be in the midst of the argument."[38]

Welcome to (a new) Tijuana.

Notes

1 For more on Nortec, see Alejandro Madrid, *Nor-Tec Rifa! Electronic Dance Music from Tijuana to the World* (Oxford University Press, 2008); and José Manuel Valenzuela (ed.), *Paso del Nortec: This Is Tijuana!* (Trilce, 2004).

2 Daniel Cohen, *Globalization and Its Enemies* (MIT, 2007), 6.

3 Thomas P. M. Barnett, *The Pentagon's New Map: War and Peace in the 21st Century* (Putnam, 2004).

4 Harm de Blij, *The Power of Place: Geography, Destiny, and Globalization's Rough Landscape* (Oxford University Press, 2008), 32.

5 To be clear, we do not believe that tourism and globalization are mutually exclusive economic and cultural regimes, but that they are in fact very much entangled with one another. It's a theme that the essays in this collection constantly grapple with: the relationship between the new cultural networks and social structures that emerged in Tijuana in the 1960s as a direct result of border industrialization and previous cultural regimes tied to the binational flows of tourist dollars and tourist fantasies.

6 Leslie Sklair, *Assembling for Development: The Maquila Industry in Mexico and the United States* (UCSD, 1993), 27.

7 Jesús Blancornelas, *El Cartel* (Plaza y Janes, 2002), 39.

8 David Harvey, *Spaces of Hope* (University of California Press, 2000), 78.

9 Saskia Sassen, *Territory, Authority, Rights: From Medieval to Global Assemblages* (Princeton University Press, 2008), 1.

10 Alejandro Lugo, *Fragmented Lives, Assembled Parts: Culture, Capitalism, and Conquest at the U.S.-Mexico Border* (University of Texas Press, 2008), 2.

11 Saskia Sassen, *Globalization and Its Discontents: Essays on the New Mobility of People and Money* (New Press, 1999), xx; for a helpful treatment of different "world-city" and "international city" approaches, see Steven Erie, *Globalizing L.A.: Trade, Infrastructure, and Regional Development* (Stanford University Press, 2004).

12 Kathryn Kopinak (ed.), *The Social Costs of Industrial Growth in Northern Mexico* (UCSD Center for US-Mexican Studies, 2006).

13 Sklair, *Assembling for Development*, 11.

14   George Yúdice, *The Expediency of Culture: Uses of Culture in the Global Era* (Duke University Press, 2004), 288.

15   Margath A. Walker, "The Cultural Economy of a Border Renaissance: Politics and Practices in the City," *Space and Polity* 11, no. 2 (2007): 185–200.

16   Ibid., 191.

17   Tijuana Economic Development Corporation, http://www.tijuana-edc.com.

18   For a different take on the ciudad de paso as it is manifest in Tijuana's oldest residential neighborhood, La Libertad, see Omar Pimienta's outstanding poetry collection *La Libertad: Ciudad de Paso* (CECUT, 2006).

19   Lawrence Herzog, "Global Tijuana: The Seven Ecologies of the Border," in Michael Dear and Gustavo LeClerc (eds.), *Postborder City: Cultural Spaces of Bajalta California* (Routledge, 2003), 120.

20   Cited in Alexis McCrossen (ed.), *Land of Necessity: Consumer Culture in the United States–Mexico Borderlands* (Duke University Press, 2009), 34.

21   Harvey, *Spaces of Hope*.

22   Ibid., 3.

23   Andreas Huyssen, *Other Cities, Other Worlds: Urban Imaginaries in a Globalizing Age* (Duke University Press, 2008), 15.

24   Michael Stepner and Paul Fiske, "San Diego and Tijuana," in *Global City Regions: Their Emerging Forms* (Spon Press, 2000); Kevin Lynch and Donald Appleyard, *Temporary Paradise? A Look at the Spatial Landscape of the San Diego Region* (Report to the City of San Diego, 1974).

25   Lawrence Herzog, "The Transfrontier Metropolis," *Harvard Design Magazine*, no. 1 (Winter/Spring 1997), 2.

26   Dear and Leclerc, *Postborder City*.

27   Ruth Wilson Gilmore, "Fatal Couplings of Power and Difference: Notes on Racism and Geography," *Professional Geographer* 54, no. 1 (2002): 16.

28   Josiah M. Heyman and Robert Pallitto, "Theorizing Cross-Border Mobility: Surveillance, Security, and Identity," *Surveillance and Society* 5, no. 3 (2008): 318.

29   Alejandro Lugo, *Fragmented Lives, Assembled Parts: Culture, Capitalism, and Conquest at the US-Mexico Border* (University of Texas Press, 2008).

30   Tito Alegría, *Metrópolis transfronteriza: Revisión de la hipótesis y evidencias de Tijuana, Mexico y San Diego, Estados Unidos* (COLEF, 2009), 24.

31   For just two of many examples of the press attention paid to Tijuana's "hot" arts and culture scenes, see William L. Hamilton, "It's Hot. It's Hip. It's Tijuana?" *New York Times*, August 25, 2006; and Elisabeth Malkin, "Tijuana Transforms into a Cultural Hotbed," *New York Times*, June 8, 2006.

32   Heriberto Yépez, *Made in Tijuana* (ICBC, 2005), 67.

33   Néstor García Canclini, *Culturas híbridas: Estrategias para entrar y salir de la modernidad* (Grijalbo, 1990), 233.

34   In his 1990 book, Michael Dear, *The Postmodern Urban Condition* (John Wiley, 2000), 174–75, continues this idea by making Tijuana a key case study for his analysis of postmodern urbanism.

35   Diana Palaversich, *De Macondo a McOndo: Senderos de la postmodernidad latinoamericana* (Plaza y Valdes, 2005), 172.

36 For example, see Guillermo Gómez-Peña, *Warrior for Gringostroika* (Graywolf, 1993); and Gomez-Peña, *The New World Border* (City Lights, 1996).

37 Palaversich, *De Macondo a McOndo*, 172.

38 Nicolai Ourossoff, "Shantytowns as a New Suburban Ideal," *New York Times*, March 12, 2006.

Roberto Castillo

Welcome Tu Tijuana

Ladies and Gentlemen
Welcome to Tijuana,
The most mythical place on earth,
Where tongues love each other and unite
In the "aló," the "oquei," the "babai" en the verb "tu bi";

Where the free zone exists,
The *fayuca* and the little gifts
For the boss, the secretary,
The horny friend, the wife
And the unbearable children;

Where the pizza boys in motorcycles,
The cops, the taxi drivers,
The *narcojuniors* and their buddies
And the ladies with California license plates
Don't respect lights or stop signs.

Friends,
Welcome to Tijuana,
The city farthest from centralism,
Where the *clamatos* and parties have flavor
Where the junkyards and the muffler shops flower

Where the blocks
Are spaces for pharmacies
Liquor stores, *casas de cambio*
Taco stands, Oxxos everywhere
And seafood restaurants

Where the regional food
Is *carne asada* and beer,
The lobster and the fish tacos,

The Caesar salad, the pizza
And the Sunday Chinese food;

Welcome to Tijuas
The place with emergency architecture,
Where the women are houses,
Moles are offices
And *sombreros* are restaurants;
The marvelous space
Where used tires
Are transformed into steps,
Into swings, into retaining walls,
Pots or huarache soles;

Where the department of tourism
Thinks that the only important things are
The Chapu towers, the Cecut ball, the plaza rio,
The Jai Alai, the Revu and the minaret's plaza.

Ladies and gentlemen,
Welcome to Tiyei
Where the cholos, surfers, and punks,
Drug dealers, mercenaries and federal police
Make leisure their business;

Where politicians, businessmen,
maquila bosses and customs agents,
salesmen and money exchangers
"loteros" and policemen,
are the true illegals;

Where the polka becomes cumbia,
"norteño" becomes techno,
"mofleros" are sculptors,
painters are graffiti artists (taggers?)
and the culture is in the Zona Norte;

Gentlemen and young ladies,
Welcome to Tijuana,
Where "compiures" and hearts unite
The new technology and the old
And the donkeys have stripes;

The northern zoo
Where coyotes and "polleros"
The "chiva," the "perico" and the "gallo,"
The "tigres" and the "tucanes"
Are millionaire animals;

Where the beautiful calafia
Legendary queen of California,
First was transformed into wine
And now, sad and forgotten
Has become only public transportation;

Welcome to tijuana,
The city of lights
And home of Juan Soldado,
The migrant's saint,
Lord of the little miracles;

Home of the "leche Jersey,"
De kid with the "beisbol" hat
And the fortified smile
That substitutes the mother
In childhood feeding;

Where "doing line"
To cross to the other side to go shopping
Becomes a two-hour torture
Or a sour eternity of horn honking
And "agandalles" to get a spot

Welcome to tijuana,
Promised land for migrants
National and foreign,
Where life is worth a lot
And death is a business;

Where unknown heroes
Decorate avenues with "glorietas";
Where it's the same to have Lincoln,
Cuauhtemoc, saint rocket or
An incomprehensible sculpture;

Welcome to tijuana,
The street, the unexpected phrase,
The "hornyness" and the binary system,
The border crossing, the "albur,"
The going "there" and coming "here."

Humberto Félix Berumen

Snapshots from and about a City Named Tijuana

On the Discourses That Made Tijuana an Unmistakable Icon

Over the course of the years, what are the discourses that have built the contemporary perception of Tijuana? There are several different discourses and it would serve us well to take this opportunity to review them, even if only briefly. These discourses are enumerated below in a quick and succinct list. It's true they are contradictory, in opposition, and ambiguous, but at the same time, they are complementary, perpetually in conflict, and in a process of negotiation.

Tijuana, Synthesis of the Nation

This discourse is based on the enduring metaphor of the city as a barely updated version of the border melting pot (the "crucible of races"). Put in another way (in its more widespread and accepted version): the city is thought to be a mosaic of every possible tradition, of all the experiences brought by a continual stream of immigration over the course of several decades.

For the proponents of this discourse, Tijuana has almost been the emblematic symbol of a city in which diverse Mexican traditions coexist without significant conflicts. Every region of the country is said to be found in the city: they argue that it is, and has been, a home for everyone. Customs, traditions, forms of speech, regional foods, and social types all have been melded and muddled within the human mosaic that is contemporary Tijuana. The city is the northernmost point, a place where each of the states that make up the great Mexican nation converge and are integrated in brotherly unity. Because, just as the sociologist Martín de la Rosa has succinctly stated: "We come to Tijuana from everywhere, the difference is that some of us came first and others later" (*Marginalidad en Tijuana* [Marginality in Tijuana], 1985). This is an idea which the Argentine writer Manuel Puig would reiterate in the film script for *Recuerdo de Tijuana* (Souvenir from Tijuana, 1985): "We come to Tijuana from everywhere."

In fact, for an important sector of society, Tijuana has come to represent—and this is how several local authors have imagined it—the social laboratory from which will arise a new Mexican: an extravagant synthesis of all the cardinal points of the country. Each one has fed the cultural life of the city. As Antonio Pompa y Pompa discerned years ago in his essay titled *Visión de Baja California* (1979): "and so [the city] both shapes and constitutes in and of itself a baroque visage of the nation, an embryonic display of authentic Mexicanness. Because of this, California has been converted into a laboratory of the Mexican of tomorrow."

Many authors declare with false nationalist pride that Mexico's diverse cultures have melded together in Tijuana, even though it is not exactly clear what this phenomenon might mean. But in its less idealized version, it alludes to an undeniable fact: the cultural and linguistic heterogeneity that gave birth to this city. Tijuana's syncretism is recognized as an important marker of the identity of the city.

Tijuana, Land of Promise

Above all, this view is maintained in the official version of the city as a place with minimal unemployment and a low rate of illiteracy, wages above the established national minimum, the existence of multiple opportunities flowing from the proximity to the United States and the presence of numerous maquiladoras that utilize (and exploit) a low-wage workforce. This version of Tijuana seems to comprise what would be the closest thing we have in Mexico to a land of promise—even if it seems to be permanently out of reach.

Because of all this, it has been said on more than one occasion that Tijuana is an atypical city, which is "inhabited by the most middle-class society in Mexico" (Jorge A. Bustamante). It has even been asserted that it is the most cosmopolitan, dynamic, and progressive of the cities on the Mexican border; however, the poverty and extreme marginalization in which a large part of its population live is consistently forgotten. This is a situation which, even though seen in other places, is quite paradoxical for a city considered to be the model of a modern, egalitarian society.

At its heart lies a discourse popular in the business world, or which the primary commercial groups have promoted with particular resolve. They have spread a more idealized, less realistic vision in regard to Tijuana. There is a lot of Manichaeism in this vision, a false veneration of the city, and statements made by people blinded by the many interests at play. There is no other way to explain the arguments wielded, for example, by the businessman José Galicot. He expressed these views in his flawed book (flawed because it was badly written and devoid of interest) titled *Presencias de la ciudad* (Images of the City, 2001): "This is the Tijuana that I love: industrious and working productively in factories and maquiladoras. The fame of the high-quality Mexican worker has grown around the world and created more opportunities for the many unemployed Mexicans who stream into the city each year."

Tijuana, *Ciudad de Paso*, City to Pass Through

This discourse exposes Tijuana's existence as a border city, as a city open to the exploitation of U.S. tourism ("Tijuana, the most visited city in the world" prays the cheap mythomania of a publicity slogan), of commerce and large foreign investment. Its best expression is to be found in the Zona Libre, or redlight district, today experiencing a steady and unmistakable deterioration.

Tijuana is also a ciudad de paso, or a city to pass through, from another perspective entirely: as a result of the crisis in the Mexican countryside, people have been driven into a permanent diaspora and doggedly seek an opportunity to cross over to the "other side" for as long as they are able to stay there. Some of these people will end up swelling the ranks of those who have perished trying to cross. Others, after being deported from California, will end up adding to the steady expansion of the illegal settlements or *asentamientos irregulares* as they are called in Spanish. Tijuana is also a transit zone for the drug-trafficking groups that have converted the city into a beachhead for the distribution of illicit drugs.

A no-place (city one passes through, with no roots or traditions) that the anthropologist Guillermo Bonfil Batalla describes with a keen eye: "A city that is still in pieces." Wide avenues, towering hotels, and a background of arid mountains scaled by all kinds of constructions (up and down, along the canyons), the majority of them precarious. An unfinished Tijuana, without its own defined image—or, perhaps, this is its image: a new city of the border (the border crossing with the greatest movement).

Despite this, for the deceased poet Eduardo Arellano, Tijuana rather than "a no-place is the place of saturation. As such, it accepts and continually incorporates foreign elements, because, in fact, it would seem that nothing is foreign to the city. And a particular ambiguity arises within this incredible abundance of humanity that gives places like this city a feeling of perversity. This ambiguity makes these places exceptionally favorable to diverse expressions of the human, ranging from happiness to art" ("Estación Tijuana").

Tijuana, Symbol of Cultural Postmodernity

This is a discourse with academic origins. For a large group of social re-searchers, writers, and anthropologists, Tijuana has been the paradigmatic symbol for explaining the phenomenon of deterritorialization of cultural and economic processes at this turn of the century.

According to this well-known interpretation, Tijuana becomes the symbol par excellence of urban, cultural postmodernity. Authors like Néstor García Canclini ("This city is, along with New York, one of the major laboratories of postmodernity") and Guillermo Gómez-Peña, among others, have insisted that hybridity is part of the cultural identity of Tijuana. This would lead later to the contention of Santiago Vaquera-Vásquez (paraphrasing Walter Benjamin) that "Tijuana is the capital of the twenty-first century." This same vision has been repeated by other authors: "Tijuana is the city which best represents the twenty-first century, precisely because of its border nature and because it is a generator of so many itinerant identities. Tijuana is a markedly postmodern city" (Lauro Zavala).

Nevertheless, if the metaphor of cultural hybridity presupposes fluidity and cultural mixture as inescapable prerequisites, or rather, as the image of disintegration of cultural repertoires—the "settings without territory" to which Néstor García Canclini alludes—in the particular case of Tijuana, there is an image of a city of permanent nomads without any social roots. This is exactly what the writer Juan Villoro has warned, when he reminds us that "Tijuana has the temporality of a campsite, a space where everything signals its transitoriness and where tradition is improvised from minute to minute."

But the image is not completely accurate. "Although it is true that Tijuana, like other border cities, has a significant floating population, and that it is in fact the busiest border in the world, for a large part of its population Tijuana is, without a doubt, a home—with all of the positive and negative connotations of the word—a place full of history and memory" (Diana Palaversich). In summary, this is a vision we could only accept with some difficulty; the reality of Tijuana is not fully explained by the idea of rootlessness or by the transitory nature of its social relations.

In any case, we are dealing with an insufficient postmodernity, in large measure belated, subordinate, or which still has not fully established itself, in other words, embryonic. Tijuana is principally a premodern city with multiple deficiencies, but also it is paradoxical and contradictory. As Heriberto Yépez has stated quite clearly: "Tijuana is the failed project of postmodernity."

The Literary Discourse of Tijuana

Tijuana has occupied a privileged place in literature since the first years of its foundation; the city has been mentioned, invented, and reconfigured in the literary imagination. It is the archetype par excellence of a vilified city, due to the social violence and drug trafficking evident in a wide array of stories and novels. The subject matter in many of them is unimportant; even the details of their respective plots matter little.

The literary importance of Tijuana is definitely considerable and has transcended all territorial boundaries; it even possesses the semantic density of a new literary myth with its own unmistakable identity. And much more than that: it constitutes a symbol, since it always means much more than the direct or literal meaning signified by the word itself.

The Cinematic Discourse on Tijuana

Since the beginning of the twentieth century, American film, and later Mexican and Chicano film, constructed and propagated the primary stereotypes that came to define the representation of Tijuana in the imaginary. They dedicated themselves to the work of projecting the configuration of Tijuana as a heterotopia (from *héteros*, other, and *topos*, place) through the cinematographic imaginary—that is, as a place in contraposition to the morality and culture of the United States. A place also in contraposition to the morality and culture of Mexico, as disseminated from the center of the country. *Verbi gratia.*

An other-space conceived and configured based on cultural and political differences, but above all, by the necessity to exclude everything American (and also Mexican) society considered reprehensible at the time. Tijuana: a territory liberated of moralistic pressures in order to curry favor with the ravenous tourists from San Diego and Los Angeles, California. The myth of Tijuana as the ultimate city of vice is the result of the articulations and distribution of American cinema in the 1920s and 1930s.

Tijuana Engulfed in Violence

The glaring headlines of the media have played a primary role in structuring and distributing a discourse that portrays the city as extremely violent. This discourse has emphasized above all the idea of a territory outside of the reach of the law and controlled by criminals. The lack of public safety as a symbol of social identity. And it has been said that "organized crime is embedded in Tijuana society; it is part of the city and its identity" (Jorge Santibáñez Romellón).

In its mass-media reproduction, Tijuana has taken on the face of a city immersed in daily violence and with little or no public safety. This has given rise to the appearance of the verb *tijuanize* and, consequently, the gerund *tijuaniz-ing*, for example, in the following epigram published in the newspaper *La Jornada*: "The increasing power of the drug cartels is *tijuanizing* Mexico City" (March 25, 2000).

Tijuana, Nation between Two Nations

In a few years, we have moved from the idea of the city as a symbol of cultural rootlessness and denationalization to the concept of a city as being completely different from the center of the country. The discourse that imagines a different city assumes the existence of a space increasingly disconnected socially and culturally from the rest of the nation, be it called Third Nation, Third Country, Mexamerica, Amermexico, Nepantla, Ecotono. . . . The names vary and in their very diversity they reveal the difficulties inherent in confronting a city that is itself a border.

In summary, there is a discursive city, the result of different discourses that have constructed it through the course of the years. A city that alludes to history, projects and utopias, dreams and distinct visions, but which is also explained by the relationship its inhabitants have with the urban space, their passions and their fears. Through all of these, we can perceive the superim-posed, multiple faces of a heterogeneous city. One for every occasion, accord-ing to the particular demands of the moment.

To put it succinctly, it is a kind of palimpsest made up of multiple voices that have contributed to diversify its own social physiognomy. Sometimes in a much more convincing way than the real city.

From the Cinematic City to the Distribution of an Archetype

> The 1929 stock market crash economically destroyed Tijuana. This explains the presence of produc-ers filming low-cost pornographic movies whose main characters were old, perverted European prostitutes and Mexican teenage girls. —MIGUEL ÁNGEL MORALES, "Tijuana, escenario clandestino. La meca del cine porno (1930–1943)" ["Tijuana, Clandestine Stage: The Porn Movie Mecca (1930–1943)"]

No one can say exactly how many there are. They come in all types and genres. Both domestic and foreign. Silent and talking. High and low quality. Film noir and gay film. Harmless musical comedies or unimaginably bad, fake border thrillers. The plots can be as unbelievable or as strange as in any other movie. Many were filmed in Tijuana; others were produced on tempo-rary, papier-mâché sets built just for that purpose.

But while some of these films alluded to the city in an indirect way, as if they wished to hide a certain shame, many others mentioned the city in the actual title, perhaps in order to reaffirm their most immediate intention (*A Day in Tijuana*, 1925; *The Tijuana Story*, 1957; *Tijuana caliente* [Hot Tijuana], 1981; *Asalto en Tijuana* [Attack on Tijuana], 1984). In any case, film would become a formidable catalyst for the creation of myths about the city's public image of vice and indulgence, especially during and beginning in the 1920s and 1930s. Without their productive contribution, it would not be possible to explain the continuity and the persistence of the archetype that converted Tijuana into a city of immorality and indiscriminate violence.

And in view of the fact that the large majority of these films have explicitly mentioned the city's name, they have used it almost always as if it were the unquestionable symbol of vice and indulgence. Several hundred movies have helped to create the myth, the image of the vilified city, and then they have reproduced it repeatedly without the slightest remorse. And it is easy to understand why: who the hell would possibly care about what happens to a city with a past so unworthy of respect?

In the majority of the films, there is an obvious tendency to emphasize the moral corruption, misery, or sordidness of the Tijuana underworld. The exceptions are found in a few Mexican movies, but they are very far from actually countering the cinematic archetype that was so arduously constructed: *El jardín del Edén* (The Garden of Eden) by María Novaro, for example. To summarize, a film noir for a city with a reprehensible, dark past.

Despite this, these are the movies that speak to us today about Tijuana, movies that have contributed in one or another way to forging the mythical visions that now hold sway over the city. The movies show the way that Tijuana has been patiently imagined, conceived, valued, or maliciously exaggerated. All of them could form another chapter in the history of international film. Or, in any case, they could form the "Tijuana filmography." At this time, their quantity is certainly considerable.

Even if the distinct stereotypes that appear in these movies are different in each of them, almost all of them seem to faithfully obey the same (mythical) cultural code: the image of the quintessential cities of perversion, Sodom and Babylon. I'll quickly list the most notable cinematic stereotypes, among many others that very well might be mentioned in an analysis more detailed than this one.

The Border Nightclub

Conceived from the beginning as a gigantic brothel located at the edge of the Mexican border, American film in the 1920s and 1930s found in Tijuana the appropriate backdrop for many of its movies. In fact, Tijuana became the ideal place for Hollywood to go since there were few reasons not to: whether it was to use it as a summer resort or to openly promote its stars and directors, whether as a setting for its cinematic fictions or finally to include it as part of the plotlines of its movies. For whatever reason, Tijuana played the part of the despicable city, a hardly altered version of the diabolic cities. For some, this could be summed up by the incontrovertible image of the *leyenda negra* (black legend) in Tijuana.

In fact, the legend was initially constructed on the celluloid screen, ever since the first examples like *Riders Up* (1924), *A Day in Tijuana* (1925), *Tell It to the Marines* (1926), *Golf Widows* (1928), *The Speed Classic* (1928), and *The Champ* (1931), and then moving on to *In Caliente* (1935)—filmed in the old casino of Agua Caliente, with Dolores del Río and a momentary appearance by Margarita Carmen Cansino (later known as Rita Hayworth)—and many others whom it would be too tedious to mention now. Tijuana is portrayed as a brothel infested with dive bars, in some movies more so than others, but all of them set out to safeguard the "Puritanism" of the immoral American citizens.

During the following years, the cinematic vision of Tijuana hardly changed at all. This is because, as Emilio García Riera wrote in his indispensable work *México visto por el cine extranjero, 1894–1940* (Mexico as Seen in Foreign Films, 1987), Hollywood continued "to see Tijuana as the most sinful—and attractive—of the border no man's land." Just as one example, the movie *Charlie's Angels: Full Throttle* (2003) is nothing more than a continuation of the cinematic stereotype erected in the mid-1920s. For its part, Mexican film did much the same.

The City of Smuggling

Ever since the first Mexican talking movie, *Contrabando* (Smuggling, 1931)—in part set in the casino of Agua Caliente and filmed several months before *Santa* would be filmed in Mexico City—smuggling has been one of the favorite subjects both for businessmen and film directors, both foreign and Mexican. Since then the title of the first Mexican movie would seem to reaffirm the vocation and the fate associated with Tijuana.

In time, a new cinematic subgenre was born: the so-called *narcopelículas* or drug movies that created what Jorge Ayala Blanco would later call *la frontera grifa* or "the stoned border" (referring to marijuana).

Smuggling, whether it involves people or drugs, is still a substantial part of the thematic repertoire of the majority of movies that mention Tijuana. It is the same, whether one is talking about Mexican film or American film (*Traffic*, 2000), or a smaller subset of American production, Chicano film (*La Bamba*, 1987, and *Born in East L.A.*, 1987).

Ciudad de paso, City to Pass Through

Both from the interior of Mexico and from the United States, for Mexican immigrants and for fleeing Americans—for the latter group, escaping the justice system in their country and hungry for all types of entertainment, Tijuana would seem to be a refuge they can run to without any major obstacles. For the Mexicans, simply fleeing the misery and unemployment that dominates Mexico, Tijuana has been the sum total of all the unexpected mishaps that must be dealt with before being able to reach American prosperity, or even just to leave the country for as long as possible.

Among the more recent movies are *Losin' It* (1983), *Born in East L.A.*, and *La Bamba*. In the last movie, the singer Richie Valens finds the source of musical inspiration in Tijuana. Here, for the first time, he hears a Mexican group playing "La Bamba," the song that later he would record with considerable success. And among the Mexican films are *La tumba del mojado* (The Wetback's Grave, 1985) and *Santitos* (1999), based on the novel of the same name by María Amparo Escandón and which includes a dialogue that is quite faithful to it. Esperanza, the main character, takes a bus to look for her teenage daughter who supposedly is somewhere in Tijuana. A girl the same age as her daughter is sitting next to her on the bus. Esperanza asks her: "What are you going to do in Tijuana?" The answer, despite initially seeming ambiguous, leaves no doubt: "What everybody goes to Tijuana to do!"

The City of Violence

One of the most common themes of Mexican cinema in recent years is the projection of an extraordinarily violent city. The list of such movies is extensive and it would be tedious to mention each and every one of them individually. Nevertheless, *Asalto en Tijuana* (Attack on Tijuana, 1984), *Tijuana Jones* (1985), *El fiscal de hierro* (The Iron Prosecutor, 1988), and *Largo camino a Tijuana* (Long Road to Tijuana, 1989) stand out from the long list of other films.

The Mecca of Pornography

In the 1930s, without actually trying, Tijuana became the mecca of porn. The majority of these pornographic films were underground projects with very low budgets. According to Miguel Ángel Morales, El bohemio (The Bohemian, 1930), Pancho: Como quiere un mexicano (Pancho: How a Mexican Loves, 1932), and El satario (1932) were filmed at that time; in all of them, we see the talents of the Mexican Rin Tin Tin. Thus, a new and unknown global film market was discovered: canophilia. The Mexican double for the Hollywood German shepherd also starred in La dama de negro (The Lady in Black, 1932) and Mexican Lady and Dog (1933). Presumably, a passionate and worthy representative of Agua Caliente later starred in Wild Gal (1933).

Other movies of the period are Genie (1935 or 1936), Mexican Dream or Mexican Dance (1935), Toreador (1935 or 1939), La víbora (The Snake, 1939), the anti-clerical Mexican Honeymoon (1935 or 1939) or Shirley Temple enamorada (Shirley Temple in Love, 1939), related to pedophilia. Other movies featuring dog lovers include El perro masajista (The Dog Masseuse, 1935), Un cazador y su perro (A Hunter and His Dog, 1939), and Pretty Pup or Super Dog (1939). These were in addition to lesbian flicks like Tortilla Girls (1943), films about passionate wives, Office Wife (1940), or films set in gypsy camps, like Gypsies (1943). We should also mention several movies that could have been filmed in Tijuana: The Lady and the Maid and the one christened in the Film Center of La Universidad Nacional Autónoma de México (UNAM) as Las cazadoras (The Huntresses).

Tijuana is a city that is continually reinvented, recreated, and imagined by and through the cinema. It is possible that the urban landscapes, the streets and familiar neighborhoods are the least important, which in large part they are. It could also be true that the reasons really matter very little, as in fact is true for the majority of these movies; cinematic objectivity is of minimal importance. It could also be that no one cares about their relative faithfulness to the reality of the setting or the details of the physical environs. What is most important in the end in all of these movies is the images that come off the screen; those that the viewer accepts as if they were a simple transposition of social reality.

The image of Tijuana that these movies have helped to create is not very different from the image offered by literature or by the actual corridos of drug trafficking. In every case, they repeat almost exactly the same stereotypes that the social imaginary has already converted into part of the Tijuana imaginary. Invariably, it is the prototype of the city of vice, of moral corruption, of drug trafficking, of indiscriminate violence, of . . .

On How Tijuana Became a Narratable City

Some people say Padre Truquitos opened a gambling casino—underground of course—in Tijuana. And other ones even venture to say he hooked up with Valverde's people. Valverde was an ex-drug dealer who was practically made into a saint with an altar and everything.
—PEDRO ÁNGEL PALOU, *Memoria de los días* (Memory of the Days)

Every city is made of bricks, stones, cement, and, fundamentally, words. These words, like ancestral myths and beliefs, come from the archives that make up the collective imaginary. This is true even in those cities with deep and well-established geographic roots, with their own architectural style, or even a defined character. All have been constructed out of the same illusory material as the famous fictional cities.[1] It is the same situation, whether it involves Macondo or Paris, Yoknapatawpha or Dublin, Comala or Mexico City, Ciudad Delicias or Tijuana. There is already a long list.

If such cities exist, it is because they have been previously imagined, re-created, invented, dreamed, and modeled. As Michel Butor has said, these cities have a considerable literary weight. It is the literary city, made out of words that is the mediatized city of fiction—the one that exists in and through the different stories that have shaped the city in literary spaces. Because of this, it is a world exposed by the literary text, but which does not exactly correspond to a simple narrative transposition. It is, in turn, the result of a dense frame of voices and discourses that are layered on top of one another so that the city is able to speak or be spoken.

Like all cities or almost all cities, Tijuana has also been established through the written work of its numerous and contradictory narrators. It exists in the literary texts that have given it life and substance—a city constructed more by its writers than by the bricklayers and carpenters who erected its buildings. The fact that the city is made of words is due both to the writing itself and to the interpretations derived from that same writing, which have ended up shaping a now unmistakable face. It has been elevated to the level of a universal myth, articulated in large part by literary fiction.

It would seem that Western literature about urban life has revolved around three themes: nostalgic tropes of the lost Garden of Eden, the deferred dream of heavenly Jerusalem, or the abjection symbolized by the mythical city of Babylon. However, the writers who have written about Tijuana have almost always had the last one in mind as their primary model. Tijuana embodies the archetype of urban debasement, a new Babylon whose mythical referent has always been the city wholly dedicated to immorality and vice. For that reason, Tijuana, perhaps more so than any other Mexican city, has taken the brunt of condemnation and criticism. In fact, in a large number of stories, Tijuana appears to be portrayed as the perverted city, as the example of vice and corruption with no limits.

These stories refer to the myths of perverted and diabolic cities, namely: Sodom, Gomorrah, and, principally, Babylon. In a quick list that does not attempt to be exhaustive, but rather meaningful, we could enumerate the following imagotypes of the intangible literary city, which combined have sketched the most recognized and accepted literary profile of Tijuana; the city visited and revisited in literary fiction. To put it another way: a literaturized city.

The Leyenda Negra

The idea of the leyenda negra emerged out of a book: an allegorical, naturalist novel called *Tijuana In* (1932) by Hernán de la Roca—a pseudonym of Fernando de Corral. The other book is *Border Town* (1935), a novel by an American, Graham Carroll. In the first case, we find a novel with a moralistic tone; Tijuana is portrayed as "a cruel and evil goddess who poisons and steals without mercy." Compared to San Diego, Tijuana is a place "infested with the plagues of lust and the vice of drunkenness." As a consequence of its moralizing vision, Hernán de la Roca (Fernando de Corral) only ends his story once he has imagined the wretched place cleaned up once and for all. The solution he proposes is emblematic of his obvious religious symbolism: the city is destroyed by the flames of a fire that will end up purifying it.

In the novel by Graham Carroll, we read the following lines: "Baldy had dealt in the Klondike and in Montreal, New York, Chicago, New Orleans, Juárez, Tia Juana and numerous other cities. He had but one vice—gambling." This is nothing different from what we have seen in other sources; for example, it is repeated in the novel *Corpus of Joe Bailey* (1953) by Oakley May. This is just to mention a couple of novels that have left their mark forever on the literary imaginary of the city.

The Mother of All Vices

In *Calle Revolución* (1964), a novel by Rubén Vizcaíno Valencia, the Avenida Revolución (and consequently, Tijuana), is portrayed in the narrative as a place of absolute filth and immorality. The judgment that the narrator reaches is categorical in the extreme, perhaps so as not to leave any doubt: "That street was hell." Tijuana embodies the undeniable appeal of all that is sinful and despicable. Because hell is more convincing than heavenly promises.

   In his dramatic work *La madre de todos los vicios* (1965), and in the voice of one of his characters, the author insists on the unquestionable truth of his moral verdict; he leaves no doubt here either about the place's malignant nature: "Tijuana is the mother of all vices." Luckily, as he would maintain later in his poem titled "Bendición" (Blessing):

Ninguna alma
es completamente criminal,
como ninguna ciudad
podrá ser ruin eternamente.

¡Bendito sea Dios
que dispone las cosas!

(No soul
Is completely criminal,
Just as no city
Could be eternally lost.

Blessed be to God
Who arranges all things!)

The Obscene, Shameless Main Street

Avenida Revolución occupies a central position in practically all the literature written in and about Tijuana; it is an indispensable reference, unavoidable and highly symbolic. And it's easy to understand why: it has been the scene of all kinds of cabarets and brothels, cantinas and strip clubs. Since the 1920s, the space has been set up to provide entertainment to American tourists, a space freed from all legal and moral restrictions.

   So, while Dashiell Hammett sees it as a "dirty, dusty street that wound through two nonstop rows of bars and cantinas" (*The Golden Horseshoe*), for Raymond Chandler, it ends up being a place that "is nothing: all they want there is the buck. The kid who sidles over to your car and looks at you with big wistful eyes and says, 'One dime, please, mister,' will try to sell you his sister in the next sentence" (*The Long Goodbye*, 1953). For the Mexican José Revueltas, the Avenida Revolución was simply "the obscene, shameless Main Street of Tijuana, surrounded by hordes of gringos, prostitutes and drunks" (*Los motivos de Caín* [Cain's Motives], 1957).

The Drug-Trafficking Paradise

People trafficking all types of illicit drugs are forced to pass through Tijuana, and more than a few writers have also found it one of their favorite locations. Álvaro Mutis, for example, refers to the city as "paradise for drug traffickers and cardsharks, the vast brothel that is open day or night, with the deafening noise of its jukeboxes and under the lights of a thousand neon signs" (*Diario de Lecumberri*, 1975). In much the same way, Rafael Bernal, in his police novel *El complot mongol* (1969), mentions that his main character is planning to go to Tijuana to "look for a few buddies who were smuggling marijuana."

"'I came to Tijuana because they told me that the man who lived here killed my father,' said Bonilla." This is how Mauricio Electorat's story "I've Never Been to Tijuana" begins, a story included in the book *I've Never Been to Tijuana and Other Stories* (2000). A story whose backdrop is also drug trafficking begins in Santiago, Chile, and reaches its climax in Tijuana with a murder. In reality, revenge. Bonilla, the son of a soldier who refused to collaborate with the repression, comes to Tijuana to kill his brother-in-law. In addition, in the Electorat story, a character named Teodocio Jara, "nicknamed TJ, i.e. Tijuana" is a typical Mexican hitman and, apparently, the first fictional character with that nickname.

The Paradise of Illicit Practices

Tijuana has also been a paradise for divorce and fly-by-night marriages, for trading in immigration documents, for back-alley abortions—as Ross McDonald wrote about in his novel *Black Money* (1955)—or, in more recent years, for the alleged trafficking in human organs, as portrayed in a novel by Eduardo Bofil, *Bajo mi piel* (Under My Skin, 1998), and in *Tijuana City Blues* (1999) by Gabriel Trujillo Muñoz.

Because, in the end, and according to the novel by Mempo Giardinelli, "Tijuana's like that: an undeniable paradise of gambling and corruption" (*Santo oficio de la memoria* [The Holy Labor of Memory], 1991). Or as James Ellroy makes clear, "The Tijuana police were vultures dressed in black shirts who barely spoke English . . . but who understood perfectly the international language" of corruption (*The Black Dahlia*, 1993). James Ellroy is also the author of the novel meaningfully titled *Tijuana, Mon Amour* (Tijuana, My Love, 1999).

The Wicked Border Brothel

Part of the previous interpretations is the constant tendency to see Tijuana as the huge brothel of the Mexican border. There is no lack of fictional narratives in this regard as well. Although the versions can differ from one author to another, or from one book to another, the result has invariably been the same. For Dashiell Hammett, the "whores in Tijuana don't beat around the bush" (*The Golden Horseshoe*), but for Henry Miller, they seem to be "hard and soft at the same time. Whores, of course."

The City of Love

There is also no lack of declarations of love, but it is a love that embraces the idea of the city as wicked and extraordinarily violent. As the main character of Juan Hernández Luna's *Tijuana Dream* (1997) puts it, "*Wacha*, pig. *La Gran Tiyei*, you know? The sexiest city in the world, *guey*. I love that city with everything I got. Take a good look at her and tell me she's not a cute, little bitch. Answer me, *cabrón!*"

Or as is explained in the "novel" by Tomás Perrín Escobar, *El agua de la presa* (The Water behind the Dam, 1985): "Tijuana was never a whore, son—he continued—never a whore like Miller's Paris. It was and still is an excellent saleswoman who constantly switches out her merchandise and the decorations in her shop window, who does whatever the market in the North asks for and follows the idiotic regulations that come from the South."

The Ironic, Playful Celebration

Although it is less frequent, it is worth mentioning the ironic approach to Tijuana, for example, as in the case of Parménides García Saldaña, who described Tijuana as a "store selling groceries, chorizos and liquor open 69 hours a day to serve you prostitution and vice" (*Pasto Verde*, 1968). But if during the daytime Tijuana can fake a certain decency, for Paco Ignacio Taibo II, the night makes Tijuana once again "a gateway city to the other side and gives it back its heroically won fame as a city of vice, an illegal city for the timid, fearful gringo adventure-seeker, looking for nasty sex, exotic delights for their dicks only about twenty miles from San Diego" (*Sueños de frontera* [Border Dreams], 1990).

The Slighted City

While it is not the only one, perhaps Guillermo Cabrera Infante's slight against Tijuana is the least acceptable—above all because it's based on a historical lie and his own personal aversion toward Tijuana: "One must remember as well that on the continent that Columbus (and the Pinzón brothers) discovered, Havana is the closest to the urban areas of the USA—unless one wishes to insult Tijuana by calling it a city" (*Mea Cuba*, 1993).

In these cases, the imagination wins out over actual knowledge, the bad public image beats any fondness for truth. The novel *El recurso del método* (Reasons of State, 1974), by Alejo Carpentier, is a good example of the former.

Tijuana as a Metaphor for Urban Chaos

Tijuana can also be a space for apocalyptic nightmares, dark, dystopian visions of urban life, as is clear in the pages of "Neon City Blues" (2001), a story by Emiliano González:

> TIJUANA, 1989
>
> The smell of fried fast food and border brothels. Trash in the streets, in the wind, in the clouds. A few angels sweep the sidewalks. Mexican whores lift up their skirts to show us the syphilitic thicket where mosquitos, larvas, beetles and centipedes make their nests. There are greasers sticking their butts out of the windows of their rooms and shit on the people walking by. A hot cake seller in the street cooks it a while and sells it, covered with honey, to a pair of tourists who devour it without saying a word, maybe because they're scared the locals won't like them.

Apocalyptic Fiction

For the same reason, Tijuana has not been exempt from apocalyptic visions of the end of the world. Two examples will illustrate this type of story. In *Cristóbal Nonato* (Christopher Unborn, 1987) Carlos Fuentes imagines a country wracked with social disasters, a nation divided and conflicted: "from the Pacific coast to the Gulf coast, one hundred miles to the north and a hundred to the south of the old border, from Sandy Ego to Antijane to Cofferville and Kilmoors." Sandy Ego is none other than San Diego, and Antijane is without a doubt Tijuana.

The other example is a novel by Pedro Angel Palou, *Memoria de los días* (Memory of the Days, 1995). In this novel, the narrator points out, "Some people say Father Truquitos opened a gambling casino—underground, of course—in Tijuana. And other ones even venture to say he hooked up with Valverde's people. Valverde was an ex-drug dealer who was practically made into a saint with an altar and everything."

Of course, the list is not limited to the authors mentioned above. Many more writers have made their own individual contributions to the process of imagining Tijuana. But it would take a long time to list them all, and, besides, what would that possibly achieve? The invention of Tijuana in the narrative imaginary is a fact that transcends numbers and specific cases. Because, as Jorge Luis Borges said, "It never was exactly like its legend, but it kept getting closer." In our case, the legend ended up larger than the reality.

The Epic of the Corridos of the Drug Trade

Beginning in the 1980s, the corridos of the drug trade—which are also the corridos of smugglers and the mafia—began to propagate many different kinds of popular myths (including the myth of the social bandit, among others), create lasting legends (like Camelia la Texana), provide updated values and beliefs to a vast sector of the population, disseminate basic attitudes in regard to the incidents reported in the crime news, and revitalize a musical genre in decline (the corrido norteño) and convert it into a profitable pursuit for musical groups, record companies, and radio stations.

Despite their few lyrical or poetic discoveries, the *narcocorridos* are the dramatized stories of the exploits of those people who choose to live life out of the reach of the law or those who, wishing to get out of poverty as soon as possible, look for the only accessible alternative. Perhaps because of this, as Luis A. Astorga maintains in his notable work, *Mythology of the Drug Trafficker in Mexico* (1995), the corrido reproduces a continual process of "sublimation and mythification of a way of life." The subjects are recurring, and not necessarily in the same order: violence as an essential part of the environment, the ever-present dangers in the random daily work of the drug trafficker, the desire for easy money as a compensation for the lack of work opportunities, the apologias of the antihero, the bravery that is or passes for being synonymous with a general coldness toward life, and the border as an indispensable stage for illegal operations. For the drug traffickers, the corrido has been responsible for taking what yesterday was seen as crime news and turning it into what today is seen as legendary exploits.

In its own way and without deliberately setting out to do it, the narcocorrido has become an important part of the epic that has grown up to recount the (real and fictitious) events involved with the illegal smuggling of drugs. For that reason, as a narrative genre, the narcocorrido also belongs to the epic song, to the popular epic that the listeners know or have heard previously because it has been written about in the news on crime, in the newspapers that confirm what everyone knows or believes they know. Because of this, the person who "sings (hears, memorizes) the life and death of a *narco* does not sentimentally exalt a social bandit, rather he only states the obvious: he does not feel morally superior to the characters of the corrido" (Carlos Monsiváis).

Also, and on another level, the corridos made a huge contribution toward propagating "a biased image of the northern border" (José Manuel Valenzuela Arce). It is usually a violent and pernicious vision. In all these instances, we notice above all the repetition of an image that (though not new) found in the corrido the perfect way to reinforce the public reputation: Tijuana as a mandatory gateway for the drug trade, the setting for a large quantity of illicit transactions. But above all, the corrido provides a refrain for the image of a city immersed in social violence.

In order to examine the "musical image" of Tijuana, I will look at a body of corridos—as small a group as possible, but that sufficiently illustrate my point—to illustrate what, at this stage, is already a very recognizable theme: Tijuana as an active symbol within the mythology that surrounds illegal drug trafficking. The symbolic violence carries the gravest consequences.

Curiously, two violent women, both of them dedicated to the lucrative business of drug trafficking, are the first formal protagonists of a series of corridos that made Tijuana a well-known musical subject. Both women are also part of one love story that weaves together a violent narrative of love and breakups, betrayal and revenge.

The first woman is known by the nickname Margarita la de Tijuana (Margarita, the Woman from Tijuana). The corrido with her name as the title—made popular in the 1970s—contains all the elements that would be developed later: the subject matter, the attitude toward the drug trade, and the musical tone of many corridos from and about Tijuana.

Margarita de su bolsa
le enseñaba un cargador
Yo descargué tu pistola,
presentía tu traición.
Sonaron cuatro balazos
Julián bien muerto cayó
y aquél fajo de billetes
Margarita se los llevó.
Por tener cuentas pendientes
a Tijuana no volvió.

(Margarita flashed the butt
of the gun in her bag.
I shot your pistol,
I knew you'd betray me.
Four shots rang out
Julian fell dead
and Margarita took
that bundle of bills.

Because the score was left unsettled,
she never came back to Tijuana.)

The other woman is even more famous. Camelia la Tejana was a fictional character that became famous first during the 1970s. To date, several corridos and other movies filmed over a little more than the last three decades recount the exploits of this intrepid woman. The movies include *Contrabando y traición (Camelia la Texana)* (Smuggling and Betrayal [Camelia the Tejana], 1976), *Mataron a Camelia la Texana* (They Killed Camelia the Tejana, 1976), *La hija del contrabando* (Smuggling's Daughter, 1977), *La mafia de la frontera* (The Border Mafia, 1979), *Emilio Varela vs. Camelia la Texana* (1979), *El hijo de Camelia la tejana* (The Son of Camelia the Tejana, 1989), *Ya encontraron a Camelia* (They Already Caught Camelia), and *La muerte de Camelia* (The Death of Camelia). And the corridos include "Contrabando y traición," "Ya encontraron a Camelia," and "El hijo de Camelia." Of the three, the best-known one is definitely the first. The lyrics are so well known that I do not even need to reproduce all of them here:

Salieron de San Ysidro
procedentes de Tijuana.
Traían las llantas
del carro repletas
de yerba mala.
Eran Emilio Varela
y Camelia la texana.

(They left San Ysidro
coming from Tijuana.
The tires in the car
were stuffed
full of marijuana.
It was Emilio Varela
And Camelia la Texana.)

In the epic of Camelia la Tejana, as fantastic as it is extensive, we can immediately recognize the media perception that later would feed the musical and cinematic legend of the northern border (and as a consequence Tijuana) as the center of operations for illicit drug smuggling.

La banda la perseguía
en la Unión Americana.
También mandaron su gente

a buscarla hasta Tijuana.
Sólo Dios podría salvar
a Camelia la Tejana.

(The gang went after her
into the United States.
They also sent their people
to look for her in Tijuana.
Only God could save
Camelia la Tejana.)

The end is predictable. In the geography of the drug trade portrayed in the corridos, Tijuana would quickly become an important stopover. According to several well-known versions, it is a mandatory stop on the risky road that drug traffickers have to follow in order to reach their consumers. There is no question about the underlying message:

Por kilos o toneladas
yo siempre trabajo igual
por Tijuana o Mexicali
mis tráilers logran pasar
mi contrabando es muy fino
es coca de calidad.

(I always work the same
whether it's kilos or tons
through Tijuana or Mexicali
my trucks get right through
my goods are top notch—
high-quality coke.)

And Tijuana, as a gateway city, became something more than a point of reference. It is an important part of the narrative plot, as articulated in a series of corridos that continually reiterate the hardships involved in drug trafficking.

Cuántos hombres sinaloenses
pasan hoy la Rumorosa
la frontera de Tijuana
pero rodean Santa Rosa
llevando su contrabando
desde hierba, goma y coca.

(How many men from Sinaloa
drive through the Rumorosa
and the Tijuana border
but drive around Santa Rosa
carrying their illegal cargo
weed, hash and coke.)

As if this weren't enough, all kinds of stories are born out of the illicit trade in
drugs. But without exception, all of the stories that refer to Tijuana reproduce
the image of a scene of indiscriminate violence. It is always the same image
whether it refers to the violence among different groups fighting for control
of the drug trade or the violence arising out of clashes between the gangs and
the police. In any case, the corrido is practically the same as a tabloid crime
story or a fake police thriller:

Volaban las avionetas
con cargas de hierba mala
unas para Houston, Texas
otras allá por Tijuana
de diferentes estados.

(The small planes flew out
from different states
with weed as their cargo
some headed to Houston, Texas
others over there near Tijuana.)

The portrait that finally emerges is that of a city mixed up in the international
circuit of illicit drugs. Tijuana is not only the trampoline for drugs that many
assume it to be, nor simply a mandatory stopover for illegal cargo. In the end,
it is the quintessential symbol of the drug trade. A large number of people
have fallen dead, and more than a few are in prison. The corrido is clear:

Ahí lo vieron por Sonora
iba con rumbo a Nogales
lo encontraron en Tijuana
por Chihuahua y Ciudad Juárez
en busca del Gallo Negro
el que le mató a su padre.

(They saw him around Sonora
he was headed toward Nogales

they found him in Tijuana
around Chihuahua and Ciudad Juárez
looking for El Gallo Negro
the one who killed his father.)

The corrido as a discursive genre has another important element that is easily demonstrated; it possesses a certain power that could only be called performative, because there is no other way to describe the effect its distribution has produced. In its own way, the corrido, like literature or film, dramatizes, constructs, feeds, and confirms the image that is held about the border and the cities mixed up in the international drug trade. And Tijuana takes first place.

Note

1 Rosalba Campra, "La ciudad en el discurso literario" [The city in literary discourse], *SYC*, no. 5 (Buenos Aires, May 1994): 5–39.

Tijuanologies

An Urban Essay

There are more cantinas in Tijuana than buildings.—*The Nation* (1888)

On the other side of the dry river bed, liminal, held in common by the two countries, a dusty road is visible, and, after a short distance, leads to a small, dilapidated wooden ranch house, designated on the maps by the name, Tijuana.—JOSÉ VASCONCELOS, "Visiones californianas" (Californian Visions, 1919)

Tijuana is a *play box*. At least in its storefronts, which, because of their mystery, could easily be entirely something else. . . . The thing is that in Tijuana you only see a street, a street at nighttime where a cabaret is next to a bar, the bar beside a fake curio shop, the shop next to another cabaret, then a bar, then a hotel, and later another cabaret and another bar. . . . It's just like that for an entire kilometer, difficult to traverse without losing your stomach. —FERNANDO JORDÁN, *El otro México* (The Other Mexico, 1950)

I like the movement of modern cities like New York . . . but in San Diego, the density is just not there; which is part of the attraction we feel for Tijuana, crossing the border, where the old sensation of a city is still very much alive. There's a density to the streets and the people that I really appreciate. —JEROME ROTHENBERG, *The Riverside Interviews* (1984)

From the beginning of this century until fifteen years ago, Tijuana was known for a casino (abolished during the Cárdenas government), cabarets, dance halls, and liquor stores where North Americans came to elude their country's prohibitions on sex, gambling, and alcohol. The recent installation of factories, modern hotels, cultural centers, and access to wide-ranging international information has made it into a modern, contradictory, cosmopolitan city with a strong definition of itself.—NÉSTOR GARCÍA CANCLINI, *Hybrid Cultures: Strategies for Entering and Leaving Modernity* (1989)

Tijuana and San Diego are not in the same historical time zone. Tijuana is poised at the beginning of the industrial age, a Dickensian city with palm trees. San Diego is a postindustrial city of high impact plastic and desperate dieting. And palm trees. San Diego faces west, looking resolutely out to sea. Tijuana gazes north toward the future. San Diego is the future—secular, soulless. San Diego is the past, guarding its quality of life. Tijuana is the future. . . . Taken together as one, Tijuana and San Diego form the most fascinating new city in the world, a city of world-class irony.—RICHARD RODRÍGUEZ, *Days of Obligation: An Argument with My Mexican Father* (1993)

Tijuana is in the middle of an artistic flowering that has drawn attention from television executives and museum curators from New York to Tokyo. Artists of all stripes are re-examining the hybrid culture of Tijuana that exists between the glitz of San Diego and the factory life Diego Rivera could have painted.—"The World's New Cultural Meccas," *Newsweek* (2002)

At Customs: Would You Like to Know What It's Like to Live on the Border? (Tijuana Is the United States of Mexico: *Yeah, Right*)

They say there's an aphrodisiac called the "Spanish fly" and one or two drops will send someone into a state of uncontrollable, sexual frenzy. No one I know has seen a Spanish fly, except for one friend of a friend (oh, right, I forgot to mention that every rumor's source is the friend of a friend of a friend . . .). But he told me you could purchase the Spanish fly in Tijuana. You can purchase anything in Tijuana. That, by the way, is another rumor. —LEWIS BALTZ in *Urban Rumors*, a project curated by Hans Ulrich Obrist (Switzerland)

Tijuana kills. If so many writers have drafted a few paragraphs or a few sentences about the city, it is because more than a city, Tijuana is a religion or an execrable mythology. Tijuana is a maddening woman, a woman who can't be forgotten, even by insulting her or lying about her, a passionate and terrible woman, a city that consumes and destroys herself.

In my lifetime, I have not felt a love as profound as the confusing passion that I feel for Tijuana, an obsession that does not preclude criticism and which more accurately provokes sudden repudiation. Tijuana elicits a crazy love, a narcotic love. Tijuana is addictive.

No Mexican city has provoked as much morbid interest as Mexico City or Tijuana. Mexico City because of its frightening size, the weight of its ancient pyramids; Tijuana because of its sinister youth, because of the black shadows of its streets, and above all, because of the fear it inspires in us, what it truly represents in regard to our whole culture. A city representing the entire future of the globalized world, but without any prospects. Like any city that is alive even in its deepest depths, Tijuana is an assassin.

Richard Rodríguez has explained it wisely: "Tijuana is an industrial park in the suburbs of Minneapolis. Tijuana is a neighborhood of Tokyo. Tijuana is a sweatshop in Taiwan" (*Days of Obligation: An Argument with My Mexican Father*, 1992). Tijuana is not a city. Tijuana is a symptom of contemporary urbanity. Tijuana is a posturban condition, in which the battles of attraction and resistance have been made almost impossible. Tijuana is a magnet that bleeds.

For this same reason, the city belongs to the scattered archives of international literature, since living on the border is not only living among unbelievable statistics, and, at the same time, among irrefutable images in the street, but also existing on the border means putting up with pseudoproblems and imitations.

To live here is to return to the greatest myth of all myths, to be required to profess—before certain visitors, certain neighbors, certain experts—a second-rate esotericism.

Write something about Tijuana and you will be quoted. Write something about that city and you will soon be addicted to her self-deception. To her thirst to continually fall to new lows. Tijuana is an empty city. None of us can deny that.

That is the reason for her taste in drugs, partying, murder, and, at the same time, the anonymous life of the maquila. Tijuana is a narco. Tijuana is a prostitute. Tijuana is hope.

To talk about the border is to convert oneself into a corner mystagogue. The border is this and this and this; the border according to so-and-so is that, but not that. The discourse about the border has gone mad.

Gringos, Mexicans, Spanish, it doesn't matter who it is, Tijuana is a whore about whom you can say whatever you want. Anything can be proven about her.

In terms of ideology, Tijuana is a nightmare.

To live here is to be a character, because on the border, there are no inhabitants, just archetypes. The border has no life: it has metaphysics—thou shalt hear her bullshit.

Presenting, the Coyote,

Presenting, the Tourist,

Presenting, the Whore,

Presenting, the Hybrid,

Presenting, the Migrant.

Each person becomes histrionic, or, better stated, an online nickname. To talk about the Border is to use capital letters. To be up to date with journalism, bibliographies, the latest theories. Oh, and to always know the latest neologism. Typical of the academic gang. Which criminal was recently honored.

Debate Bilateralism, Division, Postmodernism, the Borderline.

Living here is not knowing if, all of a sudden, the people at the next table will start using high metaphysical jargon or typical border slang in their conversation: you hear them talking about the Border, about crossing over to the Other Side, you hear them describing the three steps of mysticism: "Walk a Long Way," "Sleep under the Stars," "Discover the Point of It All"; you hear them talking about the Return of the Prodigal Son, about the Woman Waiting on the Other Side, you hear them talking about the Leap, and after a romantic fling being sent back by the Migra.

On the Border, we are all, albeit against our will, mystagogues.

To live on the Border is to reside in the middle of an unexpected atheology. An embezzled ontology. The suspicion that all this will soon be either less or more than a city, the laboratory of what is to come. Everything in this place is dragged along in terms of phenomenology or mysticism.

A Triple X mysticism, by the way.

From Tia Juana's Ranch to Television Town: Hell as Seen from the Inside

> Immediately, cantinas and vice-ridden establishments proliferated all along the Mexican border, including in Tijuana. The city's celebrated cantina, "La Ballena," opened in this period; its bar, 560 feet long, was proudly advertised as the largest in the world. —DAVID PIÑERA, *Historia de Tijuana* (History of Tijuana, 1985)

Tijuana is situated at the extreme left of Mexico and Latin America. The last stop for the Spanish language and the northernmost Latin American city, and the southernmost city where English is deconstructed, as some others would add. It's a city located in an arid region, not favorable for natural development, a factor that has not prevented it from becoming the city with the most maquiladoras in the country. Perhaps in the world. The worst thing about Tijuana though is that she is destined to be substituted in the imaginary by other Tijuanas, even worse cities. It's not an accident that the red-light districts, redolent of social collapse, whether in Central America or in the mind, are called Little Tijuanas.

Of course, her aliases include maquilopolis or maquilalandia. Tijuana has many nicknames. One for each of her characteristics. "Taking away any one of her aspects would make the city less Tijuana. More than a city, Tijuana has become a concept," writes Luis Humberto Crosthwaite. Tijuana is already several cities and, in fact, is a city that is splitting in two. The old Tijuana, the one that is the object of all the legends, and the Tijuana behind the red mountain, the Tijuana of the demographic boom, the most recent invasions, that area that at the end of the twentieth century had almost a million inhabitants and had begun to be called New Tijuana. But we will talk about that Tijuana on another occasion. In this book, we are speaking of a symbolic Tijuana, of the Tijuana from the discourse of the turn of the century. Of a dying city, shedding its snakeskin.

"TJ" belongs to the Baja California peninsula, the most isolated corner of the Mexican Republic. A portion of the population has always thought that the peninsula should separate off from Mexico. Others are almost sure that the maps are lying and that the peninsula is, in fact, already an island.

When the San Andreas fault separates the tectonic plates, that dream will be realized.

To the north, Tijuana borders San Diego, California, and to the west is the Pacific Ocean and its freezing waters, which don't attract many tourists, seeing as it is polluted by raw sewage and waste from numerous transnational companies located in the area. Tijuana is a combination of extreme situations. Perhaps it is the most reliable proof that we could survive the apocalypse.

The name probably means "dry land" in the Yumana language (yantijuan) or is derived from another indigenous linguistic family, one of the languages of the nomadic groups who lived in the region before the arrival of the Spanish missionaries. In this sense, Tijuana means wasteland, paramo, or desert. Having a name like this, being mocked in this way is another coincidence in a fucked-up life. We live in a city whose name means Wasteland.

Nevertheless, it's odd that the name is commonly explained by the existence of a powerful female landowner named Juana. La Tía Juana. Aunt Juana. As if we wanted to make ourselves believe that we lived in a woman, or came from the maternal, and not from this modern disorder, from this merciless city. It has been established that the founding of the city dates back to 1889. But that is no more than a retrospective date. By that year, the city was already known in the United States as a city with more cantinas than houses.

The cover-up of the real etymology of Tijuana might seem like an apparently insignificant fact, but it actually suggests one of the key points of border culture: we prefer to erase all of the indigenous symbols from the sign, Tijuana, and for that reason the idiotic legend was invented that the name came from a mythical rancherwoman named Tía Juana, a theory that has now been completely discarded by Tijuanologists. Complete ranchero ridiculousness.

And unlike other parts of Mexico, the mestizaje of the original habitants does not seem to have been systematic. Practically all of the indigenous groups of the region (killiwas, cucapás, pai pai, cahuilla, and akuala) are in the process of disappearing and live in far-flung communities, very similar to the way that Native Americans live in the United States. Tijuana, as a city, is not interested at all in its indigenous past. In that sense, Tijuana is more a Californian city than a Mexican city. Tijuana is the capital of Wanna Be California.

At one time, Mexico had 170 languages. When Tijuana was founded, it had 100. In 2000, the nation only had 62 left, which makes it the nation with the second-largest number of languages, behind only India. The languages native to the border are disappearing, and in a few years, there is no doubt that none of them will exist, since part of the project of "Tijuana" as a political fantasy is the continuation of an imperceptible genocide, a kind of genocide lite. Tijuana is a city that believes it has no roots, a city with the roots pulled out. Perhaps this is the reason why the new Zapatistas made the decision to name their plan to unite civil society La Realidad-Tijuana. Nevertheless, this new Zapatismo has little reverberation in Tijuana. Tijuana is sick of it.

In regard to the lack of racial mixing between the indigenous people of the region and the immigrants, the relationship that was established with the native inhabitants is definitely inspired more by the North American model than by what occurred between the Spaniards and the Mesoamerican native peoples. Indigenous people are invisible in the contemporary border society. In fact, one of the glorious myths of local racism boasts that one of the genealogical highlights of Baja California is that mestizaje never existed. The Spanish priests who came here to convert the natives to Christianity were brutal. There was more than one rebellion against them. But as with all brutality, the Conquista won out.

At the end of the nineteenth century, the economic boom in California inspired the initial development of urban life in Tijuana. The construction of houses began around Calle Olvera, which afterward came to be known as Avenida Revolución, famous worldwide for its cheap and no-holds-barred nightlife. A horizontal moment to *cheap tourism*. People always say the city looks like a typical Old West town. There is not very much historical documentation from that period. The only certainty is that the town looked toward San Diego and turned away from the rest of Mexico. Tijuana was born a motherless city, an orphaned beggar girl, her own pimp.

A few deceptive city maps and, above all, tourist postcards tell us the history of Tijuana. When historians propose researching the city, the majority of the documents they find are trash, fantasies, as if it were impossible to write a history of this city, and only literature were possible.

Or even worse, *Tijuana Bibles*. Those adult-oriented, household publications that were the precursors to *Playboy* or *Hustler*. Perverted cartoons from the beginning of the twentieth century that adopted the name of Tijuana in order to be even more obscene.

The 1900 census counted 242 residents in Tijuana. In the period since the naval base opened in San Diego in 1898, there must have been times when there were more tourists than *tijuanenses*. In that era, people could cross the border with no documents. The border was porous in both directions.

During this first decade, Tijuana established itself, slowly, as a city of vice. There was gambling and racing. In 1908, a federal administration was even created to oversee these activities on the border. But it had to be disbanded because of American insistence; they said that such measures by the Mexican government would make it possible for the border region to fill up with people of doubtful reputation. This was completely false, seeing that the region was already full of these beautiful people. Since the turn of this century, Tijuana has gradually fallen under the control of the Mafia. In 2004, the Mafia took over the Palacio Municipal (Tijuana's city hall). When Jorge Hank took power, a man accused of murdering the journalist Héctor "El Gato" Félix and embroiled in all kinds of rumored illicit activities, it represented the return of the Institutional Revolutionary Party (PRI) to the mayor's office. This "red tide" as it was called (owing to the color that was used in all of their propaganda) made it known that Tijuana had arrived at a crucial moment in which it would show its bloodiest side and show just how infatuated with death it was. Tijuana wrote its own sentence at the polls. It declared itself proudly corrupt.

And so, at the beginning of the twenty-first century, the gangsters of organized crime literally came to power. By that time, the Tijuana Cartel had for two decades not only controlled drug trafficking but also was the most powerful criminal organization in Latin America, with more power than even the Colombian cartels. At the beginning of the twentieth century, this state of affairs had already been set into motion with the first gambling *top cats* and the growth of business in prostitution and alcohol.

Paradoxically, as Tijuana elected its worst, people began to call for protecting its Good Image in a way previously unknown. The *leyenda negra* that officially took power in 2004 had, nevertheless, been born more than a century before.

The first event of the region's official history took place in 1911 when the celebrated Mexican revolutionaries Ricardo and Enrique Flores Magón focused their struggle on the region—parallel to Madero's uprising in the south of the country. For a while, they were able to establish and run an independent anarchist commune in Mexico with the help of an errant band of foreign *filibusteros*. In this way, they realized the long-held plans for Baja Californian autonomy and tijuanense culture. According to the Plan of the Liberal Party, the only ones who were excluded from that heterotopia were the Chinese.

The Flores Magón brothers, who had been imprisoned in the United States for violating the laws of neutrality, were released at the end of 1910. Just after returning to freedom, they decided to take up arms. One of the first measures taken by their forces (by the way, commanded by Anglos) was to reopen the cantinas and gambling parlors in order to increase their funding.

Despite this, a few months later, the anarchist forces were overthrown, due to their partial disorganization. Even today, the Flores Magón brothers are accused of selling out their country; there is even a monument in Tijuana dedicated to the forces of the dictator Porfirio Díaz, who "defended" the nation. This is one of the first outrageous border stories that unjustly linked the region with "foreignness" and *malinchismo* and a supposed innate desire in the region to be culturally annexed by the United States.

The city's economic reality, by necessity linked to the state of California, would add fuel to the fire. In the same year, 1911, bars and horse race gambling were prohibited in California and in 1920 the Volstead Act went into effect, making the production and sale of alcohol illegal in the entire country.

The so-called Ley Seca or Dry Law gave a fabulous boost to the development of nightlife in Tijuana. Already by 1916, the Agua Caliente Racetrack had opened and, throughout the decade, it maintained its central role in the illegal activities and nightlife that had begun during the nineteenth century.

Thanks to the Ley Seca, the city was accused of wanting to become part of the United States and betraying the nation during the Magonist revolution. Because of this, Tijuana became the metropolis of perdition; everyone and everything was seen as Americanized: from the employees to the tourists, from the street signs to the hotels.

> During the 1920s, the panorama that established the archetype of Tijuana as the city of vice par excellence is unmistakable: dozens of cantinas ready to sate the thirst of the refugees of the Ley Seca, caravans of automobiles crossing the border each day to lose themselves in the complicity of the night, recreation centers that allow the investment of free time (gambling parlors) or favor gregarious attitudes among their clientele (brothels), internationally famous casinos frequented by professional card sharks, movie stars, or wanna-be stars . . . and their counterparts: drug trafficking, a raucous night life, Russian roulette, greyhound and horse races. (Humberto Félix Berumen, "*Tijuana In*: La parábola del mal o la creación de un mito" [*Tijuana In*: The Parable of Evil or the Creation of a Myth], 1998).

In the gangster period of the 1920s, the so-called leyenda negra de Tijuana, or Tijuana's black legend, was born. This legend (now in its Windows XP version) continues to determine the perception of the Mexican border within the United States. (TJ: The scene of all those murders.) In regard to this legend, one of the definitions of Tijuana actually has been as a stomping ground for the famous. During the 1920s, Tijuana was the place for the Hollywood after party. Unable to let it all hang loose and drink ridiculous quantities on American soil (the Dry Law ruled the land and sent the alcoholics other places), they organized their binges, parties, and all-nighters in the former ranch of Tía Juana, who, even if she never existed, no one ever doubted had made an amazing party hostess.

Thanks to the contact with Hollywood and the Volstead Act, Tijuana made itself into a cultural photo op for the international who's who list. They were all here—Buster Keaton and Al Capone, Charlie Chaplin and Clark Gable, the Marx Brothers and the Flores Magón brothers, Bing Crosby and Rita Hayworth, formerly known as Margarita Cansino. Hayworth came out at the famous casino to open La Tarde Mexicana leading around a burro by a rope—the same hot burro that later in the erotic imagination of the tourists fucks dark-skinned, sexy Mexican women in bestiality-ridden cantinas, to which local taxi drivers are more than happy to drive you.

Tijuana was dog-loving, cheap, and "Mexican." Tijuana had been created by force, like a virgin who, on the day after being raped, has to take over the position of madam. Tijuana already was an irredeemable city. A city that grew to satisfy machismo, Tijuana was a lost city, an addict.

Russian roulette in a mini-neo–Old West, doctored drinks, Americans buying off the local sheriffs, all this was the basis for the leyenda negra stereotype that (temporarily) ended when "Tata" Lázaro Cárdenas, the Mexican president most symbolic of nationalism, outlawed gambling in 1935. Afterward, the Casino de Agua Caliente was actually converted into the only federal high school in the country! The local chronicles tell the story of Tijuana's ancestral greatness, about its gangsters, dog racing, light aircraft, and stardom (the Casino de Agua Caliente is our Quaternary period with ghosts and everything). Americans controlled all of these businesses, just as they continue to dominate contemporary nightlife in Tijuana.

But the fame continued unabated thanks to the Second World War. With the war, the great Tijuana nightlife was reborn, after a brief lapse: the city filled up with marines coming from San Diego. Before they headed out to the Orient to kill Japanese, they slurped tequila and Mexican women in Tijuana. Since then, the writers who come to the city continue to see the marines (even though they don't come as much) as a natural symbol for the "most vice-ridden city on the planet."

In the modern-day Plaza Santa Cecilia, a small downtown plaza, merchants sell their plaster sculptures and other little, useless items next to gay bars and old-time cantinas where the bohemian intellectuals get together to argue about who among them is the hottest diva. Up until a short time ago, there was an embarrassing walk of fame in that plaza that was trying to imitate Hollywood's in the worst ranchero kind of way. Perhaps the most notable hands in the cement were those of José José, the Mexican singer known for his romantic pain and alcoholism, which was in the process of becoming cocaine addiction. That walk of fame, by the way, was destroyed when McDonald's arrived in 2001 and installed a clock tower in this traditional Mexican plaza, an arch that looks just like the arch of this transnational company. Today, the local joke is that the city is symbolized today by an allusion to the Arc de Triomphe of Ronald McDonald. The Cuban poet José Kozer, on a visit to the city, very accurately called it McTijuana.

An artificial city with postmodern architecture, commercial anarchitecture, and chaotic self-construction.

This raucous city uses folkloric anecdotes to generate continual updates to its mythology of decadence and strange notoriety. For example, the urban legend about the quintessential 1970s guitar-playing rocker, Carlos Santana, who left Tijuana and went straight to Woodstock, or the fact that Tijuana is currently the largest trash dump for used tires in the whole world. The city of perpetual recycling. Tijuana Re: Re.

Tijuana is the best example of a hub in the civilized world—a city made for passing through and visiting. Because of this, the postcard is our most representative artistic genre. (The photographs prove that I'm not lying.) There are cities one travels to in order to get to know them. Those cities are like Paris, London, Lima, or Seattle. There are cities that people go to not to get to know them (in fact, there is nothing worth seeing), but rather to say that they have been. (The cities modern Tourism invented.) *I was here, he and she were also here, everybody at one time or another has been here, anyway. . . . I was here* is the mental graffiti we all resort to at one time or another in order to confirm that we can all have our fifteen minutes of fame. In the future, we will all have fifteen days in Tijuana that will make us famous! Come and get your picture taken.

On the other hand, this explains the constant visits by intellectuals from other places that come to Tijuana looking for intense emotions (a typically North American behavior, which is not that different from any teenager). They persist with this tradition of coming in and leaving their mark on

Tijuana. All of us, at one time or another, have wanted to spend some time in Tijuana, to let everyone know that I *was here* and as proof, here are some catch-phrases, some fantastical descriptions, the insanity of fearless people, chronicles of the urban barbarity. Tijuana has become a rite of passage.

What is Tijuana's appeal? Being here allows you to enter a select elite of personalities who have visited and written about this place. It also gives you the chance to live alongside the city's dehumanized masses immigrating and heading north. What an amusing combination: the *happy few* and the lumpen-migrants. Who could resist such a magical formula? For just this reason, Krusty the Clown, Fernando Jordán, Charles Bukowski, Cabrera Infante, Manu Chao, Alejo Carpentier, Raymond Chandler, Manuel Puig, Henry Miller, Juan Goytisolo, Jay Leno, José Revueltas, and Javier Cercas have all had something to say about Tijuana. Perhaps due to this proliferation of discourses, at the end of the century (1997), the municipal government of Tijuana thought it intelligent (*sic*) to register the name "Tijuana" in order to prevent the discourse about the city from expanding without any controls, continually linked to drug dealing or illegality in general. Isn't it unusual that the name of the city be registered as a brand name? Of course, the proposal failed and was itself illegal. But it says a lot about how Tijuanological speculation has proliferated, from TV to the academic world.

Why have so many people said so much about Tijuana? I think it is because Tijuana has become a symbol representing their fears and subconscious desires. Tijuana plays an important role in the making of the official national discourse. The middle class and their supporters like to hear about, write about, and visit Tijuana because they see in her the opportunity to convert Reality into a Show. Tijuana is the city of shows. (The mecca of *la Neta*—the truth, the real deal.) The most overhyped striptease shows in the world take place here, even though the adult industry is much more developed in the central part of the country than in Tijuana. (When a depraved tijuanense goes to Mexico City, he feels underdeveloped.) But prostitution in Mexico City doesn't surprise anyone because the industry there is made up of sex workers. While here on the other hand, the stars are the *beautiful ladies, come down sir, we have a nice show for you.* A large part of Tijuana's appeal is her language. That language of hybridity, remix, and the end of all symbols, that impurity in which the other is assimilated into the cheapest kind of cliché.

Her constant sabotage of all meaning. Her linguistic perversion.

Everything that is boring elsewhere is spectacular in Tijuana. That is the secret agreement. The same occurs with the migrants. The migrants are the favorite show for the entire central part of the republic, who don't remember that up until three days ago, those migrants were their monotonous, fucked-over neighbors. What's amazing about Reality being a Show is that it is more comfortable. If we are not in the world, but instead in a show, then we aren't responsible, we are spectators (*¡qué chingón!*). You have no reason to feel guilty (oh, man, what a relief to hear that). Just sit down, watch, and have fun. Watching a news report about Tijuana is better than watching *Big Brother*. Tijuana is not a metropolis; instead, it's a *reality city*. And in that hyperreality, we can all be actors or *web cams*. So let's buy the plane ticket.

As far as I can tell, we are all in agreement that Tijuana is a show the spectator watches with a remote control, in which existence becomes the live broadcast from the scene of the crime. At the very least, we tijuanenses should be paid a salary (as actors, extras, cameramen, or makeup artists, whatever each person's particular part is). They should subsidize us or give us grants to keep putting on this show whose purpose is to provide nighttime entertainment and a tragicomic report to the Great People of Mexico and to the West, a report on things of which they are already perfectly aware. Or, if it's possible and a producer is listening to me right now, then we should all agree that Tijuana should stop being a city and become an interactive telenovela. (I propose that this historic soap opera be called *Ustedes los pobres*.) Besides, Tijuana already has a profound relationship with Television: seven out of ten televisions in the world were made in Tijuana. (This has been another episode in our series *Numbers to Surprise, Amuse, and Confuse Your Homies* brought to you by the company Statistics to Tell People Even Though They Seem Unbelievable.) (*Exploit the Data!*)

However one looks at it, Tijuana is Television Town. So, then, let's all Tijuanize ourselves as soon as possible. Welcome to globalization. Globcult TJ Style!!!

Oh Border, You Know You Like It! *Neocostumbrismo* in the Chronicle of the City That Says Yes

Monday, November 9 (1:30 pm)
I ran across several interesting facts about Mexico.
    If it doesn't make sense it isn't logical.
Why Mexican diplomats all drive in Mercedes Benzes.
    If it isn't logical it may still be funny.
The President of Mexico gets a commission.
    It makes sense.

                    DAVID ANTIN, "The November Exercises," in *Talking* (1972)

Coming to Tijuana on an intellectual tour assumes the old concept that walking in the streets can provide us with a special gnosis. In this sense, visiting Tijuana to write about Tijuana is a nostalgia that makes sense. (Once upon a time we were decadent and wore Nike sneakers.) The sin of naïveté is believing that tourism (the lowest category of perception), given certain circumstances, could be elevated to Husserlian phenomenology. And in Tijuana, everyone seems to agree that those circumstances exist. Just observe, intellectual or tourist, because the eidetic is on full display. Simply watch a Mixtec woman selling flowers, at the English-Friendly store window, look at the plaster statues. The essence of these things is but skin deep. We are all Humboldt at the corner of Avenida Revolución and Calle Primera. Strolling around Tijuana, Mexican intellectuals behave the same as Japanese videotourists. They want to get to the heart of things, but they end up getting the same things as everyone else.

The city is a miraculous topic. Even clichés can become fancy turns of phrase when you're talking about Tijuana. The border is a topic that encourages sensationalist and oversimplistic statements. (For yellow journalism, everything that glitters is gold.) When it comes time to describe Tijuana, the adjectives used by fashion columnists or California movies seem to be the most applicable descriptors. We are a "multicolored, multifaceted, postmodern" metropolis. We are "hybridity," a "collage," a "prism," an "Aleph," et cetera.

My suspicion is that all of these chaotic words are used as a stylistic strategy so as not to reflect too deeply. If Tijuana is a "prism," it obviously does not necessitate a detailed analysis; rather quaint phrases and portraits of local color will suffice. A series of random and exotic observations that prove that this is a multicolored set. The brilliance of my puns is simply astonishing!

The authors of chronicles, energized by the copiousness of postmodernism, "live" Tijuana like a theme park that must be seen in one day, a *road movie* in an unpaved country. Or they experience it through a never-ending stream of cable channels, remote control in hand, zapping zapping zapping in pursuit of Netaphysics, the metaphysics of la Neta, the real deal, street truth. They contemplate the city, moving through it like a desperate teenage party, watching video clips that in the end present only "curiosities," arbitrary visions, hallucinogenic, decontextualized, of a reality that they had already decided to experience in fragments, never as a slow or total experience, but rather as just a flow of images. "From the greyhound races to the lobster tacos, the Tijuana bazaar exceeds all inventory" (Villoro). The car window and a lightning-quick visit to a cantina, relishing the speed. *Too much is not enough, and too fast is just too little.*

Another reason for the national fascination with the border (from the press to literature) is because this seems to be the last opportunity to believe in the picturesque, in noetic tourism. That's why her Cultural Peculiarity is exaggerated, her Pataphysical nature. We know globalization erases all difference, and with its disappearance, the wonderful genre of the chronicle is at risk of vanishing. The Border is the last Reason to write Profiles, Vignettes, Phraseology, and the Last Chance to grab the attention of the disbelieving. The Border is used (faked) as the last opportunity for perception to be carnavalesque (Oh, Saint Walter Benjamin! Let me be the last flaneur!) and for prose to once again get permission to be costumbrista. Didn't I tell you, carnal, that my paintings of local color are all old-fashioned now?

Making Tijuana into an exceptional city is evidence of our hypocrisy or of our myopia. It's not exceptional because the border is a universal condition. It's been years since the border condition stopped being a geographic reality. The media and mass consumption make cities in the interior, which are far from another country, equally or more like a border town than those actually next to a foreign country. New York is more of a border town than San Diego. Acapulco is more of a border town than Tecate. Tijuana isn't the biggest border crossing in the world, the Internet is. To say that Tijuana is the border of borders is no more than an outdated, pre-electronic asseveration.

Tijuana is relevant because it combines conditions present in other cities. Tijuana isn't strange. It's the mirror of our various present realities and immediate futures.

So if someone thinks that something Completely Strange is happening in Tijuana, this doesn't mean that we are an exotic city; instead, it means that the observer doesn't understand the least about what's happening in the country as a whole. The tendency is to judge life in Tijuana as something foreign or to isolate its cultural phenomena from the rest of the country. If previous observers of border cultures looked at it merely in passing, from the outside, in order to criticize it from a perspective of Marxist nationalism or Christian morality, today they look at it through their windshield, not to openly disparage it (serious criticism, in the Baroque Age, is not in fashion anymore), but to proclaim its extreme otherness, its singularity placed in epoché. This decontextualization is especially at play in the approach to the subject of migration. On my drive by, I feel like my car gives me a heightened awareness. From my car, I can take the world apart and rearrange it; I can put the woman from two blocks ago on top of that table of used clothes; I can put that balcony into the next policeman's arms.

The massive migration to the United States (logically) is not something that is happening just to Tijuana, but rather is happening across the breadth of the country. Every day, there are 2,000 Mexicans trying to cross, not 2,000 tijuanenses. In Tijuana, the vast majority of the people do not put any attention on what is happening near the border fence. Not even 5 percent of the population would be able to answer the question: How many people have died trying to cross the border since the gringos launched Operation Gate Keeper? (Hundreds have died . . . as I write this at the beginning of the twenty-first century.) This separation tijuanenses have from their immediate reality is the same type of separation that makes someone from outside of Tijuana surprised to see so many guys in hats sleeping in the street, poking through some hole in the fence, waiting for the Migra to move away, so they can all jump up and run en masse. They are surprised, as if this "show" were something local and anomalous and not the reality for the entire country. Only someone who lives on another planet could find this phenomenon strange, seeing as how it is the same across the country, a phenomenon that does not begin or end in Tijuana. (In fact, all the phenomena of transculturation taking place in Tijuana are happening to a larger degree in the rest of the republic.) The government and semimorbid intellectuals would like for immigration to be a border phenomenon, preferably tijuanense, to free themselves from their responsibility or to be astonished by this diaspora of Others.

The phenomenon of illegal border crossing is not something that is only happening to Tijuana, but rather throughout the entire country; nonetheless, it is easier to present the images and stories of illegal crossing as one more phenomenon in the problematic, most-visited city in the world than to contextualize it as it should be. But to contextualize this phenomenon would mean to stop attributing it to the leyenda negra of Tijuana in order to locate it as an effect of the national crisis. This, of course, is of no benefit to the government or to its voluntary and involuntary information lackeys.

The poor, confused writers who come to visit the city in order to write about the latest fashionable topic really do think they have to buy a plane ticket on Aeroméxico or Delta to see migration. (In fact, now, thanks to the many Web sites they don't even have to make the lightning visit to "Margaritaville.") What stupidity—it could have only cost them the price of a Metro ticket. It would've been enough for them to go to the airport or the Central Bus Station in Mexico City or to Barcelona's dirty corners. Of course, consciously or unconsciously, they classify this "situation" as one of the distinctive features of the city and period. No one says anything and, besides, this extraordinary decontextualization sells magazines. You know, *Welcome to Tijuana, Tequila, Sexo y Mariguana.* Oh, and, of course, anything else you can think of, right?

City Fiction

> From my first visit to Amparo Dávila, la Verdadera, I remember more than anything the invasion of eyes. I had left the coast two hours early, because, even though I wasn't going directly to the Ciudad del Sur, I knew how slow and, sometimes, how stiflingly hot it was to enter the city. I had to deal with the incredibly slow traffic at the checkpoints; I had to show identification cards and do my best to smile: I had to show that I was a sensible and productive individual and not another desperate man looking for cheap medicine and easy women. —CRISTINA RIVERA GARZA, *La cresta de Ilión* (Ilion's Crest, 2002)

The most interesting documentary about Tijuana is *Frontier Life* (2002) by Hans Fjellestad: illegal car races reusing American automotive parts; water recycling on the border and the origin of the electronic fusion music, Nortec. In the documentary, the city is portrayed as a paradise of cultural mixture, from migrants to technologies. The documentary opens with a quote from the multidisciplinary artist Torolab: "Tijuana has more to do with science fiction novels than with Mexican history books." The idea summarizes and improves upon the fantastic philosophy of the most daring Tijuanology: Tijuana as an ahistorical entity, an imaginary city.

The person who has crafted this vision best, the idea of Tijuana as a volatile urban conglomeration slave to the present or the gravity-less future, is Guillermo Fadanelli. I place an extensive quote here because his text is one of the best literary portraits that have been written about the city.

> In no other place have I felt the strength that a territory inspires in its residents as much as in Tijuana. The city has been called to belong to everyone and one senses a strange pride in the city, perhaps because it is one gigantic hotel with no doors. The fact that it was never imagined as a real city, but rather as part of a strategy, not as an end but rather as means, stripping away that aura of "lasting forever" that the majority of cities have. There is a sensation that at any moment, everyone will leave and emigrate to the middle of the desert or to another border. Even the Zona del Río, which is supposed to be the seat of modernity, has the look of a set design, an ephemeral set-up, a location where endless movies and simulacra will be shot, but where nothing will actually happen, because all the people are

actors, not by vocation or by choice but by contagion, because they know they are in the midst of a territory lacking both history and future, a territory in which everything is movement, continual flux. A fake, invented city, Tijuana is a city in which everything real is wiped out by an excess of performance. Everything is there, at hand, at whatever price and whatever hour: one only has to stroll the streets of the Zona Norte at night to realize that pleasure is an endemic disease: La Estrella, El Chicago Club, La Ballena are some of the clubs that make up that ruthless geography in which everything seems to be at the point of collapse, the climax of an ahistorical decadence: the anatomy of a junkie. On the other hand, the rivers of humanity that cross the border every day have ended up passing on the migrant's inherent impatience to the entire city, an impatience that is contagious and infects every step. Tijuana is like a mirage, only there for the person who desires to see her and is able to visit her. For the majority of people, though, she is transparent, she doesn't exist: our gaze, from this side of the border, passes right through her and is fixed on California, the Promised Land, the glamorous paradise of dollars. The Californian gaze is stalled in Tijuana, constructing a false, funhouse image of Mexico; for us, Mexicans, Tijuana is transparent, for them she is a myth: two different ways to deny reality, to avoid her actual existence. Even the steel fence, the Line that cuts along the border, seems to be an artifact more appropriate for science fiction than as a tool to divide nations. The spotlights lighting up the border, the helicopters spiraling across the desert in search of Mexican deserters, fleeing from their land and its precarious economy, the inherent tension of a line that unites such different, divided lands, all of this form a set from a typical Nintendo hunting game, unmistakable and violent, cynical and spectacular: the border seems to be more like a series of images from virtual reality, than a racial or economic conflict. One has to be there to see it. (Guillermo Fadanelli, http://www.fadanelli.blogspot.com, 2003)

This conception of the city seems tempting, poetic. But, unfortunately, Tijuana has a history too. Another fantasy projected onto this metropolis is the imaginative construction of a place with no past and possibly no future. Tijuana is the myth of a nonexistent city, yet people still live there despite that fact. Tijuana: Utopia. No-place. A city that is pure space with no temporal existence. Instant Tijuana.

The border has become a favorite topic of discussion in Mexico and the United States because of strategic reasons stemming both from globalization and the historical relationship of the two countries, but, above all, because of an internal, national process of change. Tijuana was used as a laboratory example for so-called Hybridization only after a long national process.

Tijuana was born at the end of the nineteenth century when a conglomeration of binational interests acquired its external image; at the beginning of the twentieth century when it was used as a hotspot for alcohol-soaked, nighttime entertainment for American tourists. Since then, despite the fact that the city has become much more complex than an All-Night Party Zone for gringos, the image has stuck. In the past few decades, several factors coalesced to reify this pseudo-definition of the city as *maldita-malinchista*, cursed and Malinchist, in the imaginary, namely: drug trafficking, constant passage of migrants headed to the United States, prostitution, organized crime, poverty, familial disintegration, the social marginalization of the majority of the population, and the arrival of the maquiladoras. This definition was believed not only by those viewing the city from outsider positions, but also in the minds of its own residents. It is as if the city were one big crime tabloid, inhabited by two million people, all potential criminals or victims. All of them recently arrived, all of them utterly predictable.

The world needs immoral cities in order to be able to feel more virtuous and less chaotic. And Tijuana, just like other cities (Hollywood, Paris, Havana, Medellín, New York, Delhi, etc.), has been chosen as a container for everything that the other cities/cultures deny being. Tijuana, specifically, is the media scapegoat for Mexicans and some foreigners.

Is Tijuana more "gringoized" than Mexico City? No. But the geographic location of Tijuana makes it a perfect target. This is my position in regard to the discourse about Tijuana: the national and foreign Tijuanological discourse would like to define this city as the model of "gringoization" and urban collapse. This exaggeration allows them to avoid acknowledging their own situation, and so they can attribute the deterioration to the Others, the tijuanenses, those Strange Ex-Mexicans, those Border Barbarians, those Semi-Citizens. The Neo-Chichimecas who want to found Tecnotitlan.

We are the Malinche of an untruthful national discourse. According to this discourse, our immorality or other metaphysical reasons account for border identity. Here We've Decided to Speak Spanglish! Here We've Decided to Become a City of Whores! These lies purport that tijuanenses have become wildly eccentric and thus solely responsible for their Physical, Linguistic, and Political Immorality. They are the only ones to blame, no one else: take photos of them before they disappear into the nightclubs!

All of this is a disrespectful myth, taken almost directly from the "Tijuana Bibles," those porno manifestos that used the city's name to appeal to the American libido. They never realized the Tijuana Bibles were not made in Tijuana, but in the United States itself. Tijuana assures us that the whore is someone else's mother, not our own, like in Ray Loriga's novel or in almost all of the quotes about this speculative city: itself a mirror.

It is true that the proximity of the United States has defined a large portion of the northern border's economy, society, and politics, but the decisive factor for the culture of the city has not been its closeness, but instead the decisions that the Mexican state has made. Tijuana is not a product of the United States, but of Mexico.

Despite this, the Mexican state does not want to assume responsibility for the border's poverty, its colonias with no public services or guaranteed education, its pollution, its social disintegration (which makes possible phenomena like the hundreds of women murdered in Ciudad Juárez, that other mythical border city, or the thousands of people who have died crossing illegally into the United States), its enslavement by the mass media, and its lax approach to national identity.

What Tijuana has become: a collapsing city. Not so much because of its closeness to the United States; rather as a consequence of the decision by the Mexican state to take advantage of its proximity to ally itself with corporations and the American government for material gain. And so, to erase its political responsibility, the state promotes the image and the discourse that Tijuana is a city that has become a disaster due to its immorality, its personal alliance with the Gringos or as an unpreventable or natural effect of globalization. The Mexican government's corruption allows the Americans and the Japanese to exploit the half-dead populations of Tijuana. Tijuana is, more than anything else, a logical consequence of the erroneous course taken by the national project in the twentieth century.

In the last few years, interest in the border has skyrocketed, but it has principally been defined from the perspective of its cultural relationship with the United States, of its post-Mexican denationalization. This perspective ignores the fact of the city as a direct consequence of Mexican corruption, not of an ahistorical hybridization per se.

Tijuana was not invented by the Chicanos, the Gringos or by Us, the Hybrids. Tijuana was created by the seventy-year-long "perfect dictatorship" (Vargas Llosa dixit) of the Institutional Revolutionary Party and by the arrival in 2002 of the right-wing National Action Party. Tijuana is the evidence of the internal decadence of the Mexican, beginning in Mexico City and ending at the border. But since they do not want this to be at the center of the debate, the idea is popularized that the border is only one topic and that topic is going out of style already. Let's move on to another.

Coda or Eleventh Commandment:
Thou Shalt Not Tell the Truth about Your City

> Tijuana is a synonym of mediocrity. It has given nothing of any worth to the world. Not artists, not renowned intellectuals, nothing, in reality, nothing of any importance. The tijuanenses, like good Mexicans, are very proud of foolish things, like the invention of the Caesar salad or the copyright for a feminine drink baptized the "Margarita." Both are restaurant specialties that sell very well with foreigners and Mexican visitors, but they are still just stupidities of which only *losers* could be proud. A salad or a drink . . . it would be better if Tijuana never existed at all.
>
> Does it exist?—ESTHER GASCA, "Apuntes de una fugitiva" (Notes of a Fugitive Woman, 1998)

The truth is always insipid and colorless. Misery is what all human beings have in common. Because of this misery, we will never miss an opportunity to make ourselves seem like we are extraordinary individuals living in exceptional locales at an amazing moment in history. This is what happens with tijuanenses who, far from the development of the national capital and incapable of accessing our American neighbors' progress, take advantage of the opportunity to exaggerate the supposed extraordinary condition of our border culture. We perform for a national and international public who are either gullible, our unconditional fans, or receiving some kind of personal gain for publicizing the strangeness of the Other.

Prostitutes, merchants, children, workers, housewives, smugglers, drivers, writers, we all act in such a way as to make *them* believe that we are another race of people entirely. A central part of the tijuanense identity is this: to know how to sell yourself, to know how to cultivate a bad image as a commercial advantage. And, at the same time, to claim that the good image should be recovered. In one way or another, Tijuana denies that Tijuana is true.

If a tourist guide—some of them Americans, by the way—promotes the idea that Tijuana is dangerous and dark, it's because he needs that discourse to sell his services. The same thing happens with its literati, academics, artists; all of them have a good number of charlatans in their ranks. The deficiencies of the infrastructure in Tijuana are made up for by the Neobaroquism of the discourse. Post/Pop beats Third World.

Convinced by our performance for them and by our testimonials, the visitors or exegetes then write all those novels, articles, film scripts, commentaries, and lectures that they take back to their countries. In their work, they make a record of the city's good or bad, extraordinary condition. Everyone believed our dog and pony show. Or they didn't believe it, but they used it. In the end, when fiction has become believable, the truth is unbelievable.

People from Mexico City and gringos want desperately for us to prove to them that we are exotic. So what do we do? We prove it to them! Who in their right mind would refuse to be an exceptional being, linked to drug trafficking, to the legend of a New Babylon, to a Hell stuck between two worlds or, as they're saying nowadays, the mero mero laboratory of postmodernity? Tell me who would deny such outstanding titles just for living in a city that is the subject of such damning myths? Who wouldn't fall for this mythomania when the prize is fame, or at least a tip? All of you want fantastic stories and sociological news, well, okay, I'll make them up for you, of course, my pleasure. How many do you want? The discourse of Tijuanology is much too attentive to its leadership, to its insane dialogue with the other. Tijuanology wasn't developed for autognosis, but rather as a discourse-for-the-other. All of us are no more than tour guides.

To tell them the truth, to tell them that we are like everyone else, to tell them that you are us, and we are you, to tell them that Tijuana looks like the mixtures of culture that you find wherever you live, that Tijuana is the sum of its projections, that Tijuana is whatever and nothing, would be cruel. How could we disappoint them? The tijuanenses and the Tijuanologists are like those tribes that make things up and lie to the anthropologists that ask them about their sex lives or their Lévi-Straussism.

It's been a long time since the natives have had the opportunity to exaggerate about their lives or to daydream, so they decide to say everything that comes into their heads, speaking their lies straight into the interviewer's tape recorders or notebooks. Sociologists, anthropologists, and journalists are always willing to believe anything they are told, forgetting that informants or tourist guides are less trustworthy than auto salesmen. We tijuanenses pretend to be unusual specimens and we show the city's seven peculiarities to these "dupes"—those individuals who act like they believe other people's fantasies in order to comply with their social function. That's what the public demands, and you have to give them what they want.

Children want us to scare them when they ask us to tell them a story. So, one makes up a scary story. Is there anything possibly more human than lying to gullible people? Lying is a way to take pity on them and a minor entertainment for ourselves.

"Tijuana" is nothing more than a philosopheme. An entelechy that doesn't exist at all, except for a plethora of quotes and a pile of articles. Someone at some time started to investigate Tijuana to try to find her essence, and his successor swallowed the tale that such an entity even existed. In this way, several intertextual generations take up the task of arguing over the essence of a supposedly mythical city named Tijuana, which in reality is nothing more than an imaginary border. I have done it myself, I accept that. I myself do not believe in the existence of Tijuana, and, despite that, I enter into the discussion. What else could I do on a cloudy Saturday?

Tijuana doesn't exist. It's just an Internet site.

To be frank, I argue that Tijuana is such a cliché that in order to escape the monotony of life, sometimes someone (either me, you, or someone else) has to take on the miserable task of "the vindication of the frivolous image of the city" (denying the leyenda negra and its gray aftereffects). But then, the next day, the same person fervently dedicates himself or herself to spreading the concept of "the vicious and nocturnal nature of this mysterious city." If she or he didn't do it, who would?

The Tijuanologists face a situation similar to the one faced by a provincial philosopher, who, in order to get a little attention, wrote a book against God. When he saw that no one cared about his thesis, he decided to stir up some controversy by writing a theological treatise to refute his own book (attributing it to someone else). Tijuana is an Onetti character who wants to convince everyone else that he is a Borges character.

This is the way Tijuanology works. It's our last way to make ourselves and the rest of the world think we're interesting. The city is all too normal, but what can we do? Confessing that would be boring and people need to entertain themselves somehow. Let the party carry on. We'll buy the beers and the myths. ¡Salud! Never confess what you know: you are Tijuana. And Tijuana is a lie.

Recommendations for Crossing Successfully into the USA
(from the Simplest Way to the Most Complicated)

Try to cross legally.

Pick a time of day with little traffic.

Before crossing, have a reason to tell the agent, a good reason, a true one, or at least a believable one.

Drive a good car that looks classy or that says: I'm middle class.

Drive a good car without provoking suspicions about where you got it from.
 If you are dark-skinned, drive a car that corresponds to your status.
Cross by bike in the special line.
Take a magazine when you cross on foot.
Take two magazines when you cross on foot.
Pick the line that is moving the fastest.
Don't bring fruits or vegetables.
Don't bring metals.
Don't tell jokes about terrorism.
Don't say "ojalá."
(Ojalá sounds Muslim.)
Don't take a lot of luggage or stuff.
Dress well.
Don't sweat excessively.
Don't have nervous tics.
Cross by yourself so you don't have to wait for anyone left behind.
Bring receipts that prove that you are investors.
Be an elegant Mexican politician and bring special identification recognized
 by the United States.
Be a refined, attractive woman—with white skin to appeal to Anglo tastes or
 dark skin to appeal to their global fantasies.
Be an elderly person in a wheelchair.
Don't be too dark-skinned or short.
Try to guess which agents are racists or which ones are in a bad mood at that
 moment.
Talk as little as possible.
Don't be drunk.
Don't have a criminal record.
Don't have any scent in your car or clothing that upsets the trained dogs.
Don't wear a turban or insignias that are hostile to the United States.
Don't look like a Mexican drug dealer.
Don't look like a drug dealer.
Don't look Mexican.
Don't write about, draw, photograph, or film what is happening at the
 checkpoint or during the trip across.
Don't look the Immigration agents in the eyes while you're in line.
Don't hesitate as you answer their questions when it's your turn.
Don't reveal that you are going to work or study without the appropriate
 permit.

Don't be rude when you answer.

Don't have guns on you.

Don't have drugs on you.

Don't cross with an obviously false passport.

Don't cross through the desert by yourself or through the mountains during rainstorms.

Don't drive through really fast in an armored car trying to avoid the gunfire.

Don't threaten the agents with a bomb in your hand.

Don't enter in a light aircraft without authorization to cross into the airspace of the United States.

Be married to an American.

Be an American on your way home.

Kathryn Kopinak

Globalization in Tijuana Maquiladoras

Using Historical Antecedents and Migration
to Test Globalization Models

Mexico's economy is undergoing a stunning transformation. Five years after the launch of the North American Free Trade Agreement (NAFTA), it is fast becoming an industrial power. Free trade with the U.S. and Canada is turning the country from a mere assembler of cheap, low-quality goods into a reliable exporter of sophisticated products. . . . "This is a completely different economy than Mexico had a decade ago" says sociologist Federico Reyes Heroles. . . . NAFTA "has given Mexicans a new vision of the world" says Clemente Ruiz Duran. —SMITH AND MALKIN, *Business Week* (1998: 50)

The "policy of isolation," . . . which ceased when the Congress passed the Colonization law of 1883, was the most dangerous policy to Mexico. To exclude immigration or tolerate it only under intolerable conditions, forced foreigners to cast covetous eyes on the Mexican domain. It alone gave rise to constant schemes of annexation and revolutionary separation. To forbid or make difficult and insecure the entry of capital and labor from without, necessarily united capital, labor, and enterprise in hostility to Mexico, and led to schemes against the integrity of her territory. To welcome capital and labor and make both secure makes these her friends and allies, and unites them in a common interest with her. —NORDHOFF, *Peninsular California* (1888: 99)

Mexican maquiladora industrialization, which began along the northern border in the 1960s and grew quickly in the interior in the 1990s, is often thought to be part of globalization. The latter is understood as the transregional connection of social, political, and economic activities, making decisions taken in one place relevant for people elsewhere. Several theoretical ideas recently put forward by hyperglobalists, transformationalists, and skeptics about global flows and their limits are used in this chapter to assess the extent to which maquiladora industrialization in Tijuana can be considered globalization, the kind of globalization it might represent, and/or to what extent it may be part of a more regionally based economic form (Held et al., 1999: 3–27).

Hyperglobalists conceive of globalization as a totally new and primarily economic reorganization of human action, driven by technology and comparative advantage. Transformationalists understand globalization trends as a historically unprecedented reordering of interregional relations, and see them as caused not only by technology, but also by conjunctural and political factors which make it difficult to predict their final character. On the other hand, the skeptical school of thought tends to view the turn of the twentieth century as the period of greatest world economic integration and current globalization as highly exaggerated. To the degree that skeptics acknowledge contemporary forces of globalization, they tend to see them as a distinct phase of a recurring phenomenon.

Hyperglobalists believe that globalization, which they view as progressive, will lead to a denationalization and homogeneity of world cultures. Similarly, they think that governments will be forced to curtail state spending in order to be competitive, and that this will lead to the demise of redistributive measures characteristic of the welfare state. Transformationalists disagree and point to examples of cultural hybridization, and show that in some cases, national governments which are open to globalization can mediate its negative impacts on their populations, depending on the strategies they adopt and their relative power in the world. Skeptics, on the other hand, are convinced that social movements which oppose globalization can be effective in limiting its scope, and argue that globalization can be successfully contested.

The two quotations above, published 110 years apart, reflect different positions on when one of the world's most successful export processing regimes actually began. The first one, heard most often today, indicates that maquiladora industrialization is a totally new economic phenomenon for Mexico. The second is an echo from the past which indicates that at least at the western tip of the border between Mexico and the United States, this process has deeper historical roots.

This chapter investigates the extent to which maquiladora industrialization at the head of the Baja California peninsula is a totally new phenomenon in the context of the three schools of thought regarding globalization put forward above. It is often thought that Baja California has little history of its own because of its adjacency to the very populous region of Southern California, the fifth largest market in the world in the U.S. state of California. This chapter investigates the background of current globalization trends.

Previous research has focused on the flow of goods such as supplies and finished products as indicators of the extent to which maquiladora industries are a form of globalization (Kopinak, 1998, 2003). Using the spatiotemporal dimensions of globalization—extensity (stretching), intensity, velocity, and impact—put forward by Held et al. (1999: 16), it concluded that the kinescope corridor located right at the border from Tijuana, Baja California, to San Luis R.C., Sonora, represented thick globalization because it was high on all of the spatiotemporal dimensions. However, the rest of the Baja California peninsula was more representative of thin globalization, since much of the rapid and intense exchange of goods between Mexico and the United States and many Asian countries is limited to the area right at the border near the ocean. Finally, there is strong support for the idea that much trade activity associated with maquiladoras is not global at all, but tightly linked to Southern California, especially San Diego.

In contrast to the focus on the flow of goods across distances, there has been little attention by researchers to how maquilization is related to the transregional flow of people, even though, as Held et al. (1999: 283) indicate, human migration is the form of globalization that is more ubiquitous than any other. Mexican maquiladora industries have required more employees here than preexisting labor markets could supply because they represent the largest economy ever to rise up in this territory. In the second half of the chapter, the extent to which migration has been responsible for filling these jobs is examined, as well as the implications this has for consolidation of the new economy based on production for export. We use the same spatiotemporal dimensions as previously applied to analyze the flow of goods—extensity, intensity, velocity, and impact.

The focus of this chapter is on the Baja California peninsula because it is one of the areas on the border that was transformed earliest and to the greatest extent by production for export. Tijuana has more maquiladoras than any other city in Mexico, and is second only to Ciudad Juárez in numbers of people employed by them.[1] It became Mexico's fifth-largest city in the mid-1990s, and is home to two-thirds of the state's maquiladora industries. Outside of Tijuana, there are two agroindustrial corridors—one between the cities of Ensenada and San Quintín, and the other in the Valley of Mexicali (Map 4.1). These agroindustrial corridors produce tomatoes and other vegetables and fruit for export to the United States with labor forces made up of migrants from southern Mexican states such as Oaxaca.

Historical Roots of Export Processing in Baja California

Capitalist expansion in this part of the world began in the late nineteenth century, but the obscuring of borders that is so characteristic of current

Map 4.1. Cities and municipios at the head of the Baja California peninsula.

globalization trends began in this part of the world long before that. I will show in this section that the current Mexican promotion of export-led development via maquiladoras is sometimes undertaken in a nationalist spirit of rebalancing the effects of previous territorial losses. This is not a pre-Columbian kind of Montezuma's revenge, which might be predicted as the orientation of Mixteco families compelled by economic and political forces to migrate from Oaxaca *milpas* to toil over exported designer fruits and vegetables in San Quintín. Instead, it is a self-confidant "Sí, *se puede*" orientation held by *norteños*, who trace their ancestry to European roots, after long years of co-existence with gringos at the border.

Baja Californians cannot easily forget that the U.S. state of California was lost to them in the Treaty of Guadalupe Hidalgo ending the Mexican American War in 1848, since it meant that their peninsula was cut off from the Mexican mainland and they would have to be documented to travel to other parts of their country overland through the United States. After the war, the only train connecting Baja California to other parts of Mexico went through the United States. This war was provoked by some U.S. nationals wanting to take all of Mexico after the conflict ended, as implied in the phrases "constant schemes of annexation" and "schemes against the integrity of her territory" in the Nordoff quotation at the beginning of the chapter. The U.S. state of California used to be the Mexican state of Alta California, which was divided from Baja California a little to the south of the current municipio of Rosarito (see Map 4.1). The Baja Peninsula was occupied by Americans during the Mexican American War, and many Mexicans who favored annexation returned to the United States with its troops, or left for the California Gold Rush soon after.

Like other northern areas of Mexico, Baja California was sparsely inhabited after the Mexican American war. In order to settle it, the federal government passed the Colonization Law in 1883, which allowed foreigners and nonnative Mexicans to own, develop, and settle Mexican land. Passed originally under President Gonzalez, it was subsequently promoted by President Porfirio Díaz, who integrated it into his broader opening of Mexico to foreign capital. Aguilar (2001) argues that under Díaz's policies to attract U.S. capital, Tijuana was transformed from a ranch to an urban settlement due to the economic boom in Southern California at the end of the nineteenth century. Colonists were granted many privileges, including exemption from military service, all taxes, import and domestic duties on provisions, tools, equipment, and so on, and from duties on exportation of fruit for a decade. One U.S.-based railroad company had special ownership and administrative status on the land from San Quintín northward to the U.S. border, which did not preclude ownership by individual colonists (Nordhoff, 1888).

However, development did not really take off in the northwest under these policies. By the time the Mexican Revolution began in 1911, Tijuana, Tecate, Mexicali, and Ensenada together were inhabited by less than 2,000 people, most of whom lived in the then-capital of Ensenada, and relied on San Diego for their provisioning (Melo de Remes, 1964). After the revolution, Tijuana grew as a tourist center with the attractions being casinos, bars, and racetracks, whose owners and patrons were all U.S. nationals. The clientele was motivated by U.S. laws prohibiting the sale of alcohol, and transformed Tijuana into a "gilded gambling spa for the Los Angeles movie colony," according to Davis (2000: 26). The social distance between those patronizing tourist attractions and the local Mexican population was immense, and the economy which arose around tourism was an economic enclave, just as modern maquiladoras have been so categorized because they include few local inputs.

Excluded from most jobs, Mexicans were employed only as construction workers, waiters, and street sweepers. When the racetrack outgrew its original quarters and expanded to a bigger facility, the unionized Mexican workers employed in its construction, revolutionary veterans in many cases, invaded the old stables and renovated them for family housing, since there was no infrastructure for the local population (Bustamente, 1990). In the Valley of Mexicali, the Colorado River Land Company, owned by U.S. nationals, controlled agriculture. It hired only Chinese, Japanese, and East Indian workers (Valenzuela, 1991: 63).

Between 1935 and 1937, President Cárdenas closed the casinos and outlawed gambling, nationalizing some foreign- and Mexican-owned land for the unemployed, as part of his *conversión* of the export-led development strategies of the Porfiriato to import substitution. He also declared this area a free trade zone to restimulate the economy. In Baja California, this meant getting the same kinds of revolutionary veterans who had invaded the stables for housing, now mobilized by the ruling party's unions, to use their constitution to reclaim national territory previously dominated by foreigners. The 1980s reversal of Mexican government policies from import substitution back to export-led development by making maquiladoras one of the main cornerstones of the Mexican economy was called *reconversión*.

Sklair (1989, 2000) has shown how a transnationalist capitalist class throughout the border has been an important causal factor promoting globalization. We add here that there is also a group of intellectuals in Baja California attempting to assist the link of maquila industries' growth to external markets. Alegría et al. (1997: 197–199), for example, have suggested that the contemporary maquiladora boom is not without local roots, arguing that local entrepreneurs in Mexico's northern border cities who had imported commercial products from the United States since the 1930s contributed to maquiladora growth by negotiating border development policy, and transferring surpluses from one sector to another in their own investment portfolios.

An illustrative example we suggest in this chapter is Conrado Acevedo Cárdenas, a well-known Baja California businessman and cultural promoter, responsible for building a Historical and Cultural Centre in Calafia, south of Rosarito, and also Nueva Tijuana-Ciudad Industrial, the first large, modern industrial park in Tijuana, providing about 10,000 jobs, and building housing nearby for 125,000 employees (Arce, 1999). The historical center in Calafia is a profitable hotel built on the supposed site of the boundary line between Alta and Baja California drawn in Mexico in 1773, with a museum of ersatz artifacts harkening back to Baja California's colonization by missionaries. The industrial park and its housing for employees integrates Tijuana into the global economy since it houses some of the largest maquiladora factories in Tijuana.

Acevedo Cárdenas's stated goal at Calafia is the creation of a cultural space on the Mexican side of the border in which both native Baja Californians and migrants from the interior can strengthen their sense of belonging to the nation.[2] He is representative of those who insist that promoting globalization does not have to mean the loss of sovereignty or the adoption of a homogeneous global culture, as the hyperglobalists would suggest. Castillo-Curry (1998, 2001) argues that the recreation of sites lacking historical integrity is a way of preserving a collective memory of identity in the face of rapid industrialization and social change.

In this chapter, I interpret the products this developer has created as a form of cultural hybridization, as predicted by the transformationalists (Held et al., 1999: 374). It is not an oppositional recovery of local knowledge, such as the cosmopolitan localism of the Zapatistas in Chiapas which the skeptics might predict (McMichael, 2000: 271). Instead, the ersatz artifacts at the Calafia hotel are a passive display of museum culture reinforcing national myths. They represent a recreation of local culture that gives evidence of an earlier history than the popular and globally homogeneous mass culture produced by a maquiladora located only a few kilometers up the coast, Estudios de la Playa, owned by 20th Century Fox in Beverly Hills, Southern California. The studio was built in 1996 to shoot the wetter parts of Titanic and was later used for Pearl Harbor and other seascape films. It also has a museum displaying props and techniques used in making the films (Ellingwood, 2001). The Calafia hotel and 20th Century Fox's maquila are neighboring businesses which display local and global culture side by side, offering them both up for mass consumption.

Contreras, Alonso-Estrada, and Kenney (1997) have documented the new decision, making roles played by Mexican engineers and administrators in the maquiladora industry part of the process they call endogeneización. They found some Tijuana maquiladoras managed by young Mexican northerners educated in local postsecondary institutions. They argue that by the 1990s, these technocratic personnel were acting as social agents, mediating multinational corporate policy and its local requirements. Their professional development as a group has contributed a local dimension to industrial expansion which enhances the attractiveness of the northwest corner of Mexico to foreign investment. They have risen professionally in the larger companies that not only assemble but also manufacture, and in a few cases do some design. The electronic maquiladora cluster, particularly the Asian-owned subsector which gives this area its global links, is unprecedented in providing highly skilled jobs for some tijuanenses.

This is in contrast to 20th Century Fox's maquiladora which employed only fifty Mexicans in 1998 and imported the rest of its personnel from Los Angeles, a short three-hour drive away. Aspiring Mexican actors complained that they got the smallest parts as extras in the filming of *Titanic*, such as jumping into the cold ocean at night, because they did not look sufficiently European to fit the script. This maquila was apparently not set up to access cheap Mexican labor, since Fox persuades its Los Angeles mechanics to relocate to Rosarito for the temporary period it takes to shoot a film by paying them substantially extra for working "off shore." Fox may have relocated not only for the seascape on the Baja California coast but also to reduce its environmental costs. Local fishermen in the nearby village of Popotla have accused the studio of endangering their livelihoods by polluting local waters. In some ways, the Fox maquila harkens back to the tourist economy of the 1920s and 1930s in its enclave character and strong connection with the entertainment industry. Although "big gamblers and their Hollywood friends" moved to Las Vegas, Nevada, after Tijuana's casinos were closed (Davis, 2000: 26), there is a tendency to recreate the link because of geographic proximity.

This section suggests that while the growth of internationally connected maquiladora industries has been precipitated by the technological advances (e.g., microelectronics) and comparative advantage (e.g., low wages) emphasized by the hyperglobalist model, it has roots that go back before even the beginning of the twentieth century, which is the important turning point which the skeptics identify. What is novel about current industrial growth is its rapid boom since the 1980s and the weight of non–North American capital, which has consolidated here mainly due to conjunctural and political factors emphasized by the transformationalists and skeptics, such as trade agreements, and connections to large U.S. markets. Asian firms have to transfer more than simple assembly to North America, and make highly skilled jobs available to technically trained Mexicans, who have the resources to organize, protect, and perhaps even expand their class interests. The addition to the stratification system of what Max Weber would call a nonmanual middle class which maintains its cultural traditions is not dissimilar to the growth in the state middle class and managerial classes in French Canada earlier in the twentieth century, when English-speaking multinational capital penetrated the northeastern part of the continent (Millner, 1978). The longevity of the endogeneización of international capital in this part of Mexico depends not only on the talents of new occupational groups such as Mexican engineers and managers, but also on the future course of globalization, since the Canadian example indicates that such classes can be quickly "hollowed out," even after several decades of prominence (Arthurs, 2000).

Maquiladora industrialization has undoubtedly contributed to the unprecedented rise of Tijuana and San Diego to a position of greater prominence in the

hierarchy of cities in this region and in the larger continent. This can be explained via the application of the newest model articulating the relationship
between time and space known as spatial-temporal simultaneity. This model
highlights the fact that technological innovation has permitted interconnected
phenomena to occur on different parts of the earth's surface at the same time
(Hiernaux, 1999: 15). Thus, different parts of shared production, carried out by
maquiladora industries and the companies from which they subcontract, are
occurring in more than one place at the same time. For example, an order
placed for a computer in the United States can stimulate the simultaneous production of computer parts in several locations of the continent, and the finished product can be assembled and delivered to the customer in a week or so.

We would argue, however, that this is not a totally new phenomenon, but
very similar to earlier attempts to develop the area's economy via colonization
in the nineteenth century and tourism in the 1920s and 1930s. Different articulations of space with time can coexist, and a recognition of the historical roots
of the current export-led maquiladora economy illuminates the existence of the
circular model of the relationship between time and space which is characterized by repetition and reconstruction. This model has a certain permanence in
that spaces remain, although not always in the same form. Time may be measured in a particular space by the layers of different reconstructions, as with
the pre-Hispanic pyramids of Mesoamerica, which archaeologists have found
to have been reconstructed on top of each other on the same site by different
generations whose conception of the divine varied (Hiernaux, 1999: 18).

Distributional Impacts:
Migrant Workers Absorb the Social Costs of Maquilization

> La americanización del lado mexicano es, en primer lugar, en términos económicos, la
> hispanización, mejor dicho, mexicanización de las ciudades estadounidenses es de-
> mográfica. —AGUILAR (2001)

The incredibly rapid growth of Tijuana's population is part of the northward
movement of Mexicans in search of work within Mexico and the United
States. Tijuana first became an important destination for internal migrants
when the Bracero Program began in 1942 to allow Mexican male agricultural
workers to work for part of each year in U.S. agriculture. This program was
initiated because U.S. farm labor was engaged in the war effort, and in Southern California it was especially employed in the establishment of San Diego as
the main port for naval operations. Braceros' families sometimes accompanied

them as far as the border and set up households in Tijuana to wait for their return. Aguilar (2001) says that in the postwar era, the attraction of migrants to this part of the border continued to grow until Tijuana was incapable of providing enough jobs, leading to the formation of an enormous sector of the population which was poor, living marginally in irregular settlements.

When the Bracero Program was unilaterally cancelled in 1965 by the United States, the Mexican government took advantage of U.S. tax laws to set up export-processing operations in the form of maquiladoras. Mexicans continued to migrate to Tijuana to take these new jobs, but often considered their work as transitional, while they waited to cross the border or find a better job in Mexico. Historically, Tijuana has been one of the main crossing points for undocumented migration to the United States. The boom in maquiladora employment beginning in the 1980s supplied more jobs, which were very badly needed by Mexicans who had lived in the interior and been displaced by the economic opening of Mexico. In 1980, Tijuana had a population of 461,257, growing by 62 percent to reach a population of 747,381 in 1990 (Mendoza, 2002).[3] By 2000, it had grown by 70.5 percent to reach a total of 1,274,240 people.

These statistics and other findings reflective of the spatiotemporal dimensions of globalization suggest that migration to this area is reflective of thick globalization. First, this is a very intense and rapid flow of people. It also has high extensity, since the Tijuana area is known to attract migrants from farther away than other maquiladora cities with migrant labor forces such as Nogales and Sonora, which tend to recruit workers from within their own regions (Kopinak, 1996: 105). Or, in some cases, the presence of migrants from very far away attracted maquiladoras. This was the case with the first maquiladoras in the clothing sector which set up shop in Ensenada, which came to hire the female relatives of male Mixteco agricultural workers who have a reputation for excellent sewing. In Tijuana, Mixteco women may be most visible as street vendors, but Lestage (1988) reported that they also often work in maquiladora factories temporarily or permanently to supplement or double their husbands' income, when a family needs to build a house, or pay unusual expenses.

Although this migration is transregional, most of it occurs within the Mexican nation-state. There are no data on the numbers of international migrants coming to Mexico to work in maquiladoras, but they can all be considered elites, working in managerial positions. Mexican migrants are much more numerous and make up all of the labor.[4] This phenomenon is reflected in the quotation at the beginning of this section by Aguilar, which notes that the Americanization of the Mexican side of the border is mainly economic, whereas the Hispanicization of U.S. cities is demographic. This differs from the early colonization period, when foreign labor was an important part of the attempted settlement, as the quotation from Nordhoff at the beginning of the chapter indicates. It is part of the greater mobility of capital in the modern period, in comparison to the mobility of labor. In the past, industries imported labor if there was not sufficient available locally, whereas now they are more likely to move to the location where that labor is available.

Although there has not been much research on the relationship between maquiladora employment and migration, there is no doubt about the newness of much of the population which has come to take up maquiladora jobs. The findings of studies using varying sampling techniques at different points in time show that a high proportion of Tijuana maquiladora workers were born outside of the state of Baja California. Carrillo and Santibáñez (1993) found that 75 percent were born out of state; Quintero (1997) found that 83 percent were; Contreras (2000) found from 60 to 64 percent; and Coubès's (2001) results were 72 percent. The situation at the eastern end of Mexico's border with the United States is quite different in terms of migration, with Matamoros having only 24 percent of its maquiladora workers born outside the state in 1990 (Quintero, 1997).

Approximately 80 percent of those employed in maquiladoras are direct workers and 20 percent indirect. Only about 1 percent of the labor force is made up of managers. Since Tijuana does not have a history of industrial entrepreneurialism, there have been shortages of both direct and indirect personnel, and migrants who work in maquiladoras can be considered to represent both elite and mass migration. Carrillo, Mortimer, and Alonso (1999) show that in the north of Mexico, in the TV and autoparts sectors of maquiladora industries, Asiatic companies would especially prefer to have local suppliers in order to take advantage of economies of scale. Their main recommendation is that apprenticeship be internalized, with Mexicans with proven entrepreneurial ability in other parts of the country moved to the northern regions without entrepreneurial cultural traditions. The alternative, foreign managers, are also migrants since they usually do not live in Tijuana. Most maquiladora companies prefer to have non-Mexican managers living on the U.S. side of the border for security reasons, and most managers themselves prefer to locate their families there as well. Maquiladora managers who commute each day from their U.S. homes to work in Mexican plants have become a newest component of the borderlander population, which is the name Martínez (1988, 1994) has given to people living in the immediate region of the international line.

Although Held et al. (1999: 313) note that it is difficult to assess the economic impact of migration on the labor market and wage rates, there are very specific examples of migration being used by maquiladora employers in Tijuana to prevent independent unionization and keep down wages. In the famous case of the maquiladora Han Young, a subcontractor for Hyundai, new workers were brought all the way from Veracruz in 1998 to replace workers fired for supporting an independent union which had been legally recognized (Bandy, forthcoming). Simonelli (2002: 164) found that between 1990 and 2002, Veracruz had displaced Jalisco as the second most frequent place of origin of migrants to Tijuana, but the workers brought from Veracruz to Tijuana by Han Young had signed very specific contracts agreeing to have travel and other expenses deducted from their pay. Many of the workers supporting the independent union were longtime residents of Tijuana who live in a *colonia* that is well known for its high level of community organization. Some years before the unionization drive, they had defended their neighborhood's land rights against government efforts to assist Hyundai's expansion. The *veracruzanos* supported the CROC, a union subordinated to a large central union which, unlike the independent union, was not interested in bargaining with the company for safer working conditions and higher pay. The company's efforts to defeat the independent union failed and the maquiladora closed.

The remainder of this section suggests that one of the most important distributional impacts of maquiladora industrialization in Tijuana has been to pass many of the costs associated with constructing a competitive labor force on to workers and their communities, especially migrant workers and their families. Their absorption of these social costs has impeded their settlement in maquiladora cities where they work and has compromised their upward mobility. This often leaves them socially excluded and marginalized in Mexican border cities where they make up the majority of the population, and likely to try to take advantage of better employment opportunities within Mexico or north of the border if they are available.

As Hualde (forthcoming) has indicated,

> although maquiladoras have created jobs that require various skills in some professional and technical sectors, an important segment of direct workers continues to be devoted to simple routine tasks. . . . Profession-

als and technicians are a very minor part of a labor market characterized by low educational levels with stagnated wages and skills throughout the nineties. Data also indicate that the labor market is increasingly polarized. Highly educated people and professionals improved their incomes in the nineties in contrast to the less educated.

The poor quality of the average maquiladora job is quite clear to the popular classes who comprise the vast majority of its maquiladora labor market, since they avoid maquiladora jobs if they can find other types of employment. In a study of the labor trajectories of low-skilled, low-paid workers in the services, and maquiladora sectors of the economy, as well as the self-employed, Coubès (2001: 215) found two distinguishable groups of people following different paths within the Tijuana labor market: migrants from rural locations with low education, who worked exclusively in maquiladoras, and the better-educated natives who were able to avoid work in maquiladoras and had taken only service jobs. The latter were more likely to have an urban social background and were able to use their familial networks to get jobs in the service sector, whereas migrants were more likely to have found their maquila jobs themselves, by answering a newspaper ad, or responding to a "help wanted" sign outside a factory. Coubès (2001: 215) characterizes the differences between these two groups, both of which are low-wage workers, by saying that maquiladoras play the role of a *verdadero refugio* for migrants arriving in Tijuana, while the native born more easily avoid working in maquiladoras altogether.

For those maquiladora workers who stay in maquiladora centers such as Tijuana rather than returning home or migrating to the United States, the quality of life is often marginal at best. Ward (1999) dedicated his book on self-constructed housing with the following words: "for *colonia* residents in Texas and Mexico, who with or without public-sector support have had to bear the brunt of the social costs of housing themselves." This is a powerful way of recognizing that when there are insufficient or nonexistent public funds for essential services such as housing, and little support from the private sector or unions, social costs are often absorbed by individuals and families. While recognizing the resilience of those who construct their own housing, and arguing that Texas has a lot to learn on this issue from the Mexican side of the border, Ward (1999: 129) is critical of the self-help house-building process because it is a manifestation of the "high rates of poverty and lack of development resources." In a study of self-constructed housing in Tijuana, Hiernaux (1986: 132) is more specific about the role of the maquiladora industry in displacing poorer residents. His research demonstrated that even the probability that U.S. companies would locate maquiladoras in the city moved speculators to buy up the best land, causing prices to rise to levels which average tijuanenses could not afford.

Not only do low wages make it difficult to afford adequate housing, but the insufficient stock of housing means that even those with higher wages may not meet their needs for shelter. Sánchez (1999: 59), citing a study by Browning and Zeteneno, argues that "few maquiladora workers with less than three years of residence in Tijuana have access to adequate housing or basic public services. While access increases with their term of residency in the city, the proportion of maquiladora workers with such access remains below the comparable figures for workers in non-maquiladora sectors." Sánchez notes that while maquiladora industries are not legally responsible for providing housing, government suggestions that new taxes be levied to help provide housing have been resisted by industry organizations.

There are many dangers associated with the precarious, often self-built housing, in which maquiladora workers often invest a great deal of their time and resources in order to supply themselves with shelter. Land invasions, or squatting on unclaimed land, is a common way of getting access to property on which migrant workers build their own dwellings. The Regional Workbench Consortium, which includes university personnel, government agencies, and private businesses in the San Diego–Tijuana region, has a project to bring public and private resources together in a community-based planning program to provide basic services such as lighting to one such area in Tijuana, the Colonia 10 de mayo (see www.regionalworkbench.org). This neighborhood is located a little to the east of the industrial park. Ciudad Industrial, which was built by Acevedo Cárdenas as noted above, and many of its households are headed by single women who work in maquiladoras. Innovative attempts to improve the quality of life, such as those of the Regional Workbench Consortium, are necessary because maquiladoras have historically paid almost no taxes. Tax reform in 2001, which levied a special tax on salaries, was recently struck down by the Corte de Justicia de la Nación as unconstitutional. The tax was perceived to be acting as a profound disincentive for new investments in the maquiladora sector of the economy (Sourcemex, 2003). Nevertheless, the single women heads of households have organized themselves well and have lobbied their maquiladora employers to build a school in the Colonia 10 de mayo. Their next goal is a park, but maquiladora managers have been reluctant to donate funds for such a project for fear that the park would not be adequately maintained.

In the summer of 2002, the Tijuana municipal government carried out a very controversial program of actually destroying substandard, irregular housing which it judged to be in overly precarious locations, and which would lead to disasters when the next heavy rains fell. According to Betanzos (2002a), from 250 to 300 houses in the Colonia Puerta al Futuro were demolished in August 2002 which did not have building permits and would be flooded in the coming rainy season. Only eighty to ninety of these dwellings were inhabited, but 500 persons were left homeless by the demolitions. Unlike the Puerto al Futuro demolitions which simply left people homeless and did not consult them ahead of time, later plans by the municipality to relocate 600 families living on the washes of the Arroyo Alamar and 300 families which lived in the Cañón Las Torres included relocation (Salinas, 2002). The PRI alderman Carlos Barbosa, who decried the demolitions, said that if this was to be the way in which the city government was going to deal with all of Tijuana's irregular settlements, they should begin with the rich neighborhoods which were responsible for an immense number of irregularities (Betanzos, 2002b).

While poorer residents have been displaced to the periphery by higher land prices, as noted above, many newcomers arriving in the city and taking up maquiladora jobs often invade land very near to their workplace and build housing there. The Arroyo Alamar, referred to above, is a little to the south of Ciudad Industrial and much of the area around it settled by migrants to Tijuana who work in maquiladoras (Kopinak and Barajas, 2002: 237). Tijuana maquiladora workers who are migrants are more likely to live in the same colonia as the plant that employs them, or an adjacent colonia, than are workers born in Tijuana. This can be problematic, since they are likely to be living very close to sites where the highest-risk hazardous waste is generated (Kopinak and Barajas, 2002: 235, 237).

In the case of families living downstream from the most dangerous brownfield site of abandoned hazardous waste on the border, the former Metales y Derivados factory located on the southwest side of Ciudad Industrial, migrants invaded this land because they did not have the resources to purchase land, and they have dug shallow wells even though the groundwater is contaminated. This area has one of the highest concentrations of children under fourteen years of age in the city. Those living closest to their workplace tend to have migrated from the areas of Mexico which have experienced the deindustrialization and/or economic recession in the 1980s and have sent large numbers of their inhabitants elsewhere: central Mexico, the states of Aguascalientes, Guanajuato, Hidalgo, Mexico, Morelos, Querétaro, and the Distrito Federal.

A rare example of a grassroots organization mobilizing local people to petition government and industry to clean up brownfield sites such as Metales y Derivados is the Colectivo Chipancingo Pro Justicia Ambiental, an affiliate of the Environmental Health Coalition in San Diego, which is supported financially by a grant from the North American Commission for Environmental Cooperation. Activists tend to be long-term residents. In public speeches, members of the Colectivo talk about the fact that their community existed before industry came to Ciudad Industrial in the 1970s, and they can remember when the Arroyo Alamar, now very polluted by industrial contaminants, was clean enough to wash and swim in. It is their observation that health problems within their community have skyrocketed since the arrival of industry, and especially since the abandonment of lead and other toxic heavy metals and the failure to contain much of it at the Metales y Derivados site.

People who are more recent migrants, however, do not have long-term memories of their current communities on which they can draw, which contributes to their social exclusion. The *Report on Environmental Conditions and Natural Resources on Mexico's Northern Border* says that

> another factor that contributes to these problems [infrastructure deficiencies] is that many of the people who migrate to the border don't establish roots there or adopt a "border" identity. They feel that their stay on the border is only temporary and that one day they will return to their place of origin. This attitude creates an obstacle to their contributing in a real way to solving the problems of their cities. (ITESM and InfoMexus, 2002: 61)

Nevertheless, the costs of maquiladora pollution in terms of human health have been estimated to be high. In a study of the health damages attributable to particulate emissions from two sample maquiladoras in Ciudad Juárez, Blackman (forthcoming) estimates the cost to be $25 million per year, and to be incurred much more on the Mexican side of the border. He argues that although the value of health damages from non-maquiladora industries, such as brick kilns, is much higher, policymakers should pressure maquiladoras to further control air pollution because the resources for pollution control are scant, and it would be less costly to change the behavior of the two maquiladoras than the hundreds of small brick kiln operators.

Although very little research has been done on the impact of maquiladoras on public health, the first article surveying what little is known shows that vital statistics at Mexico's northern border compare unfavorably with the Mexican average (Harlow, Denman, and Cedillo, forthcoming). Life expectancy is slightly higher and the percentage of low-weight births is lower in the country as a whole. Baja California especially shows higher rates of age-standardized mortality, infant mortality, and perinatal mortality. Chihuahua also had higher age-standardized mortality and infant mortality, and Sonora also has higher infant mortality. There is also a much higher prevalence of obesity among women in the northern states, increasing their likelihood of developing diabetes, the fourth leading cause of death in Mexico.

Discussion

The findings in this chapter that other forms of export-led development preceded maquiladora industrialization in Tijuana do not support the hyperglobalist understanding of globalization as a totally new phenomenon. It is also clear that new technologies are not the main force underlying maquiladora industrialization here. Moreover, the strong representation of Mexican entrepreneurs, managers, and engineers in the maquiladora labor force makes denationalization and the adoption of any homogeneous world culture difficult.

The findings might seem to support the skeptical orientation to globalization, which argues that current trends of economic integration are not as unique as those which took place earlier in history, especially at the turn of the twentieth century. The Porfiriato was such a clear case of export-led development policy that Mexico's embrace of maquiladora industrialization as a way of linking itself to external economies may seem like going back historically, and not really embarking on a new path. The closure and downsizing of maquiladora industries since the end of 2000 would also support a skeptical orientation by giving rise to doubts about the permanence of maquiladora industries.[5] The latest use of the term *reconversión* observed by this author refers to foreign investors actually leaving Mexico in response to the latest U.S. recession. Ernesto O'Farrill, president of Bursametrica Management, a partner of Standard and Poor, said, "A la industria maquiladora se le caen los pedidos, despide gente, cierra plantas e incluso companies globales aprovechan esas circunstancias de contracción para realizar lo que llaman su reconversión, que no es otra cosa que cambiare sus plantas de país" (*Frontera*, April 17, 2001). After this statement was made, the tightening of security at the border in response to terrorist attacks and the war in Iraq plunged maquiladora industries even further into decline. This suggests that thick globalization, which was found to be present in the kinescope corridor right at the border, will be limited to that one area.

On the other hand, some of the biggest maquiladoras in Tijuana have announced new investments, which weakens support for an interpretation of this area which would coincide with a skeptical orientation to globalization. At the beginning of 2003, Samsung announced that they would invest as much as they had in Tijuana ($30 million) in a new factory in Querétaro making refrigerators and air conditioners (*Frontera*, January 19, 2003). Their Tijuana factories have moved some production to China, but also added new employees. At that time they also said they had plans for another electronics factory in 2004 and still another in 2005. Their goal is to sell more of their products in the Mexican market. Likewise, Toyota is building a large plant at the eastern end of Tijuana.

Held et al. (1999: 17) do not take a skeptical point of view, but suggest that "globalization may differ between historical eras," which is much closer to a tranformationalist understanding of globalization, seeing it as contingent on conjunctural forces and contradictory. We suggest here that maquiladora industrialization constitutes a particular historical form of globalization, which Held et al. (1999: 17) define as "the spatio-temporal and organizational attributes of global interconnectedness in discrete historical epochs." Spatiotemporal simultaneity has been made possible by communications technology which only recently came into existence, allowing for different parts of a production process taking place in different locations at the same time. A very unique part of the organization of this historical form of globalization at the head of the Baja California peninsula is the construction of a labor force made up by very high levels of migrants from other parts of Mexico. Moreover, we argue below that most of these migrants will probably not return to their places of origin, even if rates of unemployment continue to rise within maquiladoras.

Very little is known about how migrant maquiladora workers respond to unemployment since there has been no research on the topic. However, there are several reasons to believe that workers would not return to their places of origin:

1 Unemployment rates are probably still higher in their places of origin than at the border. Most have acquired material goods necessary for life (e.g., refrigerators, land, dwellings) which tie them to the city in which they acquired maquiladora work.
2 Leaving their place of origin was based on a formal or informal understanding that they would bring back economic support when they returned, and if they are unemployed they probably do not have the wherewithal to meet their families' expectations in this regard.

3 Maquiladora workers are quite young, and probably search for other work in the formal and/or informal economies of maquiladora cities, as well as taking advantage of work in the United States if they have a possibility of crossing and contacts on the other side. Operation Guardian, by which the U.S. government has invested millions of dollars into new surveillance equipment and Border Patrol personnel, makes it unlikely that those intending to migrate to the United States will do it in the Tijuana area, but farther to the east where the risks of injury and death are very high.

Having concluded that maquiladora industrialization represents a particular historical form of globalization in this area, further research needs to be done to understand in what form it will be consolidated in the future. Alonso, Carrillo, and Conteras (2002) have identified several kinds of learning trajectories in Tijuana maquiladoras, many of them very advanced and highly skilled. However, they conclude that these trajectories could be interrupted by the downturn in maquiladora industries caused by the weak U.S. economy and flight of some production to China. Hualde (forthcoming), on the other hand, finds Baja California's maquiladora regime weakened from within by the failure to train the vast majority of workers in highly skilled techniques. The low-skilled character of most of the maquiladora labor force will make it difficult for them to compete with other areas of the world where the multiskilled aspect of lean production models has been implemented more thoroughly. As demonstrated in this chapter, the migratory status of many maquiladora workers compounds this situation, since they are too burdened with absorbing the social costs of this new form of globalization to invest in their own human capital. One of the clearest examples of this is the lack of adequate housing, leading migrants to invade unoccupied land and build their own dwellings. This has been a constant across different historical forms of globalization in Tijuana, with workers in the tourist economy of the 1930s taking over abandoned stables to renovate as housing, and maquiladora workers in the 1980s and 1990s often using materials discarded by maquiladora industries as building supplies.

Notes

Part of this chapter was presented at the conference on Economic Integration and Migration, Mexico and the US. Sponsored by Migration Dialogue in La Jolla, California, January 9–11, 2003.

1   INEGI reported that in March 2003, Baja California had 1,057 maquiladoras out of a total of 3,251 in all of Mexico. In March 2003, Baja California had 218,882 people employed in maquiladoras out of a total of 1,090,547 in the country (Industria maquiladora de exportación, May).

2   Acevedo Cárdenas is not only a successful businessman, but has worked as a public administrator and published several books about the area. One example is *El Rancho Tijuana, consideraciones en torno a una calumnia* (Tijuana: Tipografía Mercantil, 1963), which defends Tijuana's reputation against the stereotype that it is only a center of vice and crime.

3   The municipio of Rosarito is included for statistical purposes.

4   There are no data on the numbers of Mexicans who have migrated internationally by moving up the corporate chain, leaving maquiladora employment for better jobs in the multinational in another location, although this is known to have occurred.

5   Between 2001 and 2002, the number of maquiladora plants in Baja California dropped from 1,267 to 1,055. In March 2003 there were 1,057 plants. Between 2001 and 2002, the total number of persons employed by Baja California maquila plants dropped from 261,505 to 221,311. In March 2003, 218, 882 persons were employed (El Instituto Nacional de Estadística y Geografía [INEGI], 2003).

References

Aguilar, Jesús, 2001, "Centros y fronteras: una interpretación de las centralidades urbanas en Tijuana 1889–2000," *El Bordo* 7, http://kino.tij.uia.mx/publicaciones/elbordo/vol 7.

Alegría, Tito, Jorge Carrillo, and Jorge Alonso Estrada, 1997, "Restructuring of production and territorial change: a second industrializaton hub in Northern Mexico," *CEPAL Review* 61, Santiago.

Alonso, Jorge et al., 2002, "Aprendizaje tecnológico en las maquiladoras de México," *Frontera Norte*, 14, Tijuana.

Arce, Rosa, 1999, "Promueve espacios culturales," *Frontera* August 4, http://www.fronteratij.com.mx, Tijuana.

Arthurs, Harry, 2000, "The Hollowing Out of Corporate Canada," in J. Jenson and Bonaventura De Sousa Santos, *Globalizing Institutions: Case Studies in Regulation and Innovation*, Aldershot, Ashgate.

Bandy, Joe, forthcoming, "So What Is to Be Done?, Maquila Justice Movements, Transnational Solidarity and Dynamics of Resistance," in Kathryn Kopinak, *The Social Costs of Industrial Growth in Northern Mexico*, Center for U.S.-Mexican Studies, La Jolla, Calif.

Betanzos, Said, 2002a, "Derrumban 250 casas de invasión," *Frontera*, August 8, Tijuana, http://www.fronteratij.com.mx.

———, 2002b, "Reprochan destrucción," *Frontera*, August 9, Tijuana, http://www.fronteratij.com.mx.

Blackman, Allen, forthcoming, "Maquiladoras, Air Pollution and Human Health in Ciudad Juárez and El Paso," in Kathryn Kopinak, *Social Costs of Industrial Growth in Northern Mexico*, Center for U.S.-Mexican Studies, La Jolla, Calif.

Bustamante, Jorge, 1990, *Historia de la colonia Libertad*, El Colegio de la Frontera Norte, Tijuana.

Carrillo, Jorge et al., 1999. *Competitividad y Mercado de trabajo. Empresas de autopartes y televisores en México*, UAM, México.

Carrillo, Jorge, and Jorge Santibáñez, 1993, *Rotación de personal en las maquiladoras de exportación en Tijuana*, Secretaría de Trabajo y Previsión Social y El Colegio de la Frontera Norte, Tijuana.

Castillo Curry, Maria Eugenia, 2001, *The Binational Preservation Front, SOHO Newsletter*, February.

———, 1998, *Historical Integrity from a Social and International Perspective*, presented at the Second National Forum on Historic Preservation Practice, March 15, Tijuana.

Contreras, Óscar, 2000, *Empresas globales, actors locales: producción flexible y aprendizaje industrial en las maquiladoras*, El Colegio de México, Centro de Estudios Sociológicos, Mexico.

Contreras, Óscar et al., 1997, "Los gerentes de las maquiladoras como agents de endogeneización de la industria," *Comercio Exterior* 47, no. 8.

Coubès, Marie Laure, 2001, "Trayectorias laborales en Tijuana: ¿segmentación o continuidad entre sectores de empleo?" *Trabajo* 2, no. 4, Mexico.

Davis, Mike, 2000, *Magical Urbanism: Latinos Reinvent the US City*, New York.

Ellingwood, Ken, 2001, "Fox Opens Movie Park in Baja," *Los Angeles Times*, May 21.

Frontera, 2003, *Va Samsung por liderazgo*, January 19, http://www.fronteratij.com.mx, Tijuana.

———, 2001, *Pega a México crisis de Estados Unidos*, Frontera, April 17, http://www.fronteratij.com.mx.

Harlow, Siobán et al., forthcoming, "Occupational and Population Health Profiles: A Public Health Perspective on the Social Costs and Benefits of Export-Led Development," in Kathryn Kopinak, *The Social Costs of Industrial Growth in Northern Mexico*, Center for U.S.-Mexican Studies, La Jolla, Calif.

Held, David et al., 1999, *Global Transformations: Politics, Economics and Culture*, Stanford University Press, Stanford, Calif.

Hiernaux, Daniel, 1999, *Los senderos del cambio*, Centro de Investigaciones Cientificas y Plana y Valdés, Mexico.

———, 1986, *Urbanización y autoconstrucción de vivienda en Tijuana*, Centro de Ecodesarrollo, Mexico.

Hualde, Alfredo, forthcoming, "Segmentation of Skills and Social Polarization in Tijuana's Maquiladora Industry," in Kathryn Kopinak, *The Social Costs of Industrial Growth in Northern Mexico*, Center for U. S.-Mexican Studies, La Jolla, Calif.

Instituto Tecnológico y de Estudios Superiores de Monterrey (ITESM) and Instituto de Información fronteriza México-Estados Unidos (InfoMexus), 2002, *Report on*

Environmental Conditions and Natural Resources on Mexico's Northern Border, Gila Resources Information Project (GRIP) and the Interhemispheric Resource Center (IRC), http://americaspolicy.org/rep-envt/.

Kopinak, Kathryn, 2003, "Maquiladora Industrialization of the Baja California Peninsula: The Coexistence of Thick and Thin Globalization with Economic Regionalism," International Journal of Urban and Regional Research 27, no. 2.

———, 1998, "Industrial Exchanges across the U.S.-Mexico Border: The Export Platform Thesis Reconsidered in Tijuana and San Diego," in Frontera Norte 8, no. 10, Tijuana.

———, 1996, Desert Capitalism: Maquiladoras in North America's Western Industrial Corridor, University of Arizona Press, Tucson.

Kopinak, Kathryn, and María del Rocio Barajas, 2002, "Too Close for Comfort? The Proximity of Industrial Hazardous Wastes to Local Populations in Tijuana, Baja California," Journal of Environment and Development 11, no. 3, La Jolla, Calif.

Lestage, Françoise, 1988, "Los indígenas mixtecos en la frontera norte (1977–1996)," in Notas: Revista de información y análisis, no. 4, INEGI, Aguascalientes.

Martínez, Oscar, 1994, Border People: Life and Society in the U.S.-Mexico Borderlands, University of Arizona Press, Tucson.

———, 1988, Troublesome Border, University of Arizona Press, Tucson.

McMichael, Philip, 2000, Development and Social Change: A Global Perspective, Pine Forge Press, Thousand Oaks, Calif.

Melo de Remes, Maria Luisa, 1964, ¡Alerta, Baja California!, editorial Jus, Mexico.

Mendoza, Cristobal, 2002, "Migración, empleos y vivienda en los municipios y condados de la frontera internacional México-Estados Unidos," final project report, CONACYT (301)-S.

Millner, Henry, 1978, Politics in the New Quebec, McClelland and Stewart, Toronto.

Nordhoff, Charles, 1888, Peninsular California: Some Account of the Climate, Soil, Productions, and Present Condition Chiefly of the Northern Half of Lower California, Harper & Brothers, New York.

Quintero, Cirila, 1997, Restructuración syndical en la frontera norte, El Colegio de la Frontera Norte, Tijuana.

Salinas, Daniel, 2002, "Tumbarán casas de 1000 familias," in Frontera, August 16 http://www.fronteratij.com.mx, Tijuana.

Sánchez, Roberto, 1999, "Sustainable Development in Tijuana: A Perspective on Options and Challenges," in Sustainable Development in the San Diego-Tijuana Region, Center for U.S.-Mexican Studies, La Jolla, Calif.

Simonelli, Carlos Ernesto, 2002, "Cambios recientes en la migración y en la inserció laboral en Tijuana, entre 1990 y 2000," Papeles de Población 34, 2002. 159–189.

Sklair, Leslie, 2000, Free Trade and the Future of the Maquila Industry: Global Production and Local Workers, presented at IME: 2000: COLEF, October 19–21, Tijuana.

———, 1989, Assembly for Development, Unwin Hyman, Boston.

Smith, Geri, and Elisabeth Malkin, 1998, "Mexican Makeover: NAFTA Creates the World's Newest Industrial Power," Business Week, December 21, no. 3609.

Sourcemex, 2003, *Supreme Court Rules against Special Tax; Decision to Affect Government Revenues*, 14, no. 20, May 28.

Valenzuela, José Manuel, 1991, *Empapados de sereno. El movimiento urbano popular en Baja California (1928–1988)*, El Colegio de la Frontera Norte, Tijuana.

Ward, Peter, 1999, *Colonias and Public Policy in Texas and Mexico: Urbanization by Stealth*, University of Texas Press, Austin.

Fiamma Montezemolo

(Conversation with) Néstor García Canclini, on How Tijuana Ceased to Be the Laboratory of Postmodernity

F.M.: Néstor, when I asked you for an interview for the book that I was working on about Tijuana, you responded by saying that it seemed like a good idea, but you also pointed out that you had undertaken your last research in the city in 2000. "Since then," you said, "I have continued to follow its process of disintegration and transformation in newspapers, in academic articles, and through friends' stories. I would say that for me, Tijuana is no longer, as I wrote in *Hybrid Cultures*, a laboratory of postmodernity but rather perhaps a laboratory of the social and political disintegration of Mexico as a consequence of a calculated ungovernability."

Within this statement, there are several points that I would like to tease out with you. The first one is this: Why were you interested in Tijuana in the 1980s?

N.G.C.: I first went to Tijuana in 1979 to give a talk as part of a series organized by the National Institute of Fine Arts in Mexico in border towns. At that time, within the federal government (under President López Portillo) people were beginning to argue that it was necessary to strengthen Mexican identity in the border region because it was thought that there was a lack of Mexicanness in that area due to its proximity to the United States. I was doing fieldwork in Michoacán about craftwork and its transformation due to contact with the city and with tourism, with factors outside of indigenous communities. I was fascinated to find a very different Mexico in the border region, one with a discourse very distinct from that of the rest of the country. It was clear that the border towns had more of a relationship with the United States than with the Mexican capital. Many people had never been south of Guadalajara.

Later, in 1984, I was invited to do a study of the public served by the Centro Cultural de Tijuana (CECUT). The Centro had been built in 1982 as part of a project to strengthen identity and to develop local cultural facilities. We observed that CECUT existed primarily as a building and only later as a cultural program. We agreed—with two other anthropologists—to do a study not only of CECUT's audience, as they asked us to do, but also to try to understand Tijuana's cultural needs. I also worked with a photographer, Lourdes Grobet, taking pictures in many parts of Tijuana and later suggesting, through focus groups with people in a variety of professions, that they select the most representative parts of the city. We found interesting evidence that their perception of Tijuana was not strictly territorial: for example, when we asked which parts of the city they preferred or which for them were most representative of the city, someone answered "Balboa Park," which is in San Diego. There was a certain transterritoriality or urban transnationalism.

Through interviews and fieldwork with artists, intellectuals, academics from the Colegio de la Frontera Norte, journalists, and photographers, we proved that the city already was an extraordinary cultural and economic force. It's significant that while Mexico experienced no economic growth during the 1980s, Tijuana experienced a leap of approximately 10 percent.

F.M.: That's what they say: when Mexico does badly, Tijuana does well.

N.G.C.: The image of Tijuana that emerged through fieldwork was very different from the one which appeared in U.S. or Mexican newspapers, which was based on stereotypes held by people in both countries. In the 1980s, Tijuana was for many a synonym for the emigrants from all over Mexico that came to form a kind of synthesis or condensation of Mexicanness, and at the same time an incredibly dynamic place of business, tourism, and sexual spectacle. All of this gave rise to complex interactions, a diversity of cultural demands and expectations in regard to what a cultural center as large as CECUT could offer, very different demands from the ones we had found while studying audiences of museums and cultural centers in Mexico City.

Afterwards, in the 1990s, I started going to Tijuana again, this time to participate with inSITE, an important binational artistic event organized in Tijuana and San Diego. I worked with Manuel Valenzuela on a study of the repercussions of "border art" and "public art," which experimented every two or three years with new aesthetic, urban, and institutional configurations. I was very interested in the complexity of migratory processes, the existence of several borders on the Mexican side and also, of course, on the U.S. side as well: the cliché of the Mexican-U.S. border was just starting to come undone, and it was recognized that there were very different perspectives, not only between Tijuana and San Diego, but also between San Diego and El Paso or between Tijuana and Ciudad Juárez.

In part because Tijuana represented the synthesis of contemporary processes which were challenging for the social sciences and the arts—restructuring of relationships between metropolis and periphery, interethnic creativity, the change from national cultures to globalized flows—Tijuana as a multicultural city was held up as an emblem of postmodernity. Many of us who shared those experiences or studied them saw in the border, along with the drama of immigration and the violent asymmetries between the United States and Mexico, a space in which the dying certainties of nationalism were being destabilized and an unforeseen creativity might emerge. This perspective was developed in the analyses of Latin American critics and curators, as well as in the articles about inSITE by *Art in America* and *Artforum*. Sociologists like Larry Herzog asked themselves if Tijuana "could become the next Hong Kong."

Nevertheless, in the following years, I began to notice that that notion of Tijuana as a laboratory of postmodernity, besides having the typical problems of postmodern thinking in regard to sustaining an empirical consistency, also ran other risks. Speaking of my description of the border as a place where the territorialized stereotypes of Mexicanness were breaking down, I remember that John Kraniauskas, the English cultural critic, made a very pertinent point: he said that I was paying much more attention to the phenomenon of deterritorialization than to the reterritorialization sought by the migrants, who were now converted into new residents of the border.

Changes in the Conceptualization of Borders

F.M.: At one time, did Tijuana seem like a vanguard to you?

N.G.C.: I don't know if I would say vanguard, because I saw Tijuana as a very advanced place but also with serious social and economic backwardness. If one considers the structures of work in the maquiladoras, for example, or social disintegration, the brutal effects on families torn apart by migration, those who remain on the Mexican side and those who are able to make it to the United States, this process can't be simplified to fit into a single historical direction. I would not use the word *vanguard*, but without a doubt those contemporary contradictions were made visible in a more obvious way, a more intense way, than in other regions of Mexico.

As time passed, it became necessary to oppose certain hasty thinking that was referencing cities like Tijuana or borders like the one between Mexico and the United States as a way to justify their theories about the predominance of nomadism. Even in areas where migration and borders made the oppositions, conflicts, and the difficulty of crossing from one country to another very obvious, a way of thinking emerged which celebrated the fluidity and the permeability of the border. Some artistic movements, while still motivated by the exaltation of nomadism, attempted a new kind of analysis. The changes generated during the development of inSITE represent this shift quite well. The time artists and intellectuals from many countries spent living in this area, after being invited by the binational program to carry out projects, gave them the opportunity to discover the variety of situations and actors. They didn't arrive with previously completed work; rather they went through a process of immersion in the area before beginning their production, even though they were not required to explicitly refer to the border. By following these processes and seeing the ambivalence that they generated, the artists took positions or avoided the question of the border, and thereby made the diversity and the ambivalence clear. One of the contrasts that I first noticed was that while the foreign artists used the public space of Tijuana with much more freedom, contrasting their search for forms with the local culture and border conflicts, many Latin American artists, when they went to San Diego to make their artwork, ended up hiding it in a basement: it was as if the urbanism of San Diego, and getting a grasp on that urban fabric, made their interventions that much more difficult. Some artists have used the open spaces, above all Chicano muralists, but there were in general few instances of public art within the city. The lack of urban structure in Tijuana seemed to be more propitious to the utilization of space than the layout of isolated neighborhoods in San Diego, linked together by highways.

F.M.: If we are all positioned subjects—in the sense of the term provided by Donna Haraway, Renato Rosaldo, Trinh Minh-Ha, and other cultural theorists—what was the influence of your own "positional-ity" in relationship to your reading of Tijuana in that historical pe-riod? I am referring to the concepts of deterritorialization and hy-bridity in particular. For example, do you think you grasped that idea because you came from a condition of deterritorialization and hybrid-ity as a result of your own migration from Argentina to Mexico?

N.G.C.: Yes, beginning in 1976, when I left Argentina after the military coup and moved to Mexico, I experienced several migration processes: one was the change in country; another was the disciplinary migra-tion because I was schooled in philosophy and in Mexico I began to do fieldwork as an anthropologist. We worked on Michoacán with a group of researchers, with the idea to study their communities not only in isolation in their own territories, but also while migrating, traveling to sell their craft products, to go to distant festivals, to visit relatives. For me, it was vital to the anthropological project at that time not only to study communities in and of themselves but also to recognize the multiple outflows and exchanges that in the end redefined Purépecha culture.

F.M.: To put an end to the myth of an isolated and completely self-sufficient community? And on a personal level?

N.G.C.: Those migrations across disciplinary and national borders made me feel like an outsider in regard to conventional methods of investigation.

F.M.: Because I imagine that you, being from Argentina, would have had a bit of a different relationship with Mexico, at least initially, than that of a Mexican; that is, we're talking about a Mexican nationalism that can be quite strong.

N.G.C.: Yes, and with a role played by the state that I had never known in Argentina. . . . Many people have asked me about the cultural shock I experienced in Mexico when I arrived, and I always say that there wasn't much confrontation, because the strong feeling of ter-ror I brought with me from Argentina contrasted with a very wel-coming Mexico. . . . I quickly found work, good conditions for put-ting together research teams, funding for going into the field, for publishing—I was even able to get two books published which were not able to appear in Argentina due to repression and censorship. Mexico was a country with steady rates of development due to the single-party hegemony of the PRI and at the same time was begin-ning to open up to dissident thought.

So, it was about a few years later—when I began to reflect on what was happening to me in relation to Mexico—I wrote a few pages about my own disaffection or about my difficulty adapting to Mexican ways of being and acting. It's apparent above all in the book *The Imagined Globalization*, for which I decided I should write an appendix to explain my subject position in relation to this text about globalization. I wasn't speaking from a neutral place, but rather out of the tension between a number of cultures, that is of an Argentinian who studied in France, who went to Mexico as an exile and admired certain lifestyles in the United States and Europe and rejected others, discovering the relativity of each culture and the necessity of thinking interculturally.

Tijuana and the Debate about Hybridization and Ethnicity

F.M.: Of course, you know that your theory of the hybrid has provoked a number of reactions both at a local level and internationally. Some have adopted it with enthusiasm and others have interpreted it as a theory out of touch with the "real condition" of the city. There are two problems: on the one hand, the "internal" vision, which is opposed to someone who doesn't come from the same culture and sees the interpretation of others in this way, as an "other," an outsider who has the power to speak about us and make decisions without our consent about what we are and what we aren't; on the other hand, there's the problem laid out by *tijuanense* writers like Heriberto Yépez, who feel that the theory of the hybrid is somehow a pacified Hegelian synthesis dressed up as something new, referring to a lack of resistance. It's a fact that the theory of the hybrid has had more success outside of the city than in the city itself. And it's also a fact that sometimes there's an exaggerated defense of local identity against everyone-who-comes-from-far-away-and-defines-us-without-knowing-us. How would you respond to those criticisms?

N.G.C.: Some of those critiques are comprehensible. They have helped make clear to several of us who work on hybridization that, by interpreting social processes with that category, we run the risk of covering up the contradictions. I wrote a new introduction to the book *Hybrid Cultures* in 2001 in order to debate that question and other methodological points, returning to the very intense debate about hybridization, which took place both in Spanish and in English during the

1990s. Many works appeared, for example Homi Bhabha's book, and an enormous amount of magazines, entire issues devoted to the topic, books, international debates. I began to notice certain theoretical consequences of the concept of hybridization not only as a central process of modernity and postmodernity, but also as a notion that had to be articulated with others, like the concepts of contradiction and inequality. In the same way, there was a need to differentiate hybridization as an initial process of fusion, of synthesis, from the consequences which later emerged as it was unpacked. When there is a migration and there emerges what anthropologists in another period called "cultural contact," there is almost always hybridization, but it is not enough to look at what can be fused together: we must also consider what is left outside, other processes of contradiction and of conflict. Hybridization is not a synonym for reconciling things that are different or unequal.

F.M.: I also feel that the work on hybridity implied a political thought in the sense that it did not have to do with reconciling but rather with getting beyond those dualisms, those very Western oppositions of traditional/modern, white/not-white, feminine/masculine. There's a certain categorization of the same and the other which is implicit in these dualisms and is now very much in question, since it always implies a certain hierarchy.

N.G.C.: Yes, the emphasis on hybridization was an effort to oppose identitarian essentialisms, nationalism in Mexico and in other countries.

F.M.: In the United States as well, I would say.

N.G.C.: Yes, in opposition to the segregating multiculturalism which compartmentalized ethnic groups and immigrants. All of that was there, but as time passed I realized that from an epistemological and methodological point of view, the concept of hybridization is a descriptive concept. It allows us to describe multiple processes of fusion which can be religious syncretism, ethnic *mestizaje*, musical and cultural fusion, et cetera, but in each case we have to specifically analyze how those fusions are always partial—that they leave a great deal out—how they operate in the midst of conflicts and social inequalities that persist and sometimes are made worse by the very contact. So hybridization is not the destination, it is not the only concept for describing a societal state, and much less a satisfactory state, it is the recognition that cultures cannot develop in an autonomous way, isolated from what is happening on the global stage.

F.M.: Do you think that hybridity and a less solid conception of identity, an overly plural conception of identity, could weaken a politics of resistance or of self-determination? There is a certain fear that the politics of differences is going to destroy the politics of opposition. I still feel quite close to Paul Gilroy, who suggests the possibility of moving beyond these two oppositions through the notion of anti-antiessentialism, that is, in the notion of an identity which is neither monolithic and essentialized nor completely useless, because of being too fragmented by difference. We are talking about a third possibility: an identity which is sensitive to differences, while at the same time open to the possibility of alliances based on situational affinities. For example, I am thinking of the antiglobalization movement that in Genoa and on other occasions was able to bring together feminists, environmentalists, pacifists, and immigrants, all of them united for a moment by the common goal of opposing something else.

But even with this Gilroyan vision, a more general problem is still present in my thought, the problem of reconciling hybridity with hegemonies and subalternities that continue to exist in the relationships between nation states that do not seem to be collapsing; how to reconcile the amount of biopolitics present on the border with the theory of multiplication of identities. How do we reconcile the discourse of autorepresentation with the discourse of the hybrid?

N.G.C.: I am under the impression that there has been a certain evolution within the social sciences in the last ten to fifteen years, which has meant that certain key concepts have been altered. Today, we speak of identification, more than identity, of processes of identification, and we even speak of interculturality, more than of hybridization. What significance do these conceptual changes have? *Identity* always carries with it the risk of overvaluing self-affirmation and of essentializing it, freezing it. We know that all identities are temporary sedimentations of processes that have been changing and are going to continue to change. So it does not mean much to say "we do this in the name of Chicano identity" or "we act this way because of our Brazilian identity." These national and group identities designate abstract fusions of certain particularities, which in a certain historical moment were able to organize themselves into a nation but which continue to change in different ways in different regions of the same country and depending on contact with the outside world.

We can localize this analysis in regard to what we were saying just a moment ago about Tijuana in the 1980s. I am referring to the conflict between those who promoted the culture of Tijuana with its complexity and its heterogeneous makeup, and the unifying cultural policies emanating from Mexico City, which sought to establish the canons of Mexicanness for northern residents.

In that period, there was a conflict between—more than two identities—two modes of identification, about which one could be more effective in relation to sociocultural and political projects, one regional and the other national. If we speak of processes of identification, we can understand that in Genoa, as in other places, globalization movements have brought together groups with different identifications, distinct identities defined more by ethnicity, environmentalism, gender, et cetera. The relationship with identification is more dynamic and requires us to take as a reference point that with which we identify ourselves, not to think of identity as something that we possess, as if it were a self-contained substance that belongs to us as a group. I'm thinking of Arjun Appadurai in *Modernity at Large*, about his criticism of essentialist conceptions of identity and culture.

F.M.: That it is accepted almost in a naturalized way.

N.G.C.: Naturalized and naturalizing . . .

F.M.: It's more of a process.

N.G.C.: Something similar is happening with the evolution away from the concept of hybridization to that of interculturality. I continue to insist on the importance of examining the processes of hybridization, but talking about interculturality allows us to understand that cultures act among themselves without predefining what is going to happen or what is happening. We have to analyze the many forms of interculturality that imply acceptance, rejection, dominations, hegemonies, a multiplicity of forms of interaction. We know that there are historical moments in which the affirmation of a community, of a group, is valuable and necessary for survival.

F.M.: We say that it's necessary to essentialize at times in order to move to the level of politics, for example.

N.G.C.: We can understand the importance and the value of processes of identity affirmation, understood as the ethnic and national affirmation in Bolivia, in this moment, although from a theoretical or more general point of view, we would prefer the productivity of intercultural processes that work with the appropriation of multiple cultures, that is, a more fluid interaction with what is outside the actual nation. But I understand that—after five hundred years of *criollo*, white domination, subordination, or exclusion of indigenous people—the fact that there is not only an indigenous president, but also a completely indigenous cabinet, is a historic event. It would be beneficial if they had time to articulate this historical bloc we call Bolivia on new axes.

F.M.: You're making me think of when I worked on Zapatismo in the early 1990s, and I noticed their dynamic use of the "ethnic" in their communiqués. The first communiqués put much less emphasis on a certain "indigeneity" or "Mayanness," while the later communiqués made greater use of that concept, because it was understood that the use of ethnicity would not necessarily isolate the group, but rather would strengthen them in a globalized world, which feared dominant homogenization. A certain identity-based localism was very attractive for many lost souls (including myself), from a West that was looking for alternatives to itself. Zapatismo and its ethnic specificity came to be understood as a possibility for resistance.

N.G.C.: We would also have to include in the analysis the marginalization of the Zapatistas within Chiapas by the Mexican state and the army, which made it difficult for them to construct a national or international alternative. In the first communiqués, Zapatismo had three agendas: a local one for Chiapas and the indigenous communities; another agenda for the country; and let's not forget that the insurgency began on January 1, 1994—when NAFTA went into effect, it also proposed an international agenda for Mexican relations with the world. That last part later became diplomatic relations: looking for solidarity from foreign countries. Inside Mexico, they began to fail for many reasons that are not solely due to the Zapatistas, but rather due to the Mexican political system and to its social movements: their calls for solidarity organized an alternative power base and that also contributed to them rooting themselves more deeply in the indigenous, the ethnic, and in more local demands.

F.M.: Doesn't it seem interesting to you that a city renowned as "postmodern," "Bajalta," a megalopolis tied together with L.A., shows such obvious signs of an industrial reality (like that of the maquila) generally associated with the modern, Fordist era? A city in which half of the population still does not cross the border and in which the other half crosses mainly to shop or to work, much less to share a kind of "Bajalta-ness," unless it has to do with family relationships or specific friends, possibly among the upper middle classes? In five years of experience in Tijuana, I realized that certain theoretical concepts like hybridity and transculturation or transnationalism operate more effectively in relation to certain social classes or specific ethnic groups, for example, young people of the upper middle classes who have access to the Internet, who have passports and access not just to their own surroundings. Or we see that the idea of a more open border is more in use from a Chicano point of view than from a specifically *fronterizo* perspective. As we said previously, there are many people in Tijuana that never cross the border and for whom the border remains simply a wall, a wall which unfortunately is not at all porous.

N.G.C.: Transculturality, or the transcity or the transborder, was overexaggerrated. It exists more as a circuit than as a space, more as a possibility of a constant and fluid exchange, sometimes with great obstacles, than as a shared culture. When one crosses from Tijuana to San Diego or from San Diego to Tijuana, one immediately notices the differences in the spatial layout, in the care of the yards, in the traffic on the streets.

F.M.: Even in the attitude. . . . My tijuanense friends, almost invariably, when they cross the border into San Diego drive differently, not with the sense of transgression from before, but rather embodying a respect for the law and for the traffic signals. . . . They're more careful.

N.G.C.: In that sense, perhaps the notion of Bajalta, of transborder, isn't very productive. It is more helpful to talk about circuits, which are important. In regard to the organization of industry, looking for cheaper prices to produce goods and an ease of coming and going, not only between Mexico and the United States, corresponds to global movements that also occur with Jakarta or African countries. This allows the mobility of capital, objects, and goods, which circulate and accumulate in a way that is very different from Fordism.

F.M.: Yes, that's true . . . but in regard to the local working conditions in the maquila . . . I was referring more to this: without unions, without rights, with women in a majority because they are less educated, they are more vulnerable, and thus easier to manipulate. In my opinion, they are fixed in a historical moment that we thought was already over; that is, I would differentiate the dynamics of the finished product from that of the production itself. Those two conditions would seem to belong to two different periods, which paradoxically continue to exist contemporaneously in Tijuana.

N.G.C.: But this is a characteristic of capitalist development in most of the world. In the central countries, despite the current economic crisis, a higher level of well-being in labor terms persists, like better conditions in collective bargaining contracts, while when the same companies work in peripheral countries, they impose the most unjust conditions, not only on production but also on services. The great transnationals like Walmart, for example, exploit workers in Latin American even more because the legal structure in these countries is weaker and it's easier to corrupt the authorities.

F.M.: Yes, and it's well known that now the maquiladoras are moving from Mexico to China because there are even more advantages there for the companies.

Again, it seems to me that Tijuana is caught between two different kinds of violence: the violence of the border and of the Foucauldian biopolitics/biosecurity mentioned by Paul Rabinow and the violence of the drug traffickers and the kidnappings that are taking place across Mexico right now. What do you think? How did this condition arise? Did events in the United States (September 11) and others in Mexico itself create this explosive situation?

N.G.C.: It is a process which began previous to September 11. The repression of immigrants, the organization of KKK-like groups, laws restricting rights . . . all of this was already evidence of a social and cultural uneasiness in the United States and forms of racist discrimination previous to the extension of the border wall ordered during the Bush administration. It also has to do with the increase in emigration of labor from Mexico and other Latin American countries due to the reorganization of agricultural production stemming from deindustrialization and free-trade agreements. Along with those processes of social and economic regression, during the last decades of the twentieth century, there was a steady acceptance of the advance of informality and illegality in labor relations, the growing power of drug traffickers, and they even were conceded political protection. The death of Colosio in 1994 took place in Tijuana, but he was the candidate of the PRI for the presidency of the entire country and it was never cleared up in an acceptable investigation what national forces were implicated. That's why it's possible to say that from that time on Tijuana was the laboratory of the sociopolitical disintegration of Mexico as a consequence of a calculated ungovernability. With that disintegration, the volume of migration increased, and also the possibility of sending remittances to relatives who stayed in Mexico: a very precarious equilibrium was maintained in this way between the population which was lost and the survival of those who stayed behind.

F.M.: Remittances make up the third highest source of income for the Mexican economy, right?

N.G.C.: But they are decreasing. It seems that the level of remittances at $25 billion a year is not going to be seen again and the immigration specialists provide several explanations: one is the recession and the loss of jobs in the United States; another cause is that by the second or third generation of immigrants in the United States, with all of their local commitments (paying for the car, the house, the kids' education), they don't have much money left and their relationship with Mexico is weakened. Then, there are also the barriers: there are increased controls for crossing the border or for sending money.

These facts at least partially explain the repositioning of Tijuana and other Mexican border towns in relation to the worldwide restructuring of the markets. The impact of the recent economic crisis in the United States is greater in Mexico, thanks to NAFTA and an increased and more consolidated dependency on the United States. More than 90 percent of Mexican trade is with the United States, unlike other Latin American countries, like Argentina or Brazil, who divide their commercial relationships in a different way: a third with Europe, a third with the United States, and a third with their regional neighbors. At the same time, the way in which the free-trade agreement was established with free passage of goods but not of people has a large influence. The Mexican government was not able to include migration in the treaties. At the same time, there has been a growth in informality throughout the country, as demonstrated along the border by the illegal trafficking in goods and people, in shady businesses of all kinds, drug trafficking, immigrant exploitation, kidnappings, cruelty in the dispute for public space and commercial networks.

F.M.: Are we seeing a resurgence of the *leyenda negra*?

N.G.C.: But it is no longer the same leyenda negra from the last century, which stigmatized Tijuana in particular. What's happening in Tijuana is in some way what is happening throughout Mexico: incredibly violent killings, dismembered bodies, corruption at all levels of the police and the state. The conflicts between mafias, the decapitated cadavers, and the police and political complicity are reproduced in regions far from the border: Acapulco, Michoacán, Mexico City.

F.M.: I think that the main difference involved in the violence in Tijuana is that—as I was saying before—the city is caught between two violences: the one that it shares with the entire country, and the border one, that violence which is also biopolitical, related to hyperidentification like fingerprinting, iris scans, handing over power to the other to look inside me, in my body, for proof of my citizenship and of my intention to return to my country after my visit to the other side. The example of secondary inspection is very illustrative in this sense.

In practice, a secondary inspection is an obsessive review of your identity, your "legality," and your intentions on crossing the border. Through the figure of the border guard and the symbolic geopolitical divide, any attempt at intrusion by an undetermined identity is put into question, an identity which, in order to be monitored, must first be obsessively defined in one sense or another. The first agent at the border crossing carries out an inspection which is less strict and largely ritualistic, with repetitions of words and gestures; but the second "inspection" examines the tiniest details of your person, your mode of transportation, and your trustworthiness. There is a logic in the feared secondary inspection; it is very strict but at the same time rooted in the concept of belonging and of the nation-state. A logic that (despite the oft-mentioned hybridities and flux at a theoretical level) forcefully marks the divide between the "first" and "third" worlds: it is the logic of the script, interrupted if not executed in the correct way. Not even the slightest ambiguity is permitted. If you are Mexican, you will be admitted, but only under certain conditions: you have to have money in your bank account and you have to prove it; be in transit or have a specific reason that you need to first explain to the consulate; your legal record must be impeccable and your intentions more innocent.

If NAFTA were able to alter the relationship among the several Americas and to unify the continent, this doesn't seem to have changed in the slightest the destiny of those people who do not know how to play the correct role in the script, the role of one who belongs to a certain "nation."

The only passenger that does not appear fearsome is the "alien" who crosses the border temporarily and with an explicit time frame.

So, for example, a Mexican family with a bulging wallet and with essentially laudable motives: that is, going shopping.

The statistics speak of illegal migration and the commuters but also insist on telling the stories of the 42 percent of people who wait in line for hours under the glaring sun to "go shopping." Many Mexican consumers are infatuated with spending their savings in San Diego or *en el otro lado*, in stores selling clothes, electronics, and groceries. This topology shines a light on the "most agreeable and inoffensive" category of visitors, of which we spoke previously, a visitor who is not an ambiguous nonresident, who is possibly middle class, with a light skin tone, with an understandable English, and who, after an afternoon of shopping, goes back home, to his/her own territory of juridico-political belonging.

Borders become mise-en-scène in two ways: besides the border guards who patrol the script and the particular characters, there are also those characters who have an understanding and a familiarity with the system of "crossing the border"; they know how to carry themselves, what to say. The nation is represented in two different senses, to the outside in the United States and to the inside within Mexico itself. The "white" upper-middle-class Mexican, schooled in certain educational environments, economically stable, a "consumer" who knows that it isn't difficult to play the role of the useful "alien," is the same character who is generally well accepted inside Mexico as well—a country which at times reproduces historical racial dynamics very similar to those of Western countries. It is this ambiguity which creates this sense of danger, the strange, uncertain identities, or the shady intentions both inside as well as outside the nations of belonging, the same motives for provoking the suspicions of the agents on any border that seek to preserve the imaginary homogeneity of a nation-state. In this sense, the border continues to be a highly biopoliticized place, not only as an obvious judicial system of inclusion/exclusion, but also as a stage for the national projects of Mexico and the United States.

Lost Creativity and the Appropriation of the Different

F.M.: All right, Néstor, I'd like to move on to another question now: Tijuana lives between two myths that sometimes characterize the perception not just of the city but also of the "third world" in general:

creativity and violence, the "noble savage" of Rousseau, and the other as a dangerous and dark man who has been spoken of from Sally Price to Jim Clifford. It would seem that a certain West has not stopped perceiving a certain "other" in this double vision: an "exceptionalization" of the other, whether in a positive or a negative way, in the end comes to the same end: a distorted perception. Tijuanense artists became relevant without any real sense of discrimination (often independently of their real value, which in certain cases is indubitable), because the West still needs its noble savages. Their creativity becomes something "natural," innate, in opposition to a West considered functional and rational. It is as if a certain West kept looking for its Josephine Baker, the exploitation of the other through a creativity which is seemingly out of reach for oneself. A trend that has taken the postcolonial and the other peripheries to the peak of fashion and which tomorrow—capricious and unpredictable—will consign these internal and external others once again to a new oblivion. . . . Do you have a feeling about all of this?

N.G.C.: Yes, partially. We find various processes in what you are saying. On the one hand, there are international movements which broaden the field of legitimacy of the artistic mainstream and have continually incorporated a selective sample of African, Asian, and Latin American artists. The majority of the art that is produced on these three continents circulates on a local or national level, but there is no doubt that a larger number of artists are being invited to the biennials and there are even biennials being developed in the so-called third world: Johannesburg, Sao Paolo, and so on. In Tijuana we can also see the development of a cosmopolitan culture, in part thanks to inSITE. In Tijuana in the 1980s, that kind of artistic and cultural development didn't exist and artists had more difficulty showing their work. Hardly anyone crossed the border to show their work on the other side—they would go as spectators. That also changed because now Tijuana, with a better educational system and sustained quality production, has local audiences and international resonance.

F.M.: Among other things: the new art school at the Universidad Autónoma de Baja California.

N.G.C.: Yes, publications, shows, visits, and residencies by mainstream artists. All of this has attracted the attention of international art magazines, of U.S. curators, to find out what's happening in the city.

A new type of author and artist appears who doesn't write as a tijua-nense or about Tijuana anymore, but rather with a certain style that has international echoes: I'm thinking of Marcos Ramírez ERRE, Luis Humberto Crosthwaite, and others. It's not that they cease to represent a place, but they speak of the place while insisting that "they have to recognize me, not because I'm tijuanense, but because I'm an artist that produces work of a certain value." The phenomenon of the collectives also seems very interesting to me, like Bulbo, for example, a media collective, with anthropological interests. The inter-vention of artists from outside the city is also important, like Judith Werhein, from Brico, who did the tennis shoe to cross the border. So then it is not talking about a place from a naturalist perspective, but rather positioning oneself as they would somewhere else. I'm think-ing of the work of ERRE, the Trojan horse left for a period of time next to the immigration checkpoints between Tijuana and San Diego: a gigantic, wooden horse with two heads, one looking to-ward the United States and the other toward Mexico, which was later reproduced in Valencia, Spain, to talk about borders between Europe and Latin America, and was adopted as a symbol of the Biennial, *En-cuentro entre dos mares* (Encounter between Two Seas).

F.M.: My criticism is more directed at a certain way of curating. . . . I re-member an artist from Tijuana who told me: "The curators just aren't interested in art that's not related to the border. That's why if one wants to enter a certain circuit, one has to produce works about the border."

N.G.C.: That process of exoticization continues to be widespread even when there is more recognition of Latin American artists. No one asks for a passport from a German, French, or U.S. artist. No one demands that they represent the place they're from.

F.M.: It's a fact that there are not many Roman artists who are concerned with their Romanness or who are asked to produce this type of work.

N.G.C.: The most internal artist from Mexico, Gabriel Orozco, is almost forced—despite his best efforts to distance himself from Mexicanness—to represent, to provide signs of Mexicanness no matter what.

F.M.: Is this obsession with a certain Mexicanness, that always has to be associated with Mexican artists, related to a discourse of alternative modernity?

N.G.C.: We see different situations. In some cases, exoticizing is necessary to reaffirm a culture that is thought to be in decline: there are those who, to shake up the market, offer something which is somehow novel or provocative. In addition, there's a desire on the part of peripheral artists to be accepted by hegemonic circuits. We can't forget that the art market has become a place for very safe investing for huge sums of money or also as a way to write off taxes. But what has been happening in the last few years—unlike the period of neo-Mexicanism—is that after 1989 and the fall of the Berlin Wall, Europe has started to look more to the East than to Latin America. After the emergence of the Asian countries in the Western art world, Latin American artists have been steadily displaced by new actors from China, India, Korea . . .

Artists as Anthropologists?

F.M.: The possibility of an ethnographically related art in Biennials and artistic events geopolitically positioned in strategic areas, possibly third world areas, would seem to be difficult: I am thinking about Hal Foster's criticisms and what I have personally experienced while collaborating with them. In many of these events, perhaps the name of the city—normally situated in the margins—finally emerges but with local skepticism because the event ends; the curators and visitors leave, and the conditions remain the same. Another criticism revolves around the real impossibility of interaction between visiting artists and the communities they attempt to involve temporarily in their projects. Involving an "other" that is supposed to be important because, as Foster says, the "other" is *dans le vrai*, just because of being from those cultural, ethnic, economic, social, or gender margins.

N.G.C.: An aspect is what Foster calls the "ethnographic turn" in contemporary art, which of course is very attractive to me as an anthropologist. I think that this is more interesting right now than a sociology of art or a sociological art. It makes us rethink the differences between sociology and anthropology. We know that the differences are partial, but in general sociology tends to work with structures and social situations, and anthropology with more interpersonal, intersubjective questions, paying more attention to the subjective variations of behavior, experience, and not only what is determinative. In this sense, art, as a work focused on the evolution of the I and on the alterity of the other, as a discipline is also interested in the experience. It's closer to anthropology.

Another coincidence that allows us to talk about an ethnographic art is that both art and anthropology have dedicated a lot of work for a long time to unmasking the institutions that sediment or freeze objects and social and interpersonal relationships. Anthropological criticism of the institutionalizing codification of museums is analogous to that of a lot of artists.

In the same way, it seems to me that in this ethnographic turn we find what Foster calls "a nostalgia for the real," the search to reinsert art into life, as the vanguards said in the first half of the twentieth century. Turning back to everyday experience, to have the spectators participate as actors, to listen to society from the inside again. I find similarities between what is happening with the ephemeral interventions of artists and what is happening with anthropological work. Even though ethnographic work tends to be more long-term, there is a moment when the anthropologist leaves, writes, and teaches based on what he/she saw and on the people who lived in that place. The capacity of the anthropologist, we know, is limited as far as what can be accomplished, but often he/she aspires to modify society or intercultural relationships between societies. The artist wants to intervene, but more on a symbolic level. The anthropologist's question is: "What have I revealed? What did I discover in this aspect of social life? How can it change? Is my description useful or not?" On the other hand, as far as art intervenes in symbolic relationships, what the artist can provide is rather a change in the way society is perceived and represented, providing the possibility to see in a new way.

As far as the symbolic is a part of society, there is a possibility of intervening in the real, while acting on the symbolic. But all of this is, of course, very uncertain. What we call ethnographic art has increased the role of art, avoids reducing it to elitist circles, only for specialists, and suggests other ways of relating socially. In other cases, deconstructionism of the institution—or of border codification, like in Tijuana—can be converted into a game for the well informed that takes up the most inscrutable artistic practices once again.

As far as what you were saying in regard to artistic and ethnographic practices in the peripheral countries, discrimination is prevalent because we live on the divide created by the hegemonic control that comes from a mainstream of metropolitan art and the separate and alternative developments without access to that mainstream. But there are also other experiences that, although they are not called ethnographic art, occur within Europe and the central countries. I am thinking of the intervention of Santiago Sierra in the Venice Biennial in 2003, when he closed the Spanish pavilion with a wall that closed off the main entrance and a sign that said, "if you want to come in, you must enter through the back, where armed guards will request a document proving Spanish national identity." He shined a spotlight on the exclusion of foreigners from Spain, and also, in a way, speaks of the difficulty of representing a country, the pointlessness of an artist taking on the burden of national representation in a globalized event.

F.M.: You're making me think of the world fairs at the end of the nineteenth century, the ones that Walter Benjamin mentions, with the "primitives" on display.

N.G.C.: This takes us to an art that more than being an ethnographic art is one that intervenes in the ways we perceive the national within the global and what a country is versus the way it is represented abroad.

F.M.: Or even within the country. . . . It seems impossible to me that a single Spaniard would think himself or herself capable of representing the entirety of a country, all of Spain. As Stuart Hall said, "Just being black doesn't mean I can represent any black person."

N.G.C.: Of course, that's true as well! In reality, there are many avenues artists are trying out. In the particular case of inSITE and Tijuana, what we find when we study the reception of the event in terms of public intervention in 1997 and 2000 is that its effect was much greater in international magazines than at a local level. Not only because the artists spent a limited amount of time there—they made their pieces and they left—but also because the society did not have much ability to absorb that experience. The local artists were not well organized, there were few organizations that could support their experiences and also, of course, the difficulties that arose from the border situation, the boundaries imposed by security policies, the lack of respect for Mexicans by the United States. But I don't know if it is right to ask art to occupy the space left empty by politics. Perhaps the real work of the artist is that of producing experiences or making hidden experiences visible and interpreting them and suggesting forms of thinking and memory, projections into the future without having to produce measurable results. It's the most devious and elliptical design of the symbolic.

F.M.: At the same time, there are artists who are looking to change their point of intervention. But it's not so easy, if you involve a "community"—with all the risks inherent in that definition—it's unsure if that will change its conditions, typically underprivileged, as a consequence of the intervention and artistic involvement. So there are those who ask themselves: Who is this experience for? Only for the artist's audience? It's difficult to say it's for the community in question, which—when the artist is gone—returns to its daily situation of uncertainty. The artist takes his success away, perhaps even someone from the community involved in the event does too, but sometimes it doesn't seem possible to get beyond a certain narcissism and notoriety. I have a lot of doubts about relational art, in situ. . . . I feel like the ethical remains outside of it. . . . for example, that wonderful video produced by Itzel Martínez in inSITE about the street girls. What will it take to the girls when inSITE ends? Specifically, what will it take them that could help in their incredibly difficult daily lives?

N.G.C.: There is still another aspect: the relationship between the artist and the media. A large part of the artistic circuit has become eloquent through their relationship with the media. Many artists aim to perturb, to surprise, so that the media covers their work, providing it a media boost so their work has greater reach. But this is complicated, because in part this requires subordinating oneself to the logic of the media, which is ephemeral, which almost never generates community, but rather simply a show, with a manipulated message. Even so, it is not an option we can discard that easily, for an interaction between art and the media has at times produced interesting results. I am thinking of the work of Krzysztof Wodiczko in Tijuana when he projected the stories of women from the maquila onto the huge "ball," the CECUT building, his stories of their abuse at the hands of their bosses, husbands, men in general. He worked with psychologists in Tijuana to do the interviews. The women gave their testimonies and their faces appeared in the video that was projected. The criticism that was leveled was that the artist was going to leave and the women would stay in Tijuana and could suffer vengeful attacks for their public denunciations. For the artist, this work was very successful; for the women we don't know. . . . We would have to speak with them.

F.M.: A piece about the post-artwork seems to be called for, about its effects once it was over. That is the ethical aspect I was talking about. It leaves me perplexed. But of course, this also happens with the anthropologist. It's not like staying for more months or years that the anthropologist doesn't face similar questions that arise in the course of doing ethnography . . . in his or her "heart of darkness," as Conrad said.

N.G.C.: It's analogous, even though the interventions have different purposes. Another recourse that has been considered is for the artists, instead of creating their work alone, to involve local organizations of women or migrants, with the hope that the local organization could capitalize in part on the work.

F.M.: But the problem would remain as to why would one choose women, indigenous people, that is, it maintains this idea of the subject of alterity—now in fashion and previously rejected and perhaps tomorrow rejected once again—who has the truth for all of us who do not belong to that specific alterity. Besides, it gives power to certain organizations or actors that the artist chooses for their dialogue instead of others, thus creating more hierarchies locally between those who participated in the project and those who were left out.

N.G.C.: I ask myself what would have happened if Krzysztof Wodiczko had dared to interview the men who were accused of doing these things, the bosses at the maquiladoras or the husbands.

F.M.: It would be interesting to include more contradictory voices in the work.

N.G.C.: In this sense, the emphasis that we place on interculturality and on not speaking from one single place removes us from the period of Lukács and the subalternists when it was thought that there were social positions that generated truth: the proletariat in capitalism, women in the condition of gender, indigenous people as possessing the truth about the interethnic society. It seems to me that the truth, or the representations which most approximate it, must be in more places, in interactions.

F.M.: We say that the comparative turn can multiply points of view, providing more partial truths. I'd like to conclude with a question about certain geopolitical categories, that we could judge as being less rigorous but still more utilized and born in the post-Bandung era: Is Tijuana, Mexico City, Mexico in general "first" or "third" world or both?

N.G.C.: These are categories that are less and less precise, even though they continue to be utilized. The category of third world, which includes Asia, Africa, and Latin America, spans continents which are different from each other and within each one of them. It includes a reality so immense as to lose meaning. I would say that it is a category which was useful in order to unify those excluded from the perspective of the "metropolis": "people who are like us." But the "us" is not homogeneous either, not even inside of Europe. We can look at the problems the European Union has had making its members identify themselves as European.

Santiago Vaquera-Vásquez

Postcards from the Border

In Tijuana, Revolución Is an Avenue

si usted es un sureño en busca de trabajo
y camina cabizbajo por calles de anuncios y ofertas
con un morral de colores chillantes y bolsillas rotos,
perseguido por ser ilegal,
encarcelado por ser ilegal
condenado por ser ilegal,
pásele, pásele

ROBERTO CASTILLO, "La última función
del mago de los espejos"

Tijuana Postcards: Güelcome to Tijuana

Tijuana: city of more than a million on the most-crossed border in the world. Tijuana: postmodern city, caught in the cultural crossfire from Mexico and the United States. Tijuana: dog races, beaches, Avenida Revolución, tourists, cheap liquor, flashy discos, maquiladoras, neighborhoods of cardboard houses, American armed servicemen on weekend leave, the Border Patrol, narcopolitics, drug killings, Colosio. Tijuana is the laboratory of postmodernity, so says Néstor García Canclini. Every city looks like Tijuana on a Saturday night, so says Guillermo Gómez-Peña. Tijuana looks toward the future, so says Richard Rodriguez. Tijuana is the "mecca of syncretism," so says Juan Villoro. Tijuana reinvents Mexico, so says Heriberto Yépez. Tijuana is the center of the universe, so says Luis Humberto Crosthwaite. Tijuana in postcards.

The metaphor of the postcard employed here is similar to that of the "establishing shot" as used by Claire Fox in her excellent study, *The Fence and the River*. Briefly, she refers to "a two to three second take of a building exterior or landscape that is inserted at the beginning of a scene . . . meant to be unobtrusive keys that help the viewer to locate action within a larger space" (1999: 46). The postcard, as used here, functions in a similar way. Postcards are meant to be unobtrusive objects passed around, sent to friends, fitted in an album. Often, they reduce the complex realities of a place to a set of markers, creating a further distancing between the object viewed and the viewer. They establish, or fix, a place in time and space. It is in this aspect that I argue for an approach that is similar to what Fox aims for in her study of the U.S.-Mexico border. At the same time that the postcard situates a place—much like an establishing shot in film—it also serves as foundation for approaching that place. The postcard creates a narrative that can remind us that, as Patricia Price argues, "place . . . is a processual, polyvocal, always-becoming entity" (2004: 1). In the second half of this chapter I will focus on "postcards" that operate on a metaphorical level. That is, I discuss objects that are not necessarily postcards but serve in the establishment of a particular place, in this case Tijuana's main tourist drag, Avenida Revolución. The first image will be a tourist postcard, the second an aural postcard, and the third a narrative postcard.

I will begin by telling a story about Tijuana and its cultural representations, rendering the city not as a global city, but rather an antiglobal middle-world outpost. It merits emphasizing that Tijuana is different things to different people; it is—like the border itself—not easily contained within one dominant gaze. It calls for a tangential approach. Thus this chapter necessarily moves through various—postcard—(re)presentations of the city, interrogating the types of imaginative geographies that are constructed out of the space of the city. The guiding principle is that a work that focuses on Tijuana is not "telling it like it is," that is, simply reflecting a mirrored reality of the topography, but rather, it is "telling it like we are," in the words of Trevor Barnes and James Duncan. Writing about a place "reveals as much about ourselves as it does about the worlds represented" (1992: 3). Güelcome to Tijuana.

The Antiglobal City

As a border city founded at the end of the nineteenth century, Tijuana's identity owes much to movement. To arrive in Tijuana, as is the case for other major urban centers, is to be preceded by others.[1] The types of border crossers and people in the city include:

- Tourists who cross the border to "know" Mexico, or at least an idea of a fictional Mexico. They search for Mexico in Tijuana's principal avenues and in its black velvet Elvises, Bart Simpson piggy banks, and painted donkey carts. Looking, according to Mexican border writer Rubén

Vizcaíno, "for their identity. . . . They see Third World poverty—the skinny dogs, the people begging, the indígenas kneeling before them—and they prove to themselves that they are great" (Martínez 1993: 92).

- The American military and underage college students who cross by night guided by the magnet of the Avenida Revolución where they can get lost in the bars and the gigantic discoteques.
- Writers and the artists who come to carnival Tijuana to partake in the culture clash of the border.
- The millions who cross back and forth, the waves who use Tijuana as a way station, working in the maquilas or shopping in its stores. The millions who migrate from south to north, hoping to cross, standing at the line and waiting for that opportunity to leap across. Some go, some return, and many wait.

In this city, affirms Martín de la Rosa, "we are all immigrants. The only difference is that some came earlier and others later" (in Castillo 1989: 199). It is in these crossings that Tijuana becomes a city of imagined cities that are written in the wanderings through the streets of the city. Cities captured in postcards, Greetings from Tijuana, images of Avenida Revolución, the beaches, the tower of Agua Caliente, the giant Mexican flag waving over the border.

Tijuana sits on multiple borderlines. It is the meeting of the Californias, the point of union and division between Mexico and the United States, and the juncture where the Pacific Ocean meets North America. It is also a city in which Mexican and American cultures meet, clash, and mix. It is—literally and figuratively—in the cultural crossfire between Mexico and the United States. It is a mirror that reflects back on both Mexico and the United States by subverting Mexican national identity and offering up a vision of global mixing. In this respect, Tijuana, and the northern border in general, threatens the monolithic national image that the central power, Mexico City, wants to project over the country.

Despite the celebrated phrase by the Mexican performance artist Guillermo Gómez-Peña, Tijuana cannot be considered a global city. At least not as proposed by Saskia Sassen, where she defines these types of cities as "centers for the servicing and financing of international trade, investment, and headquarter operations" (2001: xxiii). Tijuana is, literally and figuratively, a peripheral city, situated by its history and location on the margins. However, given this peripheral standing, Tijuana, Mexico's northern frontier in general, is a participant in a global economy and forms a part of a global corridor, bridging global cities like Los Angeles and Mexico City.

Conceptualizing this city as one that is always peripheral, Tijuana can be seen as an Antiglobal City, or as an outpost in the middle world. This term, borrowed from Breyten Breytenbach, refers to a world between the first and the third, a liminal space where "truths no longer fit snugly and certainties do not overlap" (2001: 13). He emphasizes that though the middle world is everywhere, "belonging and not belonging," it is not "of the Center . . . since it is by definition and vocation peripheral; it is other, living in the margins, the live edges" (2001: 14).

To further clarify we might turn to Edward Soja and his definition for the postmetropolis. He argues that the changes in contemporary urban spaces have been "so dramatic that we can no longer simply add our new knowledge to the old. There are too many incompatibilities, contradictions, disruptions. We must instead radically rethink and perhaps deeply restructure—that is, deconstruct and reconstitute—our inherited forms of urban analysis to meet the practical, political and theoretical challenges presented by the postmetropolis" (1997: 21). To understand postmodern urban spaces he proposes a perspective in which both a localized—the "view from below" epitomized by the walker in the city and championed in much contemporary cultural studies—and a macro perspective, the overall structure of the city, are combined (Soja 1997: 22). In a way, to take in such cities is analogous to reading a text or as a network of texts each corresponding to different urban needs and concerns: the text of the city becomes unraveled in walking the tangle of streets and buildings (de Certeau 1988).

Michel Butor has written of cities "que tienen un peso literario enorme" in that they are often written about.[2] These textual cities impact not only on a purely literary level; they are also containers of other texts: graffiti, street signs, billboards, and advertisements. Butor promotes a textual metaphor for the city in which straying emphasizes chance and uncertainty, foregrounding the incidental, indefinite flows of people, cultures, and texts of postmodern urban metropolises. The type of flaneur in the postmodern city that is implied in his reading would have to accept the possibility of never arriving at a complete knowledge of the city; he must instead seek out the ephemeral and the transitory.[3]

The Wandering City

A city like Tijuana, an outpost in the middle world, delights not in the totalizing gaze of a singular reading but rather in the multiple answers it presents to questions posed by those who practice it. As a site of representation,

Tijuana, "la casa de toda la gente" in the words of García Canclini, is a pa-limpsest of routes, histories, and images. Because, as such geographers as James Duncan and Jonathan Smith have noted, places are intertextual sites.[4]

In the meetings of cultures that exist at the U.S.-Mexico borderlands, one notices the itinerant, or what I have referred to in other works as a poetics of wandering. It merits emphasizing that I am not referring to aimlessness, or to being lost. To get lost, as Walter Benjamin writes, "requires ignorance—nothing more" (1986: 8). What is at issue is rather a straying, a wandering in which the walker is guided by the city, in which "signboards and street names, passersby, roofs, kiosks, or bars must speak to the wanderer" (Benjamin 1986: 9). These all form part of the text that is inscribed within the city and the text that is read and written by the city walker. To wander, stray, in the city, then, is to experience it for oneself, to write one's story with one's footsteps, to con-struct a city within the city. At the same time, the overall structure of the city is constantly changing, in a continual process of reinvention.

Wandering is at once both deterritorializing and reterritorializing. Both forces are apparent in the northern Mexican border region. There is a deter-ritorializing of hegemonic notions of nation, and a reterritorialization of a border identity that is, at one level, forged by a condition of liminality. As Lauro Zavala defines it, this refers to "the paradoxical and potentially pro-ductive condition of being situated between two locations. These locations may be physical locations, languages, literary genres, cultural traditions, or stages of development. The concept of liminality erases hierarchical separa-tions" (1997: 9). Liminality, as an expression of wandering, implies hybridity. The Mexican cultural critic Sergio Gómez Montero proposes four structural axes—or dimensions—for studying border cultural production: borderiza-tion, intertextuality, vanguardism, and biculturalism-bilingualism (1993: 96–98). As culturally specific strategies produced by marginalized commu-nities they "express the need to distance themselves from the tradition inher-ited from their predecessors while encoding that preceding discourse in an ironical, double-voiced way" (Zavala 1997: 10). Each one of these structural axes can be analyzed separately as a line of flight to study a text, and each one can be a study in itself; not all of them will always be present in a border text.

Belonging to various regions, liminal texts express hybrid narrative strat-egies that can be related to liminal communities. That is to say that hybrid strategies—for example code switching, ironic forms of writing, transcul-tural forms—lend themselves, according to Zavala, to "the expression of lim-inal, hybrid, transitional and paradoxical historical conditions. . . . These writing strategies express the cultural need for new languages not yet created, especially those of emerging communities" (1997: 10). Cultural liminality opens up an interstitial space that transforms, paraphrasing Iain Chambers, the myth of a single temporal order (be it "Modernity," "Progress," "United States") into multiple orders and histories.

It merits noting that recurring to liminality or to wandering is not simply a celebration of hybridity: this would greatly reduce the complexity of the borderlands. Hybridity is but one tool that could be used to approach the border. Lavie and Swedenburg note that hybridity is the result of a long history of "confrontations between unequal cultures and forces, in which the stronger culture struggles to control, remake, or eliminate the subordinate partner" (1996: 9).

At asymmetrical borders, like the one between Mexico and the United States, the inhabitants who find themselves in a subordinate position "have frequently managed to divert the cultural elements they were forced to adopt and have rearranged them for their own sly purposes within a new ensemble" (Lavie and Swedenburg 1996: 9). An example of this can be seen in the ways that the physical border on the Mexican side has often become a canvas upon which border citizens express themselves: through graffiti; through artistic installations, such as those set up during the inSITE festivals; since the creation of Operation Gatekeeper in 1994, the wall on the beach of Tijuana has been filled with the names of those who have died attempting to cross; and, for a while in the 1980s, through the pickup volleyball games that were played, with the old chain-link fence serving as the net. To use the border—an institutional barrier constructed to delimit the line between two nations—in these ways illustrates the ways in which the local community attempts to subvert controls by national centers that would attempt to lay claim to a region. In effect, punch holes through the border, create openings through the middle world. As Breytenbach notes, "Middle Worlders, paradoxically, have a sharpened awareness of place . . . as with the nomads the environment may be constantly changing and you do not possess it, but it is always a potentially dangerous framework with which you must interact, and therefore they will know cloud and well and star and fire better than sedentary citizens do" (2001: 19).

Tijuana, viewed as a wandering city, is marked in the itineraries of the people who use it. It is a wandering city not because of its migrant communities, but because of its constantly changing character. Tijuana as outpost posits a cardinal rule for the Middle World: "you can only survive and move forward by continuing to invent yourself" (Breytenbach 2001: 19). Wandering implies movement from one position to another. By focusing on wandering, notions of a point of departure, or of arrival, become less important: what matters is the journey.

What needs to be noted is that wandering does not imply aimlessness, but rather a process of becoming; a journeying along multiple trajectories. More specifically, we can focus on wandering as a deterritorializing strategy. That is, to wander is to change the emphasis on identity as being rooted in a place but also being built on movement, on routes. The identity that arises is not one based on territory; rather, the border identity that is proclaimed is forged between national cultures, in a migrant movement that is situated in an intervening space.

Revolution Is a Street in Tijuana
(or All Roads Lead to La Revu)

Tijuana, as a peripheral city, can be viewed—for a particular segment of the population—as a nomadic city that is created in its practice—in its use—in the itineraries of the people who walk/move/use it. For many, the introduction to the city is through its main tourist drag, Revolution Avenue. In Mexico, the naming of streets after important Mexican historical events, heroes, and places serves to unite a national narrative literally at street level. Every urban area has a street named Niños Heroes, or Revolución, or 16 de septiembre. This naming functions within a project of national unification—all urban areas partake in the nation of Mexico—but these meanings often become lost as new significations are ascribed to the streets by those who walk them.[5] In Tijuana, Avenida Revolución serves for many as an introduction to "Mexico." But it is a Mexico that responds to the perception of the viewer: arriving in Tijuana is to be preceded by the imagination of others, as well as by the multiple narratives that have been told about it.

If Avenida Revolución constructs a fictional Mexico, it does so through an appropriation of styles from all over the world. In a fragmented text that reads less like an essay and more like a collection of one-liners (or a zapping of television stations, in keeping with a fragmented narrative of the border), Yépez writes, "Space Invaders could easily define Tijuana. It is a city of 'anarchitecture,' a city of self-destruction. . . . Its official architecture is pure simulacrum, pure kitsch. Tijuana existed long before Baudrillard" (2005: 46–49).

Avenida Revolución, "La Revu," is a site of contact, of meeting, where, in a sense, all roads lead. In regard to its urban architecture, it is a mishmash of styles. It unfolds for the walker as a stream of consciousness; its mash-up of architectural styles brings us into a sense of heightened perception. Juan

Villoro notes that its landscape "cambia como si respondiera al *zapping* de la televisión" (2000: 16).[6] Anchored—if it can be called that—on one end by the Frontón Jai Alai, a large structure with a vague Moorish air, it ends—if it can be called that—at a small triangular plaza where the mariachis meet, across from the Zona Norte, Tijuana's red-light district. In between these two zones: mega-discos; open markets—with the air of a bazaar—that sell a dizzying number of items (sign over one: "Cheap Liquor. Public Bathroom. Welcome to Mexico. Want to buy a blanket?"); liquor stores; curio shops; restaurants (Cesar's the birthplace of the Caesar salad in a large vaguely art deco palace); donkey carts. There is a sense of placelessness, as there seems to be no architectural unity. While there are markers that evoke Mexico—a plaza where mariachis meet, the signs that welcome you to Mexico, the images on the donkey carts—at the same time the visitor is placed in a zone that evokes Mexico and a lot of other places. As Lawrence Herzog states, "Revolution is carnival—buildings decorated like zebras or Moorish castles, flags and colorful blimps floating overhead" (1999: 208). Reminding us, too, that in Tijuana, Revolution is an avenue.

Tijuana Postcards: The Border Is . . .

In the following "postcards," I focus on the narratives that they generate about a place, in this case Tijuana. These narratives—the tropes that they construct—can be positive or, as they often are, negative. Norma Klahn has written of a "South of the Borderism" trope in U.S.-Mexico relations, which refers to the ways that the United States culturally constructs its southern neighbor: often, the Mexican becomes "everything the Anglo was not" (1997: 123). A similar process has taken place in Mexico, in what Socorro Tabuenca has called a "North of the Borderism" (1997). In each case, this cultural "othering" becomes self-serving, affirming national identities and generating meaning about the neighbor. In the case of the United States, South of the Borderism justifies the myth of manifest destiny and the continued militarization of the border; while for Mexico, North of the Borderism vindicates cultural nationalist projects to combat the spread of American culture. These two tropes—stating what "the border is"—also shape the most common negative stereotypes about the border as a zone of danger or of vice.

In political discourse, not only from Mexico City but also from Washington, DC, Tijuana, as also the rest of the border, is a danger zone. On the U.S. side of the fence there exists a type of border machine that attempts to set limits to the border. Border Patrol operations, as Operation Hold the Line or

Gatekeeper, not only militarize the border but also function as strategies to maintain the line, protect the nation from its southern Other. On the Mexican side, federal practices to inscribe the north into a national narrative—through the creation of writers' programs, for example—function in a similar way, to maintain the homogeneity of the nation, to keep the Other back, to protect the border.[7]

As stated, these tropes attempt to ascribe meaning to a particular region: they instill a narrative on a landscape. But landscape also generates narrative. As Price reminds us, "Landscapes are scripts that discursively construct particular understandings of place" (2004: 23). Much of the negative tropes that arise from North/South of the Borderism come from outside the border region; in what follows I focus on "postcards" (narratives) from the border.

Tijuana Postcard: Tourist Photo

Years ago, living in Texas, I constructed an altar of sorts to connect with my California home. It consisted of photos tacked to a wall in my office at the university. There were posters for bands, flyers for events, photos that I had taken of my family. In the center was an old black-and-white photo of tourists partaking in one of the emblematic images of Tijuana, having their photo taken on one of the donkey carts. In the photo there is a pregnant young woman with a two-year-old child in front. They are both seated on a donkey painted as a zebra (what Yépez calls the "zonkey") in front of a cart. The zonkey riders, the young woman and the child, both wear sombreros. His, "Cisco Kid," hers, "Tijuana." Despite the fact that the photo is in black and white, I know that the *carreta* is painted with bright colors and features a large bucolic image. A woman in a *huipil*, a traditional dress, does laundry by the side of a river in a tropical jungle setting. She is looking (approvingly?) up at a man seated on a horse and dressed in full *charro* regalia. It is an image that represents México, the kind seen: in Mexico's golden age of film—its *cine de oro*—as captured by the likes of Gabriel Figueroa; in that of the national tourist agency promoting Mexico in the travel sections of major newspapers in the United States; in that of the national myth. In that of "México, rrrrrrrrrooooommmmmaaaaanntiiiiccc México," as the border *brujo* Guillermo Gómez-Peña would sing.

In *Passport Photos*, Amitava Kumar asks why readers of newspapers so readily accept photographs as truthful representations; "why do we so drastically reduce the immense complexity of reality, its wide heterogeneity and scope of dissent, by what we so quickly accept as the singular truth represented in the shallow frame of an image?" (2000: 45). In this old photo we only see tourism in Tijuana. It is also one of the most common images from Tijuana, tourists on a holiday: hopping across the border to experience Mexico. Yet the imaginative geography that constructs this Mexican postcard is complex. This is Mexico, romantic Mexico. Smiling tourists, tropical jungles, women contentedly washing by the side of the river, and men on horseback looking as if they should be backed by a full mariachi complement. The representation of Mexico painted on the donkey cart contrasts with the region where the photo was taken: Baja California, northern Mexico, a region that is largely arid. In Tijuana, the only tropical forests are the ones painted on the donkey carts.

I was almost two when the photo was taken, my mom and me, at the end of spring, spending time with my grandparents on the border. That would be the last time that it would just be us. My father would come to take us back to California; my sister would be born in a couple of months. There would also be a change in the history of the country, but this was beyond our comprehension as we sat for the photo. Beneath the bucolic image painted on the donkey cart was painted the words, "Tijuana 1968 México."

The many zonkeys that are posed for photographs on Avenida Revolución lead carts that are usually adorned with the imagery of "traditional" Mexico: images of volcanoes, pre-Columbian cultures, and the national symbol of the serpent and eagle on the cactus—imagery that has very little do with the reality of Baja California. A *tijuanense* states, "ante la falta de otro tipo de cosas, como en el sur, que hay pirámides, aquí no hay nada de eso . . . como que algo hay que inventarle a los gringos" (García Canclini 1989: 28).[8] The result is a city covered by the texts of a Mexico that never existed in that region, an atopical Mexico superimposed in a city crossed by itinerants.

In covering the city with these hybrid cultural texts there is not only the invention of a history for the tourists, but the inscription of the city, and the Mexican border region, into a national narrative. Tijuana becomes, then, a mirror that reflects the whole country, marking out the differences between this and that side of the border.[9] Avenida Revolución, as a fragment of the mirror, creates an idealized Mexico: "a fantasy land that is a caricature of what Americans might think Mexico is (land of bullfights, sombreros, burros, and mission-style churches), insulated from the real Mexico, but with just a touch of a veiled sense of mystery and foreign intrigue" (Herzog 1999: 210). It is the marketing of Mexico through its history (pre-Columbian imagery) and culture (the bucolic premodern countryside that offers a respite from the chaos of modern urbanism). And the marketing of culture, as Arlene Dávila reminds us, "is central to tourism" (2004: 97). Tourism demands dif-

ference, which are what the zonkey carts and the many curio shops on Avenida Revolución offer. At the same time, it has to be made safe, comfortable,
and entertaining for the tourist. La Revu encompasses Mexico in a few
blocks, but it is a represented Mexico, a narrative that corresponds to what a
tourist hopes to find on "the other side." At the same time, the zonkey carts
offer up a counternarrative: while the imagery that they represent serves to
affirm notions of nation, the zonkey itself—a hybrid creation made in the
meeting between donkey and black paint—erodes that meaning. The zonkey,
more precisely, its painted hide, affirms that Tijuana is different, from Mexico and from the United States. By injecting this difference into the landscape, the zonkey, like Tijuana, resists narrativization.

Tijuana Postcard #2: ". . . It Had to Happen in Tijuana"
It all began, if the story is to be believed, with audio scraps in a recording
studio in Tijuana. A techno musician who went by the name Bostich sampled
those scraps, bits of norteño music, with some beats of his own. That mash-up
of Mexican regional norteño with electronica laid the groundwork for the
Nortec sound: a sound that reflects and creates the soundclash of the border.
Alongside the zonkey, and its visual representation of a border, there is this:
the border is sound.

This soundscape is in the sounds of the cars waiting to cross; in the crowds;
in the mix of sounds from the mega dance clubs and the honky-tonks steps
away from each other in the border cities. Cruising Revolution Avenue in
Tijuana on a Saturday is a trip across a varied aural landscape. The urban
sounds connect distinct places. By disrupting notions of national homogeneity
(if such a thing ever existed), the mixed sounds and languages coming from
the megadiscos, nightclubs, and the stereos of passing cars negate the physical
material border instituted by nations trying to impose border controls. The
soundscape of Tijuana, of the border.

The electronica collective known as Nortec maps out musical geographies
that unite disparate places. Through the use of tape loops of northern Mexican banda mixed with European techno, the collective constructs a soundtrack
for another type of migrant passing through the middle world: the migrant
that follows the global flows of electronic music. There are various narrative
tropes of the groups that form the collective, including Fussible, Bostich, Hiperboreal, Panóptica, and Clorofila.[10] Touch upon: Tijuana as a city of vice,
Tijuana as a city of drugs, Tijuana as a rave scene. Above all, they reflect the
image of Tijuana as hybrid. As an outpost in the middle world, its various

elements come together in exciting ways. As the tijuanense cultural critic José Manuel Valenzuela states, "Tijuana's status as a sort of intermediate location, neither here nor there, allowed it to create nortec" (2004: 57).

Their second production, *Tijuana Sessions, Vol 3*—the first was *Tijuana Sessions, Vol 1*; there was no volume 2—constructs a musical geography that touches upon the various representations of the city. The opening track, "Tengo la voz" by Bostich, sets the tone for a record that showcases more norteño rhythms than in the previous *Tijuana Sessions*. Fusing a beat that is composed of tuba, accordion, a Herb Alpert Tijuana Brass–style trumpet, laid over a drum-n-bass beat, the only sampled dialogue in the song states, "Tengo la voz." The opening serves to guide the listener into the hybrid urban soundscape that the collective mines for musical references. The second track, and possibly the most commercial song, Fussible's "Tijuana Makes Me Happy," also fuses various musical elements—an accordion being the most obvious element—into a lighter, more pop beat. Over this joyful beat, an anonymous guest singer sings—in English:

Some people call it the happiest place on earth.
Others says it's a dangerous place.
It has been the city of sin.
But you know I don't care.
What I care about is to see you again.
And to dance that song.
From the record that I love so much.
Tijuana makes me happy.

While alluding to the negative reputation of the city—despite the quote from *The Simpsons'* Krusty the Clown, who once called Tijuana "the happiest place on earth"—the song reflects the positive fusing of sound and place. Criticized for being the most commercial track on the album, it could also be argued that this overt use of commercialism—slick pop beats, smooth vocals—is ironic. This homage to Tijuana undercuts the negative representation of the city and belies its image as loud, brash, and violent.

The following tracks flow along these hybrid rhythms, creating an aural soundscape layered over/under/in-between the urban landscape and constructing what Josh Kun refers to as an audiotopia that is "sonic spaces of utopian longings where several sites normally deemed incompatible are brought together not only in the space of a particular piece of music itself, but in the production of social space and mapping of geographical space that music makes possible as well" (2000: 6). It is in this kind of soundscape that connections can be made between the hybrid social scene of this border city and a larger globalized music scene. That the Nortec collective is an homage to Tijuana and what one might consider its soundclash—street mariachis performing alongside bandas norteñas while hip-hop, punk, and pop music blare from passing cars—is further strengthened by the titles of songs on their latest album, "Dandy del Sur," "Bar Infierno," and "El Fracaso." These titles are also the names of three bars in the Zona Norte, Tijuana's red-light district.

The Mexico that the collective connects with is diverse, crossed and recrossed by sounds and images from all over the world. That it all comes together in this border city makes sense for its musicians, especially since the city has been a musical center in Mexico for decades. Nortec reflects the Tijuana of the twenty-first century. Uniting Mexican regional rhythms with European electronic music, they lay bare the connections across borders, and align themselves with histories of migration, both northern and southern. What the Nortec collective does is cut up not just the musical DNA but scramble and reconfigure it to show off the borderlands' aural landscape: they remind us that the border is sound.

Tijuana Postcard #3: You Only Say You Love Me
When You're Drunk

In Luis Humberto Crosthwaite's story, "Where Have You Gone, Juan Escutia," the border is presented as a wall of protection against the invading north. This subverts one of the perceptions from the center of the country: Mexico's north is not really "Mexico," because it has been overrun by the United States. Significantly, the story is structured against one of the founding national myths, that of the niños héroes: during the U.S. invasion of Mexico City in 1848, while the U.S. forces led by Winfield Scott advanced upon the military academy in the Castillo de Chapultepec, six young military cadets chose to leap off a cliff wrapped in the Mexican flag rather than have their flag—and the nation's sovereignty—captured. Of course, the academy was taken, and the U.S. flag was hoisted over the capital of Mexico, signaling the end of the war and the creation of the U.S.-Mexico border.

The story is preceded by a note from the author who talks about how unimportant September 13 was for his school group. That date commemorates the niños héroes. But for the narrator's school, that day meant that "nos ponían de pie por estatura y todos formaditos entonábamos el ciña oh patria de la misma manera" (Crosthwaite 1988: 25).[11] In other words, the historical account is erased and replaced with a meaningless—for these children—ritual.

Until.

"Uno de los maestros de historia, el más despiadado, nos puso frente a frente con la realidad (ah, ¿qué no lo sabían?): los niños héroes fueron derrotados en aquella famosa batalla, los gringos los hicieron caca. Seis años de asambleas y jamás lo habían dicho" (Crosthwaite 1988: 25).[12] The children felt deceived. They were thirteen years old and they felt that they had been beaten. Thirteen becomes an important age for this story, because it was not only the age of one of the child heroes, Juan Escutia, but it also marks an important turning point in the lives of the protagonists.

Three soldiers on military leave decide to cross to hit the bars and revel in the vices that Tijuana offers. They cross like the conquerors they believe themselves to be, "como Winfield Scott en busca de los niños héroes, seguros de lo que hacen" (Crosthwaite 1988: 27).[13] Walking along Revolution Avenue, they are on their way to its logical end: the Zona Norte. At a bar they hatch out schemes of taking a prostitute without paying. Their plans of invasion are foiled as the one thing they had not counted on conquers them: Mexican beer. The next morning they find themselves shirtless and penniless on the street. Defeated and in retreat they return across the border to San Diego, vanquished. Early in the story, the narrator states: "Si Winfield Scott, general en jefe del ejército invasor, hubiera entrado por estos rumbos, en lugar de hacerlo por Tamaulipas o Veracruz, tal vez el Castillo de Chapultepec no fuera tan visitado o el xalapeño Santa Anna, fundador de la frontera norte, todavía estuviera en la presidencia (pierna de palo sustituida por biónico, *made in Japan*), hablando sobre el clima capitalino, gozando de salud perfecta" (1988: 28).[14]

In "Where Have You Gone, Juan Escutia" we note various parodic levels. At one, there is the parody of the historical narrative of the niños héroes. Hutcheon stresses that "parody's 'target' text is always another work of art or, more generally, another form of coded discourse" (2000: 16). I would argue that what is being parodied in this particular story by Crosthwaite is not so much the historical event as the historical telling, or reinscription.

The account of the niños héroes has become one of the narratives that has helped form the national identity, just as other narratives have done: the Revolution, the pre-Columbian past, and so on. These "boy heroes" were recodified long before Crosthwaite wrote his parody. They were molded into one unit, their lives erased. The six boys, last names of De la Barrera, Márquez, Suárez, Montes de Oca, Melgar, and Escutia, have become simply, "los niños héroes." Crosthwaite comments on this by focusing on the youngest, Juan Escutia. The title of the story presents then a series of readings. It refers to the erasing of the historical identities into one, and it refers to a note from the narrator where he writes about how as a child a series of commemorative stamps for Mexican history were released. He goes on to note how among him and his friends abounded stamps to Aldama, Maximilian, and Obregón, but not a single one to Juan Escutia. The narrator asks, "¿Sería otra nefasta idea del presidente Echeverría o alguna conjura siniestra de la CIA para apoderarse de la juventud mexicana?" (Crosthwaite 1988: 29).[15] The boy hero, Juan Escutia, represents, then, the youthful idealism that is lost. The book of historical stamps is filled with dictators, but no Juan Escutia. Mexico loses the battle to General Scott at Chapultepec castle, the boy heroes are beaten. The narrator and his friends feel themselves beaten at the age of thirteen when they discover the truth about the niños héroes. By parodying the account in the story, Crosthwaite recontextualizes and places into question the narratives that give rise to the national identity: he subverts the tropes of North and South of the Borderism.

The story short-circuits different mythologies; the niños héroes, the construction of national identity, Tijuana as playground in which everything can be had for cheap or for free, and the border as region ripe for conquest. References abound to the niños héroes throughout the text, and what begins as an all-too-familiar scene of the American military on weekend leave in Mexico is reconfigured into an ironic inversion of a national myth of identity through a wandering story that continually disrupts its own narrative.[16] The object here is not so much the myth, but the way that the narrative shapes the nation. By parodying the account in the story, Crosthwaite recontextualizes and places into question the narratives that give rise to the national identity. At the same time, he praises Tijuana, precisely for its image as a city of vice, in the process subverting another conception of the border.

"Ain't This the Life": Tijuana in Postcards

As a large ever-expanding city, the image of Tijuana that arises from these three representations is one of fragmentation: there is no conception of a total Tijuana. In this sense, Tijuana is known, but only in passing, never as a unit. The tijuanenses reflect and constitute their urban and borderland existence. Tijuana, as viewed through the narrative postcards discussed here, is separated from its historical moment—blasted out of the continuum of history in the Benjaminian sense—or that ephemeral event that caused its constructions, and displaces its history to become an empty sign within which other significations can be added. The city is an empty sign, not because it has been drained by the evanescent, the saying; it is empty because it is oversignified, the multiplicity of texts that cover it are meaningless cyphers, partial snapshots in a box full of photographs. A box of postcards, each telling a different story.

To read Tijuana as a wandering city, an outpost in the middle world, is to be in a city that is constantly reinventing itself: Tijuana as a palimpsest, as a space of transition, a city filled with texts that invite the visitor, the inhabitant, or the reader to act out on its urban stage, as in Roberto Castillo Udiarte's poem, "La ultima función del mago de los espejos" in which a tijuanense barker invites the different urban identities at play in Tijuana to "step right up," to partake in an upcoming show in which they themselves are put on display.

How best to represent Tijuana? Tijuanense writers offer their own representations, the tourists passing along Revolución offer others, and the migrants who come waiting to cross offer still others. To see it this way, then, Tijuana is known by passing through it, becoming a player in the border show. If you are a scholar of the oh-so-trendy Border Studies, and walk among the *bordos culturales* pondering the image of Tijuana and its multiple representations, photographed on a donkey painted as zebra, caught in the lights of La Revu, lost in the stellar nights of La Estrella, *pásele, pásele*.

Notes

1 The history of Tijuana is based on the waves of migration from the South to the North. These first began in the years following the Mexican Revolution and the subsequent Cristero revolt and then the lure of the U.S. Bracero Program of the 1940s. The massive deportation of Mexicans from the United States caused the migration to turn back southward. In 1950, Tijuana's population was 60,000. In the mid-1960s there was another influx of migration from the south as the government established the maquiladora system, creating new jobs in the border cities. Compounding the number of people seeking jobs there is also the fact that the city has been used by millions as a conduit for entering the United States. By the end of the 1980s, the population had exploded to more than a million people. For a more detailed history of the rise of Tijuana, see Herzog (1990).

2 "That bear a heavy literary weight" (translation mine).

3 John Lechte writes, "The *flâneur's* trajectory leads nowhere and comes from no-where. It is a trajectory without fixed spatial coordinates. . . . The *flâneur* is an entity without identity: an entity of contingency and indeterminacy" (1995: 103). For the flaneur, then, the postmodern city, covered in texts and itineraries that fragment it, presents a plurality of entrances and exits, a multiplicity of gazes.

4 See, for example, the introduction to *Writing Worlds: Discourse Text and Metaphor in the Representation of Landscape* (Barnes and Duncan 1992); "Sites of Representation," by Duncan (1993); and "The Lie That Blinds," by Smith (1993).

5 Michel de Certeau points out that as the original signification of the name of a street is worn away and inscribed with another signification, "they [the streets] become liberated spaces that can be occupied. A rich indetermination gives them, by means of a semantic rarefaction, the function of articulating a second, poetic geography on top of the geography of the literal, forbidden or permitted meaning" (1988: 105).

6 "Changes as if it were responding to the zapping of a television" (translation mine).

7 For an extended discussion of these tropes, see the work of Tabuenca (1997), as well as Vaquera (1996, 1998) and Insley (2004).

8 "Because of the need for certain types of objects—like in the south where there are pyramids, we don't have anything like that here— . . . it's as if we need to invent something for the gringos" (translation mine).

9 But it is a poor likeness since—as Baudrillard states of a simulacrum—"it bears no relation to any reality whatever" (1983: 11). Tijuana subverts, then, both national narrativization and the border.

10 Originally, there were two other bands in the scene, Plankton Man and Terrestre. By the release of the collective's second record, the groups had been narrowed down to five.

11 "We were forced to stand according to height and then all lined up we had to intone 'el ciña oh patria' in that way" (translation mine).

12 "One of our history teachers, the cruelest one, forced us to face the truth—what you didn't know? The child heroes were defeated in that famous battle, the gringos flattened them. Six years of school assemblies and nobody had ever told us this" (translation mine).

13 "Like Winfield Scott in search of the child heroes, filled with purpose" (translation mine).

14 "If Winfield Scott, chief general of the invading army, had entered through these parts, instead of through Tamaulipas or Veracruz, maybe Chapultepec Castle wouldn't be so visited or our man from Xalapa, Santa Anna, founder of the northern border, would still be president (wooden leg substituted by a bionic one, made in Japan) and talking about the weather in the capital and enjoying perfect health" (translation mine).

15 "Could it be another of President Echeverría's nefarious ideas or some sinister plot by the CIA to take over our Mexican youth?" (translation mine).

16 For an extended discussion of this type of story, see Vaquera (1996) and Zavala (1997).

References

Augé, Marc. 1995. *Non-places: Introduction to an Anthropology of Supermodernity.* John Howe, trans. London: Verso.

Barnes, Trevor, and James Duncan. 1992. *Writing Worlds: Discourse, Text, and Metaphor in the Representation of Landscape.* New York: Routledge.

Baudrillard, Jean. 1983. *Simulations*. Paul Foss, Paul Patton, and Philip Beitchman, trans. New York: Semiotext(e).

Benjamin, Walter. 1986. "Paris, Capital of the Nineteenth Century." *Reflections: Essays, Aphorisms, Autobiographical Writings*. Edmund Jephcott, trans. New York: Schocken, 146–62.

Bhabha, Homi K. 1994. *The Location of Culture*. London: Routledge.

Breytenbach, Breyten. 2001. "Notes from the Middle World." *McSweeney's* 6: 13–23.

Butor, Michel. 1993. "La ciudad como texto." *Universidad de México* 504–505: 7–10.

Castillo, Roberto. 1989. "La última función del mago de los espejojs." *La pasión de Angélica según el Johnny Tecate*. Tijuana: CNCA, CECUT, 23–26.

Certeau, Michel de. 1988. *The Practice of Everyday Life*. Berkeley: University of California Press.

Chambers, Iain. 1994. *Migrancy, Culture, Identity*. London: Routledge.

Crosthwaite, Luis Humberto. 1988. "Where Have You Gone, Juan Escutia." *Marcela y el rey al fin juntos*. Mexico: J. Boldo i Clement / UA Zacatecas / Centro de Estudios Literarios de la Dirección de Investigación.

Dávila, Arlene. 2004. *Barrio Dreams: Puerto Ricans, Latinos, and the Neoliberal City*. Berkeley: University of California Press.

Duncan, James. 1993. "Sites of Representation: Place, Time, and the Discourse of the Other." *Place/Culture/Representation*. James Duncan and David Ley, eds. London: Routledge, 39–56.

Fox, Claire F. 1994. "The Portable Border: Site-Specificity, Art, and the U.S.-Mexico Frontier." *Social Text* 41: 61–82.

———. 1999. *The Fence and the River: Culture and Politics at the U.S.-Mexico Border*. Minneapolis: University of Minnesota Press.

García Canclini, Néstor. 1989. *Tijuana la casa de toda la gente*. Mexico: INAH-ENAH, Programa Cultural de las Fronteras UAM-Iztapalapa / CNCA.

Gómez Montero, Sergio. 1993. *Sociedad y desierto. Literatura en la frontera norte*. Mexico: Universidad Pedagógica Nacional.

Gómez-Peña, Guillermo. 1993. *Warrior for Gringostroika: Essays, Performance Texts, and Poetry*. St. Paul, Minn.: Graywolf.

Herzog, Lawrence A. 1990. *Where North Meets South: Cities, Space, and Politics on the U.S. Mexico Border*. Austin: CMAS, University of Texas Press, 1990.

———. 1999. *From Aztec to High Tech: Architecture and Landscape across the Mexico-United States Border*. Baltimore: Johns Hopkins University Press.

Hutcheon, Linda. 2000. *A Theory of Parody: The Teachings of Twentieth-Century Art Forms*. Urbana: University of Illinois Press.

Insley, Jennifer. 2004. "Redefining Sodom: A Latter-Day Vision of Tijuana." *Mexican Studies/Estudios Mexicanos* 20.1: 99–121.

Klahn, Norma. 1997. "Writing the Border: The Languages and Limits of Representation." *Common Border, Uncommon Paths: Race, Culture, and National Identity in U.S.-Mexican Relations*. O. J. Rodriguez and K. Vincent, eds. Wilmington: SR Books, 123–41.

Kumar, Amitava. 2000. *Passport Photos*. Berkeley: University of California Press.

Kun, Josh D. 2000. "The Aural Border." *Theatre Journal* 52.1: 1–21.

Lavie, Smadar, and Ted Swedenburg. 1996. *Displacement, Diaspora, and Geographies of Identity*. Durham: Duke University Press.

Lechte, John. 1995. "(Not) Belonging in Postmodern Space." *Postmodern Cities and Spaces*. Sophie Watson and Katherine Gibson, eds. Oxford, UK: Blackwell.

Martínez, Rubén. 1993. *The Other Side: Notes from the New L.A., Mexico City, and Beyond*. New York: Vintage.

Price, Patricia. 2004. *Dry Place: Landscapes of Belonging and Exclusion*. Minneapolis: University of Minnesota Press.

Sassen, Saskia. 2001. *The Global City: New York, London, Tokyo*. Princeton: Princeton University Press.

Smith, Jonathan. 1993. "The Lie That Blinds: Destabilizing the Text of Landscape." *Place/Culture/Representation*. James Duncan and David Ley, eds. London: Routledge, 78–92.

Soja, Edward. 1997. "Six Discourses on the Postmetropolis." *Imagining Cities: Scripts, Signs, Memory*. Sallie Westwood and John Williams, eds. London: Routledge, 19–30.

Tabuenca, María Socorro. 1997. *La frontera textual y geográfica en dos narradoras de la frontera norte mexicana: Rosina Conde y Rosario Sanmiguel*. PhD diss., State University of New York at Stony Brook.

Valenzuela Arce, José Manuel. 2004. "Paso del nortec." *Paso del nortec: This Is Tijuana!* Mexico: Trilce Ediciones, Consejo Nacional para la Cultura y las Artes, Oceáno, Colegio de la Frontera Norte, UNAM, 56–105.

Vaquera, Santiago. 1996. " 'Cuál es la onda': vagando por la ciudad posmoderna." *El cuento mexicano. Homenaje a Luis Leal*. Mexico: UNAM, 439–57.

———. 1998. "Wandering in the Borderlands: Mapping an Imaginative Geography of the Border." *Latin American Issues* 14: 107–32.

Villoro, Juan. 2000. "Nada que declarar. Welcome to Tijuana." *Letras libres* 17: 16–20.

Yépez, Heriberto. 2005. "Tijuana: Processes of a Science Fiction City without a Future." *Tijuana Sessions*. Mexico: CNCA, SRE, Comunidad de Madrid, UNAM, 44–51.

Zavala, Lauro. 1997. "Toward a Dialogic Theory of Cultural Liminality: Contemporary Writing and Contemporary Cultural Identity in Mexico." *Arizona Journal of Hispanic Cultural Studies* 1: 9–22.

Illicit Acts of Urbanism

> We have different legal systems, but the basic rules are the same.
> —Tijuana Mayor JESUS GONZALEZ REYES (2001–4) on the Mexican laws
> that U.S. tourists break

Tijuana is primarily a result of illegal or illicit acts.

Since its conception, illegality has been the driving force behind Tijuana's dystopian condition, a prevalence of conflicting processes that have become the modus operandi of urban transformation. An illegality separated from morality and sometimes put into
practice according to need or necessity—a way of survival.

In Tijuana, illegality produced a legendary saga, forming and re-
shaping the numerous mythical narratives of the contemporary city.
A city conceived by conflict (Mexican-American War) and endorsed
by a shady deal (Treaty of Guadalupe Hidalgo), events that became
the symbolic impetus for the future evolution of its urban space.

Illegality has been the crux of a city caught in a dialectical tension
between desire and condemnation.

Debunking Utopia

Following the Mexican-American War of 1846–48, Ricardo Orozco, a
young engineer from Mexico City, was hired by the Argüello family to
give order to the various ranches they had established in the valley of
Tijuana. The plan was part of an agreement to settle a land dispute
between members of the Argüello and Olvera families, original settlers of the valley. Litigations ended in 1889, which became the date
adopted as the founding of the city. Orozco was trained at the famous
Academy of San Carlos in Mexico City, an institution influenced by
French concepts in urban design during an era described as the belle
epoque, a style adopted in the late nineteenth century by emerging
Latin American cities. Orozco laid out the plan along the U.S.-Mexico
border and adjacent to the Tijuana River valley. The plan included a

series of diagonal boulevards that connected parks and public spaces, as well as a diverse set of block types for residential and commercial functions. Positivism and a Haussmann sense of urban order were meant to replace the old colonial checkerboard grids, common in most Mexican cities, and negate the generic homogenous block plans of neighboring San Diego. As Antonio Padilla, Tijuana's leading urban historian, writes, "one of the prime relations between the map and the ideals of positivism influenced by Augusteo Comte, was the rejection at the outset of a return to a historical tradition typified by the Hispano-Colonial model conformed by a grid with a center as the seat of religious and political power. The plan of Tijuana is part of a rational and philosophical order based on man's liberty and not only subjected to rational logic."[1]

As soon as the beaux arts plan was laid out and implemented, it went through radical changes. Topography interrupted the philosophical order and form, and the desire for greater profits became the stimulus for illegality. Forceful confrontations arose in places where the street diagonals touched a parcel. Landowners began to transgress the axial paths by building into them in order to increase their parcels' area. By 1921, the plan and its axial avenues had become a crippled desire of order and control, a failed plan to produce Cartesian logic. In contrast to the positivist ideals of Orozco, his new plan for Tijuana marked the beginning of the dystopic myth of the city.

Today, the only remnant piece of the plan's diagonals is Plaza Santa Cecilia, located on the verge of decency near the red-light district of Zona Norte and the once "family" oriented Revolution Street. There would be one more attempt in the 1970s to bring order to the urban chaos from years of informal planning with the imposed plan of a new downtown area known as Zona Río, an area that left a distinct scar in the organic fabric of contemporary Tijuana.

Bargain Basement of Sin

In 1915, while San Diego was organizing the San Diego Panama-California Exposition and constructing the pseudocolonial buildings of Balboa Park, Tijuana came up with its own Mexican festivities and featured around-the-clock entertainment such as cock fights, alcohol, gambling, and many other venues for the prohibited desires of Californians. Corroborating once again that while San Diego was nostalgically looking for a past, Tijuana was the happiest place on earth. The Tijuana racetrack began construction during this time, a project mostly financed by Californians, and opened its doors in 1916. James "Sunny Jim" Coffroth, son of a California senator and a boxing promoter, headed south from San Francisco and its moral climate looking for a profitable business deal south of the border in Old Mexico. He became a major investor in the construction of the racetrack. The track became an unrivaled tourist attraction in the border region and many raced down to Tijuana once the bars were closed indefinitely in California. San Diego closed its border at nine o'clock trying to stop the Anglo diaspora, yet tourists still got away through the famous hole in the fence, a secret breech that was well known by visitors, racetrack employees, and the "twenties version of contemporary coyotes in reverse who shuttled visitors back and forth from north to south across the border."[2] Tijuana during this time had a population of less than 2,000 and there were probably more visitors to the track during the racing season than inhabitants of the city. In multiple occasions the track suffered damages from the torrent waters of the Tijuana River yet it was such a profitable business that the track was rebuilt every time. This gambling venue alone sparked the economy and nightlife of downtown which for the next fifty years became the epitome of hedonistic gringo entertainment across the U.S.-Mexico border. David Jimenez Beltran, the track's biographer, said it best: "Without the racetrack Tijuana would have had a difficult time economically. The growth of the city can be traced to one word, hipodromo, or racetrack."[3] Since then it has been part of a violent and unlawful history. Though horse racing no longer takes place at the track, to this day it continues to be in the spotlight of various controversies.

During Prohibition in the United States, Tijuana became an accomplice to bootlegging and drunkenness by becoming an oasis of bars and liquor stores that served Americans during the era of the Volstead Act of the 1920s. It was then that many establishments—from La Ballena beer hall (considered to have the longest bar in the world) to a series of saloons, brothels, and other illicit Edens—began to cater to tourists who came as far as from the Hollywood Hills and as close by as San Diego. Baja California's wine industry also took off to meet the intoxicating needs of the gringo. Today the wines of the valley of Guadalupe are world renowned, all thanks to Prohibition. Yet again, Tijuana took advantage of the disobedient actions of its neighbor and embraced the situation as a successful business enterprise. In 1928, American entrepreneurs trying to strike a profit by making Tijuana the precursor to Las Vegas founded the Agua Caliente casino. The casino pampered Hollywood celebrities such as Buster Keaton, Bing Crosby, and Rita Hayworth, along with mafia boss Al Capone. Wayne McAllister, a young eighteen-year-old draftsman from San Diego, and his wife were given the task of designing Agua Caliente, a luxurious casino and resort second only to Monte Carlo. Designed with an eclectic palette of Spanish Mission architecture, art deco interiors, and Moorish accents, Agua Caliente was a $10 million investment that in today's economy would sum a $2 billion price tag.[4] Caliente became very lucrative and had daily jackpots in the thousands of dollars and its fame aided in the proliferation of many bars and hotels across the river into downtown. McAllister would later design the first major casino in Las Vegas, El Rancho (also known as the "Caliente of Nevada") and his work continues to adorn the famous strip with casinos such as the Freemont and the Sands. In his last interview, published in Spanish, McAllister remembers that Agua Caliente was such a profitable venture that it created enough tax revenue for the total budget of the Northern Territory of Baja California.[5] During the U.S. depression, the casino expanded and the new commercial strip of downtown Tijuana flourished economically, yet all of this would come to an end in 1939 when, by presidential decree, all gambling was prohibited in Mexico and Agua Caliente was converted into a school. Soon after, the money, glory, and legend of sin city moved to its new home—Las Vegas.

Fluvial Tabula Rasa

During the Second World War, the United States sent its young laboring men into the military service, leaving the fields of California without hands to work the land. The Bracero Program of 1942 became another incentive to immigrate to Tijuana and work in California. Immigration quadrupled the city's population in a decade and originated the phenomena that still plague it today: uncontrolled growth, informal development, and illegal immigration. Even after the war, Americans felt obliged to hire illegal workforces in agriculture, construction, and low-paying service jobs. Many of these immigrants settled illegally in different parts of the city, but the most problematic settlement grew along the banks of the Tijuana River: *cartolandia* or Carton-land. The relocation of people from this area became a twenty-year endeavor for city officials that ended with a violent act in 1979, which would launch the city of Tijuana into modernity, a malevolent plan concocted by the federal government in Mexico City. During that year, heavy rains came down upon the city and the Rodriguez Dam, located on the city's east side, had a significant amount of reserve that according to state officials needed to be released and, without previous notice, the water swept away the cardboard shacks. The Tijuana River Canal, a deep cut dividing the city in two, a *voie triomphale* of concrete and sewage, memorializes this event today.

The city of Tijuana has always turned its back on the only river that transects the city's urban fabric from east to west. Since its conception, Tijuana has always gazed north toward the border and struggled with the frantic development along the Tijuana River until major federal efforts proposed its channelization. The Tijuana River Canal proved to be a monological solution to control yearly flooding and informal development along its edge. The concrete canal violently divided the urban fabric in two areas and created a no-man's land in its interior that today even police don't dare to enter. The accelerated development of the periphery, brought about by the installation of manufacturing parks, produced communities lacking basic urban services such as sewer infrastructure, that had no alternative but to use the Tijuana River Canal as an outlet for sewage discharge, mixing with the toxic fluids from adjacent manufacturing plants.[6] The canal runs across the U.S.-Mexico border, releasing this concoction of toxic waters into the Tijuana River Estuary Reserve in the United States and the Pacific Ocean. This crisis, of environmental and binational consequence of the shared ecology between San Diego and Tijuana, prompted authorities to plan a series of sewage treatment plants, of which only two have been built and are currently operational. Only recently has the Tijuana city government been able to install sewer infrastructure in the many squatter communities adjacent to the river. This has prompted the urgent task of rethinking the relationship between the canal, the river, and its urban development. City officials, however, seem to think that more channelization is the answer to the problems created by the rapid growth along the banks of the river. In the last two years there have been alternative plans to restore part of the river: removing concrete in parts of the canal, using the river as a public space during the dry season, and installing trains for public transportation on the shoulder of the canal. Many of these plans have failed or have not been studied in detail, leaving the future relationship of Tijuana and its river unresolved.

Drag-and-Drop Urbanism

Modernization and progress are supposedly what foreign industries were to offer Tijuana. Maquiladoras are manufacturing plants that take advantage of cheap labor and relaxed environmental regulations that find the dumping of hazardous materials overlooked by the Mexican authorities. Acids, solvents, and other poisons spill into the canyons along the industrial parks of Tijuana and into nearby informal housing developments.[7] The maquiladoras promoted jobs and security to an incoming population that settled rapidly in the eastern part of the city, an informal process that began through property invasion.

A reactionary antidote to the expedient squatter settlements was a government-subsidized program for the acquisition of homes built by private developers. Today private developers are building, under the banner of social housing, serialized housing developments that even the UN has deemed unfit for dignified living. In comparison to these communities, the informal developments tend to improve with limited infrastructure as years pass and some have morphed into consolidated communities. In a 2000 study published by COLEF, Mexico's border think tank, 50 percent of all housing stock in the city was found to have begun as an illegal settlement.[8] At the same time, the "legal" constructions of greedy developers are a product of faulty government zoning codes where loopholes become the main conduit of shady legality.

The informal settlements have woven themselves into multiple spaces, each with its distinct form of identity, which as of today has produced the most heterogeneous places within the city. Yet the conflict arises when these informal and rhizomatic systems of development are confronted with "planned" alternatives of serialized housing for hundreds of thousands of people, using methods of mass manufacturing that produce monological containers, a homogenous archipelago, where the pursuit of diversity is an illicit endeavor. These communities were part of a drag-and-drop urbanism by which, after twenty years, only some have been successful in breaking away from the mold of top-down urban planning and inflexible land-use policy. The spatial differences between both informal and formal developments vary in that one is capable of absorbing individual perceptions of what constitutes a partial yet autonomous right to the city. Subsidized developments tend to produce a condition of entropy within serialized communities and as a result individual needs and wants have to be attained through forms of resistance against capsular sub-urbanization. Size, boundaries, and the concept of ownership are part of the discrepancies found between both formal and informal models. A typical serialized development is made up numerous enclaves; for example, the oldest developments of this kind are composed of approximately eight sections, sometimes defined by walls and access control gates in the manner of upper-middle-class gated communities. Their limits are defined, yet the concept of ownership is redefined by a new system of credit while failing to promote opportunities in community building. Meanwhile, in the informal communities, the city bureaucracy has not been able to completely "legalize" them because of their constant flux, leaving boundaries to be negotiated between each member of the community. Ownership is achieved through a system of channels of communication. Therefore, the boundaries within informal developments change due to the constant reorganization of the area. Most of these communities share a desire for a better future and organize strong political groups that can guarantee votes for city council seats.

These days, land is scarce and the waves of arriving settlers have fewer options in settling in, especially if they don't participate in the low-income housing market. As the city extends toward the east and topography limits access to buildable land, new informal communities tend to decrease. Yet there is an increase in the second-hand rental market in informal areas where small rooms and back houses are rented to incoming migrants. New extensive areas of informal settlements have decreased but existing ones have begun a process of densification.

Hybrid Mutations

The new sectors of the city made up of a combination of informal (shanty-towns) and formal (developer housing) developments have reached a critical mass. This eastern zone of the city was described a few years ago as La Nueva Tijuana, the New Tijuana.[9] It is where half of the population now resides, approximately one million people. It became a zone of immigrants from diverse socioeconomic levels and distinct regions of the country, with each bringing their own customs and traditions into a mix of tastes and fantasies in the city epitomized by the famous Porfirio Díaz quote, "so far from God and so close to the United States." The first serialized housing developments created twenty years ago are no longer discernable. The need to transform both informal and formal developments has created an ambiguous urban space of improvised informal markets, multifamily zones (once single-family residences), Internet cafés and countless incompatible programmatic assemblies based solely on consumer trends and needs. "New Tijuana" became the poster child of informality, where academics, artists, and social scientists catalogued, documented, and photographed the creative methods of construction, resiliency, and survival. New Tijuana is made up of different *delegaciones* (boroughs) and its urban fabric moves across jurisdictional boundaries that fight for revenue against other more affluent areas of the city.

Public safety is compromised for this reason and these zones have become some of the most crime-ridden areas of the city. Recently they have been host to drug cartel groups that take advantage of the large rental housing stock used for operation centers, hostage detainment, and armories—an estimated 40,000 abandoned low-income homes have been taken over by organized crime in the northern states of Mexico.[10] The infamous Arellano Felix cartel ex-lieutenant who was operating with his own commandos, Teodoro Garica Pimentel, "El Teo," was said to have complete control of the east side of the city before his capture by federal police in early 2010. An area of the city once known for its self-styled architectural creativity (the recycling of garage doors, tires, and many other surplus items from the United States for incredible vernacular constructions) is now the government's target against a large black market arms trade coming from bordering states in the United States. The New Tijuana has been transformed from the laboratory of postmodernism to one of the nation's most important battlegrounds of the war on drugs—nearly an independent state with its own culture, law, and development strategy.

Recently, the rest of the city has suspended its fascination for the east side as a space of inspiration. New Tijuana has ceased to be "the Mother of Invention."[11] The struggle of the working class from incomplete programs of urbanization and other top-down planning policies is no longer looked upon as a rightful method to achieve an urban society. Even the categorization of the east side as a product of bottom-up urbanism is no longer championed as the struggle of a disadvantaged class against neocapitalist and free-market urbanism (manufacturing, free-trade zones, private development).

From a cultural perspective, the New Tijuana begins to become irrelevant as a celebratory image of hybridity due to the impulsive autonomy that extended the appropriation of the city to all social groups including organized crime. The urban imaginary of the city has changed since it was baptized in the 1990s as a laboratory of postmodernity by the celebrated sociologist Néstor García Canclini, which helped encourage the creation of academic and artistic events and symposia that brought together world-renowned artists and thinkers.[12] One of the most successful art programs to build on the idea of Tijuana and the border region as hybrid and postmodern was inSITE, a binational in-situ art installation event and symposium where international artists and theorists came together every three years to research and discuss art practices in the public domain in the San Diego / Tijuana border region. Tijuana artist Marcos Ramírez ERRE illustrated the fractured essence of Tijuana urban and social space with his reconstruction of an informal house for InSITE 1994. He recreated a dwelling typical to the ones built in the informal settlements of the city on the esplanade of the Tijuana Cultural Center (CECUT). Designed in the late 1970s by the renowned Mexican architects Pedro Ramirez Vazquez and Manuel Rosen Morrison, CECUT represents the institutional modernism of the PRI, the political party that ruled Mexico for more than seventy years. *Century 21* intended to decontextualize both structures by making apparent and visible the formal and spatiotemporal tension inherent in the large context of the contemporary city. During InSITE 2000 and within the same context of the CECUT, the Polish-born artist Krzysztof Wodiczko projected images of women maquiladora workers on the exterior of the large spherical structure of the center's Imax theater. The work exposes the employment abuses of these women who work long hours in the maquiladoras and live in the precarious company towns near the industrial parks. Wodiczko's project, like the Ramírez intervention, emphasizes the fractures between the global and local, and between nation-state politics and the political realities of the border.[13]

Mea Culpa

In 2002 *Newsweek* magazine named Tijuana—alongside Cape Town and Kabul—as one of the top emerging cultural centers in the developing world, a so-called World Cultural Mecca.[14] By 2006, Tijuana's cultural boom would begin to fade as its reputation shifted toward its being one of the most dangerous urban areas in northern Mexico. Homicides, cartel shoot-outs, and kidnappings became daily ordeals across the city from east to west; Tijuana had been subjugated to the reign of the AK-47. That same year the U.S. Department of State warned its citizens of the violence and made an effort to restrain them from traveling to the city.[15] The warning was extended to many of the same academic institutions that had only recently established Tijuana as their Latin American petri dish.

By 2008, Tijuana was considered the third most violent city in the country.[16] The entire city was now dealing with the extreme rise of violence, and numerous cultural projects and curatorial efforts began to publicly question the validity of art and culture as a means of social activism. In 2008, curators Lucía Sanromán and Ruth Estévez organized *Proyecto Cívico* / Civic Project, which constructed an argument based on the theory of states of exception to critically present the need for society to become active participants, via cultural production, in the reformulation of the political and the city. According to the curators, "Tijuana has been historically established as a series of exclusions from the legal constitution of the country that have created conditions that closely parallel the concept of a state of exception as defined by Giorgio Agamben, a suspension of law that nevertheless ratifies the rule of law and the hierarchy of the sovereign."[17] Our continued tolerance of the illicit as a way of survival has crippled our participation in the construction of a democratic and integrated society. We are now, as a society, participants in the decay of our system of illicit acts.

This attitude was clearly evidenced in one of the works exhibited in Proyecto Civico / Civic Project by the artist Marcos Ramírez ERRE. Ramírez, the same artist known for his *Century 21* project in the plaza of the Tijuana Cultural Center for InSITE '94, prepared a short video performance of an organized crime murder for hire. In the work titled *Todos somos el mismo (El bueno, el malo y el feo)* / We Are All the Same One (The Good, the Bad and the Ugly), Ramírez impersonates a mafia hit man, known in the drug cartel world as a *sicario*, and in a second scene reappears as the murdered mystery man in a black Suburban and at the end of the performance plays the federal officer investigating the murder scene. In this short video performance Ramírez suggests that we as a society are incriminating ourselves as participants in the dissolution of society's values and construction of a destructive public consciousness. The enemy is among us. We have succumbed to a debilitating psychosis of our own hyperdystopia.

We are now experiencing the city not as a laboratory of postmodernism, but more as a state of exception. Our sociocultural strategies are now geared toward healing the social fabric and if possible the reconstruction of our institutions as more democratic and heterogeneous points of interaction. Based on the success in the mid-1990s of Bogotá's model of community building implemented by the controversial mayor Antanas Mockus and later the restructuring of public space and institutions by his successor Enrique Peñalosa, a group of artists from Tijuana made public their desire for civic change in a proposal titled *Plan de Cultura para Tijuana* / Tijuana's Plan for Culture 2010.[18] The group was formed by writers, painters, video artists, architects, and representatives of various nonprofit organizations, and the premise of the plan was to entice a new way of making cultural policy through various social groups with vested interests in the local community. This policy was then shared with political candidates from all parties running for the Tijuana mayor's office in 2010.

The plan has five central core objectives. The first makes a strong effort to encourage the dispersing of cultural programs and institutions throughout the city, thereby decentralizing state-run programs. The second objective argues for a "cultural healing of community and public space" which involves combating visual and auditory contamination and a cleansing of the city of discriminatory violent propaganda. Ironically, some of these same intolerant acts of urban life were celebrated by the advocates of the postmodern Tijuana less than a decade ago and left their influence on some aspects of cultural projects such as the Nortec Collective (who, for example, often incorporated images of Tijuana criminality in their live performance visuals). The plan is a draft that needs more concrete trajectories for its deployment, yet it is important to recognize that it considers the politics of exclusion as one of the conditions that has allowed organized crime to appropriate the social imaginary.

This new attitude toward Tijuana's social fabric and public space has been a guiding factor in the evolution of a new urban imaginary with a decidedly self-critical point of view. After decades of external signifiers that have some way or another shaped the perception of the city, various social groups are interested in forging a new type of citizen with a critical and self-referential point of view. These include organizations that foster new social ties between policies and community, reclaim public space, and promote environmental practices that take care of our shared natural ecology. The potential of the city lies in its innate state of expediency and resiliency that's been honed over the one hundred years of its history of surviving illicit acts of urbanism. Its future is rooted in its ability to reimagine itself from within, to believe that new cultural and social paradigms can be part of a new era of change.

Notes

1 Antonio Padilla Corona. "El centro histórico de Tijuana." In *Tijuana Identidades y Nostalgias*, ed. Francisco Manuel Acuña Borbolla, Mario Ortiz Villacorta Lacave, et al., 121–36. Tijuana: XVII Ayuntamiento de Tijuana. 2006.

2 Jim Miller. "Just Another Day in Paradise?" In *Under the Perfect Sun: The San Diego Tourists Never See*. Mike Davis, Kelly Mayhew, and Jim Miller. New York: New Press. 2005.

3 David Jimenez Beltran. *The Agua Caliente Story: Remembering Mexico's Legendary Racetrack*. Lexington, Ky.: Blood-Horse. 2004.

4 Chris Nichols. *The Leisure Architecture of Wayne McAllister*. Layton, Utah: Gibbs Smith. 2007.

5 Pablo Bransburg. "Entrevista a Wayne McAllister." In *Tijuana Identidades y Nostalgias*, ed. Francisco Manuel Acuña Borbolla, Mario Ortiz Villacorta Lacave, et al., 287–302. Tijuana: XVII Ayuntamiento de Tijuana. 2006.

6 "Tijuana River Pollution." Trade and Environment Database (TED). January 11, 1997. http://www1.american.edu/TED/tijuana.htm.

7 Ibid.

8 Tito Alegría. *Legalizando La Ciudad Asentamientos Informales y Procesos de Regularización en Tijuana*. Tijuana: El Colegio de la Frontera Norte, 2005.

9 Fiamma Montezemolo, René Peralta, and Heriberto Yépez. *Here Is Tijuana!* London: Black Dog. 2006.

10 Fernando Damian. "Se Apodero el Narco de 40 Mil Casas de Infonavit." Milenio Online, July 20, 2010. http://impreso.milenio.com/node/8802605.

11 René Peralta. "Tijuana: Mother of Invention." World View Cities Online Report, Architectural League of New York. 2005. http://www.worldviewcities.org/tijuana/main.html.

12 Néstor García Canclini. *Hybrid Cultures: Strategies for Entering and Leaving Modernity*. Minneapolis: University of Minnesota Press. 1995.

13 A. Roberto Gonzalez. "Ensalada Tijuana? Welcome to the Gritty Landscape of Globalization." In *Cruelty and Utopia: Cities and Landscape of Latin America*, 254–60. New York: Princeton Architectural Press. 2003.

14 Adam Piore, et al. "The World's New Cultural Meccas." *Newsweek*, Atlantic Edition. September 2, 2002, 56.

15 U.S. Department of Defense. "Travel Warning U.S. Department of State Bureau of Consular Affairs." July 2010. http://travel.state.gov/travel/cis_pa_tw/tw/tw_4755 .html.

16 Mosso Rosario Castro and Enrique Mendoza Hernandez. "Ejecuciones Imparables." Zeta Online. July 4–10, 2008. http://www.zetatijuana.com/html/Edicion 1788/Principal.html

17 Ruth Estévez and Lucía Sanromán. "Una Suposición que se Desvanece." In *Proyecto Civico/Civic Project*, 18–43. Tijuana: Conaculta/CECUT, 2008.

18 "Plan de Cultura para Tijuana." June 7, 2010. http://plandeculturatijuana.blogspot .com/2010/06/propuesta-de-cultura-para-una-nueva.html.

The Transborder Metropolis in Question

The Case of Tijuana and San Diego

The population living on the U.S.-Mexico border is concentrated in binational pairs of adjacent cities. In the literature on border urbanization, in the mass media, and in the political dialogue of both countries, these adjacent cities are often called "twin cities," a "border region," or "transborder metropolises." The two cities of Tijuana and San Diego are the most well-known example because they are the cities with the greatest population on both sides of the border and have received the most attention in the literature. The idea that a transborder metropolis exists—that each pair of neighboring cities forms a sole city or region—implies that both cities have similar futures and interests. This idea emphasizes their proximity and the interactions between both sides of the border as arguments to sustain the concept of the oneness of the two sides. On the other hand, by highlighting the structural characteristics that stimulate urban growth—characteristics that are different on both sides of the border—it is possible to make a case for the oneness of each side.

This study proposes that the idea of the transborder metropolis has a weak theoretical and empirical foundation. Evidence is presented that suggests we are looking at two adjacent, but different urban units. This text first presents the idea of a transborder society, region, and metropolis and then presents the critiques of those ideas and empirical evidence that backs up those critiques.

Transborder Society and Metropolis

Transborder Society

Until the end of the 1970s, border problems were looked at as national processes in the Mexican literature on the subject. The analysis of urban development and the policies stemming from it were not exempt from that focus: the urban border activities were considered as local-national processes as in any other city in the interior of the country, without taking the binational praxis of said processes into account in order to explain the development of the border and its cities.

In 1981, what was perhaps the first transborder vision of the conceptualization of the border was proposed (Bustamante 1981). In this proposal, the border area is defined as "a binational region geographically demarcated by the empirical extension of the processes of interaction between people living on both sides of the border" (39). Using a Weberian conception of social class, the binational region was conceptualized as a transborder social structure with a social stratification spanning both sides of the border. The oneness of the social structure of the area demarcated by the interaction is defined through a number of social development indicators. The differences between both sides of the border do not appear as a rupture, but rather as a stratified continuity in the border region's binational social structure (41).

This conceptualization is based on three main ideas: (1) the "border region" is binational; (2) that region has the same social structure regardless of the border; and (3) both sides of the border have similar economic and social processes. The binationality of the border region is here a geographic-social definition and not a political-administrative one. This clarification allows for two types of implications. First, in the theoretical aspect, the geographic-social definition presupposes a contradiction between the national way of elaborating and implementing public policy on the border and the binational way the region spans the border. The border is a political-administrative impediment to resolving the problems affecting society in the entire binational border region. Considering the existence of the border as invariable, the solution to the problems of this region requires transborder coordination in public policy on each side of the border. The second implication, on a practical level, is that, if the concept of a binational region were used in an incorrect way in the elaboration of public policies on the border, that is to say, if the concept were used in the political-administrative sense, it could give rise to situations detrimental to the national sovereignty of either nation. In a later work, Bustamante (1989) considers this second implication. The idea of a region defined as a territory delimited by interaction is still present, although the term binational region is rejected due to the potentially "risky" possibility of it being used in border relations with the United States.

Transborder Metropolis

In the same way as "binational region," the urban pair Tijuana–San Diego has been considered as an urban binational unit due to the existence of a continuous urbanization and of a consistent relationship between the two urban units. Several authors and media outlets have named this a binational space (Ganster and Valenciano 1992; Gildersleeve 1978) or twin cities (Kearney and Knopp 1995; *Economist* 1992). Several European authors have proposed a similar notion in terms of other urban border areas (Anderson 1983).

Lawrence Herzog (1997, 1991, 1990a) has proposed the concept of transborder metropolis to understand the urbanized area of Tijuana–San Diego, according to the author, a concept generalizable to all of the binational pairs of neighboring border cities. In addition, Herzog has used that concept to interpret diverse urban border phenomena (2003a, 2003b, 2000, 1999, 1990b). From his point of view, the urban area spanning the border is considered as an urban region whose integration is based on the existent interactions between the two sides in the binational pair of adjacent cities.

From the point of view of economic geography, this author classified the relationships between both sides of the border in terms of transborder global manufacturing, the transborder job market, the transborder market for consumption, the transborder tourist market, and the transborder market in housing and land (Herzog 2003a, 1997). From the point of view of urban geography, this author classifies relations between both sides of the border as falling within seven global ecologies: zones of global manufacturing, spaces of transnational consumption, global tourist districts, post-NAFTA neighborhoods, places of transnational community, spaces of conflict, and invented connections (Herzog 2003b). The author posits that transnational corporations are leading the process of integration of Tijuana into the global investment market, homogenizing consumption, architecture, urban space, and cultural patterns (making them more similar to San Diego). In this way, the international boundary as a dividing line between the cities on both sides of the border has been weakened.

In the construction of the concept of a transborder metropolis, Herzog explores two subjects that are fundamental to our understanding of border cities: the first is the process of convergence/integration or divergence/independence of the two societies that meet at the border; and the second is the possibility and necessity of policies elaborated in a binational way for the border cities. Thinking about these matters leads the author to the question of whether a "transborder social system" exists that creates a community of interests along the border. In his proposal, there is an explicit affirmative response in that he constructs a definition of *transborder metropolis*. What Herzog does not explore is whether relationships in existence between both sides of the border—in his proposal, evidence of integration—are a product of the differences or similarities between both sides of the border. Paradoxically, his discourse is imbued with the supposition that in the end, but not now, both sides will be similar and integrated. For Herzog, the border has two types of functions that are intrinsic and antagonistic. The first is to divide two cultures and two urban structures, reproducing the respective, different national patterns along the border. The second function is to unify both sides of the border in an ecological and social way. These aspects of unification are the basis for the phenomenon he qualifies as a "transborder metropolis."

The first function—as a dividing/differentiating force—affirms the differences in the spatial and political patterns between the cities on both sides of the border. In this sense, each border locality looks more like the rest of the cities in its country than its neighbor on the other side of the international divide, in terms of both its spatial structure and its process of change. These differences define them as elements of "friction" or confrontation between the postindustrial North and the industrializing South. For Herzog, this dividing/differentiating role of the border has been relatively stable across time and is relatively independent of the changes in the porosity of the border for existing relations between the two sides.

The second function of the border—as a unifying force—becomes apparent in its porousness. According to Herzog this second function is in fact particular to the second half of the last century and has intensified recently with the worldwide expansion of the capitalist system and globalization. The permeability of the border is made material in the flows of people, goods, capital, and environmental elements between each binational pair of neighboring cities, which occur primarily due to transborder proximity. Proximity is the main catalyst of integration within the transborder ecological system. This integration is defined by the author as "fusion" between the two neighboring cities.

The idea that interaction gives rise to integration and, along with it, a metropolis that crosses the border is shared by other academics. One variant of that idea appears in Dear and Leclerc (2003, 1998). From the point of view of cultural geography, these authors consider processes of globalization, network society, hybridization, and privatization (processes classified as "hard border") to be forces for integration on both sides of the border. As these forces intensify over time, so too does integration. With the strengthening of these forces, the space formed by transborder interactions becomes a place itself: the container for the transborder society which the authors designate as "Bajalta California" and define as a "postborder megalopolis." Although they consider this megalopolis to be one place, it (Southern California and northern Baja California) actually contains various different and distinct places within it. The inclusion of diverse places in one sole unit is derived from the subjective perception of the geography of this space held by its inhabitants. For the authors, the construction of the perception of a transborder "we" is being consolidated as an imaginary community, and minimizes the obstacle of the international border.

Another variant of the transborder idea is presented by Pezzoli and his partners (2001) from the perspective of urban environmental planning. The authors adhere to the concept that San Diego and Tijuana form one transborder city-region, although they do not develop it. Their position is that planning in both cities should be done in conjunction since they share three common problems: extensive urban growth, fragmented infrastructures, and unequal development.

The idea of a transborder metropolis also supports intentions in the development and land-use plans in several border cities of both countries, as in San Diego and Tijuana for example. The San Diego Association of Governments (SANDAG, a countywide group) considers San Diego and Tijuana to be a binational border region (SANDAG 2003). In 2002, the Committee on Binational Regional Opportunities (COBRO) was founded to serve as a working group of the Borders Committee of SANDAG, which makes recommendations on transborder planning projects. Matters considered as transborder by SANDAG and which have an intervention proposal in its 2003 plan include jobs and housing accessibility, transportation, energy, water, drainage, air quality, economic development, and homeland security. In Tijuana, the Municipal Planning Institute asserts in its *Program for Urban Development of the Population Center of Tijuana, 2002–2025* that Tijuana and San Diego form one sole region due to the fact that they share problems that require joint solutions (IMPLAN 2002, 100). Although IMPLAN recognizes the same relevant transborder issues as SANDAG, the specific plans for facing the problems thought to be held in common are in fact local plans for each city. The only transborder plans underway (water and drainage) are administered by the Mexican federal government and the water agency of San Diego. The intent to undertake local transborder planning, which undergirds the rhetoric of the plans, confronts the reality of an absence of an adequate binational legal framework and of divergent planning priorities of the two cities.

Critique of the Transborder Metropolis Vision

The idea that neighboring border cities, like San Diego and Tijuana, make up a binational metropolitan unit can be critiqued on several levels. Now I move into a discussion of that idea from the perspective of social structure, economic structure, regional divergence, and metropolitan structure.

About the Transborder Society

In order for the concept of transborder continuity of social structure to withstand theoretical scrutiny, three assumptions are needed, which were not made explicit in the formulation of the transborder region (by Bustamante) reviewed earlier in this chapter: first, that social groups on both sides of the border present similar social practices; second, that individuals on both sides of the border have a similar awareness of the roles of social groups and the resulting symbolisms; and third, that the conditions that allow for the reproduction of the social system operate indistinctly on both sides of the border. Let's look at these assumptions in more detail.

The concept of transborder continuity in social structure presupposes that the social groups on both sides of the border present similar social practices. This similarity implies three characteristics in regard to the relationship between social agents and the social structure (Cohen 1991): (1) social actors in collectivities on both sides of the border are familiar with similar procedures for action; (2) social actors on both sides of the border interpret and apply the semantic and normative aspects of these procedures of action in the same way; and (3) social actors on both sides of the border have access to the same type of resources. But, as the evidence shows, these conditions of social structuring are not all found on the border.

In the first place, the procedures of action are not similar on both sides of the border. Half of Tijuana's population does not have the legal right to cross the border and definitely does not cross it. This spatial factor in and of itself makes it impossible for Tijuana's population to have a similar awareness of the procedures for social action as San Diego's population. Also it is difficult to make the case that the majority of San Diego's population, who have crossed over to Tijuana one time or never, would have a praxis of action similar to that of Tijuana's people. The interaction between both collectivities is weak, as is the mutual awareness of their social praxes. (The complaint about mutual incomprehension and lack of knowledge between the collectivities on both side of the border frequently reappears in the manifestos of the handful of binational projects.) Social practices on both sides of the border are separate and appear related only in some aspects. The reproduction of social practices requires a shared awareness of the ways of doing things; for that reason, they are limited by time and space. The international border is in fact a powerful institutional constraint, preventing the practices of agents from both collectivities from developing in the same space and having a relationship.

For the people who can cross the border and overcome this institutional barrier, the use of two languages (Spanish and English) is another obstacle to the establishment of shared knowledge that could serve as both a foundation and a stimulus for the realization of similar social practices. In communicative acts, through which individual actions are coordinated, "pretensions of validity" accumulate that are invariable within a culture (Honneth 1991). These pretensions imply affirmations—which are generally implicit—relative to (1) authenticity and sincerity in gestures as manifestations of subjective experience, (2) affirmations related to efficiency and effectiveness of gestures as indicators of the means by which an end is pursued, and (3) affirmations related to the rectitude of actions from the perspective of relevant norms (Turner 1991). In this way, in social interaction, materialized in communicative acts, a subtle process takes place, generally implicit, in which each party asserts their sincerity, efficiency, and rectitude. The "pretensions of validity" exist as such in the interaction only if a person appeals to the shared knowledge of norms that establish (1) what behaviors are sincere, and (2) which relationship between means and ends is culturally acceptable. The existence of more than one language in the transborder space not only prevents the sharing of knowledge of these norms, but also limits the existence of pretensions of validity in the interactions. Due to the lack of these pretensions, a great effort must be made to have transborder interaction, and, when it does occur, the efficiency of the interaction is usually minimal. The result is that there is little communication between groups on both sides of the border, even among those people who can legally surmount the barrier to international crossing. And as a corollary, the shared knowledge of social practices is also minimal.

The second characteristic of the relationship between social actors and their social structure is that social practices are, in each case, accompanied by particular interpretations of the semantics and social norms involved in said practices. Nevertheless, these interpretations are specific to the side of the border under consideration and different from the interpretations developed on the other side due to spatial constraints on the reproduction of social practices that intermediate between agents of both collectivities.

A social structure is at once the instrument and the result of the reproduction of the practices. In order for the practices to replicate themselves, the agents have to share the same semantic interpretation of the ways of doing things and of the resulting signs. The relative semantic homogeneity in a collectivity is not a product solely of sharing practices limited in time and space, but rather principally the result of a negotiation of meaning between the agents. The necessity to negotiate meaning between agents arises out of a quick assessment of the consequences and implications of a particular interpretation of the practices. The negotiation of meaning occurs around the struggle for the resources of the place, that is to say, the maintenance or improvement of the relative position of each agent in relation to the rest. The negotiation that arises out of the imperative for a shared interpretation of the social practices produces a shared sense of the social order, which is made material in meanings. In this way, the construction of meaning is intrinsic to the shared interpretations, without depending on an external body. There is no administrative (institutional) production of the meaning of the social order (Habermas 1989).

When they interact, individuals act under the assumption that the orchestration of gestures communicates a specific line of behavior to others. To reduce tension and loss of time, individuals come up with shared conceptions about the diverse types of roles. For each individual, these are replicated, shared, and recognized by others. The construction of these roles is only possible if people share a common repertoire of self-perceptions and definitions, which depends on a shared knowledge and interpretation, that is to say, of a similar sense of the social order. The shared construction of roles is only possible in one particular society.

The negotiation of meaning between the collectivities on both side of the border is not ongoing, but rather sporadic and focused on particular aspects of exchange or externalities. Between both communities, in Tijuana and San Diego, the transborder exchanges can be interpreted differently by the residents of each locality. This dual interpretation is possible because in that exchange, what is at stake is not the legitimacy of the relative local position of the agents and their roles in each society, but rather economic gain. The possibility of not negotiating meaning during transborder interactions allows for the perpetuation of different social structures on both sides of the border, one next to the other.

The third characteristic of the relationship between social agents and their structure establishes that the resources of a place are the means or the basis of power to which an agent can gain access and manipulate to influence the course of interactions with others (Cohen 1991). In modern societies, resources are derived less and less from natural sources and are increasingly produced by society itself. The resources to which an agent can gain access are the result of previous practices, and because of this, are delimited in time and space. The greater or lesser possibility of gaining access to resources establishes the relative position of each agent in relation to the rest within a social structure. The possibility of some agents gaining access to resources produced in other spaces is realized as a practice peculiar to their social structure and not to the structure of the space from which that resource was produced. Agents' practice of acquiring the external resource operates in the economic aspect of circulation in a moment in time. In that exchange, what agents acquire is the continuation or change in their relative position in the local structure and not in the one where they obtained the resource. The possibility of gaining access to the resources produced by the collectivity on the other side of the border is different for each social agent. When social agents gain access to resources on the other side of the border, they do not modify their relative position in that other collectivity because they have no relative position defined by their praxis. When the agents on one side of the border appear in some relative position on the other side, their position is determined by the mechanisms of social structuring of that side and not of their own, where their possibility of gaining access to resources is different. Only if there were one social structure on both sides of the border would the relative position of an agent be the same on both sides, but that does not happen on this border.

The concept of transborder continuity of the social structure also assumes that the conditions allowing for the reproduction of the system operate indistinctly on both sides of the border. The reproduction of a social system, of its internal cohesion and the sense of its interests, includes political aspects of domination. Systemic social control is necessary to guarantee the conditions for social reproduction and is exercised through political institutions whose objective practices consist of processes of integration and repression. The state is the legitimate repository of the exercise of integration and repression in the territory bounded by the borders of the nation.

The national state can only guarantee the reproduction of a social system outside of its national borders in a situation of imperial domination. Although the state of the United States has guaranteed the reproduction of a social system outside its borders (the most recent cases are Iraq and Haiti), it has not done the same, recently, in the case of Mexico. The Mexican state has not guaranteed the reproduction of the U.S. social system either. On this border, numerous unilateral actions of one of the two national states have taken place that have provoked community and/or state protests in the other country. The legitimacy of their actions is founded on the notion that those actions have been undertaken within their own national territory, even though they have led to negative effects for the interests of the community in the other country. The border is the boundary of the territorialized power of a nation-state, the boundary of the exercise of its practices of social reproduction. The reproduction of a social structure materializes itself as a national reproduction, and a binational reproduction of said structure is not possible. Contiguous regions separated by the border have different social structures with different political conditions of reproduction and for that reason have different processes of reproduction.

Urban Growth, Economic Structure, and Cross-Border Regional Divergence

In order for Tijuana and San Diego to form a metropolis, they must be integrated in a systemic way. A systemic urban unit distributes the effects of change in particular activity in a differentiated way among its other activities, whether that change originates internally or externally. The most important activities (the biggest and the ones that grow the most) affect the entire city. If changes in the most important activities of the city do not affect a set of activities (or a portion of the territory) in a continuous way, they are not related in a systemic way to the main activities. The hypothesis of the transborder metropolis carries with it the implicit assumption that Tijuana and San Diego form a systemic unit, that is to say, that the changes that occur in the principal activities of one city affect the other. Stated in terms of growth, this means that the forces that make one city grow are the same forces making the other one grow and that the rate of growth in both cities is similar. However, the evidence contradicts this assumption.

San Diego has grown as a consequence of regional and national forces; there is no evidence that it has grown due to the influence of border factors. San Diego was a small city at the beginning of the twentieth century. At that time, federal government investment in irrigation in Southern California was a huge boost to its growth, and in the city itself, military investment related to the First World War converted San Diego into an important base for the U.S. Navy (Hansen 1981). In the 1920s, the aviation industry grew rapidly, due mainly to the favorable climate in the region. With both of these defense operation activities, the city's economy blossomed during the Second World War, and the Korean War gave another important boost to its growth. In the 1960s, however, military budget cuts began, cuts that would be even deeper in the following decades, culminating in the almost complete disappearance of air, missile, and satellite industries at the beginning of the 1990s. Beginning in the 1970s, with the continued reductions to the military budget, the relationship between local economic growth and state and national growth has become ever more clear (Gerber 1993). For example, San Diego, the state, and the country all experienced a huge increase in real income and a huge decrease in unemployment in the second part of the 1970s; at the end of that decade, there was also an economic downturn. In a similar way, after an economic recovery at the beginning of the 1980s, there was a reduction in real income at all three levels, culminating in the economic downturn of the beginning of the 1990s, as can be seen in figure 8.1. In this period, 60 percent of San Diego companies that closed or expanded outside the county opened their plants in Mexico, although it is not known how many of them did so in Tijuana (Gerber 1993).

As an effort to recover from the downturn, the local planning agency, SANDAG, together with several other economic promotion groups and local universities, began to implement a strategy of clustered development (Porter 1990) in activities with higher salaries. As a result of this strategy, San Diego has seen a restructuring of its economy—a reorientation toward a high-tech economy, which has been defined as a process of endogenous growth (Mercado 2004). This restructuring has allowed the reorientation of employment growth—which had been led by low-wage service activities—toward growth of high-wage employment. For example, between 1990 and 1998, the San Diego activity clusters that added the most jobs were biotechnology and pharmaceuticals, communications, and computing and software services; they attained a level of 21 percent of the county's total new employment, with respective growth of 104 percent, 57 percent, and 101 percent in that period (SANDAG 2001).

As it increased employment in high-wage industries, this economic reorientation also gave rise to an increase in the county's real wages in the 1990s (SANDAG 2002). It is worth mentioning that transborder interaction has neither led to nor sustained this reorientation. In conclusion, as Hansen (1981) and Gerber (1993) have indicated, San Diego's border location has not had a notable impact on its economic growth; rather, this city has kept pace with the national and regional economy, like many other nonborder cities in the country. In addition, unlike the majority of border cities, San Diego economic growth has almost always been higher than that of the state or the nation as a whole.

Unlike San Diego, Tijuana's border location has always determined its economic growth; that is to say, the forces driving its growth are different from those of its neighbor city (Alegría 1992). In general, for the Mexican

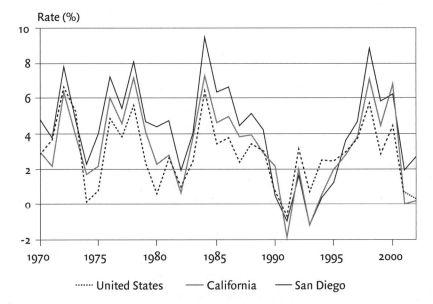

Rate (%)

...... United States   —— California   —— San Diego

8.1. Growth rates of real personal income (2004 prices). Source: Author's estimate based on data from the U.S. Bureau of Economic Analysis, and CPI (Consumer Price Index) estimates by Robert C. Sahr (2005)

border region, urban growth is determined by the geographical adjacency of the structural differences between both countries.

The border separates two socioeconomic national formations and each one has its own dynamic and structure, although they are interrelated. The structural differences are also evident in the spaces of the border. Throughout the twentieth century, parallel to the consolidation of the U.S. and Mexican nation-states, the border went from being a transition zone, where both societies overlaid one another, to a borderline drastically separating societies, markets, regulations, and sovereignties.

The structural differences can be summed up by the different capacity for capital accumulation in the two countries, differences expressed in gross domestic product (GDP), productivity, prices for goods and services, relative prices, and salaries. The differences between the two countries provide a potential for interaction, and the proximity facilitates that interaction. Crossing the border by people, goods, and capital is driven by those differences. Those crossings, or interactions, are the main forces driving the economic growth of Tijuana and all the cities along the Mexican border.

The structural differences have deepened over time, and, along with that change, their influence on the economic growth of the Mexican border region has increased. The increase in foreign trade between Mexico and the United States during recent decades, especially after the signing of NAFTA, has not slowed the two economies' divergence. For several decades, the United States has been Mexico's principal trading partner, a relationship that has intensified in recent years. In 1990, 69 percent of Mexican exports went to the United States, growing to 89 percent in 2004 (BIE-INEGI 2005). For the United States, the relationship with Mexico is of less importance, although it is also growing. The United States sent only 5 percent of its exports to Mexico in 1985 and 10 percent in 2004 (U.S. Census Bureau, http://www.census.gov /foreign-trade/balance/). Despite the growing interaction between both countries, the divergence in their economies is substantial over time. This divergence becomes clear if we represent both countries' economies in terms of the per capita GDP. In 1950, the per capita GDP of the United States was 3.5 times larger than that of Mexico, and in 2000 it increased to 3.8 times (see figure 8.2).

As a consequence of the increase in structural differences, in the last three decades, Tijuana has concentrated on transborder activities, especially in manufacturing, which became 35 percent of the EAP (economically active population) in 2000, as we can see in table 8.1. For its part, San Diego, with economic growth driven by national, not border-specific forces, has concentrated on professional services like high-tech, education, and medicine, which in 2000 employed 30 percent of the local EAP. The city's twenty leftover points tagged "Other Services" in table 8.1 are composed of information services, real estate, entertainment, and hotels and restaurants, which altogether provide a decreasing share of local employment.

San Diego's economic restructuring, which came about in the 1990s, included commercial activities. In ten years, that activity (retail and wholesale business) had a huge net loss in employment (34 percent), reaching 13 percent of county employment in 2000. This restructuring, which happened above all in retail business, increased the overall productivity (sales per worker) in both retail and wholesale business by 67 percent between 1992 and 1997 (estimates made with data from economic censuses and using constant 2004 dollars). This increase in productivity meant that the average number of people assisted by each worker increased from twelve to sixteen in those years (these figures are the result of dividing the county population by the number of workers in the commercial sector, in each year of the economic census). In Tijuana, on the other hand, commercial activity was practically unaffected by

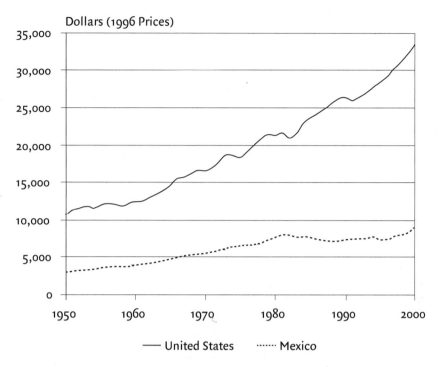

8.2. Real GDP per capita (constant prices) in the United States and Mexico. Source: A. Heston,
R. Summers, and B. Aren, *Penn World Table Version 6.1*, CICUP (2002)

that restructuring. The number of workers in retail or wholesale business in
2000 was just 1 percent less than in 1990 (see table 8.1), and their productivity
increased just 6 percent between 1993 and 1998 (estimates made with data
from economic censuses and using constant 2004 dollars); in addition, the
average number of people helped by each worker was steady at twenty during
these census years.

The effect of NAFTA would appear to be minimal, only intensifying already existing tendencies, that is to say, increased manufacturing and economic growth on the Mexican side and more services and less economic
growth in the majority of U.S. border cities (Peach and Adkisson 2000; Gruben 2001; Coubès 2003). The structural differences propel Mexican urban
border growth in two important ways, one transnational and the other transborder. The transborder and transnational activities drive urban border
growth—in an economic sense insofar as they inject investment and money
into the cities and demographically as they create jobs that are able to keep
local residents in town. The transnational forces of growth include activities

Table 8.1 Economic Structure (Percentage of Employment), 1970–2000, in Tijuana (Municipio) and San Diego (County)

SECTOR (INDUSTRY)	TIJUANA			SAN DIEGO		
	1970	1990	2000	1970	1990	2000
Agriculture, forestry, mining	10	2	1	3	2	1
Manufacturing	24	30	35	16	13	10
Construction	7	9	8	6	7	6
Commerce	19	19	18	22	20	13
Transportation, warehousing, and utilities	4	6	5	5	5	4
Finance and insurance	*	2	1	5	5	4
Public administration and armed forces	4	3	3	23	14	12
Other services	33	30	30	21	35	50
Total	100	100	100	100	100	100

* Finance and insurance included in other services in 1970.
Source: Population censuses.

whose origins and destinations are not located on the border. The two most important activities of this type are international migration and binational commerce. Border cities are the international bridges for these activities that have multiplier effects in employment and consumption. This type of activity was very important for border cities in the first decades of the twentieth century and had a decreased importance in the last decades of that century.

The second type of growth force on the Mexican side is transborder in nature and includes activities whose origins or destinations are on the border. This type of activity was important from the beginning of the border urbanization, but has increased in importance as the border has become less permeable to interaction and as the economies of both countries have become more different. Three transborder activities are the most critical for urban growth. First is manufacturing investment, attracted by lower costs on the Mexican side of the border. This investment, known as maquiladora investment, comes from the United States and a number of Asian countries, assembles products with inputs from several countries, and sells those products primarily in the United States. The Mexican border provides them a low-cost location close to the sales market. The costs are less for practically everything, from land to wages. That difference in costs between the two sides of the border, for example in wages, has increased over time. In 1987, the average hourly wage in manufacturing was $9 higher in the United States than in Mexico; that difference increased to $11.80 in 1998 (BIE-INEGI 2005 for Mexican data; Bureau of Labor Statistics [2005] for the United States). While wage differences drive the long-term expansion of the maquilas, the economic cycle in the United States (where goods are sold) drives short-term variations (Gruben 2001). This type of investment provides jobs that attract people from all over Mexico and allows them to settle in border cities; these jobs have increased at a steady rate since the 1960s when this investment began. In 2004, 156,100 people were directly employed in the Tijuana maquiladoras (BIE-INEGI 2005). In addition, this investment had a multiplier effect on employment in the rest of the city's economic sectors. For example, the estimate is that for each maquiladora job in Tijuana, another is created in other sectors (Alegría 1995).

The second activity is transborder employment, propelled by wage differences. In 1988, the average hourly salary in San Diego was $9.30 higher than in Tijuana; that difference increased to $10.40 in 1998 (BIE-INEGI 2005 for Mexican data; Bureau of Labor Statistics [2005] for the United States). *Tijuanenses* are impelled to look for jobs on the other side of the border when local Mexican wages lose purchasing power on both sides of the border. A negative macroeconomic change creates a situation (even as suddenly as the day after a negative change) in which the same level of wage in Mexico has a lower purchasing power locally (as a product of inflation) and in the neighboring U.S. city (as a result of peso devaluation): for the same work one receives a lower real wage. For every 1 percent change in the difference in wages between Tijuana and San Diego, the cross-border workers (transmigrants) increase 3 percent, in no more than three months after the change in wages (Alegría 2002). In 1998, the proportion of the employed population of Tijuana working in San Diego was 8 percent (ENEU-INEGI); however, these individuals amassed around 20 percent of the total aggregated wages of Tijuana residents (Alegría 2000b). Transmigration means direct employment for Tijuana residents and has a multiplier effect on the tertiary sector of the city economy.

The third activity is the sales of goods and services for final consumption, whose spatial market reach across the border is greater for the Mexican border city. This market reach is due to the lower Mexican prices for the majority of services, and some goods, and to the fact that Tijuana residents have a lower capacity for consumption and only 55 percent of the population has a legal means of entering the United States (Alegría 2000a). Visitors to Tijuana, the vast majority of whom come from the United States and do not need a visa to enter Mexico, are of three types: ordinary tourists who are usually in the city for less than twenty-four hours, people visiting family and friends and making purchases in the area, and people who come to purchase goods and services specifically because of a lower price, scarcity, or the way it is purchased. Tijuana is the border city with the most visitors; in 2003, it received 25.8 million visits, of which 84 percent lasted less than twenty-four hours (Bringas 2004). As a result of these visits, some of Tijuana's sectors have a larger supply of goods and services than in other big Mexican cities in the north. For example, there are twenty-five workers in the bar and restaurant sector in Tijuana for every thousand residents, while in Monterrey there are sixteen. Tijuana has four doctors (physicians and dentists) for every thousand residents while Monterrey has three (estimates based on metropolitan data from the 2000 population census).

The structural differences between the two countries have always propelled demographic growth in Tijuana, but not in San Diego. The growth rate in the last decades has not been the same in Tijuana and San Diego. Contrary to what Herzog (1990a) has argued, the two cities were more integrated at the beginning of Tijuana's growth (in 1900 it had 242 inhabitants) than now. With the exception of the 1970s, Tijuana's growth rate has been consistently higher than San Diego's. From the thirties through the sixties, the changes in rates of growth in both cities were parallel. But in the last forty years, the rate of increase has been completely opposite: in Tijuana, the rate of growth lessened in the seventies in comparison to the sixties, but in San Diego it increased; in the eighties, that rate increased in Tijuana in comparison to the seventies but decreased in San Diego. These opposite trends continued into the nineties, as can be seen in figure 8.3 (the estimate of the rate is for each ten-year period).

Although the reasons for the opposite variations in growth rates are not clear, the changes in rates are due to different causes in each city, although the main source of growth in both cities is immigration. The demographic growth of Tijuana is associated with national and binational economic conditions. San Diego, on the other hand, is affected by national and regional factors: its demographic change is associated with the economic cycle in California and in the United States.

The most convincing hypothesis for Tijuana is that the city grows (it receives internal migrants) when the national economy is doing badly (i.e., unemployment and low wages) and when there is a divergence between the U.S. and Mexican economies (differences in their per-capita GDP) (Alegría 1992).

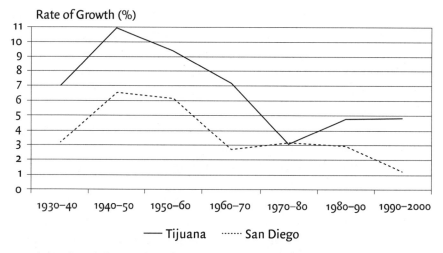

Rate of Growth (%)

8.3. Annual rate of population growth (%) for Tijuana (municipio) and San Diego (county).
Source: Author estimation based on population censuses.

With respect to the national factors driving growth, the hypothesis can be stated in the following way: demographic changes in Tijuana depend inversely on the level of wages and employment in Mexico and depend directly on the level of employment in the city. This hypothesis, besides being in agreement with theories on migration, is backed up by evidence as well. Mexico went through a process of rapid economic growth for several decades, which culminated in the 1970s with the highest real average wage in its history (Pérez and Schwartz 1999, graph 6; INEGI 1999, table 5.12). During that period of national economic expansion, Tijuana went through a constant decline in its rate of population growth, and in the 1970s that rate slowed to its lowest rate in the century. In the 1980s, the rate of population growth in Tijuana began to increase again; this was due to the fact that the country was weathering the lowest level of real wages in the previous sixty years (and in recent decades, its highest level of unemployment). In addition, the city began to have one of the lowest levels of unemployment in the country, a level that remained steady through the first years of the twenty-first century (BIE-INEGI).

The binational factors driving growth are at root a result of the almost constant increase in structural differences between Mexico and the United States and in each country's policies on binational flows. The binational factors can be separated into two hypotheses. First, for a variety of reasons, the immigration policy of the United States has become more and more restrictive in the last decades, making a certain percentage of migrants with international destinations switch to alternative sites inside Mexico, especially on the northern border. Second, the almost constant increase in economic differences between the two countries has made it more advantageous for U.S. industrial investment, making the border all the more attractive for migrants. Under this second hypothesis Tijuana can absorb Mexican migrants, and under the first hypothesis migrants are driven to the city. As a result of these two factors, residents of the municipality of Tijuana who were born outside Baja California (the state in which it is located) were 58 percent of the total in 1990 and 56 percent in 2000.

San Diego is also a city of immigrants. Out of the total number of residents in San Diego County, 61 percent were born outside California (the state in which it is located) in 1990 and 56 percent in 2000. The city of San Diego has always been the biggest on the U.S. border. In 1900, it had only 17,700 inhabitants, but by 2000 it had reached 2,674,436 people. Until the 1960s, its demographic growth is explained primarily by the draw of investment related to military bases and industries. Beginning in the 1970s, when military investment started to decline, the hypothesis is that its growth was based primarily on two factors: the U.S. economic cycle and the draw of new technology industries. As we saw in figure 8.1, San Diego has experienced economic growth similar to that of California and the nation, but almost always at a higher level. This higher level of growth has been a factor in attracting migrants for a number of decades. Nevertheless, this draw has been decreasing in strength over time, so that its rate of growth between population censuses in the 1990s was at its lowest level in the last seventy years. This demographic decline is associated with the reduction in the difference between San Diego's economic growth and national growth. In the 1970s, 1980s, and 1990s, San Diego's average economic growth rate was greater than the national rate by 3.2 percent, 2.9 percent, and 1.2 percent respectively (estimates of the author based on data from figure 8.1). Nevertheless, San Diego's economic restructuring that began at the beginning of the 1990s has allowed it to recover its higher growth rate in relation to the national level. Along with this change, it will also definitely return to its previous demographic growth by the end of the first decade of the twenty-first century. Between 1998 and 2002, San Diego grew at an average rate of 5.1 percent, 2.3 percent higher than the national rate during the same period.

In conclusion, San Diego's demographic growth has been due to national factors and to how it has attracted high-technology industries; the binational factor has had few effects on its economy and population. Tijuana's population, on the other hand, grows when the Mexican economy is doing badly and due to positive transborder effects, driven by the country's bad economic condition.

Away from the Transborder Metropolis

The vision of the transborder metropolis implicitly makes transborder interaction the same as integration and economic space the same as region. Said interaction connects local markets in both cities, but does not make these market transborder. The economic space of certain goods and services in Tijuana and San Diego is transborder, because a part of both cities' supply and demand comes from the other side of the border. However, the same market for a good does not operate on both sides of the border; each side has its own market for that good. As a result, the markets do not form one transborder "place"; that is to say, the two sides of the border do not form one sole binational border region. This statement is understood better by looking at an extreme example. If interaction integrated coffee's place of origin and its destination into one sole region, Chiapas (Mexico) and Las Vegas (U.S.) should be included in the same region since they share the same economic space of coffee. This would be a conceptual mistake, because it could be shown that both cities have different determinants of their structures and growth.

In particular, I will show below why the individual cities along the northern Mexican border (like Tijuana) do not form a sole metropolitan region with their neighbors in the United States (like San Diego). There are three aspects to the argument I present: urban transborder ecology, transborder markets, and local planning.

There Is No Urban Transborder Ecology

In the conceptualization of a transborder metropolis, there is a tendency toward homogenization (and integration) of both sides of the border as far as the organization of land use and its particular urbanism. This vision has at least three problematic, implicit assumptions. First, within this vision, the agents in the south are passive adopters of cultural patterns absorbed from the flow of trade and investment from the north. This vision does not take into account that Latin American cities have by definition been spaces where local and foreign characteristics have mixed since the sixteenth century. Since independence from Spain in the nineteenth century, these cities, some of them already fully developed at that time, have been exposed to European influences first and then to U.S. influences later. Despite that, Latin American cities have developed their own mestizo cultural systems. When people in these cities adopt foreign characteristics, they usually do it with a pragmatic attitude, resignifying the adopted styles and instruments in a local way. Second, Griffin and Ford (1976) noted how Tijuana was an architectural and urban mosaic for at least the previous four decades, with various architectural styles coexisting in the space—including Tudor, cottage, Spanish, modern Aztec, and so on. Globalization did not just bring these influences to the city recently. The third implicit assumption in this vision is that resources to produce this urban homogenized space are similar on both sides of the border. Paradoxically, the authors of this vision do recognize the lack of resources in many parts of Tijuana, which has allowed the creation of an urban landscape that is a pastiche of urban poverty and wealth, one quite different from San Diego.

There Are No Integrated Transborder Markets

In the framework of the transborder metropolis, urban markets span the border and thus are considered integrated. We can make a preliminary observation in regard to what this framework considers as a market. For example, when a San Diego resident buys a house in Tijuana, it is thought that the simple fact that the buyer lives north of the border makes the housing market in Tijuana binational. However, this is a mistaken idea. A market is not defined by the action of a number of buyers but rather by the entire set of rules that govern it (laws, zoning, etc.), the operational levels (cost per unit, wage levels, etc.), and the behavior of agents (elasticity of supply and demand). These three types of characteristics are specific to the place where the transaction takes place and are different in each country; thus there can be no transborder markets. When an agent from the north (let's assume a behavior similar to that of someone from the south) participates in a market in the south, the agent must do so under the rules and levels of the southern side of the border (where the transaction occurs), and these two characteristics are different from those of the north.

In any metropolis, that is to say a systematically integrated territory, a good (or service) has a sole market throughout its entire area. If there are two markets for one good, one next to another, then we are dealing with the presence of two urban regions.

If the metropolitan space can be traversed in a reasonable amount of time and with a transportation cost less than going to the neighboring city, it is possible for economic agents located on the far extremes of that space to compete for the same type of good, converging as suppliers and demanders. Due to the proximity of suppliers and demanders, there are few obstacles to the diffusion within the metropolis of information about quality, prices, and technology for production and commercialization of many goods and services. So all the metropolis's consumers and those who will eventually come from other places participate in the demand for the same type of good. Both the supply and the demand, coming mainly from the metropolitan area, determine the quantity of a good in a market. Its price depends on its production costs and the monopolistic capacity of the supply in the area (Krugman 1997).

Each market for a good participates in a particular relative price system in which, when a quantity of a good x is exchanged (expressed in pesos or dollars according to the side of the border under analysis), a similar amount of the good y is received in return in any place within the metropolis. When a type of good is commercialized in two different relative price systems (different amounts of y are received in exchange for a similar amount of x), this type of good has a particular market in each price system: there will be as many markets for a good as relative price systems in which it participates.

In general terms, a good participates in only one market when, first, it has just one price and second, supply and demand modify the activity level. However, on each side of the border there are usually different prices for a good or service and supply and demand on one side has a minimal impact on activity on the other side. First, due to the differences between Mexico and the United States in terms of technology, capital accumulation capacity, monopolistic capacity, income distribution, and regulations, one type of good or service participates in two relative price systems, one in Tijuana and the other in San Diego, and thus the good (or service) has two prices. For example, the price of labor, the hourly wage in 1998 in the manufacturing sector was $12.20 in San Diego and $1.90 in Tijuana (author's estimates made with data from Maquiladora Export Industry Statistics, INEGI, Mexico; and from Bureau of Labor Statistics 2005). Another illustrative example is the price of private professional services, like a dentist's visit (treatment for a tooth) that cost $140 in San Diego and $40 in Tijuana. Second, the influence of transborder supply and demand on the level of transborder activity is minimal. The markets on each side of the border for the same good or service act independently, and their level of mutual dependence is minimal, even in those markets where there is greater relative interaction. For example, in the labor market, within which people who reside in Tijuana and work in San Diego are called transmigrants, the demand for labor in San Diego has practically no effect on the level of tijuanense transmigration, and no sociodemographic characteristic of tijuanenses influences the supply of transmigrants. The number of transmigrants depends on the wage differences between the two cities (and both countries) and slightly on the level of unemployment in San Diego (Alegría 2002). In addition, the wage differences between the two cities do not depend on local conditions, but rather on those at the national level.

Since transborder integrated markets do not exist, there is no urban transborder region.

There Are Different Planning Problems and Practices

Due to the asymmetries present between Mexico and the United States, urban problems are different in their cities, even those on the border. The cities on the U.S. side of the border are almost entirely developed, while the Mexican border cities have deficiencies in almost every public service and in almost all types of infrastructure. The urban problems left to be resolved are dissimilar and separate, with the sole exception of those environmental problems that involve air and water basins. These problems, primarily the high level of contaminants in the air and sewage, are the only ones shared binationally by neighboring cities on the border (Alegría 2000b).

The way problems and urban needs are faced through planning is also different on both sides of the border. Urban planning on the U.S. side is focused on resolving land-use conflicts and is more oriented to people. Planning on the Mexican side is focused on continuing with incomplete land development and is more oriented to place. The way of undertaking urban planning and control is also different. Since local governments on the northern side of the border have much greater resources than the southern side, the plans are put into effect and are even enforced through court action. On the Mexican side, local governments have few resources and it is normal for land-use zoning to be disrespected and there are no means to prevent it. In addition, several city administrations have decided not to provide resources for planning and urban control, in favor of public works projects that often are not even mentioned in a master plan. An example of this is the investment in the so-called Ruta Troncal (Main Transit, a public transport system with buses with an exclusive designated lane approximately twelve miles long), which began in 2003 and for which there is no plan in the *Program of Urban Development for the Population Center of Tijuana 2002–2025* (IMPLAN 2002).

Transborder planning doesn't exist. There is no binational support institution for local governments, except those created in accord with NAFTA and which are oriented to financing public works on both sides of the border. There is also no legislation that would allow such an institution to exist. But the most important thing is that there is no will to do binational planning. There are two barriers in this respect. The first is that the planning priorities (problems to solve) are very different on each side of the border, except as it relates to environmental problems dealt with at the federal level. The second is the incompatibility of planning practices. On the Mexican side, plans are generally not followed, even when they are realistic, giving priority to political clientelist relationships in public expenditures. On the American side, local planning has separated the technical sphere from the economic one, which is what sets the course of the city (Herzog 1990a).

The few transborder attempts at facing problems of binational importance, like the Tijuana–San Diego International Airport, failed due to the following structural reasons: (1) the binational relationship was driven by federal agencies in Mexico and by the county on the U.S. side; the authorities involved did not know how to involve local authorities in Mexico and federal ones in the United States; (2) the lack of trust between agents participating in the negotiations about goals and the means for reaching agreement (Gordon and Rowland 1995); and (3) the lack of agreement on the allotment of the costs and benefits of a binational plan to each side of the border.

Final Summary

In the context of the border, integration, as evidence of the transborder metropolis, presupposes two urban structures joined into one systemic unit characterized by transitive and reciprocal connections (mutual determination). This implies, first, that both urban structures have responded in a similar fashion to external forces and, second, that both structures experience, directly or indirectly, the same external forces. If the systemic connections are established between critical sectors of both urban structures (which in San Diego are high-technology services and in Tijuana are the maquiladoras and part of the traditional tertiary sectors), integration assumes that over time there will be a structural convergence, according to the theory of regional growth. Nevertheless, Tijuana's urban structure changes for different reasons than San Diego's; critical sectors in the two cities do not have an institutional relationship; and globalization, insofar as it implies greater exposure to external forces, has different consequences in each city.

Since transborder, interurban exchanges are a result of the differences between the two countries, they cannot form the basis for a thesis of convergence at an interurban scale, because each city (on each side of the border) is tied to the markets and economic regulations of its own nation more so than to those of the neighboring country. The intense interurban interaction between Tijuana and San Diego does not produce urban convergence, because the differences between these cities depend on national conditions and not on local ones. Moreover, over time this interaction promotes divergence in growth, a divergence that concurrently maintains and increases transborder relations. There will be a transborder metropolis only when the economies of both countries are less different and the national regulations are less restrictive to transborder interaction.

Note

All BIE-INEGI figures are author estimates based on agency data: up to March 2012, http://dgcnesyp.inegi.org.mx/bdiesi/bdie.html; since March 2012, http://www.inegi.org.mx/sistemas/bie/.

References

Alegría, Tito (2002). "Demand and Supply of Mexican Cross-Border Workers." *Journal of Borderlands Studies*, Vol. 17, No. 1.

――― (2000a). *Estudio de Geografía Social*. First Report. 16 Ayuntamiento de Tijuana.

――― (2000b). "Transmigrants, the NAFTA, and a Proposal to Protect Air Quality on the Border," in L. Herzog (ed.), *Shared Space: Rethinking the U.S.-Mexico Border Environment*. Center for U.S.-Mexican Studies, University of California, San Diego.

――― (1995). "Efectos de la Industria Maquiladora en el Empleo Urbano." *Comercio Exterior*, Vol. 45, No. 10.

――― (1992). *Desarrollo Urbano en la Frontera México-Estados Unidos. Una Interpretación y Algunos Resultados*. Colección Regiones, CONACULTA, Mexico.

Anderson, Malcolm, ed. (1983). *Frontier Regions in Western Europe*. Frank Cass, Great Britain.

BIE-INEGI (2005). http://dgcnesyp.inegi.gob.mx/bdiesi/bdi.html.

Bringas, Nora, coord. (2004). *Turismo Fronterizo: Caracterización y Posibilidades de Desarrollo*. Research Report. COLEF-CESTUR-SECTUR, Tijuana.

Bureau of Labor Statistics (2005). Current Population Survey. http://data.bls.gov/PDQ/outside.jsp?survey=e.

Bustamante, Jorge (1989). "Frontera México-Estados Unidos: Reflexiones para un Marco Teórico." *Frontera Norte*, Vol. 1, No. 1.

――― (1981). "La interacción social en la frontera México-Estados Unidos: Un marco conceptual para la investigación," in Roque Gonzalez, *La frontera Norte: Integración y Desarrollo*. El Colegio de México.

Cohen, Ira (1991). "Teoría de la estructuración y *praxis* social," in Anthony Giddens et al., *La Teoría Social, Hoy*. CONACULTA and Alianza Edit, Mexico.

Coubès, Marie-Laure (2003). "Evolución del empleo fronterizo en los noventas: Efectos del TLCAN y de la devaluación sobre la estructura ocupacional." *Frontera Norte*, Vol. 15, No. 30.

Dear, M., and G. Leclerc (2003). "Introduction: The Postborder Condition. Art and Urbanism in Bajalta California," in M. J. Dear and G. Leclerc (eds.), *Postborder City: Cultural Spaces of Bajalta California*. University of Southern California.

——— (1998). "Tijuana Desenmascarada." *Wide Angle*, Vol. 20, No. 3.

Economist (1992). "The Mexican-American Border: Hi, Amigo." Vol. 325, No. 7789, December 12.

Ganster, Paul, and E. Valenciano, eds. (1992). *The Mexican-U.S. Border Region and the Free Trade Agreement*. Institute for Regional Studies of the Californias, San Diego State University, San Diego.

Gerber, James (1993). "Trends in San Diego and California," in Norris Clement and Eduardo Zepeda (eds.), *San Diego–Tijuana in Transition: A Regional Analysis*. Institute for Regional Studies of the Californias, San Diego State University, San Diego.

Gildersleeve, Charles (1978). *The International Border City: Urban Spatial Organization in a Context of Two Cultures along the United States-Mexico Boundary*. PhD diss., Department of Geography, University of Nebraska, Lincoln.

Gordon, Peter, and A. Rowland (1995). *Binational Airport Case Study: An Autopsy of the San Diego Binational Airport Proposal*. Research report. Lusk Center, SURP, USC, Los Angeles.

Griffin, Ernst, and Larry Ford (1976). "Tijuana: Landscape of a Cultural Hybrid." *Geographical Review*, Vol. 66, No. 4.

Gruben, W. (2001). "Was NAFTA behind Mexico's High Maquiladora Growth?" *Economic and Financial Review*, Third Quarter. Federal Reserve Bank of Dallas.

Habermas, Jürgen (1989). *Problemas de Legitimación en el Capitalismo Tardío*. Amorrortu Editores, Argentina.

Hansen, Niles (1981). *The Border Economy*. University of Texas Press, Austin.

Herzog, Lawrence (2003a). "The Political Economy of Tourism Development in the San Diego–Tijuana Transfrontier Metropolis," in Dennis R. Judd (ed.), *The Infrastructure of Play: Building the Tourist City*. M. E. Sharpe, New York.

——— (2003b). "Global Tijuana: The Seven Ecologies of the Border," in M. J. Dear and G. Leclerc (eds.), *Postborder City: Cultural Spaces of Bajalta California*. University of Southern California.

——— (2000). "Cross-Border Planning and Cooperation," in Paul Ganster (ed.), *The U.S.-Mexican Border Environment*. SDSU Press, San Diego.

——— (1999). *From Aztec to High Tech: Architecture and Landscape across the Mexico-United States Border*. Johns Hopkins University Press, Baltimore, Md.

——— (1997). "The Transfrontier Metropolis." *Harvard Design Magazine*, No. 1, Winter/Spring.

——— (1991). "Cross-National Urban Structure in the Era of Global Cities: The U.S.-Mexico Transfrontier Metropolis." *Urban Studies*, Vol. 28, No. 4.

——— (1990a). *Where North Meets South: Cities, Space and Politics on the U.S.-Mexico Border*. Center for Mexican American Studies, University of Texas at Austin.

——— (1990b). "Border Commuter Workers and Transfrontier Metropolitan Structure along the United States-Mexico Border." *Journal of Borderlands Studies*, Vol. 5, No. 2.

Heston, Alan, R. Summers, and B. Aten (2002). *Penn World Table Version 6.1*. Center for International Comparisons at the University of Pennsylvania, October.

Honneth, Axel (1991). "Teoría crítica," in Anthony Giddens et al., *La Teoría Social, Hoy*. CONACULTA and Alianza Edit, Mexico.

IMPLAN (2002). *Programa de Desarrollo Urbano del Centro de Población de Tijuana, 2002–2025*. Ayuntamiento de Tijuana.

INEGI (1999). *Estadísticas Históricas de México*, Vol. 1. Instituto Nacional de Estadística, Geografía e Informática, Mexico.

Kearney, Milo, and Anthony Knopp (1995). *Border Cuates: A History of the U.S.-Mexican Twin Cities*. Eakin Press, Austin, Tex.

Krugman, Paul (1997). *Development, Geography, and Economic Theory*. MIT Press, Cambridge, Mass.

Mercado, Alejandro (2004). "Dinámica de la integración y diferenciación económica regional. El caso de San Diego y Tijuana," in A. Mercado and E. Gutiérrez (eds.), *Fronteras en América del Norte*. CISEN, UNAM, Mexico.

Peach, James, and Richard Adkisson (2000). "NAFTA and Economic Activity along the US-Mexico Border." *Journal of Economic Issues*, Vol. 34, No. 2, June.

Pérez, Alejandro, and Moisés J. Schwartz (1999). *Inflación y Ciclos Económicos*. Documento de Investigación No. 9904. Dirección General de Investigación Económica, Banco de México.

Pezzoli, K., R. J. Marciano, and I. Zaslavsky (2001). "Transborder City-Regions and the Quest for Integrated Regional Planning: Challenges Posed by Disarticulated Infrastructures, Fragmented Ecologies of Knowing, and Uneven Development." Paper presented at the World Planning Schools Congress, Shanghai, China, July 11–15.

Porter, Michael (1990). *The Competitive Advantage of Nations*. Basic Books, New York.

Sahr, Robert C. (2005). *Consumer Price Index (CPI) Conversion Factors to Convert to 2004 Dollars*. Oregon State University, Corvallis, http://oregonstate.edu/Dept/pol_sci/fac/sahr/cv2004x.pdf.

SANDAG (2003). *Regional Comprehensive Plan for the San Diego Region*. Chapter 5: "Borders." Draft. December.

——— (2002). *Indicators of Sustainable Competitiveness*. San Diego Region. Final Report.

——— (2001). *San Diego Regional Employment Clusters*. Info No. 1, August.

Turner, Jonathan (1991). "Teorizar analítico," in Anthony Giddens et al., *La Teoría Social, Hoy*. CONACULTA and Alianza Edit, Mexico.

Teddy Cruz

Practices of Encroachment

Urban Waste Moves Southbound; Illegal Zoning Seeps into North

A Personal Reflection: Where Is (Architectural) Practice?

The transformation of my practice in recent years, in terms of my own interests, motivations, and procedures, has been inspired by a feeling of powerlessness, as our institutions of architecture, representation, and display have lost their sociopolitical relevance and advocacy. I have been increasingly disappointed at the futility of our design fields, in the context of pressing sociopolitical realities worldwide, the conditions of conflict that are currently redefining the territory of intervention. It's been unsettling to witness some of the most "cutting-edge" practitioners of architecture rush unconditionally to China and the Arab Emirates to build their dream castles, in the process reducing themselves to mere caricatures of change, camouflaging gentrification with a massive hyperaesthetic and formalist project. I certainly hope that in the context of this euphoria for the Dubais of the world and the seemingly limitless horizon of possibilities inspired by a sense of dissatisfaction, a feeling of "pessimistic optimism" remains that can provoke us, head on, to also address the sites of conflict that define and will continue to define cities in the twenty-first century.

While international urban development in major urban centers has defined the economic and political recipes that architecture practice decorates, new experimental practices of intervention in the collective territory and the territory of collaboration will emerge from zones of conflict, the margins. It is in the periphery that conditions of social emergency are transforming our ways of thinking about urban matters and the matters of concern about the city. The radicalization of the local in order to generate new readings of the global will transform the neighborhood—not the city—into the urban laboratory of our time. In this context, the task of architecture practice should be not only to reveal ignored sociopolitical and economic territorial histories and injustice within our currently ideologically polarized world, but also to generate new forms of sociability and activism.

The future of architectural practice depends on the redefinition of the formal and the social, the economic and the political, understanding that environmental degradation is a direct result of social and political degradation. No advances in urban planning can be made without redefining what we mean by infrastructure, density, mixed use, and affordability. No advances in housing design, for example, can be made without advances in housing policy and economic subsidies. As architects, we can be responsible for imagining counterspatial procedures, political and economic structures that can produce new modes of sociability and encounter. Without altering the backward exclusionary policies constructing the territory—the sociopolitical ground—our profession will continue to be subordinated to the visionless environments defined by the bottom-line urbanism of the developer's spreadsheet.

I am interested in a practice of intervention that engages the spatial, territorial, and environmental conditions across critical thresholds, whether global border zones or the local sectors of conflict generated by discriminating politics of zoning and economic development in the contemporary city. This suggests operational urban practices that encroach into the privatization of public domain and infrastructure, the rigidity of institutional thinking, and the current obsession with an ownership society. This also opens the idea that architects, besides being designers of form, can be designers of political process, pro forma economic models, and collaboration across institutions and jurisdictions.

Architecture practice needs to engage the reorganization of systems of urban development, challenging the political and economic frameworks that are only benefiting homogenous, large-scale interventions managed by private megablock development. Instead, I believe the future is small, and this implies the dismantling of the LARGE by pixilating it with the micro: an urbanism of retrofit. No intervention into the public domain can begin without first exposing political jurisdiction and conditions of ownership. Clearly, this points out the pressing need for architecture practice to reengage the invisible forces and vectors of power that shape the territory. This is the main topic of conversation and exchange that needs to take place across disciplines, but not from the isolation of the classroom or the design studio.

Moving from these broad conceptual meditations into the specificity of the San Diego–Tijuana border, one oscillates back and forth between two radically different ways of constructing city. At no other international juncture in the world one can find some of the most expensive real state, like that found in the edges of San Diego's sprawl, barely twenty minutes away from some of the poorest settlements in Latin America, manifested by the many slums that dot the new periphery of Tijuana. These two different types of suburbia are emblematic of the incremental division of the contemporary city and the territory between enclaves of megawealth and the rings of poverty that surround them. I am interested in processes of mediation that can produce critical interfaces between and across these opposites, exposing conflict as an operational device to transform architectural practice. The critical observation of this locality transforms this border region into a laboratory from which to reflect on the current politics of migration, labor, and surveillance, the tensions between sprawl and density, formal and informal urbanisms, wealth and poverty, all of which incrementally is characterizing the contemporary city everywhere.

Radicalizing the Local:
Sixty Miles of Transborder Urban Conflict

A newly reconstituted global border between the first and third worlds is reemerging as societies of overproduction and excess are barricading themselves in an unprecedented way against the sectors of scarcity produced out of political and economic indifference. The border zones along this post 9/11 "political equator" are the sites where the forces of division and control produced by these global zones of conflict are amplified and physically inscribed and manifested in the territory, producing, in turn, local zones of conflict.

The international border between the United States and Mexico at the San Diego–Tijuana checkpoint is the most trafficked in the world. Approximately sixty million people cross annually, moving untold amounts of goods and services back and forth. A sixty-linear-mile cross-section, tangential to the border wall, between these two border cities compresses the most dramatic issues currently challenging our normative notions of architecture and urbanism. This transborder cut begins thirty miles north of the border, in the periphery of San Diego, and ends thirty miles south of the border. We can find along this section's trajectory a series of collisions, critical junctures, or conflicts between natural and artificial ecologies, top-down development, and bottom-up organization.

+30 miles/San Diego. Ironically, the only interruptions along an otherwise continuous sprawl, thirty miles inland from the border, occur as the military bases that dot San Diego's suburbanization overlap with environmentally protected lands. This produces a strange montage of housing subdivisions, natural ecology, and militarization. The conflict between military bases and environmental zones has been recently dramatized as Fallujah-like mock villages, equipped with hologram technologies to project Arab subjects, are now being erected here as vernacular military training sites.

+25 miles. Large freeway and mall infrastructure runs the length of coastal San Diego, colliding with a natural network of canyons, rivers, and creeks that descend toward the Pacific Ocean. A necklace of territorial voids is produced out of the conflict between large infrastructure and the watershed. As the politics of water will define the future of this region, the recuperation of these truncated natural resources is essential to anticipate density.

+20 miles. Top-down private development has been installing a selfish and oil-hungry sprawl of detached McMansions everywhere. The conflict between master-planned gated communities and the natural topography flattens the differential landscape of San Diego's edges and encroaches into the natural cycles of fire-prone areas. This archipelago of beige tract homes also exacerbates a land use of exclusion into a sort of apartheid of everyday life.

+15 miles. San Diego's downtown has reconfigured itself with exclusive tax-revenue, redevelopment powers, becoming an island of wealth, delimited by specific zoning and budgetary borders. Luxury condos and hotels, stadiums and convention centers, surrounded by generic commercial franchises compose this stew of privatization from New York to San Diego. The proximity of wealth and poverty found at the border checkpoint is reproduced here into the conflict between powerful downtowns and the neighborhoods of marginalization that surround them. It is in these neighborhoods where cheap immigrant labor concentrates, conveniently becoming the service sector that supports downtown's massive project of gentrification.

+10 miles. The conflict between the formal and the informal emerges as immigrants fill the first ring of suburbanization surrounding downtown, retrofitting an obsolete urbanism of older postwar detached bungalows. Informal densities and economies produce a sort of three-dimensional land use that collides with the one-dimensional zoning that has characterized these older neighborhoods.

0 miles. At the border itself, the metal fence becomes emblematic of the conflict between these two border cities, reenacting the perennial alliance between militarization and urbanization. This territorial conflict is currently dramatized by the hardening of the post-9/11 border wall that divides this region, incrementally transforming San Diego into the world's largest gated community. As we cross the border into Mexico, the first sight we witness is how the large infrastructure of the Tijuana River clashes with the border wall. This is the only place where an otherwise continuous metal fence is

pierced and opened as the river enters San Diego. A faint yellow line is inscribed on the dry river's concrete channel to indicate the trajectory of the border. But as the channel moves beyond the fence and into San Diego's territory the concrete disappears, becoming the Tijuana River Estuary U.S. ecological reserve, which frames the natural ecology of the river as it flows freely toward the Pacific Ocean. What dramatizes this conflict between the natural and the political is the fact that the border checkpoint is exactly the intersection of both, punctuating the environmentally protected zone with a matrix of border patrol vehicles, helicopters, and electrified fences.

—10 miles/Tijuana. Many of the sites of conflict found in San Diego are reproduced and amplified in Tijuana. As Tijuana grows eastward, for example, it is seduced by the style and glamour of the master-planned, gated communities of the United States, and builds its own version—miniaturized replicas of typical suburban Southern California tract homes, paradoxically imported into Tijuana to provide "social housing." Thousands of tiny tract homes are now scattered around the periphery of Tijuana, creating a vast landscape of homogeneity and division that is at odds with this city's prevailing heterogeneous and organic metropolitan condition. These diminutive 250-square-foot dwellings come equipped with all the clichés and conventions: manicured landscaping, gate houses, model units, banners and flags, mini-setbacks, front and back yards.

—15 miles. The conflict between the formal and the informal is reenacted here, as these mini–tract homes quickly submit to transformation by occupants who are little hindered by permissive zoning regulations. While the gated communities of Southern California remain closed systems due to stringent zoning that prohibits any kind of formal alteration or programmatic juxtaposition, these housing tracts in Tijuana are dramatically altered by their occupants—filling in setbacks, occupying front and back yards as well as garages with more construction to support mixed use and more usable space.

—20 miles. These American-style, mini-master-planned communities are intertwined with a series of informal communities or slums, and both surround maquiladora (NAFTA assembly factory) enclaves. The conflict between cheap labor and emergency housing is produced here as these factories extract cheap labor from these slums without providing any support for dwelling. As these favela-like sectors grow out of proportion, they also encroach into the natural ecology of Tijuana's delicate topography, reenacting also the conflict between the informal and the natural.

—30 miles. And then, as we reach the sea on the Mexican side, we witness the most dramatic of all territorial collisions across this sixty-mile section of local conflict. After traveling many miles across the border territory, the border metal fence finally sinks into the Pacific Ocean, producing a surreal sight that further amplifies the clash between the natural and the jurisdictional.

It is in the midst of many of these metropolitan and territorial sites of conflict that contemporary architectural practice needs to reposition itself. In other words, no meaningful intervention can occur in the contemporary city, without first exposing the conditions, the political and economic forces (jurisdiction and ownership), that have produced these collisions in the first place.

Cross-Border Suburbias: Urbanisms of Transgression

When Kevin Lynch was commissioned by a local environmental group to come up with a "regional vision plan" for the U.S.-Mexico border zone in 1974, he dreamed of a "Temporary Paradise." Addressed to the City Planning Commission of San Diego, his binational planning strategy focused on the network of canyons and watersheds that traverse the landscape on both sides of the San Diego–Tijuana border. Lynch could never have predicted that neither the natural landscape nor city planners would define the real action plan for transborder urbanism, and that instead it would be an emergent network of underground tunnels masterminded by drug lords and "coyotes" that would quietly and invisibly efface the formidable barrier that separates the two cities. Now, thirty-four years later, at least thirty tunnels have been discovered, a vast ant farm–like maze of subterranean routes criss-crossing the border from California to Arizona—all dug within the last eight years. At the very least, this creates a "Permanent Hell" for the U.S. Department of Homeland Security.

An archaeological section map of the territory today would reveal an underground urbanism worming its way into houses, churches, parking lots, warehouses, and streets. The most outlandish and sophisticated of these tunnels, discovered by U.S. border officials in January 2010, is clearly the work of professionals: up to seventy feet below ground and 2,400 feet in length, its passageways are five to six feet high and four feet wide to permit two-way circulation. Striking not only for its scale but also for its "amenities," the tunnel is equipped with ventilation and drainage systems, water pumps, electricity, retaining reinforcements, and stairs connecting various levels. Beyond its use by drug traffickers, it was also "leased out" during off hours to coyotes transporting illegal aliens into the United States, making it perhaps the first mixed-use smuggling tunnel at the border. Some might see this as a marvel of informal transnational infrastructure, but most locals understand it as just another example of the vigorous Mexican-American economy at work.

Beyond the sensationalism that might accompany these images, it is the undeniable presence of an informal economy and the politics of density that surround it that is exposed here. As we insert the actual location of these illegal tunnels into an existing official border map, a different image of the borderline appears. The linear rigidity of the artificial geopolitical boundary, which has "flatlined" the pulsations of the living complexity of the natural, is transformed back into a complex set of porous lines perpendicular to the border, as if they were small leakages that began to percolate through a powerful dam. As these lines puncture the borderline in our fictional cartography, they almost restore the primacy of the network of existing canyons, juxtaposing the natural with the socioeconomic flows that continue to be "under the radar" in our official modes of urban planning representation.

By zooming further into the particularities of this volatile territory, traveling back and forth between these two border cities, we can expose many other landscapes of contradiction where conditions of difference and sameness collide and overlap. A series of off-the-radar two-way border crossings—north-south and south-north across the border wall—suggest that no matter how high and long the post-9/11 border wall becomes, it will always be transcended by migrating populations and the relentless flows of goods and services back and forth across the formidable barrier that seeks to preclude them. These illegal flows are physically manifested, in one direction, by the informal land-use patterns and economies produced by migrant workers flowing from Tijuana and into San Diego, searching for the strong economy of Southern California. But while "human flow" mobilizes northbound in search of dollars, "infrastructural waste" moves in the opposite direction to construct an insurgent, cross-border urbanism of emergency.

South to North: Suburbs Made of Nonconformity—Tijuana's Encroachment into San Diego's Sprawl

Millions of migrants have flowed toward the north in the last decades, searching for one of the strongest economies in the world, the state of California, with the assurance that such economic power still depends on the cheap labor only provided by them—a demand-and-supply logic. As the Latin American diaspora travels northbound, it inevitably alters and transforms the fabric of San Diego's subdivisions. Immigrants bring with them diverse sociocultural attitudes and sensibilities regarding the use of domestic and public space as well as the natural landscape. In these neighborhoods, multigenerational households of extended families shape their own programs of use, taking charge of their own microeconomies in order to maintain a standard for the household, generating nonconforming uses and high densities that reshape the fabric of the residential neighborhoods where they settle. Alternative social spaces begin to spring up in large parking lots; informal economies such as flea markets and street vendors appear in vacant properties; and housing additions in the shape of illegal companion units are plugged into existing suburban dwellings to provide affordable living.

The areas of San Diego that have been most impacted by this nonconforming urbanism are concentrated in its first ring of suburbanization. At a moment when developers and city officials are still focusing on two main areas of development—the redevelopment of downtown with an expensive project of gentrification, on one end, and the increasingly expansive project of sprawl made of an equally high-priced real estate project and supported by oil-hungry infrastructure, on the other—it is the older neighborhoods of San Diego's midcity that remain depressed and ignored. It is here in the first ring of suburbanization where immigrants have been settling in recent years, unable to afford the high rents of downtown's luxury condos and the expensive McMansions of the new suburbs, while conveniently becoming the cheap-labor service providers to both. Fifty years ago, these older neighborhoods in the midcity did not look that much different from the new rings of suburbanization of today. The older subdivisions were also following a Levittown recipe, made of homogeneity and standardization, similar to the master-planned gated communities now being built. But while the logic behind this urbanism of sameness continues to be reproduced today, it is the scale of sprawl that has changed. In other words, as the new rings of suburbanization require a version of Levittown on steroids, the midcity's small scale has made these older neighborhoods obsolete, as its postwar bungalows are not able to accommodate the current super-size-me housing market. This obsolescence has produced a void that has begun to be filled by the temporal, informal economies and patterns of density promoted by immigrants, fundamentally altering the homogeneity of this first ring of Levittown-type suburbanization into a more complex network of socioeconomic relationships.

The shifting of cultural demographics in the midcity has transformed many of these neighborhoods into the site of investigation for my practice, as the main inspiration of my research has focused on the impact of immigration in the transformation of the American neighborhood. The critical observation of the mutation of these older bedroom communities, from rigid, monocultural, and one-dimensional environments into informal, multicultural, and cross-programmed communities, opens the question: how do we anticipate density? It might be that the future of Southern California urbanism will be determined by tactics of retrofit and adaptation, making the large small.

One of the most emblematic examples of the retrofitting of Levittown is the "nonconforming Buddha." Incrementally, throughout the last twenty years, a tiny postwar bungalow in the midcity neighborhood of City Heights in San Diego has been transformed from a single-family residence into a Buddhist temple. The small decorative lawn that filled the front yard has been hardened into a fake, shiny marble plinth that serves as an altar for a huge, white statue of Buddha that encroaches illegally into the front setback. The driveway has become a dining room leading into the main interior altar, meditation space, and community room. The old setbacks that defined the separation of this house from its neighbor have now been filled with small sheds to accommodate other programs related to the temple. From far away, though, and framed by the narrow street it occupies, this small bungalow resembles another typical house. It is not the typological and spatial transformations of this small house that are really interesting here, but the fact that this house has now become a social agency inside the neighborhood, facilitating social relations, pedagogical programs, cultural support, and economic exchanges. The idea that one unit of dwelling has become a multifaceted social agency suggests that our normative idea of density needs to be questioned.

Beyond Density (as an Amount of Units per Acre)

Our institutions of representation across government, academia, and development have not been able to critically observe and translate the logic of the informal socioeconomic dynamics at play not only at the border itself, but within the city at large. The official documentation of land use at any city agency, whether in San Diego or Tijuana for example, has systematically ignored the nonconforming and self-organizing dynamics of these environments by continuing to advocate a false, bidimensional land-use convention based on abstract information rendered at the planners' table, whereby retail is represented with red and housing yellow, safely located adjacent to one another in the best of scenarios, since they are typically very far apart.

If, on the other hand, one were to map the real land use in some of the San Diego neighborhoods that have been impacted in the last decades by waves of immigration from Latin America, Africa, and Asia, examining them parcel by parcel, block by block, what would emerge is a land-use map with at least ten or more zone colors, reflecting the gradation of use and scale of the diverse social composition and nonconforming small businesses and social exchanges that characterize these culturally intensive areas of the city. We would also find a three-dimensional zoning based not on adjacencies but on juxtapositions, as dormant infrastructures are transformed into usable semipublic spaces and larger-than-"needed" parcels are illegally subdivided to accommodate extra dwelling units. In other words, the appropriation and negotiation of public and private boundaries remains anathema for conventional code regulation, ignoring the potentialities that this stealth urbanism can open. How to alter our conventions of representation in order to absorb the ambiguity of these forces remains the essential question in the negotiation between the formal and the informal city.

Similar to the cartography of cross-border illegal tunnels, then, an accurate binational land-use map does not currently exist. If we were to cut and paste the existing land-use documents from Tijuana and San Diego, a borderline—without marking the border wall itself—would again appear between the two cities as the larger land-use chunks of San Diego come side by side with the smaller pixilation of Tijuana's land-use map—two different ways of administering density and mixed uses, barely twenty minutes apart. A fictional cartography of this "collision" would invite one to speculate on an alternative way of representing the transformation of some of the San Diego neighborhoods impacted by informal patterns of development: this new land-use map would show the greater pixilation of Tijuana's three-dimensional and multicolor zoning crossing the borderline and slipping into San Diego. The "stains" of this greater pixilation are deposited in many of these older neighborhoods, beginning to form an archipelago of pockets of difference within the sea of the current homogeneous sprawl that defines this city.

What this phenomenon points out, then, is the fact that our institutions of representation are also unable to mediate the multiple forces that shape the politics of the territory and resolve the tensions between the top-down urban strategies of official development and the bottom-up tactics of community activism. The micro-heterotopias that are emerging within small communities in the form of informal spatial and entrepreneurial practices are defining a different idea of density and land use. Making visible the invisibility of these nonconforming forces and their operational potential to bridge the formal and the informal, the wealthy subdivisions and the enclaves of poverty (service communities) in the city, would be the only point of departure to construct a different idea of density and sustainability. We need to engage new conceptual and representational tools that can allow us to transcend the reductive understanding of density as an abstract amount of units or inhabitants per acre, and instead reaffirm it as an amount of "social interactions and economic exchanges" per acre.

North to South: Suburbs Made of Waste—San Diego's Levittown Is Recycled into Tijuana's Slums

While migrants go north, the waste of San Diego flows southbound to construct an urbanism of emergency. This is how one of the most dramatic and "unnoticed" urban flows across the Tijuana–San Diego border consists of the amount of urban waste that is transferred from San Diego into Tijuana. This phenomenon occurs as sections of San Diego's older suburbs begin to erode, so that developers can install a new recipe of development, while a few miles south, in Tijuana, new informal suburbs or slums spring up from one day to another.

In addition to immigrants retrofitting a large section of San Diego's midcity, other parts of San Diego's first ring of suburbanization have been replaced by larger versions of themselves. As new and large McMansion subdivisions update these older suburbs in San Diego, the first ring of suburbanization has been dismantled, piece by piece, in the last years (small bungalows are being dismembered and their pieces given away to speculators). This is how Southern California Levittown's debris is recycled to build the new periphery of Tijuana.

The leftover parts of San Diego's older subdivisions, standard framing, joists, connectors, plywood, aluminum windows, garage doors, are being disassembled and recombined on the other side, across the border. Once in Tijuana's edges, out of social emergency and housing shortage, these parts are reassembled into fresh scenarios, creating a housing urbanism of waste. But not only small, scattered debris is imported into Tijuana. Entire pieces of one city travel southward as residential ready-mades are directly plugged into the other's fabric. This process begins when a Tijuana speculator travels to San Diego to buy up little postwar bungalows that have been slated for demolition. The little houses are loaded onto trailers and prepared to travel to Tijuana, where they will have to clear customs before making their journey south. For days, one can see houses, just like cars and pedestrians, waiting in line to cross the border. Finally the houses enter Tijuana and are mounted on top of one-story metal frames, leaving an empty space at the street level to accommodate future uses. These floating houses define a space of opportunity beneath them, which will be filled, through time, with more house, a taco stand, a car repair shop, a garden. One city profits from the dwellings that the other one discards, recombining them into fresh scenarios, creating countless new possibilities. This is how the border cities enact a strange mirroring effect. While the seemingly permanent housing stock in San Diego becomes disposable from one day to another, the ephemeral dwellings in Tijuana want to become permanent.

So, as one city recycles the leftovers of the other into a sort of secondhand urbanism, Tijuana's informal settlements are shaped by these cross-border recycling dynamics and by organizational tactics of invasion, allowing settlers to claim underutilized territory. While San Diego's vast sprawl is incrementally made of gigantic infrastructure to support loosely scattered units of housing, in Tijuana's edges, dense inhabitation happens first so that incremental small infrastructure can follow.

This temporal, nomadic urbanism is supported by a very sophisticated social choreography of neighborhood participation. Hundreds of dwellers called *paracaidistas* (parachuters) invade, en masse, large public (sometimes private) vacant properties. As these urban guerrillas parachute into the hills of Tijuana's edges, they are organized and choreographed by what are commonly called "urban pirates." These characters, armed with cellular phones, are the community activists (or land speculators) who are in charge of organizing the first deployment of people at the sites as well as the community in an effort to begin the process of requesting services from the city. Through improvisational tactics of construction and distribution of goods and ad hoc services, a process of assembly begins by recycling the systems and materials from San Diego's urban debris. Garage doors are used to make walls (entire houses are made with garage doors as the main structural and exterior skin); rubber tires are cut and dismantled into folded loops, clipped and interlocked, creating a system that threads a stable retaining wall; wooden crates make the armature for other imported surfaces, such as recycled refrigerator doors, and so on. After months of construction and community organization, the neighborhood begins to request municipal services. The city sends trucks to deliver water at certain locations and electricity follows as the city sends one official line, expecting the community to "steal" the rest via a series of illegal clippings called *diablitos* (little devils). These sites are threaded by the temporal stitching of these multiple situations, internal and external, simultaneously, making the interiors of these dwellings become their exteriors, expressive of the history of their pragmatic evolution. As one anonymous resident put it: "Not everything that we have is to our liking, but everything is useful."

Ultimately, this intensive recycling urbanism of juxtaposition is emblematic of how Tijuana's informal communities are growing faster than the urban cores they surround, creating a different set of rules for development and blurring the distinctions between the urban, the suburban, and the rural. As notions of the informal are brought back, recycled by the fields of architecture and urbanism in debating the growth of the contemporary city, let's hope that it is not only the figural "image" of the ephemeral and nomadic that is once more seducing our imagination, but the complex temporal, evolutionary processes beneath them, whose essence is grounded on sociopolitical and economic dynamics.

Epilogue: Returning Duchamp's Urinal to the Bathroom

One of the most important issues underlying my research has been to produce new conceptions and interpretations of the informal, on both sides of the border. We continue to be seduced by the "style" of the informal, without translating its actual operative procedures. Instead of a fixed image, I see the informal as a functional set of urban operations that allows the transgression of imposed political boundaries and top-down economic models. I see the informal not as a noun but as a verb, which detonates traditional notions of site specificity and context into a more complex system of hidden socioeconomic exchanges. I see the informal as the urban unwanted, that which is left over after the pristine presence of Architecture with capital A has been usurped and transformed into the tenuous scaffold for social encounter. I see the informal as the site of a new interpretation of community, citizenship, and praxis, where emergent urban configurations produced out of social emergency suggest the performatic role of individuals constructing their own spaces.

But the social capital and cultural economy embedded within these marginal communities and border neighborhoods that have been the site of investigation for our practice are never included in the "official" process of urbanization and economic development. Community engagement in the theater of city redevelopment in the United States is always reduced to a symbolic gesture that transforms social participation into a "multiple-choice questionnaire" for community revitalization, a process that is ultimately co-opted by the politics of identity—in what style should we build? This is how at a time when the institutions of urban planning need to be redefined, one particular topic that needs to be considered is the value of social capital (people's participation) in urban development, enhancing the role of communities in producing housing. Housing configurations that enable the development and emergence of local economies and new forms of sociability allow neighborhoods to generate new markets from the bottom up, within the community (i.e., social and economic entrepreneurial efforts that are usually off the radar of conventional top-down economic recipes), as well as to promote new models of financing to allow unconventional mixed uses. Also, one pressing challenge in our time, primarily when the paradigm of private property has become unsustainable in conditions of poverty, is the need to rethink existing conditions of property ownership. Redefining affordability by amplifying the value of social participation: more than "owning" units, dwellers, in collaboration with community-based, nonprofit agencies, can also co-own the economic and social infrastructure around them.

But often there is a gap between the institutions of community development and the actual lived reality of these entrepreneurial energies that is seldom mobilized by top-down institutions of zoning and lending. In fact, these communities often lack the conceptual devices to understand their own everyday procedures and how their neighborhood agency can trickle up to produce new institutional transformations, shaping alternative politics and economies at the scale of their own everyday needs.

It is here where a different notion of empowerment emerges, which has less to do with the symbolic representation of people by which architectural or artistic social practices only deploy the symbolic image of the community and not its operative dimension. Empowerment here signifies an act of translation and political representation at the scale of neighborhoods: the visualization of Citizenship. These communities' invisible urban praxis needs interpretation and representation and this is the space of intervention that we are interested in occupying as architects, to design the conditions that can mobilize this activism into new spatial and economic infrastructures that benefit these communities of practice in the long term, beyond the short-term problem solving of private developers or the institutions of charity. To act as facilitators of this bottom-up intelligence means translating the ethical knowledge specific to a community into new communicational systems, radical urban pedagogy, and micropolitical and economic armatures, in essence, an urbanism at the scale of the neighborhood, and a community as political and economic unit.

Finally, in these times of crisis, empowerment also means to produce an expanded notion of practice, new ways of constructing information and conversation among ourselves, the so-called experts. We are responsible for problematizing the debate, mediating across these stakeholders and the compartmentalization of our own fields and institutions of artistic display and production. We need a critical recontextualizing of our different approaches and procedures. The transborder urban flows that have been the laboratory for my practice are the backdrop for the need to transcend our reductive and limited ways of working, by which we continue seeing the world as a tabula rasa on which to install the autonomy of architecture. Today, it is essential to reorient our gaze toward the drama embedded in the reality of the everyday and in so doing engage the shifting sociopolitical and economic domains that have been ungraspable by design. Or as artist Tania Bruguera said to me recently: It is time to restore Duchamp's urinal to the bathroom! This suggests a more functional relationship between research, artistic intervention, and the production of the city.

Community of Struggle

Gender, Violence, and Resistance on the U.S.-Mexico Border

Over the last forty years, the U.S.-Mexico border region has wit-nessed profound economic and political shifts because of the im-plementation of both national and international agreements. One result has been an increase of migration not only to the United States, but also to northern Mexico, creating a massive need for housing, health care, and education. Because of the intersecting power struc-tures of capitalism, patriarchy, and racialization (Segura and Zavella 2007), Mexican border cities have failed to meet these needs, and in-stead local residents are forced to create for themselves what the state cannot, or will not, provide. This chapter examines one community, Maclovio Rojas, located between the cities of Tijuana and Tecate in Baja California, through the oral narratives of women residents and organizers. Communities such as Maclovio Rojas that have emerged under similar circumstances are also called *colonias* and are often described as urban popular movements (UPMs). By situating women activists at the center of analysis, the case of Maclovio Rojas offers insight into the ways in which gendered state and domestic violence are negotiated and challenged at the U.S.-Mexico border.

Significantly, in their struggle for land, Maclovianas have devel-oped an oppositional consciousness (Sandoval 2000) that is simulta-neously directed both toward the neoliberal state and at unequal inter-personal relationships shaped by patriarchal practices that condone violence. I say neoliberal state because, as Fregoso (2007, 52) has ar-gued, "the Mexican state is complicit with globalization through its neoliberal economic policies and disinvestments in the public sphere," which have created the conditions for what Segura and Zavella (2007) have called "structural violence" at the border. In the face of this, these women have not only fought for a piece of land to build their modest homes, but they have learned to weave in between the "safe" spaces they have created for themselves. These *mujeres fronterizas*, or border women, demonstrate that through a commitment to collective action, they have the ability to radically change their lives.

In analyzing the narratives of women from Maclovio Rojas, I want to underscore two points. First, while there is an increasing amount of literature on border activism (Coronado 2006; Dolhinow 2006; D. Pena 1997; M. Pena 2007; Sadowski-Smith 2002; Staudt and Coronado 2002), gender and social movements (Einwohner, Hollander, and Olsen 2000; Ferree and Roth 1998; Safa 1990; Taylor 1999), and domestic violence (Bush 1992; Fine 1989), these are usually treated as separate subjects of analysis. In contrast, this chapter integrates these areas of study to address the complicated realities that these gendered, class-based, and racialized experiences entail, and to learn how women activists are developing tools for transformation through an emerging political consciousness.

Second, I highlight the physical U.S.-Mexico border as a site for change and agency—not merely as a site of passage. Much of the literature on transnationalism examines either the spaces created through transnational migration (Smith and Guarnizo 1998) or the important and necessary coalitions that are built across borders (Bandy and Smith 2005; Brooks 2007), including transnational feminist networks (Moghadam 2001). Border scholars Ortiz-Gonzalez (2004) and Lugo (2000) ask us to consider the border not simply as a transit zone but as a place of residence for millions of people. By positioning the border in this way, I am also building on the work of Ibarra (2007), who locates the border not just as a site for "leaving and arriving" but also includes within this site the lived experience and agency of these migrant women through the narratives of Mexicana border crossers. The unique sociopolitical experience of the border region creates the necessary conditions for the emergence of a woman-centered subjectivity that incites action. In this chapter I demonstrate that the border region is a space where transformative politics can take place.

Gender, Social Movements, and the Sociopolitical Location of La Frontera

Pivotal to situating my work in Maclovio Rojas is the literature on women's roles in social movements in Latin America and U.S.-based Chicana/Latina activism.[1] This literature points to the tension women experience as they negotiate the public and private spheres. For example, Bennett (1992) has demonstrated in her work on UPMs in Mexico that historically no sector of the population has been more affected by the evolution of UPMs than women.

She argues that because UPMs address issues such as housing, services, and the high cost of living—traditionally the domain of the mother-wife-housewife—women constitute the majority of participants of many UPMs. Yet although they have become "vociferous and demanding" (Bennett 1992, 256), women continue to battle sexism within the UPMs (Valenzuela-Arce 1991).

Such have been the findings of Aguilar and Chenard (1994), whose research on women in Cuba after the revolution demonstrated that women have achieved power in the public domain but not in the private. They attribute this to machismo, which they state is "a residue of a repressive macho culture which has been dragged along since colonization. The culture which grew out of this, the perceptions about men's and women's roles are still very deeply rooted" (Aguilar and Chenard 1994, 107).

Still other research has underscored the ways in which women activists are redefining public and private roles. For example, Safa (1990) found that Latin American women think their roles as wives and mothers legitimize their sense of injustice and outrage; thus they are transforming their domestic role from one of private nurturance to one of collective, public protest. In this way, they challenge the traditional seclusion of women in the private sphere of the family. Similarly, in Mary Pardo's (1998) study of Mexican American women activists in Los Angeles, she found that women's political activism was directly related to their roles as mothers and their other familial obligations. She states, "In both communities women employed gender identity to legitimate their community involvement. The fact that they used a traditional private role such as motherhood to frame new activity that is public and political deserves scrutiny. They validated their community activism by making it an extension of the traditional work they already do. This allowed them to become involved without jeopardizing traditional domestic arrangements" (161).

Pardo argues that the idea that politics is a public activity separate from the domestic or private sphere is a male-biased viewpoint. Political participation not only crosses boundaries between the public and private spheres but also relies on the relationship between the two. The research of both Stephen (1997) and Corcoran-Nantes (2003) also highlights the ways women's activism needs to be analyzed through a unity of experience and not a public/private dichotomy. Corcoran-Nantes states, "In Brazil, as in many other Latin American countries, women have created a political role for themselves based on their social status as wives and mothers but through which they have struggled for recognition of their roles and rights as workers, residents, and citizens" (2003, 127).

A useful way to characterize the contested terrain of the domestic and public spheres in women's activism is shown in the work of Diaz-Barriga (1998). He applies the borderlands concept to emphasize how, through a variety of strategies, women activists blur the distinction between the domestic and public spheres and simultaneously identify practical and gender needs. Borrowing from both Renato Rosaldo (1993) and Gloria Anzaldúa (1987), theorists who highlight the creative ways social actors navigate the intersections of social experience, Diaz-Barriga underscores how women's involvement defies dichotomous representations of domestic and public life.

Drawing on this literature, and using the borderlands concept, I emphasize that while the literature problematizes dichotomous understandings of the public and private sphere, researchers point to women's experiences as mothers and wives as informing the roles they take on as public activists. For example, in Dolhinow's (2006) study of colonias in New Mexico, she found that women who emerge as leaders are either single or in "unusually" egalitarian relationships. Yet what I found in Maclovio Rojas is that the point of departure for women activists is not the nature of interpersonal relations found within the home. Through their political and personal relationships with other women leaders in the community, their consciousness develops and they respond in ways that are true to their newfound sense of self. The spaces of women's collective struggle in Maclovio Rojas are not contained in either the public or private sphere. Rather, in this chapter I demonstrate that women's activism challenges traditional gender ideas in both spheres simultaneously.

The borderlands concept highlights how Maclovianas, through their bridging of experiences as land settlers, activists, wives, and mothers, are transforming social relations and perhaps cultural meanings as well. I also build on this concept to show how interpersonal violence is challenged in the lives of activist women. Specifically, the narratives of Maclovianas speak to the emergence of a political subjectivity that identifies the ability to act. This new subjectivity, similar to Sandoval's notion of tactical subjectivity that posits the capacity to "de- and recenter, given the forms of power to be moved" (2000, 59), allows Maclovianas to simultaneously defy the state, transnational companies, and their experiences of subjugation within the home. This analysis of the lived experiences of mujeres fronterizeras illuminates how collective struggles on the border not only work to undo the dichotomous nature of women's public and private roles, but also make evident the border as a transformative space that becomes the site where women come together to reimagine and redefine gendered, class-based, and racialized social structures.

Background: Urban Popular Movements and Maclovio Rojas

In 1961, the Mexican government launched the Programa Nacional Fronter- izo (PRONAF), or National Border Program. The program aimed to beautify border towns, build up their tourist infrastructure, and create favorable con- ditions for industrialization in the border region. The Border Industrializa- tion Program (BIP), an outgrowth of PRONAF, established the border zone corridor of export-processing industries known as maquiladoras in 1965 (Herzog 1990; Lorey 1999; Nevins 2002). Maquiladoras were the only firms exempt from Mexican law requiring majority Mexican ownership (Lorey 1999). The BIP also helped to fuel significant migration to border cities from other parts of Mexico. In a forty-year period, between 1950 and 1990, the pop- ulation of Mexican border states multiplied 3.6 times (Lorey 1999). Imple- mented in 1994, the North American Free Trade Agreement (NAFTA) and the growing liberalization of the Mexican economy also facilitated a significant exodus from Mexico's countryside. From 1980 to 1990, for example, the amount of the country's population living in rural areas declined from 36 per- cent to 28 percent (Nevins 2002). In Tijuana, the population grew by 70.5 percent to reach a total of 1,274,240 people in 2000 (Kopinak 2003).

Despite the rhetoric of a borderless global society, the border has become starker in this neoliberal context, which can be seen in strategies such as Operation Gatekeeper in San Diego and Operation Hold the Line in Texas. Migrants who intend to cross the border end up staying in border cities such as Tijuana. Furthermore, despite poor labor conditions, most of these mi- grant workers have little option but to seek employment in the maquiladoras run by transnational companies. Mexican border cities lack the necessary infrastructure to meet the housing, health care, and educational needs of the growing population of workers. Irasema Coronado (2006) has demonstrated that workers and their families who moved north in search of better employ- ment opportunities frequently find themselves living in either the same or worse conditions than those they had hoped to escape. It is this context from which Maclovio Rojas emerged. While colonias and the UPMs they inspire are not new to the border region, the conditions of Maclovio Rojas are unique in terms of who is interested in the land and the way in which the community has organized itself.

The community of Maclovio Rojas is one of the more long-standing UPMs in Baja California, where neighborhoods such as Colonia Jardin, Colonia Lib- ertad, Cartolandia, and Colonia Tierra y Libertad have a powerful history of uniting and organizing people to obtain a dignified way of life (Valenzuela-

Arce 1991). Maclovio Rojas, located between the cities of Tijuana and Tecate and thirty miles south of the U.S.-Mexico border, was founded by twenty-five families on April 10, 1988, on the anniversary of Emiliano Zapata's death. The community leaders and some of these initial families were members of an independent union of agricultural workers called the Central Independiente de Obreros Agricolas y Campesinos (CIOAC), formed in the 1940s by Ramón Danzós Palomino, a member of the old Mexican Communist Party. According to Manuel Mancillas (2002), CIOAC was the first rural-based organization to challenge the official campesino organizations, which were then largely controlled by the ruling party (the PRI) and the government. The CIOAC had a history of organizing migrant Mixteco farm workers in the tomato fields in the state of Sinaloa, and in San Quintín, Baja California.[2] Poblado Maclovio Rojas is named after Maclovio Rojas Marquéz, a CIOAC leader of Mixteco descent from Oaxaca who was killed in 1987 by a fellow organizer under orders from a frustrated grower. At the time of his death, Maclovio Rojas was the secretary of CIOAC in San Quintín. Therefore, this land movement and two others in Baja California were named in his honor (Mancillas 2002).

The land movement of Maclovio Rojas is rooted in the complicated history of agrarian reform and land tenure issues of Mexico (Mancillas 2002). When Lázaro Cárdenas came into power as president of Mexico in 1934, he set in place the institutional mechanisms necessary to redistribute land, a goal established by the Mexican Revolution and the Agrarian Reform Law (Article 27) of 1917. The Mexican poor were encouraged to solicit idle national lands for *ejidos*, the purpose of living and farming. Until the 1980s, most Mexicans believed that the Agrarian Reform Law made by Cárdenas was "irreversible and final" (William Cameron Townsend in Adler-Hellman 1994, 122). But in 1991, President Carlos Salinas de Gortari announced his proposal to amend Article 27 to permit the privatization of ejido land. The constitutional obligation to distribute land to qualified petitioners was immediately ended. Communal land would now be available for sale or rent to either Mexican or foreign companies (Adler-Hellman 1994). This move cleared the path for NAFTA, which gave multinational corporations the right to own Mexican land for profit at the expense of the racialized poor and landless Mexicans.

While these sorts of changes were taking place at the federal level, in 1989 (one year into the Maclovio Rojas land struggle), Ernesto Ruffo-Appel, a neoconservative from the PAN party, became governor of the state of Baja California. His first edict as governor was to endorse the No Invasiones (No Invasions) campaign by warning people that he would no longer tolerate land occupations. Under his regime, the state government, not the federal government, would regulate land tenureship. Ruffo-Appel's approach was to criminalize and discredit the leaders of these settlements by inventing the Crime of Instigating Forced Removal. This made being a leader of irregular settlements a crime (Lara 2003).

Maclovio Rojas was denied its communal land grant petition in 1989 and, over the last twenty years, the community and the state have been in a prolonged battle for the land. This has meant confronting repressive strategies imposed by the state government, including land invasions, and living a life with no public services such as schools, electricity, or running water. Despite the legal wrangling involved, the community has continued to grow. There are currently over 2,000 families, all migrants from the Mexican nation who have traveled north in the post-NAFTA era. The community is divided into five subsections: there are block captains and section leaders who report to the central committee. Blocked by the ocean to the west, Tijuana's urban development projects are moving toward the east and toward Maclovio Rojas. Maquiladoras, such as Samsung, Hyundai, and Coca-Cola, surround the community. The planned Boulevard 2000 (a corridor with plans to connect San Diego, Rosarito, Tijuana, Tecate, and Mexicali) will run by the section of Las Vias, which is on the western side of the community.

Although informed by previous UPMs, the case of Maclovio Rojas is unique in that their quest for land is also guided by their assertion of autonomy. By the early 1990s, the leaders realized that the state was not going to provide their infrastructure, so they set out to create it for themselves. Essentially what Maclovianos argue is that necessity, not a political ideology, drove them to autonomy. Instead, their need to have homes, roads, and schools for their children demanded that they take the task on themselves.

Apart from their homes, the residents have constructed two schools, a women's center, and a two-story cultural center called an Aguascalientes in the Zapatista tradition.[3] Many of the homes are made out of discarded garage doors and wood pallets, although newer houses are being erected out of cinder block and mortar. After years of having no electricity, the residents have created webs of electric lines that criss-cross the streets, streaming down from power poles that the government had installed on the streets for the maquiladoras but never were connected to their homes. They have also tapped into an aqueduct that carries water through the middle of their neighborhood to the nearby Samsung megaplant (Mancillas 2002). In summary, Maclovianos are confronting not only the state government but also the transnational companies interested in usurping their land. The story of

Maclovio Rojas sheds light on the ways in which communities caught at the crux of first/third world realities are responding to their predicament; indeed, it is this unique context of the border that created the conditions for the politicization of women leaders.

Method

Chicana feminist discourse (Moraga and Anzaldúa 1983; Barrera 1991; Delgado-Gaitán 1993; Flores 2000; García 1989, 1997; Martínez 1996; Russel y Rodríguez 1998) critiques cultural, political, and economic conditions in the United States. This theoretical framework embodies the goals of advocacy scholarship, which both challenges the claims of objectivity and links research to community concerns and social change. Chicana feminist discourse shapes both how I positioned myself in the field and my analysis of data. Elsewhere (Téllez 2005), I discuss how I use this framework in my research with more detail.

I conducted fieldwork in the community from September 2003 through September 2004, and again in the summer of 2006. Through participant observation, which entailed active involvement in the community's day-to-day activities (such as meetings, actions, and celebrations), extensive one-to-one interviews with ten women residents (ranging from those who were actively involved in the struggle to those who were not, and from newer to older residents), and a follow-up focus group, I obtained the data that serve as the basis for this chapter. To complement the ethnographic material, I conducted archival research through local and national press coverage, court records, legal documents, community files, and other resources.

I place women at the center of analysis because the majority of the leadership and ranks are women. Indeed, I first came to the community as an activist who supported their movement and from this position made assumptions about the nature of women's roles within the community. That said, during the first week of my field research, I was met with a disconcerting incident. One of the movement's leading organizers was being beaten by her husband, and I was asked to intervene. I felt powerless and was deeply affected by the situation, yet did not have the language to understand the contradictions of women leading a social movement when they remain subjugated in their home lives.

While my open-ended, unstructured interview questions centered on how the women had arrived at Maclovio Rojas, what their experiences with the community had been, and the nature of their roles as women in the community, it became strikingly clear through their narratives that the subject of personal violence could not be ignored. Thus as I began listening to the narratives, and las mujeres discussed their roles in fighting for their homes, their land, and the community's projects, I began to see the ways in which Maclovianas have learned to carefully navigate, and respond to, the violence that they face both in their homes and from the state and transnational companies. Of the final ten women interviewed, three shared what they described as a mutual supporting relationship, whether married or living in *union libre* (living together, not legally married), and five had left their partners/husbands as a result of the physical violence they experienced at their hands.

Juana, Maria, Hortensia, Alma, and Dora all work, to varying degrees, in the *comité*; Teresa, Luz, and Elizabeth all settled on the lands during the community's first year; Sylvia and Paula own restaurants in the community.[4] None had previously been involved in a land movement, a workers' union, or any type of community-based campaign before arriving in Maclovio Rojas. Their ages ranged from twenty-six to sixty; two had no children; and five had small children still in the home.

Las Mujeres de Maclovio

Active Actors against the Neoliberal State

Residents argue that the *lucha*, or struggle, of Maclovio Rojas has always belonged to the women, that they are the ones *al frente*, or in front. Hortensia, a community leader, says, "I think that in Maclovio Rojas, 80 percent of the struggle has been moved forward by women." Some believe that women are in front because they are *mas entronas*, or more daring, while others feel that the women's realm is more closely connected to the home, so their responsibility as women is to defend it. As Sylvia passionately articulates, "If someone tries to remove me from here, it's obvious that I will fight with teeth and nails because otherwise where am I going to take my children?!" But beyond the women being "more daring" or simply seeing their activism as an extension of their responsibilities in the home, Maclovianas recognize the larger impact of their work. For example, Dora states,

> It's big, you have a huge commitment to the people. . . . To be a part of this movement, it requires a lot of time, dedication, character, foundation, discipline, education, and if you don't have an education; then you must have practice and notions of understanding how big this is. You can't stop trying to improve yourself, to move forward. . . . Leaders of social move-

ments think about the well-being of the people. The government is corrupted but not here [in Maclovio Rojas]; here the people contribute for
themselves, and for those of us who get involved even more deeply, we give
it all without expecting anything in return.

Juana adds, "To live in an autonomous community, it's both difficult and you're
full of pride at the same time. Difficult because you don't have the necessary
services and pride because when people come from somewhere else, they're
impressed with what we are doing with our projects—schools, child care
center, etc.—without the help of the government and that's when I realize,
wow, it's true we have come far. But it's hard because sometimes we need
water, we need electricity."

As they experience and witness the repression imposed by the state, a
political analysis emerges. For example, residents are well aware of the fate
of another UPM in Baja California, Puertos al Futuro. In the summer of 2002,
the Tijuana municipal government carried out a very controversial program
of destroying substandard, irregular housing. Two hundred and fifty to three
hundred houses in the colonia Puertos al Futuro were demolished and five
hundred people were left homeless by the demolitions (Kopinak 2003).

In Maclovio Rojas, the government has also threatened to physically evict
the community on a number of occasions. Luz explains the community's
precarious position: "There are a lot of interests that the government has
here. The lands have a lot of value so we have more problems with them because they want to build state housing or factories here." The reality of the repressive pressure placed by the government is reflected in the various stories
shared by the residents. In 1998, local police forcefully tried to take over the
homes of several residents, and as residents defended their homes with their
bodies, other residents began dragging furniture onto the highway, blocking
traffic and causing severe disruption. Eventually the local police were called
off, but instances such as these have been common for Maclovio Rojas residents. Teresa concludes, "We've had some fights, some struggles. . . . It
wouldn't cost the government much to come and beat up the people."

Because physical threats of removal did not completely put an end to land
movements in Baja California, the introduction of Article 226 to the penal
code in 2002 (which makes land occupation or despojo illegal) has created a
constant stream of lawsuits against the community leaders and residents.
When a community resident or leader is charged with despojo, the police immediately seek an arrest warrant. The judicial system in Mexico works on the
principle that one is guilty until proven innocent. If a claim is made against

an individual who has not sought an *amparo* (which is almost like a bond, but literally means "protection of a right"), he or she is subject to immediate arrest. Sometimes amparos are not allowed and defendants, if caught, have to wait in jail until their case is resolved. CESPT, the department of water and power in Tijuana, has also begun to file charges against residents for the alleged stealing of untreated water from the aqueduct. With over forty-two charges of despojo currently looming over several residents, some leaders are defendants in multiple cases, scrambling to and from court appearances and meetings with lawyers.

The disruptive cycle of these lawsuits creates an insidious but subtle wave of repression not only through the creation of fear, but also by disturbing the everyday lives of those that have been charged. For example, on one of my many visits to the courthouse, the plaintiff did not show up to the hearing, and all fourteen residents who had appeared wasted yet another day of their lives tangled up in a legal mess of confusion. I drove Luz, who is being targeted for despojo, and another family there, and on our way back we talked about how this case is taking a lot of time away from their personal lives. When someone is amparado/a, like Luz, they have to sign in weekly as a form of probation. Furthermore, these lawsuits have served as a justification for sending troops into the Maclovio Rojas community to arrest leaders and cause general intimidation.

The biggest *golpe*, or hit, to the community came in 2002, which drove two prominent leaders, Artemio and Hortensia, out and into hiding and put two others, Juan and Nico, in jail. The golpe of 2002 is critical to the community's historical memory—more so, of course, for Hortensia, whose visible leadership role has made her the target of multiple attacks from the government. She has felt the brunt of repression personally in the form of arrest warrants, persecution, and imprisonment. She states, "My house was surrounded by police as if I was the worst or best drug trafficker but they didn't get me because they couldn't at the time." Governmental tactics are not hidden and Hortensia clearly explains, "The government can't do what they did in Puertos al Futuro. . . . they already tried, the last time was in 1998 and the tractors came and everything. . . . The people opposed it and put themselves in front of the machines and defended their lands against the police. They know we will defend and there will be deaths, so instead they subtly take over by creating lawsuits."

Not only do state economic policies reflect collusion with transnational companies, but their actions directly demonstrate preference for them. In the late 1990s, Hyundai Corporation was able to take over a portion of the land belonging to Maclovio Rojas after a standoff between the residents and the company. The state government did not contest legal ownership once it was out of the hands of the residents. Several storage trucks belonging to Hyundai now line the eastern border of the community. Furthermore, the other surrounding maquiladoras also "illegally" tap into the aqueduct, but no suits have been filed against them. As Hortensia argues, "There are millions of dollars at stake. We are in a strategic point where the Boulevard 2000 is going to pass and the interests of the transnational companies are there. Since we are an organized community we serve as a bad example because we might wake the consciousness of the people." But the consciousness of the residents of Maclovio Rojas has been awakened.

This is apparent when Dora says, "The government doesn't like Maclovio Rojas because it is an example for other communities. The governor gets paid to build schools and here our payment has been made by the sacrifice of the people. The government doesn't want other communities to know, from our example, that they too can organize themselves. Why would we need governors or presidents then if the people came together to organize?"

These narratives illustrate that when forced to confront the structural violence endemic to the border region, residents point to an alternative, one that challenges the gendered and racialized sociopolitical position in which they find themselves. Arguably, the residents of Maclovio Rojas came together because they simply needed a place to live. Indeed, the women described the hardships of migration, instability, and uncertainty they endured before settling on these lands. On arriving and finding the neoliberal state resistant to their rights to the land, the women emerged as leaders, and they fought back. Over the years, it became clear to them that if they needed something completed, they needed to take it on themselves to do it.

In the process, a critique of the state and the transnational companies, the same ones that employ them, materialized. Seeing themselves as political subjects allows them to recognize that they have the power to enact change. Hortensia states, "Look at my case. I'm being persecuted as a social justice fighter when I should be given respect from the government as a citizen, wife, daughter; my rights are being taken away. I'm being affected. But I'm strong even though I am still being followed. We just have to move forward."

Hortensia's final thoughts about moving forward despite their situation are representative of the community at large. Paula reiterates this when she says, "This is not just me, it's all of us. We all have the same fears that they might drive us out or whatever but we all have the same fear, not just me." The notion of being unified is extremely important to the survival of the organization, the community, and the lucha.

Transforming the Home

As these women solidify their commitment to the struggle for their land in Maclovio Rojas, they are also committing themselves to a lifestyle that demands justice in all aspects of their lives. There is a well-known *dicho*, a saying, in Maclovio Rojas: If a woman comes to Maclovio Rojas married, she divorces, and if she arrives single she will find a partner. This common practice in the community illustrates that discord occurs in traditional family life when the women develop a political consciousness through their critical engagement with the state and transnational companies. This becomes most apparent when the women negotiate their experiences of violence within the home.

Of the ten women with whom I spoke, five made the decision to leave their partners based on their experiences of violence and humiliation. All argue that becoming more deeply involved in the movement created schisms within their homes. Accusations of infidelity were common as women attended marches, rallies, and meetings. The women argue, however, that being involved in the movement allowed them to see that they did not have to remain in the violent situation they were in at home. The borderlands concept highlights the ways both the private and public spheres become politicized spaces for the women.

For example, Maria states:

> I was having problems with my husband. He felt like I abandoned our home, our children, my responsibilities with them. He was always negative because he never understood the lucha, and I say never because we've been separated now for four months and he has actually left the community never really understanding what was going on, or the work that I do. He left talking bad about the community, the organization, saying that because of the organization he lost his family; because of the organization he lost it all. I feel that it's easy to understand because even my youngest son understands and lives this experience with me and he wants to support something that my husband didn't do.

Maria made the decision to separate from her husband and chose, instead, to continue her work within the movement.

> In the end, well, maybe you could say it was a bad decision but my values wouldn't let me leave, feelings of responsibility and solidarity . . . and I didn't want to abandon the organization at such a critical time. Besides being a member of the organization, I am a community member. I have property here and so my obligation is to support the movement. If I had left,

my conscience wouldn't have let me be in peace with myself. I knew it wasn't the time. If I hadn't done it earlier when maybe I could've saved my marriage, then later just wasn't the appropriate time to leave. I was too deeply involved. . . . I don't get as stressed out because my husband's attitude always affected me negatively. The way he spoke to me ruined my thought processes, and now that I'm alone with the kids, it's better. They understand that if I have to go to a meeting or if there's a protest it's my obligation to the community. . . . They understand that at that moment I can't be with them.

Maria describes the tension felt in her relationships with her children, her husband, and the movement. Her sense of obligation to all three areas of her life never waned. It is evident that what she is articulating is that she needed reciprocity in all three relationships, which she was able to receive from her young children and members of her community. Her husband failed to see the need to understand and instead reacted with more violence. Once Maria made the decision to leave him, she never looked back.

Although las mujeres admit that their experiences have been painful, they also describe the process as a liberating one, that the movement helped them "open their minds." Juana says:

We're facing the government and it's a huge thing. No es cualquier cosa [it's no small feat], and I think you get more strength from that—even if you don't want to, because before I wasn't interested. But now by being involved in the movement you are influenced because you see the government committing so many injustices, such as salary inequalities and such. They run all over people! Here we're just trying to get ahead for our families . . . and one starts realizing more as you get more involved and as women we cannot permit this and our minds start to open up. When you start understanding more, then that's where our freedom starts. Maclovio has helped us to move forward, to face new challenges, goals, and obstacles. We have advanced both a little bit and a lot. We need to do away with the barrier called machismo.

Despite her initial disinterest in politics, Juana, through her experiences, can now articulate a critique of the state and recognizes the injustices that are imposed on workers and on the poor in general. When given the opportunity to develop a critique of the state, it is inevitable for the women to begin to critically examine their own lives. As the women draw connections between the violence imposed by the state and the violence lived in the home, political consciousness creates a fury that motivates them to act to live more "freely" and without fear. Juana says, "Before I was scared of my husband and slowly I started defending myself; you're not going to believe it, but I did and from my last child until now I don't have the same fear."

Those women who were more actively involved in the movement and made the decision to split from their partners were the ones who then created safe spaces to support each other financially, emotionally, and with child rearing. While victimization, abuse, and, in the case of two women, death at the hands of their live-in partners/husbands, all still occur in Maclovio Rojas, mechanisms in place there demonstrate that women's roles are being reconsidered. Single women are given priority for land, and wives/mothers are usually given official titles to the land, a practice that is uncommon in Mexico. Furthermore, the Casa de la Mujer, the women's center, constructed in 2002, provides child care and some workshops for women residents of Maclovio Rojas. A statue of Coatlique (the Mesoamerican goddess of life, death, and rebirth) was erected in the front of the center, a symbolic homage to women and recognition that there are needs women have that only such a center can fulfill. Juana says, "All of us that are working and supporting here are women, and it gives you security about yourself that you don't need much from your partner so that you can make it on your own."

Despite this support, the leaders argue that they are unable to move the Casa de la Mujer forward because their energies are consumed with the immediate struggle for land. Clearly, women are still responsible for the tasks accorded to them historically: housework, child rearing, and all functions within the family. Thus while it is clear that in Maclovio Rojas, women are the defenders of homes (in fact, they are the ones who attend the rallies, the marches, and the protests, and are the ones who confront the police or other invaders if necessary), this historical prototype hasn't changed. And although the call to feminism has not been made (indeed, I never once heard the women, not even the leaders, use *femenista* as a descriptor of themselves), their actions demonstrate a woman-centered subjectivity that has been engendered by their experiences. It is useful to look at Milagros Pena's (2007) research on women's NGOs in El Paso/Ciudad Juarez, where the activists defined *feminismo* as *fe-en-mi-misma* or "faith in myself."

Similarly, many of the women feel that they have become *otra*, a stronger woman, and feel that because of their ability to defend their homes they can defend themselves in their personal lives as well. Paula states, "I've learned to defend myself so that they [the government] don't take what is ours. These lands are mine and just because the government wants them doesn't mean they can take them away from me. I will defend them because I value every-thing that I have here."

Teresa says that she's learned "to be more courageous. I'm not scared of the government anymore. I can defend myself because in the beginning you do get scared but as time passes you learn more, you have more love toward what you have and you even start getting more angry. I feel good helping my community."

Maria talks about what she has learned most from living and working in the community: "I used to be very scared of Juan and I'm not anymore. I know how to confront him now. Not only am I a representative of the community but I am responsible for my children, and their security is always going to be first. So that means that I can't be scared of anything. I have to have more confidence in myself."

> Juana shares what she values most in Maclovio Rojas: "I've gained a lot of confidence being here, a lot of self-confidence, *yo sola valerme por mi misma* [to be self-reliant] with my children, and I have learned that by myself I can get ahead. If I would have lived in another community, I wouldn't have been involved in sit-ins and marches, etc., in another place this wouldn't happen."

For many Maclovianas, the journey to have a little plot of land has been a long and arduous one. And, at the time of this writing, the struggle is certainly not over. But what we can learn from the case of Maclovio Rojas is that when mujeres fronterizas are faced with the kind of gendered, class-based, and ra-cialized structural violence that is endemic to the border region, they respond with what can be described as a gut instinct for survival. Through their experi-ences, though, they develop an oppositional consciousness that critiques the neoliberal state while simultaneously, especially for those more involved in the movement, developing a woman-centered subjectivity that provides them with the tools they need to create different choices for themselves.

Conclusion

Chandra Mohanty argues that any analysis of the effects of globalization needs to centralize the experiences and struggles of communities of women and girls from the "two/third world"; that it is "precisely the potential epis-temic privilege of poor women of color that opens up the space for demystifying capitalism and for envisioning transborder social and economic justice" (2003, 250). And as Bhavnani, Foran, and Kurian (2003) and others have demonstrated, women in developing countries have actively played a role in confronting their predicaments and taking part in collective movements for change. Escobar adds that "local groups, far from being passive receivers of the transnational condition, actively shape the process of constructing identities, social relations and economic practice" (2001, 155).

Because constraints faced by women may be not only political but also cultural and familial (Moghadam 2001), the case of Maclovio Rojas offers an important intervention in the study of social movements, in particular those at the U.S.-Mexico border, where transnational and neoliberal politics, capitalism, patriarchy, and racialization create unique conditions. Furthermore, it illustrates the gendered nuances of activism such that while the goal of Maclovio Rojas is its struggle for land, an important byproduct is the woman-centered political consciousness that emerges. Maclovianas gain the capacity to self-determine their lives.

Using the borderlands concept to describe the ways Maclovianas navigate these social spheres helps us to further understand and problematize the dichotomous notions of Chicana/Latina/Mexicana activism. While Diaz-Barriga (1998) argues that women activists blur the distinction between the domestic and the public spheres, an analysis of the narratives of the women from Maclovio Rojas builds on Pardo's (1998) study, where she highlights that political participation relies on the relationship between the public and the private spheres. Maclovianas' oppositional consciousness is directed simultaneously at the neoliberal state and at the unequal relationships they experience within their homes, both being sociopolitical structures that condone violence. Maclovianas are not trying to be liberated from the private sphere; in fact, they are defending their homes and themselves. As such, they are transforming social relations and the cultural meanings attached to them.

Smith (2005) has argued that interventions to address state violence and interpersonal violence need to be developed simultaneously. Maclovianas demonstrate that both spaces are highly political, and a call such as Smith's needs to be heeded, if at a larger scale. The focus on women's agency in this chapter offers important insight into a region where most see only femicide, exploitation, or victimization. The concept of gendered borderlands aptly fits into the ways Maclovianas are negotiating their conditions but also highlights the ways they brought and continue to bring new meaning to the U.S.-Mexico border.

A possibility for future research is to examine the narratives of men in the community to provide more breadth to the analysis and to learn more about their negotiations with women and the change they are living. The work of

Kimmel (1987) outlines the ways men responded to feminism at the turn of the twentieth century, which I find largely still applicable today, particularly in Maclovio Rojas.[5] As anthropologist Alejandro Lugo argues, "when a sole feminist analyst examines, comprehensively, both men and women, new and productive categories of theoretical analysis and politics can emerge" (2000, 55). While some of the organizers and residents were able to find support in their interpersonal relationships and a setting that allowed the women to evolve both within and outside of their homes, the more common outcome, especially for those actively involved in the struggle, was a break. Thus, by creating safe spaces for themselves and for their families, these mujeres fronterizas have taken an oppositional stance toward the state, the transnational companies, and patriarchy, proving that change in all aspects of a woman's life is possible.

To conclude, I'll leave you with this quote from Maria, whose words remind me of the urgency of their struggle: "We have the right to live how we want to live. We have the right to live decently, and we can't wait for them to bring it to us—we have to fight for it."

Notes

I thank the women of Maclovio Rojas for their lessons, strength, and inspiration. The reviewers and editors of *Gender and Society* have been generous with their time and suggestions and I want to thank them for helping me shape this chapter. Finally, I thank my colleagues and friends Moira O'Neil, Anna Guevarra, Alejandra Elenes, Jonathan Xavier Inda, and Alejandro Lugo for their insightful comments and edits as they read through various drafts of this piece.

1 While the literature on social movements offers a paradigm for understanding the ways in which people mobilize for collective action and the strategies and motivations for doing so (Castells 1983; Cohen and Shirin 2000; Melucci 1989), these works largely fail to include a gender analysis, a project that Taylor begins to address. Taylor (1999) argues that gender is an explanatory factor in the emergence, nature, and outcomes of all social movements, even those that do not evoke the language of gender conflict or explicitly embrace gender change. She asks us to look at the "gender regime" of the institutional context to understand the broader set of political constraints and opportunities that impinge on social movements. Building on this work, Einwohner, Hollander, and Olsen (2000) add that social movements are gendered by their composition and goals.

2 Mixteco refers to members of an indigenous population in Mexico, many of whom do not speak Spanish and do not identify as mestizo.

3 In August 1994, the Zapatistas convened the National Democratic Convention to open a national dialogue with "civil society." To host the 6,000 people, the Zapatistas built an "auditorium" that they called an Aguascalientes, evoking the convention held in that city of central Mexico during the revolution of 1910.

Several more appeared throughout the communities in resistance. In August 2003, the Ejercito Zapatista de Liberacion Nacional announced the closure of the Aguascalientes and the opening of the Caracoles, to be the "Casas" de la Junta de Buen Gobierno (literally translated, means "homes of assembly of the good government").

4   As president of the community, and because of her very visible public persona, Hortensia's name has not been changed; all others are pseudonyms.

5   Kimmel suggests three alternative strategies for the reconstitution of gender: (1) antifeminist, which created a frightened retreat to traditional configurations; (2) the demarcation of new institutional spheres for the vigorous assertion of a renewed masculinity; and (3) men's support for feminist claims.

References

Adler-Hellman, Judith. 1994. *Mexican lives*. New York: New Press.

Aguilar, C., and A. Chenard. 1994. Is there a place for feminism in the revolution? In *Compañeras: Voices from the Latin American women's movement*, edited by G. Kuppers. London: Latin American Bureau.

Anzaldúa, Gloria. 1987. *Borderlands/La Frontera: The new mestiza*. San Francisco: Aunt Lute Books.

Bandy, Joe, and Jackie Smith. 2005. *Coalitions across borders: Transnational protest and the neoliberal order*. Lanham, MD: Rowman and Littlefield.

Barrera, M. 1991. Cafe con leche. In *Chicana lesbians*, edited by Carla Trujillo. Berkeley, CA: Third Woman Press.

Bennett, V. 1992. The evolution of urban popular movements in Mexico between 1968 and 1988. In *The making of social movements in Latin America: Identity, strategy, and democracy*, edited by A. Escobar and S. Alvarez. Boulder, CO: Westview.

Bhavnani, Kum-Kum, J. Foran, and P. Kurian. 2003. *Feminist futures: Re-imagining women, culture and development*. London: Zed.

Brooks, Ethel C. 2007. *Unraveling the garment industry: Transnational organizing and women's work*. Minneapolis: University of Minnesota Press.

Bush, Diane Mitsch. 1992. Women's movements and state policy reform aimed at domestic violence against women: A comparison of the consequences of movement mobilization in the U.S. and India. *Gender and Society* 6:587–608.

Castells, Manuel. 1983. *The city and the grassroots*. Berkeley: University of California Press.

Cohen, R., and M. Rai Shirin. 2000. *Global social movements*. London: Continuum.

Corcoran-Nantes, Y. 2003. Female consciousness or feminist consciousness? Women's consciousness raising in community based struggles in Brazil. In *Feminist theory reader: Local and global perspectives*, edited by C. R. McCann and K. Seung-Kyung. New York: Routledge.

Coronado, I. 2006. Styles, strategies, and issues of women leaders at the border. In *Women and change at the U.S./Mexico border: Mobility, labor, and activism*, edited by D. J. Mattingly and E. R. Hansen. Tucson: University of Arizona Press.

Delgado-Gaitan, Concha. 1993. Researching change and changing the researcher. *Harvard Educational Review* 63:389–411.

Diaz-Barriga, M. 1998. Beyond the domestic and the public: Colonas participation in urban movements in Mexico City. In *Cultures of politics, politics of cultures: Re-visioning Latin American social movements*, edited by S. E. Alvarez, E. Dagnino, and A. Escobar. Boulder, CO: Westview.

Dolhinow, R. 2006. Mexican women's activism in New Mexico's colonias. In *Women and change at the U.S./Mexico border: Mobility, labor, and activism*, edited by D. J. Mattingly and E. R. Hansen. Tucson: University of Arizona Press.

Einwohner, R. L., J. A. Hollander, and T. Olson. 2000. Engendering social movements: Cultural images and movement dynamics. *Gender and Society* 14: 679–99.

Escobar, Arturo. 2001. Culture sits in places: Reflections on globalism and subaltern strategies of localization. *Political Geography* 20:139–74.

Ferree, Myra M., and S. Roth. 1998. Gender, class, and the interaction between social movements: A strike of West Berlin day care workers. *Gender and Society* 12:626–48.

Fine, Michelle. 1989. The politics of research and activism: Violence against women. *Gender and Society* 3:549–58.

Flores, Lisa A. 2000. Reclaiming the "other": Toward a Chicana feminist critical perspective. *International Journal of Intercultural Relations* 24:687–705.

Fregoso, R. L. 2007. Towards a planetary civil society. In *Women and migration in the U.S.-Mexico borderlands*, edited by D. A. Segura and P. Zavella. Durham, NC: Duke University Press.

García, Alma. 1989. The development of Chicana feminist discourse. *Gender and Society* 3:217–38.

———. 1997. Voices of women of color: Redefining women's studies. *Race, Gender, and Class* 4:11–28.

Herzog, Larry. 1990. *Where north meets south: Cities, space, and politics on the U.S.-Mexico border*. Austin: University of Texas Press.

Ibarra, M. de la Luz. 2007. Buscando la vida: Mexican immigrant women's memories of home, yearning, and border crossings. In *Gender and the borderlands: The frontiers reader*, edited by Antonia Castaneda. Lincoln: University of Nebraska Press.

Kimmel, Michael S. 1987. Men's responses to feminism at the turn of the century. *Gender and Society* 1:261–83.

Kopinak, Kathryn. 2003. Globalization in Tijuana maquiladoras: Using historical antecedents and migration to test globalization models. *Papeles de poblacion*, July/September, no. 037. Toluca, Mexico: UNAM.

Lara, O. 2003. Arte, tierra y dignidad: An intervention in a subaltern community context. Honors thesis. Stanford University, Palo Alto, CA.

Lorey, David E. 1999. *The U.S./Mexican border in the twentieth century*. Wilmington, DE: SR Books.

Lugo, A. 2000. Destabilizing the masculine, refocusing "gender": Men and the aura of authority in Michelle Z. Rosaldo's work. In *Gender matters: Rereading Michelle Z. Rosaldo*, edited by A. Lugo and B. Maurer. Ann Arbor: University of Michigan Press.

Mancillas, M. R. 2002. Transborder collaboration: The dynamics of grassroots globalization. In *Globalization on the line: Culture, capital, and citizenship at U.S. borders,* edited by C. Sadowski-Smith. New York: Palgrave.

Martínez, Theresa A. 1996. Toward a Chicana feminist epistemological standpoint: Theory at the intersection of race, class, and gender. *Race, Gender, and Class* 3:107–28.

Melucci, Alberto. 1989. *Nomads of the present: social movements and individual needs in contemporary society.* London: Hutchinson Radius.

Moghadam, V. M. 2001. Transnational feminist networks: Collective action in an era of globalization. In *Globalization and social movements,* edited by P. Hamel, H. Lustiger-Thaler, and M. Mayer. New York: Palgrave.

Mohanty, Chandra. 2003. *Feminism without borders: Decolonizing theory, practicing solidarity.* Durham, NC: Duke University Press.

Moraga, Cherríe, and Gloria Anzaldúa. 1983. *This bridge called my back: Writings by radical women of color.* 2nd ed. New York: Kitchen Table, Women of Color Press.

Nevins, Joseph. 2002. *Operation Gatekeeper: The rise of the "illegal alien" and the making of the U.S.-Mexico boundary.* New York: Routledge.

Ortiz-Gonzalez, Victor M. 2004. *El Paso: Local frontiers at a global crossroads.* Minneapolis: University of Minnesota Press.

Pardo, Mary. 1998. *Mexican American women activists: Identity and resistance in two Los Angeles communities.* Philadelphia: Temple University Press.

Pena, Devon. 1997. *The terror of the machine: Technology, work, gender, and ecology on the U.S.-Mexico border.* CMAS: University of Texas at Austin Press.

Pena, Milagros. 2007. *Latina activists across borders: Women grassroots organizing in Mexico and Texas.* Durham, NC: Duke University Press.

Rosaldo, Renato. 1993. *Culture and truth: The remaking of social analysis.* Boston: Beacon Press.

Russel y Rodríguez, Mónica. 1998. Confronting anthropology's silencing praxis: Speaking of/from a Chicana consciousness. *Qualitative Inquiry* 4:15–41.

Sadowski-Smith, C. 2002. Border studies, diaspora, and theories of globalization. In *Globalization on the line: Culture, capital, and citizenship at U.S. borders,* edited by C. Sadowski-Smith. New York: Palgrave.

Safa, Helen Icken. 1990. Women's social movements in Latin America. *Gender and Society* 4:354–69.

Sandoval, Chela. 2000. *Methodology of the oppressed.* Minneapolis: University of Minnesota Press.

Segura, Denise A., and Patricia Zavella. 2007. *Women and migration in the U.S.-Mexico borderlands: A reader.* Durham, NC: Duke University Press.

Smith, A. 2005. Looking to the future: Domestic violence, women of color, the state and social change. In *Domestic violence at the margins: Readings on race, class, gender and culture,* edited by N. J. Sokoloff. New Brunswick, NJ: Rutgers University Press.

Smith, Michael P., and Luis E. Guarnizo. 1998. *Transnationalism from below: Comparative urban and community research,* Vol. 6. New Brunswick, NJ: Transaction.

Staudt, Kathleen, and Irasema Coronado. 2002. *Fronteras no mas: Toward social justice at the U.S.-Mexico border.* New York: Palgrave Macmillan.

Stephen, Lynn. 1997. *Women and social movements in Latin America: Power from below.* Austin: University of Texas Press.

Taylor, Verta. 1999. Gender and social movements: Gender processes in women's self-help movements. *Gender and Society* 13:8–33.

Téllez, Michelle. 2005. Doing research at the borderlands: Notes from a Chicana feminist ethnographer. *Chicana/Latina Studies: Journal of Mujeres Activas en Letras y Cambio Social* 4(3):46–70.

Valenzuela-Arce, Jose Manuel. 1991. *Empapados de sereno: El movimiento urbano popular en Baja California (1928–1988).* Tijuana: El Colegio de la Frontera Norte.

La Canción de Tijuana / The Song of Tijuana

That afternoon, I was ambling along looking for some shade to protect me from the slight ordeal of the 2 P.M. sun. At the corner of Avenida Constitución, a black guy, his skull criss-crossed by tense veins, was talking to an average-looking girl, staring at him with her mouth agape. He wanted to sleep with her, but his six and a half feet plus his gigantic hands made the young Mexican girl distrustful. She was scanning the eyes of the other ladies out on the street, looking for any kind of advice at all: "And what happens if you don't have a good time? You going to strangle me with those big hands of yours?" She was joking nervously, avoiding her conquistador's gaze. Let him look for a girl his own size, the malicious giggles from the other street-walkers seemed to say; they were watching what was happening out of the corner of their eyes. "You're either going to have to pull together two beds or do it on the floor," an old hunchbacked man said as he smiled and toked on his cigarette in the door of a hair salon. The black guy didn't speak any Spanish, but he just had to gesture a little and show her his dollars; she was the one who had to think through the situation and make the important decisions. I had no idea I'd find myself in a similar situation two days later; I just kept on walking toward Coahuila—a street everyone associates with their crudest dreams and most urgent urges. An endless number of doors gape open to the street, devouring people passing by, all the customers used to the fun going on forever no matter the harsh glare of the sun, which doesn't seem to bother the night at all. Rundown hotels, tenements, houses converted into brothels, cabarets with ordinary names like Chabelas, Adelitas, and La Botana make up a raunchy catwalk of vice.

That afternoon, I walked all around the streets downtown with a deep sense of calm. I was remembering my first visit to Tijuana a decade before, when I could still survive a couple straight nights of partying: at that time, I could go head to head with this city, drink in a coffin, or take jokes to places they started to get dangerous. About ten feet before I got to Revolución, I saw two blond guys from San Diego with huge beer bellies rush down some stairs that led up to the rooms of a tiny boarding house. Their smiles were almost as magnificent as their bloated bodies. They'd gotten laid an hour before lunch and an hour after leaving their Dodge truck in a dusty lot that charged twenty pesos an hour to park there. They lit up two Cuban cigars in the middle of the sidewalk—maybe as a way to celebrate their valiant copulation—and bit on them between waves of happy laughter: cheap cigars, almost always phony cosmopolitan delusions. As if they only had to cross the border to get to Cuba, the Yucatán, or Patagonia: there was nothing like strolling down Avenida Revolución in shorts smoking a Cuban cigar while they figured out which noisy dive bar they'd throw away a few dollars in. Why go any further than Revolución if they got that feeling of being in another country just by walking down this street? People from the United States think they can find all they need in Tijuana to satiate their provincial curiosity and their hankering for travel. On one sidewalk, a blond-haired woman with ridiculous freckles yells to her husband on the opposite side of the street; he doesn't hear her because he stopped to try on a Santo mask: "Hey, Bill, come over here! We've got a new pet!" There's no money left for a mask because she decided to spend it on a sculpture of a life-size dog covered in velvet. While the couple argues from one sidewalk to the other, a gang of youths from California with sickly-looking bodies debate which bar to spend the afternoon downing tequila in, listening to Madonna, and hooking up with Mexican women. From the window of a car taking me to my hotel in the Zona Río, I watch a Chinese family of twenty pose next to a white donkey painted like a zebra. According to the tiara that crowns its head, the donkey's name is Mónica. Near the Bar Animal, a person in a Spider Man costume waves his arms about to get the attention of the passersby, but no one looks at him. The heat's intense and everyone on the sidewalk looks a little dizzy. Two hours wandering around downtown have been enough to make me remember the exhausting days of my first visits, when my tijuanense friends labored to keep me in a mental state that, without anyone noticing, was pretty much the same as being dead.

It's a well-known story, but I'm going to tell it. More than a century ago, the San Diego authorities prohibited boxing matches, but the fight promoters found a way around this Puritan infamy by having the spectators gather on American soil. They put up the ring in Tijuana, a few feet from the line separating the two countries. Once the ring was set up, the boxers fought in Tijuana, but the spectators watched and bet from San Diego. After that mythical series of bouts (1886) and as the years passed, there was nothing standing in the way of all the vices conglomerating on the Mexican side: bars, brothels, and casinos were erected to receive the people fleeing from the prohibitions on the other side. Bulls, horses, and greyhounds made up the most important zoo of gambling along the border. In the 1920s, when the American Senate made gambling, boxing, and racing illegal, Tijuana became the land of Eden for businessmen, gamblers, and cardsharks who found a veritable land of opportunities in Mexico, the idyllic West where the doors would open for the first time at the Agua Caliente Casino, Montecarlo, Sunset Inn, Foreign Club, and more. The die was cast: Tijuana would be a space to practice everything Puritan morality didn't allow. All or nothing, after all it wasn't a city, but a territory in the process of being settled (Tía Juana or Ciudad Zaragoza as it was called at first). In his book *Tijuana the Horrible*, Humberto Félix Berúmen elucidates the historical roots of Tijuana, but he adds the overwhelming mythological weight to the reality of the city: that need to embody evil or to represent human corruption as the polar opposite of Puritan morality: "In the construction of Tijuana's imaginary, there is an even more important element: the biblical myth of fallen or corrupt cities."

When I get into a taxi around midnight to head back downtown, I get the feeling that, by staying in the Zona Río, I'm also on the other side of the border: sumptuous hotels, restaurants, shopping centers and office towers, wide avenues, a prosthetic city that is supposedly Tijuana, but which looks like any other city where there's progress. In the end, as Robert Walser has written, all those who attempt to achieve progress end up looking practically the same. I leave the comfort of my modern hideaway to look for and eventually immerse myself in that reality that thumbs its nose at civilized optimism, at the businessmen's dreams that become conventional models, at the hope for a Tijuana that progresses forward or tries to elude its ill-fated legend. On Paseo de los Héroes, I look up at the statue of a furious Cuauhtémoc looking north with an impudent expression on his face, like he were blaming other people for his misfortunes or his carnal weaknesses (it reminds me of El Indio Fernández dressed as a charro welcoming visitors to the Wax Museum on Calle Primera). The old Ford station wagons operating as taxis remind me of the enormous cars my father bought thirty years ago to show off in front of his friends; the Fords circulate on the streets of Tijuana like funeral hearses taking on more and more passengers as they get closer to their destination. Their underground dungeon smell doesn't dissipate even with the air streaming through the windows: not coffins, but mass graves.

Just like on my first visits to Tijuana, I start out the night drinking a beer at La Ballena. I decided not to call my friends because, at least this time, I plan to move at my own pace. That's possible in this area where no one is surprised when you ask for drugs at six in the morning or when you only have twenty pesos left to live on at dawn. Everyone seems so used to the meandering nocturnal hordes. The vendors in the area are opening the doors to their businesses while most people are still halfway through their night of partying: tons of liquor have been consumed before they sell the first yogurt in the morning or before the schoolkids take their first class. Along just one block, I count three *farmacías*: I don't think there is a comparable number of pharmacies per square block in any other neighborhood in the world: an uncontrollable epidemic of drug stores. Besides being thriving businesses, these drug stores also function as windows into infinite psychological worlds. Foreigners flock to the stores to get any kind of substance. Hundreds of drug stores. What they can't get in these windows though is crystal meth or ice (chlorhydrate methamphetamine), which are, along with cocaine, the most common drugs traded on the street. For just fifty pesos, you can get a dose of cocaine (a *globito*), enough to keep you awake for a couple days. In the middle of the last decade, I snorted crystal for the first time just to get closer to another boundary line: my nasal passages were burning, which caused a sharp pain that stopped as soon as the stupid enthusiasm set in. Crystal is a synthetic derivative of ephedrine (at the end of the day, a methamphetamine too), but at this stage no one really knows what they're buying for a few pesos: they could be selling you rat poison or ground-up bones. At that time, my friends preferred to inhale the dust through their mouths, heating it up on aluminum foil or smoking it in a pipe: no one wanted to wreck their nasal wall or leave drops of blood on the mirror. Afterward, when the harrowing hangover hit, I would hole myself away in a motel on the road to Rosarito, where I'd spend two days watching TV or scribbling on a piece of paper: I wasn't able to write anything memorable. Buying crystal is pretty simple and, in a tiny bar in the center of town, they'll even pour you a sweet little line on the table. It was just that easy a few years ago in a bar that's not there anymore: the Kin Kle, where, as I remember it, we had a transgender waiter who because of some mistakes with the silicone had grown a breast close to her belly button. Nowadays, La Ballena has changed its look: it's a bar on Calle Argüello with uncomfortable benches, carpeted walls, and a jukebox in the middle. The regulars have little in common except for the fact they've all ended up in a pretty ugly bar: a woman dressed as a cat attracts attention for just a few seconds. A man in a sleeveless shirt waits for his turn to drop a handful of coins into the jukebox: it looks like an attack of insomnia forced him out of his bed. Through the smoke, bodies become opaque silhouettes. I see an old man with a lost look on his face kicking a column with freakish rage while the other customers act indifferent, since they have already memorized his violent routine. A few seconds before he's thrown into the street, the old man launches another attack as if his ancestors or whatever caused his miserable look were buried inside the column.

At two in the morning, the movement on the streets is disturbing: shameless exhibitionism has turned this area into a hotel with no doors where nothing is off limits. On the same street, Calle Argüello, there's a bar tijuanenses know as El Turístico (the real name is even more insipid). Students, laborers, and people without any obvious work hang out long into the morning hours: the promiscuity is seductive—the cosmopolitan boredom, the lack of etiquette, a studied disinterest in anyone else's life, the scant violence despite the sinister surroundings: who's headed out and who just got back? The border as a virtual space between two extremes doesn't seem palpably real; so everyone retells the legend in their own way even if it's only to repeat the same old cliché. It doesn't matter who is looking at Tijuana; they always end up describing the city as an exception. Claudio Magris has written that the border is a necessity, because without it, there's no identity or form: "Border is form and, as a consequence, also art." The border gives definition, but is itself undefined by its very nature: it only exists to provide reality to others. And who cares about the explanations when you can immerse yourself in experience? I pour a little beer into my glass as I watch an obese woman with an inscrutable face, glued into her plastic chair, hiding her eyes behind a pair of dark glasses. The regulars know the woman as "La siete culos" or "Seven Assholes." She's nice enough to talk with the lonely guys who approach her looking for maternal company. On her late night throne, La siete culos puts up with all kinds of unwieldy metaphors without even blinking: a tragic palm reader, a retired *coyote*, or a mother asleep in a cantina waiting for her children to return.

A city without roots, Tijuana can't escape its own myth. The outsider's way of looking at the city hasn't changed and actually condemns Tijuana to just being a *ciudad de paso*, a city to pass through on the way to somewhere else, besieged by drug lords and assassins, dominated by a never-ending night: Tijuana is an open door in every sense. In addition, its politicians are now part of that delirious show, consumed like some kind of indulgent pastime. The fact that the new mayor of the city has a dark past shows that the people who elected him wanted to be governed by a *corrido* villain, an actor, or anyone who doesn't look like a sensible politician. Since the community has never in reality believed the story that it is a community—as Baudrillard says—it happily bows down to lies, because it doesn't tolerate the affectation of truth. It wants to be deceived, but not by just any politician, rather by a character, one who transgresses the bounds of sanity in every sense, a criminal or a lunatic, but not a humanist politician.

Tijuana is still trapped by the vision of the outsider that doesn't go any further than Calle Revolución, the betting halls, the racetrack, the whores of Coahuila, or the eye-catching pinnacles of the Jai Alai: a set design that is repeated even in the most superficial details. No one who believes in the existence of Tijuana is going to listen to music at a Sanborns or dance in a discotheque when the Chicago Club and the bar Zacazonapan is on Calle Constitución. After all, it's about sustaining the myth, not discrediting it, about patiently building clichés without which it would be hard to survive: because cities would be impossible to explain without the existence of prejudices. To go into the Zacazonapan, you go down a set of curving stairs that immediately empty you out into a basement where the heat from all the bodies turns the bar into a Turkish steam room. Ten years ago, I came to this place for the first time too. It was half-empty, almost half-lit, sordid but hospitable, welcoming. I remember one night when almost twenty of us were hanging out until the money was running out faster than the alcohol itself. The five of us who were left at the end had to leave a respectable writer there as a hostage, laid out on top of a table asleep, with a waiter keeping an eye on him, while we returned with enough money to cover the bill. The Zacazonapan has definitely become famous these days: writers, artists, musicians, drug-addled youths dancing on tables alongside Mara Salvatrucha gang members, cholos, criminals, or laborers waiting for an opportunity to leave their pasts behind: La Ballena, El Turístico, El Zacazonapan are a window into the human collage, promiscuity, the paradise promised by all romanticism, that is to say—in the words of Schlegel—a space consecrated to underground deities: "The meaning of creation is revealed for the first time in the drive for annihilation." The fact that the Zacazonapan closes early could be a result of its celebrity, since, as we know, once a few eyes are watching us, we start to act like something we are not. Those who live in the center of Tijuana know all the doors will never be closed: Los Equipales, Dandys, La Estrella, El Ranchero, Chez, and whatever other place you can find a few minutes later is one step closer to the sun coming up.

After a week in Tijuana, there's nothing left: the streets lose their attraction, the working-class colonias appear on the horizon, thousands of white crosses adorning the metallic wall make the border a symbolic cemetery, the whores are tired or drunk, like Elena, who came back to the Hotel Diamante with me one Sunday morning, confused by the way I was acting, by my questions: "Are you all going to rob me? Then go to sleep, relax, the hotel is paid for two days." At that moment, Tijuana becomes a junkie's dream, a turbulent trip, until everything starts up for another round. The ciudad de paso is always all too real, it looks more like life. Maybe that's why the artist is often more nomadic than sedentary. So, Tijuana is an unusual city not just because of Calle Revolución or its gambling fame or its condition as a border territory, but because its artists have survived it. The artists of Tijuana have imposed a constant state of siege on their city: visual arts collectives, music labels, fanzines, bands, videos, magazines, photographers, and even indie publishers have filled the city in the last fifteen years. It's a movement without a pre-planned course, which always finds an outlet, an original one since it takes its inspiration from its own circumstances. As Eugenio Trías has said, the city is a work of art, an erotic drive satisfied not with dreams but with production, so the artist is the creator and the city is the artwork. Because without this artistic spirit that makes the city into a human project, there is no city but rather an undefined territory or space. This Tijuana as a place where art is dominant stands in opposition to that other Tijuana—violent, with no memory, where murders go unpunished.

Elena didn't accept my invitation to go over to my hotel in the Zona Río. "You want to rob me for sure," she joked. She wanted to sleep a few hours more before heading back out to the wandering around she did every day on Calle Constitución. I went back to the model city—stable, comfortable, with perfect avenues. The taxi driver makes a mistake and drives me to the Hotel Lucerna. It doesn't matter. I'll walk a few blocks before the sun, like me, heads back to its hiding place.

Lucía Sanromán

¿Todos somos ciudadanos?

Artistic Production and Agency in Tijuana

En términos de ideología, Tijuana es una pesadilla.
Vivir aquí es ser personaje, porque en la frontera no
hay habitantes sino arquetipos. La frontera no tiene
vida: tiene metafísica—escuchad su pedo.

Con ustedes, el Pollero,
con ustedes, el Turista,
con ustedes, la Puta,
con ustedes, el Híbrido,
con ustedes, el Migrante.

[In terms of ideology, Tijuana is a nightmare.
To live here is to be a character, because at the border
there are no inhabitants, only archetypes. The border doesn't have
life: it has metaphysics—listen to its thing.

I present to you, the Coyote,
I present to you, the Tourist,
I present to you, the Whore,
I present to you, the Hybrid,
I present to you, the Migrant.]

HERIBERTO YÉPEZ, *Tijuanologías*

Con ustedes, el Curador

Curating is a tool for observation, diagnosis, and categorization. From a wider arena of visual artistic production a smaller selection is made to determine, explain, and interpret the larger whole. The conceit is that linkages between individual or collective artistic production in a specific milieu are evidence whence an accurate portrait of a moment of cultural or artistic history can be made, or from where a truthful description of a place can be drawn. Yet a measure of skepticism must be brought to this task, as curatorial frameworks delimit a much larger field of artistic production into a narrative that is digestible and concise. Needless to say, any sort of framework also provides a distorted view of the subject matter.

This is the lesson from quantum physics: the nature of the question posed to subatomic particles will determine their behavior; observation demarcates a way of looking that informs the answer given. Quantum physics is more complex than this popularized explanation, but it provides an apt metaphor to describe what happens to data under specific forms of inquiry or observation. The information responds to the question: it shapeshifts and adapts to the structure of the inquiry. All answers are approximations.

---➤

Artistic production in Tijuana has a relatively recent history, since self-identified "contemporary artists" began to move to the city in the 1960s and 1970s. Although there have been popular painters such as *constumbrista* landscape and portrait painters, velvet painters, photographers (particularly Japanese immigrant portrait and landscape photographers), and craftspeople of various sorts working in this city since its inception in the 1820s, it was in the 1960s with the arrival of paradigmatic figures like Marta Palau, Benjamin Serrano, and later Alvaro Blancarte and the Spanish painter Luis Moret—who briefly lived and taught in Tijuana during the 1980s—that an identifiable artistic conversation began to develop around individual practices and tendencies, and its transmission through art exhibitions, sales, and teaching. Although strongly defined and specific to this region, contemporary art in Tijuana does not have a long historical lineage from which to draw a self-sustaining discourse—an "art history" in the modernist sense of the term explicitly directed at expanding or evolving a connected formal or conceptual system.[1] Partially as a result, analysis of artistic production in Tijuana has been most often studied in relation to the representations and mythologies of the city, and its urban and border dynamics. An essentialized and deterministic relationship is often drawn between the geographical, political, and social contexts and the practices of contemporary artists living and working in Tijuana, or who while living elsewhere are still tied to it.

Art historians, sociologists, and curators analyzing the varied practices that have emerged in this city, particularly in the last fifteen to twenty years, have returned over and over to Tijuana as the locus and inspiration of specific approaches and themes. This exposes their methodologies and ideologies, which privilege context over other forms of analysis—such as formal deconstruction of stylistic or aesthetic tendencies, and psychoanalytic study of art practitioners, among others—but also reveals a larger malaise that is harder to diagnose: the need to refocus interpretation and analysis away from Tijuana and toward the artists that inhabit it, as visual arts practitioners who, through practice, seek to address and also to redress a city that strongly tends toward the obfuscation of the position of the citizen in the social contract, a city "where there are no inhabitants, only archetypes," as Yépez writes, and where the possibility of exercising and pinpointing individual agency is often negated.

For Gustavo Leclerc and Michael J. Dear, Tijuana as place should not be separated from the "borderlands," the geographic and cultural duality whose synergetic amalgamation has given way to a "postborder condition": "a *genus loci* of radical shifts in demographics, economics, politics and society" resulting from globalization.[2] Released from allegiance to a single overarching set of sociocultural signifiers—which are usually attached to national identity—and complicated by economic complicity with the "other," the postborder culture is marked by fluidity. Under this interpretation the culture of the "borderlands" is explained as the result of economic and social convergence between the global and the local that manifests hybrids and cross-pollinations. In this theoretical framework, artistic production references and is described by overlaps and admixtures, lending itself perfectly to the representation of hybridity through appropriation of stable and evident symbols of identity that are mixed and crossbred to find a third space of relatively peaceful aesthetic coexistence. In the worst cases of this interpretation, the supposed creativity and harmony created in the "third space" of the border is made a model of successful cultural miscegenation and consequently used as publicity to advertise the possible successful entry of "Latino" industries and products into the American and European markets.[3]

Globalization is more sharply foregrounded as the engine of a savage, all-teeth-bared, creativity by curator Rachel Teagle who analyzes the role played by the city of Tijuana, as subject, space of interpretation, and site of artistic life. "As a city, Tijuana is at the forefront of a new globalized economy and signals a new urban mode in which we all may live one day," she writes. "The city's artists see themselves as pioneering a new way of living, and with it new ways of engaging the city and making art. Their approach is one rooted in place, but is applicable to many situations: Tijuana's art may originate in site-specific material and forms of expression, but its outcome has global ramifications."[4] In the same exhibition catalog, prominent Baja California sociologist José Manuel Valenzuela Arce, one of the first academics to study the local music scene as a way to reflect on sociocultural constructions of the city, goes one step further to suggest that the visual art scene gained its coherence and prominence as a result of the national and international attention paid to Nortec, a collective of electronic music DJs that during the late 1990s gained notoriety by their intense, beat-driven sound, which sampled traditional *banda* and *conjunto norteño* music mixed with international rave styles.[5] Not so much an argument as a presentation of facts and a description of anecdotal information on the history of Nortec, Valenzuela's much-appreciated reversal of the expected top-down cultural economics—in which Tijuana simply receives culture to hybridize it, but never exports it—represents the final triumph of a beleaguered and somewhat reduced art scene that has finally caught on to its role as full participant in liberal capitalism.

Sampling, mixing, reconfiguring, recomposing, and recycling are, as a result of the theoretical constructs mentioned above, the most common and ready interpretations of Tijuana's artistic production. The DJ is the paradigmatic figure in the era of postproduction aesthetics in which originality hinges on appropriation of disparate sources whose signifiers are neutralized through cut-and-paste techniques. This practice is less about hybridization—that although impure still remains tied to origins—than about consumption of readily available products transformed into pure unreferenced spectacle.

Although much good work has been done to study Tijuana's art and music and develop appropriate descriptive languages to explain production, these interpretations tend to ghettoize practices even as they aim to make them "international" or, more precisely, globalized. There is an unfortunate consequence to the reading of artistic practices as the beneficial side effect of the voracious dynamics of the corporate city: it appears to justify the brutal economic politics and policies that have created the untenable physical and social conditions of the border by the nearly miraculous emergence of a vigorous and vibrant art scene. From this, it is but a short step to the eroticization of exotic artistic production as an easily packaged commodity—the art of *tijuanenses* is, then, a gorgeous but strange flower pushing through the asphalt of the postindustrial city.

Is it possible to establish another way of looking at the art of Tijuana? One which accepts the undeniable position that the city plays in the social imaginary but that does not reduce it to graspable iconographies, to processes and techniques that mimic industrial procedures, and to actions that ratify rather than resist liberal policies? Are there artists in Tijuana who overcome the understandable seduction of living at one of the most charged, politically construed, and emblematic sites of global capitalism to elaborate open political and social discourse with this place while allowing also the variances of individual agency in the city? Finally, can this model reverse the usual tendency to describe Tijuana's "aesthetics" as founded on difference from norms—that is, as an example of an imagined shared dystopic future, and therefore indefinitely outside of wider aesthetic discourses?

What has been largely overlooked in the positioning of place as the axis of artistic creativity in Tijuana is a fuller consideration of the relationship of the tijuanense to the city. Or, to put it another way, investigation of the category of citizen in the extreme but increasingly typical conditions of a place largely determined by international (and therefore unaccountable) corporations, suburban sprawl, migration, and fear of implicitly tolerated, nonstate violence. Around the question of citizenship, its conceptions and categories, can be established a series of questions that stretch the limits of arguments centered on place and/or ethnicity while beginning from these. This condition, rather than demarcating tijuanense practices as absolutely different from what is done elsewhere, creates peculiar alliances and connections to the work of artists not only in the rest of Mexico—where similar political vacuums are proliferating— but particularly to the strategies and approaches of Latino artists of the post-Chicano generation in Los Angeles and San Francisco and elsewhere in the United States. Artists living in Tijuana are developing approaches and strategies to reestablish their positions as citizens—that is to say, as political beings with full rights and responsibilities—in a state marked by vacuums, evasions, and erasures.

Con ustedes, el Artista

How would the capacity of the tijuanense to be a citizen be assessed—by which I mean to be an active member of a community, and able to understand, address, change, and shape living conditions and oneself? And further, how can this capacity be discernible in the artistic choices of local practitioners? The inquiry seems, to begin, overburdened with a moralistic construction that assigns an ethical intention to the artists living in Tijuana, which they may not explicitly have or which may focus only on an interpretation of their social behavior and actions. It is a short step from here to categorizing artists as "good citizens" or as "bad citizens": in this schema, those that contribute to the "common good" in some way are better people and therefore better artists than those who pursue private interests. But this is not the kind of reframing that is sought here. It is irrelevant to the purposes of this analysis whether a specific artist is a good or bad person or citizen in the common usage of the term. What is sought here is to shed light on existing practices in ways that do not reduce them to ciphers of a place and that allow a closer look at how artists in Tijuana work out forms of agency and individual and social responsibility through art production, either as empathic observation or as forms of protest, social critique, or collective action.

One might start by asking: who lives in Tijuana? A border town, it is imagined as an experiment in hybridization; the rehearsal stage of globalization; a city of factories; a place and nonplace—a passage.[6] Where are, in all these significations, its citizens? In an essay written in 2007 for the catalog of an exhibition called *Viva Mexico!* and later further explored in the exhibition *Proyecto cívico / Civic Project*, cocurated with Ruth Estévez in 2008, I argued that Tijuana does not have "citizens" as such, since this political category summarizes historically agreed responsibilities between inhabitants and government that are deficient in this context.[7] By contrast, continual permissiveness has marked Tijuana's history, and has led to a condition that, to me, closely parallels that described by Giorgio Agamben as a "state of exception"—the systematic demotion of citizens with full rights, and therefore able to count on the protection of the state, to "mere human beings" upon whom any abuse can be visited.[8]

The transformation has not been literal in the way that in Agamben's analysis, Jews, homosexuals, and gypsies were legally placed outside the law during the Second World War. Rather, obfuscation of the role of a citizen in the definition of the city in a contemporary democratic society has evolved from the historical happenstance of the environment of "tolerance" that has characterized Tijuana's history and the settlement of Mexico's northern border. From its inception as a place of vice, gambling, and sex in the 1920s and 1930s, to the establishment of the special economic zone in the 1960s, to the hijacking of its geography by unscrupulous developers, and finally the establishment of *el narco*, or the drug trafficker, as a de facto subgovernment force, a series of legal and illegal exceptions have been made in this region that have constitutionally placed its inhabitants in a remarkably disadvantageous position toward those that wield power—whether government, wealthy elites, or crime syndicates.[9] While not exclusive to Tijuana, and increasingly shaping public life in the rest of Mexico, this diagnosis shows particularly strong symptoms in the border region. Under these conditions, let us ask again: who lives in Tijuana? Not citizens certainly, but inhabitants, denizens, migrants nostalgic for elsewhere, criminals, uneasy neighbors, potential victims.

Under these conditions, the cultural production of Tijuana's visual artists has been identified by sociologist Norma Iglesias as contributing cultural capital that "plays a central role, firstly in the possibility of imagining a different city; secondly, redefining the city and its dynamics; and thirdly, in opening up the potential of real change for the city as a whole, as well as the subjects that inhabit it."[10] The phenomenon Iglesias analyzes charts the part played by art in the process of reconstruction of an urban center in crisis. Yet the question remains of how it is possible at all for artists to inscribe themselves into the social commons, to correct and change the status quo, when, as I argue here, the primary relationship to themselves and to each other as political individuals has been historically so obfuscated. Tijuanense artists, therefore, aim generally to point their cultural products toward the function of changing "the city," as Iglesias notes, addressing a desire to improve everyday conditions. But they are also increasingly responding to the current criminal crisis in the city by deploying their practices toward defining their own subjectivity in relation to a moral universe that is ambiguous at best, and where the body—its presence and absence, its defense or abjection—is often the ground zero of social exchange in this rugged "commons."

The absence of the body, its disappearance, and the occlusion of the embodied subject through erasure are therefore common motifs that resonate with the lack of a distinguishable political subject. This can be seen in the recent work of artists such as Ingrid Hernández, Monica Arreola, and Javier Ramírez Limón, among others. But the disappearing body is also counterbalanced by specific themes that have been mostly absent from representations of identity at the border, subjects that explore the complexity of personal relationships, dreams, and aspirations, as in the video and performance of Aldo Guerra, the photographs of Alicia Tsuchiya, and the appropriationist practice of Alejandro Zacarías. Finally, artists like Marcos Ramírez ERRE and Daniel Ruanova have been considering the effects of the war on drugs, and specifically of the paranoia and environment of violence it generates in the wider population.

The troubled history and current social and economic crisis in Tijuana creates a situation of disadvantageous conditions but also offers freedom from certain ideological structures that have come to define national and local identity. It is appropriate to acknowledge the common application and usage of the iconography of hybridity—the mixture of symbols of Mexican identity with "American" symbols of identity—as a strategy applied particularly in the late 1980s and 1990s by recognized visual artists, and a lingua franca of a great deal of popular kitsch crafts made and sold for the foreign market. It is also important to recognize the many artworks that deal with the border as a "clash between two cultures," but not without understanding that there is distance, unease, and irony in the relationship toward both North and South. Artists working with these themes do not position themselves as

"Mexican." Their self-identification with "the center"—meaning anything south of this region—is both distant and strategic.

Marcos Ramírez E R R E's *Toy-an Horse* (1997), a massive sculptural work that many have identified as a paradigmatic symbol of the relationship between Mexico and the United States, can also be explained as a vessel that hides its contents and intentions toward both. "Its transparency symbolized the evident mutual exchange or invasion," writes the artist in his Web site;[11] yet its permeable wooden body was not so much transparent as empty for the months it stood over the border line at the San Ysidro checkpoint during InSITE '97. The double-headed Trojan horse hid only the most obvious fact: nothing and no one was hiding within; its interior housed emptiness, the disappearance, in plain sight, from both sides. While the metaphor of double invasion is foremost, it is impossible not to feel that the territory of in-between is gone, reduced to those in the know, to the memory of its making in the hills of Colonia Libertad.

E R R E's work has not been autobiographical; it makes a critique of social and political systems that are, as it is said in Tijuana, *truqueados* (failed/deceptive) by our desires and bigotry. The assumptions and prejudices that determine the worldview of Mexicans and Americans are highly visible from the vantage point of border life, as are the monolithic power structures by which the two countries maintain control over their populations, up to and including the crisis generated by the criminalization of everyday life on both sides—one in response to the drug war and the other to terrorist and illegal immigration paranoia. E R R E's point of view is brought into focus by this to-and-froing between the cultures; it makes his best artwork sharply lucid in its critique of inequitable social dynamics and power. In 2008, however, his political work took a determined turn toward the personal with a multimedia installation produced by Artpace San Antonio. Consisting of a video work, photographic pieces, a site-conditioned installation, and wall reliefs, *El cuerpo del delito* (The Body of Crime) represented the scene of the types of drug-war crimes that are now everyday occurrences in Mexico. Somewhere in the desert landscape that characterizes the border, a narco is shot dead by a hit man, possibly a *Zeta*; hours later a taciturn police agent investigates the crime. Only three characters appear, and all are played by the artist, who considers the piece a generational self-portrait of peers who grew up with him in Colonia Libertad during the 1970s and 1980s. His was the first generation of young men to be presented with the losing wager: to take the "good" and face an increasingly unsure economic future; to join the narco, attain easy wealth, and meet violent death or incarceration; or to try to work within a corrupt governmental system. E R R E speaks with candor about this work, explaining that many of his friends are now dead or in jail, and that he, like many other people facing such dire choices, well could have been any of the three characters he played. Selfhood by proxy—I am you, and you and I are we, and we are they—is central to this piece, as is the possibility of addressing the social problem of the drug war by extending responsibility to all members of society.

In opposition, the paintings and sculptures of Daniel Ruanova react to the constant violence—mediatic and physical—that has taken over daily life in Tijuana and that drastically worsened in 2008 with the battle for control of the city between two opposing drug cartels. The son of politicians, Ruanova is one of the most actively political artists working in this city; yet his work chooses to embody the hyperhysteria of violence as capitalist culture's pop theater of the absurd by deploying in-your-face iconography closed to dialogue or response. Working in abstract styles in both his painting and his sculpture, Ruanova pushes the boundaries of acceptable imagery and of safe installations, as his works curse at the viewer with texts and titles like *DEFEND* from the Fuckoff Project (2009), and *SECURITY* (2009). Imagery of guns and other weapons prevalent in his earlier production has given way to pieces that embody the flattening effect of constant underlying fear and hostility. As curator Marcos Granados has written:

> The point that Daniel Ruanova has been making for some time in his works is overwhelmingly linked to his clarity in taking the pulse of a society like Tijuana, which exudes vitality as much as violence, recklessness as much as disenchantment, debauchery and hope. . . . Physically transferring this discourse [outside the city], besides standing out as an act of resistance, is a political act in the most Aristotelian sense, and allows him to maintain questions such as, when did we become who we are? When was the last time we felt safe? And above all: Whoever said democracy is perfect?[12]

While camouflage and concealment are often used in Ruanova's painting to provoke a physical reaction against untenable conditions, the body's occultation or absence is central to Ingrid Hernández's photographs.[13] Educated as a sociologist, she has produced five photographic series in which her academic background looms large, as they can be read as study or evidence of the informal building systems and living habits of the poorest sector of Tijuana's population. Yet in these images not a single person appears. Hernández wants to "imply human presence through its traces," she writes, adding, "in my work I do not portray the human element because I consider it important to show the configuration of spaces and the use of objects in themselves, through the arrangements and landscapes they generate that, presented in a particular manner, denote intimate gestures."[14]

As with ERRE's El cuerpo del delito, Hernández's series of photographs, which were taken over periods of years, rely upon empathic transference to create a sense of identification by the viewer. Framed by head-on, direct shots, the façades of homes of the series Outdoor are made of reused television parts, packing crates, and other detritus from the maquiladora industry, and are aesthetically pleasing compositions that do not hide the subsistence conditions of their inhabitants. Hernández approached this work as a sociologist might methodologically approach her subject—carefully building a relationship of trust, and more importantly a sense of equality and identification with the inhabitants. Her interest is not exploitative but rather investigative: the photos are a record of building systems; yet they also necessarily allude to class, both of the dwellers and of the viewer. Discomfort arises from this encounter where, as she writes, it is the viewer's own personal memory that fills the space left vacant by the resident's absent body. A later series, Irregular, emphasizes this absence even more. Tightly shot images of interiors, possibly of the same houses photographed before, form a series of still lifes of lived spaces. A body is implied in the stack of dishes drying on a rack, or in a pile of mattresses and bedding. In Irregular the problematic intrusion of the camera, and of the photographer, in homes that are unavoidably poverty-stricken is a direct provocation to rethink the one-dimensional representations of poverty most of us hold. The viewer must move beyond simple acknowledgment or guilt, as these images demand a type of intimacy with another that is in any case uncomfortable, and that solicits self-identification. Hernández's camera intervenes but also detonates a resignification of class that is as challenging as it is gentle, for it involves the capacity to see beyond the imprint of poverty in order to read the desire to build a "space of one's own" as a radical political act of self-inscription in any geographical and economic terrain.

And upon such terrain much can be inscribed. Javier Ramírez Limón explores the ground between photography as straight journalistic document and as source for conceptual and poetic interrogation of that which is captured by the lens. He attains this through breaks and alterations in the image's representational façade that take various forms: textual application, digital manipulation, and the pairing of two independent bodies of work to create a third. Expanding upon the narrative potential of the photographic document, the artist presents together two straight photographic series that, separately and using unrelated photographic techniques and conventions, document different moments in the process of migration and adaptation of

Mexican communities in the southern United States. His color portraits of the *Mexican Quinceañera* series (2006–present) capture central characters in real festivities celebrating the fifteenth birthday of adolescent women living in San Diego County—the equivalent to "sweet sixteen" parties in the United States. These images are brought together with black-and-white landscape photos taken in an area of the Sonoran desert known as Altar—a remote and dangerous region where illegal migrants and drugs are smuggled north. Ramírez Limón conceptualizes these pairings as a form of infiltration of the social and ethnographic content of one series into the other that makes the new work at once more informative and also more intimate.

The Altar landscapes were shot with a small disposable camera over a period of several months, when Ramírez Limón walked with illegal migrants toward the U.S. border in order to quietly record their trek. They were made into highly saturated black-and-white giclée prints with contrast levels pushed to the maximum, giving the images an unreal, almost textural, feel. "I needed to frame the landscape, to 'create it' in a way," explains the artist, and he adds, "I had the good fortune to come across this camera whose lens—full of all kinds of optic aberrations—locks the subjects in small blurry vignettes. This characteristic made the fragments of road and small bushes appear as if part of a stage; like instances of the world left there only to be observed. The black and white film, the optical flaws of a very basic camera, the tracks left by immigrants, and the skid marks of the trucks left on the road, together generate an allusive and reflective ambience around the phenomenon of migration."[15] These landscapes—also devoid of people—are intentionally abstract testimonials to the social phenomenon of migration that again rely primarily on identification, in this case, of the artists with those he chooses not to shoot.

Representation is informed by personal experience, and experience generates another approach to reality through the articulation of multiple and personal frames of reference built in relation to another, the artist, the spectator, or the absent figure or subject. Something similar occurs with architect and photographer Monica Arreola's multimedia work, which is a direct response to her experience working in the permits department of a social housing development company in Tijuana. Under the series *Desinterés Social* Arreola has created photographs, floor plans, drawings, text, and pieces made out of cut vinyl placed directly on the floor. The entire body of work, which was started with her sister Melisa Arreola in 2006, graphically represents the required size and program found in Tijuana's building code for social housing units, which has decreased over the years in response to an unrestrained privatized construction industry largely protected and subsidized by government. The standard size of a typical social housing unit is sixty square meters (197 square feet) but has increasingly been reduced to thirty square meters (ninety-nine square feet). Arreola's work presents a plain argument: a vinyl diagram pasted directly on the exhibition floor gives the actual footprint of a bedroom or hallway. The ridiculously small regulated dimensions are measured against the spectator's own body as she steps into and inhabits the house's outline. Avoiding anecdote and subjective observation, the piece locates the body's comfort as the basic trading unit in the economy of Tijuana's land speculation.

Varied personal scales, such as intimate relationships, family, and friendship, are also additional emerging topics that explore forms of inhabitation and claims to belonging. Aldo Guerra and Alicia Tsuchiya are two artists who have shown a marked interest in exploring human relationships, often with reference to their own memories and person. In their practice, as in Hernández's photography, objects are stand-ins for particular people with whom they associate. Tsuchiya's photographic narrative of the *Picture Bride* series (2007–8) reflects on her Japanese Mexican family in digital photos that together reveal the life and affections of her Japanese-born grandmother, who came to Ensenada in the 1920s as the mail-order bride of a Japanese fisherman. Self-identification contributes to an allusive portrayal of a history of Asian migration into Baja California that remains largely untold. Short video portraits identified with the name of their subject—*Hugo, Nubia, Azzul*—were filmed by Guerra as expansion of a likeness and self-identification, in which external objects such as a lamp, the sun setting over the ocean, or a spoon generate a minimal, repetitive performance by the subject, with the intention of testing, as the artist writes, "our relationship with what we do as individuals, with our ideas, and with our belongings."[16]

Finally, a closer look at the work of Alejandro Zacarías provides a key example of the long-term elaboration of a visual art practice within an ethical dimension of self-inscription into the city. A multidisciplinary artist who has participated and organized events, exhibitions, painting festivals, installation, performance, photography, and video shows since the 1990s, Zacarías's work is based in assemblage and recycling, and often expands the notions of public and private space. The continual positioning of himself as part of the wider, nonart community generates a visual practice in which gesture is more important than object. His pieces are often ephemeral interventions into the very fabric of the street: undocumented aesthetic actions that enter into the field of vision of the regular tijuanense as she uses the streets. Low-impact strategies allow Zacarías to engage with the dynamics of production and distribution of an informal city, rather than extract images and materials to present elsewhere, in gallery spaces and museums. He is also interested in creating methodologies and structures to express the desires of a specific person or community. An early example is an unfinished video work created in 2006 in conjunction with Tavo Castellanos and Melisa Cisneros, in which shots of the factories in the Mesa de Otay and the canal of the Tijuana River, among many other cityscape shots, are edited into a fast-paced montage that is interrupted by interviews with assembly factory workers, who are asked, "En que sueñan los empleados de las maquiladoras mientras trabajan?" (What do maquiladora workers dream of while working?). The following statement pinpoints their intentions: "Personal dreams are unquestionable, the oneiric realm is an inherent part of human individuality, and it demonstrates that automated labor does not stop thought, and thoughts are the weapons that transform a production line into something else."[17]

"Tijuana has to do with science fiction novels rather than with the books of Mexican history," accurately explains artist Raúl Cárdenas Osuna (Torolab).[18] So, do tijuanenses dream of electric sheep? In Philip K. Dick's science fiction novel *Do Androids Dream of Electric Sheep?* androids are differentiated from humans primarily by their inability to empathize, to feel another time and someone else in the imprint of their memories—by their incapacity to put themselves in the place of another. In opposition to the widespread reading of cultural production as a side effect of overwhelming and infinitely spectacular urban conditions, the recent work of the artists working in Tijuana moves in a different direction. The cases discussed in the previous pages are examples of the emergence of affect and empathy as explicit strategies by which individual visual artists working in Tijuana have begun to establish the parameters of a different type of exploration: a repositioning of the self as the axis of forms of personal and political resistance, and as a radical strategy of reinscription of the individual into the city.

Con ustedes, el Colectivo

In Tijuana the extension from the individual toward community aims, both within and outside cultural networks, to establish independent social structures that perform the functions of government and welfare agencies where those fail.[19] The need to join forces in order to exercise what David Harvey calls "the right to the city" is palpable and urgent. Harvey writes:

> The question of what kind of city we want cannot be divorced from that of what kind of social ties, relationship to nature, lifestyles, technologies

and aesthetic values we desire. The right to the city is far more than the individual liberty to access urban resources: it is a right to change ourselves by changing the city. It is, moreover, a common rather than an individual right since this transformation inevitably depends upon the exercise of a collective power to reshape the processes of urbanization. The freedom to make and remake our cities and ourselves is, I want to argue, one of the most precious yet most neglected of our human rights.[20]

"It is a right to change ourselves by changing the city." But the opposite also applies. In a condition of perennial crisis and in the absence of a historical understanding of the rights and responsibilities of the citizen toward those that govern (and vice versa), the right to the city begins by addressing first that which is most within our power: a right to change the city by changing ourselves. Communal and collective engagement offers the direct possibility of changing the city through the magnification of persistent individual actions gathered together like the cells of a self-regulated organism. Collaborative practices in Tijuana propose dialogue and activism through aesthetics in an exercise that involves changing and challenging oneself in order to work with another.

Collaboration is a buzzword in contemporary art for its democratic and egalitarian format and its ties to activism and politics. Despite this, a clear sense of how collaboration takes place behind the public façade of a specific collective practice is difficult to discern. That collaboration happens at all may even be a minor miracle, given natural tendencies toward control, personal sensitivities, and innumerable other things that can go wrong in any social exchange. A useful starting point for understanding collaborative processes is found in the notes for a roundtable held in the Dutch pavilion during the 2008 Venice Architectural Biennale. Under the title "Beyond the Singular into the Collaborative: How We Work," one moderator and four architects experienced in collaborative practice described some of the requirements. The text includes a series of steps to build trust—which is identified as the key element in successful collaboration.

Step 1 Desire to design something bigger than yourself.
Step 2 Start open-minded communications: discover each other's language and values.
Step 3 Design question: discuss urgencies and opportunities and agree on their definitions and their significance.
Step 4 Working format: understand each other's talents, skills, and past experiences.

Step 5   Reflection: consensus and conflict are part of a fruitful design process.

Step 6   Create something bigger than you: engage in a process of ongoing negotiation, trust and motivation.[21]

Torolab, La Línea, CUBO Project, Todos Somos un Mundo Pequeño, Bulbo, and Dream Addictive are six collective art groups that work through collaboration and dialogue in the conflicted social environment of Tijuana. The similarities and differences offered by these collectives reveal functional and organizational strategies established to redress and overcome the limitations of an art scene embedded in a society adverse to collectivity and participation. Each sheds light on different ways to engage the six steps toward trust described above.

Torolab is a consortium of artists, architects, and designers formed by Raúl Cárdenas Osuna with the stated aim of improving the lives of inhabitants through diagnostic analysis and intervention of specific contextual conditions. With a methodology that mixes the model of the research laboratory with that of the design studio, teams of collaborators change in response to specific projects and sites, led by Raúl Cárdenas, who initiates, conceptualizes, and develops projects, providing a loose, open structure that addresses authorship on individual willingness to participate rather than on contractual obligation.

Working within the structure of the contemporary exhibition space, Torolab expands the limits of that arena toward socially oriented art practice and proposes well-researched, poetic solutions to specific social dysfunctions, from the microscale of the body to the macroscale of the city. Dialogical exchange in conversations and formal interviews with experts and intellectuals in a given field are presented as part of the exhibition. These also form the resources that Torolab utilizes to reimagine social conditions.

Torolab's exhibition *One Degree Celsius*, created in 2008 for the University of South Florida's Contemporary Art Museum, Tampa, Florida, aimed to combat the effects of urban heat islands with a series of green interventions into what Cárdenas describes as "urban voids"—or leftover, constructed urban sites. Created specifically for Tampa's urban geography, nevertheless, *One Degree Celsius* had its origins in Cárdenas's observation of the relationship between urban warming due to the unregulated construction in Tijuana's urban core and its effects on the (darkening) mood of its inhabitants.

If Torolab employs data analysis, interviews with experts in a variety of fields—from hard sciences to social sciences and art—and formal presentation of projects in objects that borrow from furniture design as well as video, digital animation, and the architect's model, La Línea takes the word as its medium. An interdisciplinary collective whose current members are Abril Castro, Esmeralda Cevallos, Miriam García, Kara Lynch, Lorena Mancilla, and Margarita Valencia, La Línea exploits the empowering potential of language to generate a sense of self and of place.

La Línea has worked using poetry, prose, performance, video intervention, and tagging to address the particular condition of living at the border, the line as it is called in Tijuana, the term from which they take their name. With members currently located in the United States and Europe, La Línea exploits the communication afforded by e-mail, which allows for more control over the tenor of conversation and for careful measured words. All decisions are arrived at collectively in La Línea, and work is distributed horizontally without adherence to specific roles or tasks.

While projects may take place in a variety of spaces, as their Proyecto de las Morras attests, their continued documentation takes blog form, with text, photographs, and video updated by individual members according to previously set parameters. Proyecto de las Morras was created under the program Proyecto Cívico: Dialogos e Interrogantes as an exploration of situations of systematic states of exception to the law in Tijuana. In response, La Línea worked with young women at a drug rehabilitation center whose realities were very different from theirs, giving rise to the possibility of power inequality or to paternalistic indoctrination by La Línea. The collective devised conscious strategies in order to reverse or ameliorate these possible outcomes, main among them the understanding of their own political conditions as equally challenged or curtailed by generalized cultural acceptance of abuses by governmental agents, such as military and municipal police stationed in Tijuana as part of Mexico's war on drugs.

An interest in the effects of the war on drugs and its media representation is the central concern of MediaWomb, the project created by the binational collaboration between Camilo Ontiveros, who lives in Los Angeles; Nina Waisman, who lives in San Diego; and Felipe Zúñiga and Giacomo Castagnola, both based out of Tijuana. Coming together under the open framework provided by the CUBO Project, another situational collaborative whose members change depending on the parameters of the project, MediaWomb's creators expressed the need to reflect on the importance of their own friendship as a catalyst for constructive interaction. As Castagnola writes, trust as social capital is posited as an antidote to societal disturbance and distrust:

> The clearest part of this project for me is the collaboration and the application of conversation and dialogue, as exercises of community and non-

violence. More than trying to represent this locality and the events that take place here, the exercise is the necessity of dialogue, conversation, and to think about the theme. The collaboration between us took place in a very natural and fluid way, which surprised and excited me. I have always felt that in familiarity and trust is a great deal of the essence of the project—trust as social capital. Not only for the artistic or intellectual similitude we share, but also because of the fact that we are part of a small community that we have constructed, going much further than the violent context in which we live. Our answer against violence is the construction of a social basis that starts from a simple and basic relationship of friendship, that in the scale of the city or region, consolidates social structures relatively solid and active around art and culture.

Like Torolab, MediaWomb's outward aim is to function as multimedia art within the gallery space and to be situated in the context of contemporary art practice and of alternative design. Nevertheless, the trust and communication tapped by the collective in order to define and implement a project remains one of the most important aspects of its content, and becomes central to the part played by intimacy in the piece's conceptualization and design.

Formed in the wake of another form of violence, this time an intellectual attack, Todos Somos un Mundo Pequeño shares with CUBO Project and La Línea the use of intense and constant e-mail communication within the collective to set up meetings, formulate questions, generate consensus, and distribute information among a large number of diverse cultural practitioners. This collective, of which I am a member, was formed in May 2009 to protest the mismanagement of the most important cultural center in Tijuana—the Centro Cultural Tijuana (CECUT) by the political appointment of a disreputable new director.

The collective uses a variety of strategies, starting with video documentation of personal statements of protest toward the designation by prominent cultural producers in the region, as well as actions and performances with the intention of informing the general public of the case—such as the distribution of bottles of water marked with the legend "Aguas con el CECUT" (Beware of CECUT) presented outside the institution together with placards demanding an end to corruption (the action immediately generated positive response from drivers and indicated a high level of generalized disgust with all levels of government). The blog also contains an archive of texts by journalists and writers, both local and national, who oppose the arbitrary designation and who write in-depth analysis of the influence of conservative agendas in national culture and politics. In addition, similar efforts from other cultural organizations throughout Mexico, who critique the government's cultural management, are updated constantly, making this page a valuable resource for information throughout the country.

Todos Somos un Mundo Pequeño is an exercise in the organization of a civil society that represents the interests of cultural practitioners. With the intention of becoming a permanent watchdog of the management of national cultural resources, many individual artists, curators, writers, and performance and theater artists choose to engage in the remarkable effort to argue for or against a position in an open forum, to agree, and to agree to disagree in order to continue with the campaign, whose most ambitious goal is the creation of nongovernmental cultural organizations as a more permanent and reliable alternative to the partisan politics that corrupt cultural institutions in Mexico.

These collaborative practices share strategies and forms: the use of the Internet as a means of communication and as the medium for distribution of Net-specific projects and products; the foregrounding of dialogue to build trust and consensus, and to create the content itself of the collaboration; and the multidisciplinary character of these collectives and their projects, whose practitioners work in a variety of disciplines. A desire to create something bigger than the individuals that form the collaboration further guides these practices. This speaks to the frustration of living in a city whose social policies are inefficient or untrustworthy, and worse, dangerous and authoritarian. It also speaks of the opportunity to redesign culture and its means of support and distribution with dedication and patience.

Notes

1 An effort in this direction is the compilation of formalist essays on thirty-six individual artists by painter Roberto Rosique, *Hacedores de imágenes: plástica bajacaliforniana contemporánea* (Mexico City, Mexicali, Tijuana: Instituto de Cultura de Baja California, Consejo Nacional para la Cultura y las Artes, Universidad Autónoma de Baja California, Instituto Municipal de Arte y Cultura, 2004).

2 Gustavo Leclerc and Michael J. Dear, *Mixed Feelings: Art and Culture in the Postborder Metropolis* (San Diego: USC Fisher Gallery, 2002), 17–18.

3 See www.laterceranacion.com.

4 Rachel Teagle, *Strange New World: Art and Design from Tijuana* (San Diego: Museum of Contemporary Art San Diego, 2006), 106.

5 José Manuel Valenzuela Arce, "This Is Tijuana: Pastiches, Palimpsests and Cultural Sampling," in Teagle, *Strange New World*, 34–55. Valenzuela elaborates his arguments more thoroughly in his lengthy study on Nortec: *Paso del Norte: This Is Tijuana* (Mexico: Trilce Ediciones, 2004).

6 Fiamma Montezemolo, architect René Peralta, and writer Heriberto Yépez conclude that Tijuana is not this, nor is it anything else. Tijuana, they argue, is a city beyond synthesis: it never ceases to transform; and all its representations and descriptions "as hybrid, illegal, happy, Americanized, postmodern, mere myth, new cultural Mecca, are at the same time imaginary and real." Fiamma Montezemolo, René Peralta, and Heriberto Yépez, *Aquí es Tijuana* (London: Black Dog, 2006), 4–5. Translation from the Spanish by the author.

7 Magda Kardasz (curator), *Viva Mexico!* (Warsaw, Poland: Zacheta Narodowa Galeria Sztuki, 2007), 21–45; Ruth Estévez and Lucía Sanromán, *Proyecto Cívico/Civic Project,* "A Vanishing Presuposition," 19–44.

8 See Giorgio Agamben, *State of Exception* (Chicago: University of Chicago Press, 2005). The state of exception is a pragmatic response to extreme internal conflicts—generally reaction to insurrection, civil war, and resistance—by which law is suspended to redress a temporary situation. This creates a paradox by which government establishes a status that is at once within and outside the law. While the origins of the state of exception lie in the power of a sovereign who can subvert the law and holds life-and-death control over his subjects, Agamben argues that the state of exception became a working paradigm of government over the course of the twentieth century (Nazi Germany being the most notorious case). He goes on to describe how the current policies of the United States toward "terrorists," as defined by the Patriot Act, are an exercise in the creation of a state of exception by which those accused of terrorist activities are reduced to bare life: a life that, denuded of its basic political (human) rights, can be ended without incurring homicide.

9 Excepting the integration of narcos, all the conditions mentioned above have occurred as legal exceptions to the law. In the case of the establishment of maquiladoras, for example, several national labor laws were circumvented or altered—radically challenging two legacies of the Mexican Revolution and central tenets of postrevolutionary Mexico.

10 Norma Iglesias Prieto, *Emergencias: Las artes visuals en Tijuana, los contextos urbanos clo-cales y la creatividad* (Mexico and Tijuana: Consejo Nacional para la Cultura y las Artes and Centro Cultural Tijuana, 2008), 11–12. Translation by the author.

11 Marcos Ramírez ERRE, http://marcosramirezerre.com/ (October 21, 2009).

12 Marco Granados, curatorial text for the exhibition *Political Mutante Político,* Galería Arcaute Arte Contemporáneo, December 2008, in http://www.arteven.org/profile/DanielRuanova (October 22, 2009).

13 I am indebted to Marcela Quiroz's essay, "Entre el cuerpo y el discurso: El desmayo como perforación," in Estévez and Sanromán, *Proyecto Cívico/Civic Project.*

14 Ingrid Hernández, http://ingridhernandez.com.mx/espanol/statement.html.

15 Quote from brochure, *Cerca Series: Javier Ramirez Limon,* January 18–May 10, 2009, Museum of Contemporary Art San Diego.

16 Quote from statement in Archivo Baja California: http://www.archivobc.org/?secc=2&a=40&letra=G (October 22, 2009).

17 Quote from the statement for the project *Maquilando entornos,* 2003.

18 "Tijuana tiene más que ver con novelas de ciencia ficción que con libros de historia de México."

19 Norma Iglesias Prieto has exhaustively analyzed this phenomenon in her book *Emergencias: Las artes visuals en Tijuana. Los contextos urbanos glocales y la actividad creativa* (Tijuana and Mexico City: Centro Cultural Tijuana and Consejo Nacional para la Cultura y las Artes, 2008).

20 David Harvey, "The Right to the City," *New Left Review*, www.newleftreview.org/?view=2740.

21 "Beyond the Singular into the Collaborative: How We Work," in http://www.facultiesforarchitecture.org/book_latestarchiphoenix-book1.

References

Agamben, Giorgio. *State of Exception*. Chicago: University of Chicago Press, 2005.

Archivo Baja California. http://www.archivobc.org/?secc=2&a=40&letra=G (October 22, 2009).

"Beyond the Singular into the Collaborative: How We Work." http://www.facultiesforarchitecture.org/pdfs/book01.pdf.

Estévez, Ruth, and Lucía Sanromán. *Proyecto Cívico / Civic Project*. Mexico and Tijuana: Consejo Nacional para la Cultura y las Artes and Centro Cultural Tijuana, 2008.

Granados, Marco. "Political Mutante Político." Curatorial text for Galería Arcaute Arte Contemporáneo. http://www.arteven.org/profile/DanielRuanova (October 22, 2009).

Harvey, David. "The Right to the City." *New Left Review*. http://www.newleftreview.org/?view=2740.

Hernández, Ingrid. "Ingrid Hernández: Photography." http://ingridhernandez.com.mx/espanol/statement.html.

Iglesias Prieto, Norma. *Emergencias: Las artes visuales en Tijuana, los contextos urbanos glocales y la creatividad*. Mexico and Tijuana: Consejo Nacional Para la Cultura y las Artes and Centro Cultural Tijuana, 2008.

Kardasz, Magda, et al. *Viva Mexico!* Warsaw: Zacheta Narodowa Galeria Sztuki, 2007.

Leclerc, Gustavo, and Michael J. Dear. *Mixed Feelings: Art and Culture in the Postborder Metropolis*. San Diego: USC Fisher Gallery, 2002, pp. 17–18.

Montezemolo, Fiamma, René Peralta, and Heriberto Yépez. *Aquí es Tijuana*. London: Black Dog, 2006.

Ramírez ERRE, Marcos. http://marcosramirezerre.com/ (October 21, 2009).

Rosique, Roberto. *Hacedores de imágenes: plástica bajacaliforniana contemporánea*. Mexico City, Mexicali, and Tijuana: Instituto de Cultura de Baja California, Consejo Nacional para la Cultura y las Artes, Universidad Autónoma de Baja California, and Instituto Municipal de Arte y Cultura, 2004.

Sanromán, Lucía. *Cerca Series: Javier Ramirez Limon*. San Diego: Museum of Contemporary Art San Diego, 2009.

Teagle, Rachel, et al. *Strange New World: Art and Design from Tijuana*. San Diego: Museum of Contemporary Art San Diego, 2006.

Valenzuela Arce, José Manuel. *Paso del Nortec: This Is Tijuana*. Mexico: Trilce Ediciones, Consejo Nacional para la Cultura y las Artes, Editorial Océano de México, Colegio de la Frontera Norte, and Universidad Nacional Autónoma de México, 2004.

Yépez, Heriberto. *Tijuanologías*. Tijuana: Universidad Autónoma de Baja California, 2006.

Bioethnography of an Artist

Ingrid Hernández

This chapter presents a conversation between *tijuanense* visual artist Ingrid Hernández and anthropologist and artist Fiamma Montezemolo. Hernández has exhibited in Mexico, Colombia, and New York, among other places, and she has been a recipient of several grants in Mexico for her photographic work. She studied sociology at the Universidad Autonoma de Baja California and environmental studies at the Colegio de la Frontera Norte in Tijuana, while dedicating herself to designing her art practice and working in a wide range of media (photography, installation, and video). Moreover, and more important, she has consistently endeavored to resist uncritical and romantic gestures that consist of aestheticizing the poverty and violence usually associated with Tijuana. Her photographic work, in particular, is sober and patiently attentive to the inscription of the physical evidence of violence on Tijuana's public spaces. In this context, Hernández and Montezemolo discuss the aesthetic and methodological implications of the much-debated ethnographic turn in contemporary art during the 1990s and reflect on its uses and abuses in a border city that has become in recent years a paradigmatic urban location for site-specific art interventions. Over the course of the conversation, Hernández's ethnography-based photographic work emerges, unexpectedly, as a counterpoint to the paradigm of the artist-as-ethnographer. This dialogue introduces and precedes the photographic essay commissioned for this book.

--➤

F.M.: Ingrid, I'd like to start this conversation with your life history in relationship with Tijuana, this urban space which is such a presence in your work.

I.H.: My story is a typical *tijuanense* story about migration, a very female-oriented story about hard work, but still my story is quite an anomaly. If we can somehow understand that all of Tijuana is "anomalous in a normal kind of way," I can consider myself representative of the city as a whole. I was born here in Tijuana, just like my mother, but my grandmother came from Mexico City. She came to Tijuana because the situation there was very precarious. She had already been widowed twice; previously, she had had two husbands with whom she had six children. My grandfather was her third husband. So, one day the two of them came to the North together, and here we are, almost by a twist of fate, in Tijuana. They came here and stayed here. My grandmother arrived with just one box of clothes. They rented a place in the center of the city, a room where they all slept in one space; they quickly found work in restaurants, because, like everyone knows, there are of lot of opportunities to work in Tijuana. One day, she decided to stop working for other people and to start a business: she says that she borrowed money to set up her own restaurant and someone rented her a space without charging her for the first month. One woman lent her chairs, and another tables. Generous people. And that's how it all got done and she was able to start a restaurant called Licha's Place in front of the Agua Caliente Racetrack. The restaurant is named after her: Alicia. In Mexico, a nickname for Alicia is Licha. That restaurant was my home: I never lived in a house that was, say, normal. All kinds of people would come to eat there: artists, TV people, but also people from the barrio and people who liked to bet on the horses. Jockeys would come too from the racetrack—the guys that ride the horses. For me, public space was my space, it was an addition to what was my own. I felt like the street was part of my house and part of me, because my house in reality was a very large room that was under the restaurant. There was no separation between the living room and my bedroom. There was a bed with a bookshelf and an armchair that was part of the living room. There was no dining room or kitchen because we ate in the restaurant. There was no bathroom inside; the bathroom was outside. It was a little unstructured. Well, to be honest, it wasn't exactly a house!

F.M.: Could this be part of the reason for your interest in houses now?

I.H.: In houses and in families, because I was raised with a different type of family, not the kind that my classmates at school had: they had a dad, mom, siblings, and generally they all lived together in the same house. I lived in the restaurant with my grandmother and an uncle that at that time was living at my grandmother's: you know, there's always one son who goes back to his mother's house, especially here in Mexico. It happens a lot. So I saw my mom and my brother on the weekend every now and then, but sometimes more time would pass and we wouldn't see each other for weeks. I related to my mom and my brother in a weird way, like we were just relatives, like cousins. When I was born, my mom was seventeen years old. I didn't know my dad; it's a common situation, but it doesn't hurt any less because it's common. My mom was dating my dad I don't know how long, and when she got pregnant, it turned out he had another family. So my mom had to take care of me by herself, but, actually, my grandmother was the one who looked after me.

F.M.: It seems like family in your life is almost entirely feminine: mother and grandmother, with little space taken up by the masculine, represented by an absent father who also seems to be quite deceitful, according to your story. But what is most interesting to me is the final outcome of this unstable familial structure (perhaps more common than normally thought in Tijuana): your very personal relationship with public space. It seems at times you feel like "both street and a person at the same time."

I.H.: What I portray now are precisely those spaces in which people live, how those spaces are built and how they live within them; showing their families and the objects they use on a daily basis.

F.M.: Many artists from here make work that is, say, very tied up in certain urban stories. A young border space which for a long time was characterized by a lack of institutions, art schools, which are just being established now. In some ways, your art and the art of the others seems to be born out of the quotidian, out of this relationship with the city, perhaps also due to the lack of mediated relationships or of an academic discourse oriented toward predefined disciplines. Your generation—the one that basically was self-educated in an artistic sense, because, as we just said, art schools still didn't exist here—is very focused on the sociocultural implications of the city and of the subjects that you want to represent. Only now is art in Tijuana starting to shift its focus—the new generation, younger artists like Aldo Guerra—away from the city and toward masculinity, the body, intimacy, which sometimes elicits rejection from the generation that precedes them. It seems to me that you are also very influenced by a socio-anthropological aesthetic and by an almost ethnographic research methodology. Only at the end of your research—I like this a lot—the research subjects do not appear in person with their life histories, as you are right now in this conversation with me, but rather solely through their objects. It seems that you use people as means to arrive at the objects, instead of the other way around, which is more common.

I.H.: When I was growing up, I was very curious about space, people, and photography. It was something that was in my life in a latent kind of way. At fifteen, I started to take classes (there were only small workshops here) and I decided to take photos. At that time, my photos were of my neighbor's houses, all of them from the outside, nothing from the inside. After a while, I didn't take pictures of houses anymore and I focused on my friends. So I did portraits, but that was only for a short time. I concentrated on photography as a teenager and when I went to college I left it behind. I never thought of studying art. I didn't even know that there were art schools in Mexico; of course, there were none in Tijuana yet. Now there are two universities that offer a bachelor's in fine arts and I teach at both of them. A big change! The thing is that when I decided to study, I chose sociology; I was also interested in anthropology, but, just like art, there were no programs in Tijuana. I wanted to do social research. And well, during college, I left photography. I focused on sociology with a concentration in cultural studies. After I left the university, I started studying for a master's degree at the Colegio de la Frontera Norte. My master's program was interdisciplinary; we had an anthropologist, an architect, a biologist, an oceanographer, and so on. The idea was to look at environmental problems from an interdisciplinary perspective. I didn't like it, but once I was in the Colegio, I took doctorate-level classes in anthropology. That was when I decided to return to photography. After I left the master's, I started to work on making documentaries; I was a producer for *Que suene la calle* by Itzel Martínez and a production assistant for *Maquilápolis* by Sergio de la Torre and Viky Funari. These jobs took me back into urban space and into close contact with people; I was living in parts of the city that were outside of my daily routines. So once again, I started to relate to the city through my camera. I went out in my car—not on my roller-skates or my bike anymore—and took pictures of the city: the houses, the neighborhoods, the mountains covered with never-ending buildings. I remember I went out to the edges of the city to find out where it ended, what it was growing into, how it was growing, what it was like. I also went into the alleys and the labyrinthine neighborhoods near my own—places that, despite being close by, I would never have visited if I hadn't purposefully decided to go. Something like what the Situation-ists called Dérives: the kinds of trips around the city based more on a whim than on a pragmatic decision. That was how I left academia and focused on my work in photography. But of course, I couldn't shake the methodology that I learned so well in sociology and everything that I had learned in my classes on anthropology and qualitative re-search. For example, my work projects are based on an immersion in the slums; first, I make contact with the leader of the area, and only later do I show my work to the community and find out if the commu-nity is interested in participating by allowing me to enter their living spaces. My work is based on visits, talking, interviews, and photo ses-sions that combine conversation and taking pictures at the same time. All of my projects would be impossible without the people's assis-tance. Without the people's permission to go into their intimate spaces, my projects would not exist. In that sense, they are the product of my relationship with space and with them.

I could divide my methodology into the following stages: first, a writ-ten stage, that is to say, the initial document that I draw up as a first draft. This is the product of previous explorations of space and various concepts and is the initial stage of all of my projects. Next is the stage of more exhaustive documentation in which I dig deeper into my concepts. Next comes the stage of immersion in the space: examination of the en-vironment with my camera and introducing the project and conversing with the community where I will be working. Afterward, more photo sessions and more conversations. Later on comes a dialogue with the images—this is a very intimate and personal stage, that is to say, just me and my computer in my studio. After selecting and editing the images is the next stage, in which I show the photos in an informal way to gener-ate a kind of reflection. The last stage is the selection of the final images and then the exhibition, first in the community and then later in galler-ies and museums.

As you can see, this is almost an ethnographic methodology. Never-theless, I do not consider myself a researcher. I consider myself an art-ist, because, as you say, I do the opposite of what you anthropologists do: I move from people to objects and spaces. This is what I portray in my photos. I approach people and speak about them based on the ob-jects they use, the objects they hold on to and based on the spaces they construct. My intention is to make a photographic representation that is very different from the stereotype of poor places that we see in social documentary photography; this type of representation ends up provoking pity and sympathy because of the spaces it portrays, while I am looking for an approach that is more focused on the details of the objects, on the way that furniture is arranged inside the house, on whimsical ways of putting shoes in the closet or on particular meanings that each person deposits in objects.

F.M.: And what part of Tijuana are you interested in? What particular part of this space that has been so dissected—I would say, hyperdefined by artists, anthropologists, curators—do you work on and what kind of technique do you use?

I.H.: As I am deciding which space I will work in, where I will work and with whom, the first thing I do is to wander through the city, especially in places that are located on the outskirts or especially those places built by their own residents, that is to say, self-constructed. I am interested in working in spaces that do not have prior spatial definitions, but rather that are being built according to the needs and the possibilities of the moment. These spaces clearly show the whims and the gestures that people deposit in objects—what I mentioned previously. I am interested in the syntax of objects. I observe how objects are arranged and how spaces are defined by the use of a curtain as a wall or with a piece of furniture that divides one room from another. The result is a kind of photography that puts the emphasis on the arrangement of the objects, on the particular ways of relating with those spaces, and, above all, what I think is the result is that I highlight intimate gestures, the unique ways of arranging and relating to the object in question. In this way, I think that the human presence is highlighted, but without having the human body or any particular person appear. I take photographs with a digital camera, almost all of them shot from the front, at eye level. I think that this technical and conceptual approach allows me to present a more intimate and less stereotypical side of these slums and of the people that live in them. I am also looking to generate relationships with my work. I don't just arrive to the place to take pictures; no, I stay with the people for a long time and even after the project is over, I continue to interact with the people. We keep in touch even after the photographic work has ended. This is another thing that I look for in my work: to get to know people, to know the city beyond what is superficial.

F.M.: Do you think that what people say about Tijuana being so heterogenous and temporary—"a place where the ephemeral becomes permanent," as the artist Torolab says—is true?

I.H.:   What is true is that being downtown is not the same as being in Playas de Tijuana, being here in Otay, or being in Villa Fontana, right? So, I have had the access to get to know all of these Tijuanas; also, on the other hand, in terms of what is visible and not so visible, I see Tijuana as a space in which there is movement, and that is the biggest peculiarity of Tijuana. In Tijuana, it seems like business is always going on and people are constantly circulating, even though all of a sudden, you run into that barrier wall that is the border, trying to cut off your path, impede traffic. An impossible thing: you can always find a way to slip away, for example, by jumping that fence or forcing your way across a border put in place by force. This constantly renews this space, making it heterogeneous and giving it an overwhelming traffic. Even as a sociologist or an anthropologist, this place is impossible to define, to generate a picture of it; you can't say: this is it. Like when you touch water trying to give it a certain form: it doesn't work; really it just trickles away.

F.M.:   Where does the sociocultural perspective in your work come from? Is it from the city or is it you?

I.H.:   It's me, definitely. Because, as I said, I think it comes from my childhood. I am used to talking with people and seeing them. I'm really gossipy and I love to know what's going on with someone. I'm always hearing conversation, observing.

My work in photography is the product of a process that I develop, that is getting intimate with a community, with people, specifically with families; I prefer to call them families, because I actually don't work with the community, I don't search out a leader. . . . Well, I do search them out, but to say to them: "I am so-and-so, this is my work, could you help the people get to know me?" I can't show up to their house and tell them I am a photographer and that I'd like to get to know their house and take photographs of it. The first contact is not that simple. You have to build a certain level of trust with someone. And the first way to get in is by going through the leader. In this case, they are women and I love that too, because they are women who are my age who have an amazing vitality, a lot of energy invested in their organizations, their neighborhoods, and their houses. They are the bosses in their homes: the ones who take care of the house, the ones who are with the children. When I go into their homes, what I look for is to experience the spaces, to make images that talk about how they interact with those spaces and the objects. I am interested in presenting intimate images that show a very personal side: beliefs, ideas, whims that we all have and that can be seen in the things that surround us, in this case, the house. I'm not interested in holding myself up as a spokesperson that has arrived to reveal the truth to my audience, those people who have not been in contact with the families I work with and who want to know something about them. I am trying to build relationships, establish networks, and present images that are the result of my experience, of my relationship with the people I know, and my interpretation of place and space.

F.M.: What are these women's stories? Tell me a story that can represent the others.

I.H.: The most common story is the woman who is left to take care of the family . . . who is left alone. One day the husband left or she separated from her husband; whatever happened, now they are alone and have to help their children get ahead.

F.M.: Your story?

I.H.: Yes, the truth is there are very few women who have a complete family: mother, father, children, and so on. The majority have been women who escaped abusive men or the men left them with all the children.

F.M.: What neighborhoods do you go to?

I.H.: I basically work in one neighborhood. It's an illegal settlement or a slum—actually it doesn't even look like a neighborhood: Nueva Esperanza, or New Hope. Sometimes some people know it as the Alamar Arroyo because an arroyo called Alamar passes through the area and when it rains, the arroyo floods because the people throw trash in it and it gets blocked, and it floods. The neighborhood, or the settlement or slum, is very famous because the government goes to evacuate the people every time it rains. For sure, in a few months it'll be in the news. The neighborhood will be on TV because they always have to evacuate them. No one ever dies. I mean, there are no tragedies. No lives are lost; the water just comes up to a level where they have to leave their houses. And well, in any case, the tragedy is that they lose part of a wall of a house or an entire house.

F.M.: What are the houses made of? Recycled materials?

I.H.: They're completely made out of things that have been thrown away, waste material from the industrial zone. The neighborhood is just below and behind the industrial zone, which is called the Ciudad Industrial, in Mesa de Otay. It's all maquiladoras out there and they produce a lot of waste. Another neighborhood right next to Alamar called

Ejido Chilpancingo is also very well known, because it has serious problems with pollution from the factories; there are children who have been
born without a brain, people with skin diseases and respiratory problems. There is a collective that examines all of these environmental
problems, that is dedicated specifically to reporting and resolving these
issues. This neighborhood, the Ejido Chilpancingo, is right next to the
Nueva Esperanza settlement where I work. The river divides the two. So
you can just cross the bridge—which the people made themselves all out
of junk—to go from Chilpancingo to Alamar. And, well, the houses are
made out of junk as well. The spaces are very small. Inside the rooms
they are divided using sheets of fabric, and normally the bathroom is
outside the house, a pit toilet without plumbing or water, of course.
When a lot of people build their houses, they leave a space for the yard
and to keep their cars. Here in Tijuana it's easy to have a car, even if you
are lower class. A car can cost as little as $500. They're old cars that are
not used anymore in the United States. A lot of us use those cars in Tijuana. So it's strange—they leave a space for the yard, something that
you don't see a lot in Tijuana. The houses built by the government have a
very destructive structure. There is nowhere to build but up and the
square footage of an average house is very small. The space is very
limited.

F.M.:   Do you have a predetermined methodology in your work? What is the
most personal moment in the process?

I.H.:   So I have been going to this settlement for about three years, going
with my camera and walking around for hours and hours. I'd stop different places in the neighborhood, buy a piece of roasted corn. I'd talk
with the people, listen to what they were talking about. I started to get
to know the dynamics of the place a little: it's all people who work in
maquiladoras. All of them are single mothers. Some of them have
seven kids, others have five. They lose a finger in the maquiladora.
That story really affected me: they lose a finger in the maquiladora and
the maquiladora gives them like 2,000 pesos so that they don't go and
tell someone what happened. They pay them off so that they don't go
to the public health care facility because the factory, the company,
doesn't pay into the government health system for their employees.
Everyone knows this and no one does anything about it. And that is
how I enter the community little by little until I personally meet the
leader, who takes me from one house to another to meet the people.
The most personal moment in my work is when I am inside the houses,

as I am taking the photos. In that moment, I have to be very sensitive to the space, to everything and everyone inside, to the women who are talking as I am taking the pictures. The stories they tell me are very personal, so that becomes the most intimate moment of my work, because I have the camera and I am taking pictures as I listen to their stories and obviously I am also telling my own story. We exchange perspectives. The people also get to know me, because you can't just go somewhere and expect to listen to their stories without sharing your own. My work is the product of a relationship, and so that's why I am always telling my story too. It's like right now between you and I—I tell you my story but I am also finding out something about yours.

F.M.: The dialogic, something that took years to be understood in anthropology. Before, it practically was blasphemy to say that.

And these women, all of them work in the maquiladoras?

I.H.: They all work in maquiladoras or clean houses, but the majority work in maquiladoras. After that, after having spent a lot of time walking around the neighborhood, then I look for someone, normally the person who is organizing the neighborhood, the woman who hears about all the problems in the area and organizes everyone else to go to City Hall and talk to the mayor to try to resolve some issue. This is the first person I visit, this woman who is the leader. In Nueva Esperanza, I work with Vicky. She is thirty years old and I go and talk with her a lot. I ask her to tell me how she got to the neighborhood and also we start *chismoseando*, gossiping, like, "But where is your husband? Where was your daughter born? What did you used to work in? Where are you from?" A little like what you are doing now with me. Asking questions about someone's past, their life, to understand how they got where they are.

F.M.: Both of us are *chismosas*, gossipers. You being the artist spending time with your mythical "Other" and me the anthropologist spending time with you, my "informant," the Other of the Other. In the end, it's true, that's who we are: just a couple of chismosas.

I.H.: But, of course, she is also asking me questions and a whole game is started, based on relationships, exchanging stories, and gossip. After that, once I have developed a relationship . . . for example, I can go to the neighborhood and they'll ask me to eat with them and I stay and eat. Or I might stay there while they are working. Because a lot of them work right there—the ones who don't work in the factories work in their home. . . . For example, Vicky's mother sells iron. So the whole neighborhood is coming by, bringing iron to her house; people are coming in and out all day long, and they weigh the iron. That's how I start to meet other people in the neighborhood. They bring iron to her and I start to talk to them as well: "Hey, look, she's a photographer. Show them your pictures." You start showing them the picture and they say: "Hey, my house looks really pretty like that, huh?" or "I didn't know my house looked like that." "Listen, could I interview you? It's just I want to write something about the neighborhood." Because in one of my projects I am trying to figure out how people make their houses, like, what kind of materials, how they get them, how much they knew about construction before, where they get their knowledge from, if they are replicating the type of buildings that they made in the place they're from just with different materials. In the end, I'd like to make a connection between migration and their use of materials. And so, I tell them all that.

F.M.: In many of your photos, the characters are not present. The focus, as we said, is on the objects and the city. That's why it seems like we could say that you are doing a kind of "material culture art."

I.H.: Right, I don't show the people; I represent the people through their objects. I am not interested in taking pictures of people or, rather, the human body. I am interested in being able to talk to people and simply taking pictures of their intimate space, deliberately avoiding their inclusion in the image. I think that if I take a picture of a person, the image becomes much more closed because I have put a specific face on the situation; however, I think that without the people it is easier to connect with the situation and it allows you to imagine yourself as a spectator, to construct the part that isn't in the image. The people you work with become vulnerable, since you have the power. In this case it's the power that the camera provides. A power of "appearance." I do want for the people to appear, but in a subtle way. I have worked on several projects about Tijuana and the border which were about representing or self-representing people in a more direct way, but no, I don't think that is for me. I can't put myself in front of people like they do in those projects. It's a very delicate matter. . . .

F.M.: You prefer to allow the spaces and objects to speak instead of the people. It's always about biographies, as we were saying. . . .

I.H.: I think that in those spaces people make for themselves, that they build out of nothing, you have a better opportunity to see the relationships between people and objects. There is a greater sense of freedom

in self-defined spaces—in my opinion—a freedom that is direly impacted when we live in spaces that are completely predefined and that
moreover are dictated by regulations that prohibit making changes
to your housing.

F.M.: That's in the houses people build for themselves, because in the Infonavit houses, there isn't that freedom you mention. They are claustro-
phobic spaces, sometimes ninety square feet, one jammed in next to
another, completely repetitive. Not many people can fit inside one of
those houses, not even mentioning their things. In an interview that
René Peralta, Heriberto Yépez, and I did with a woman in one of those
houses, she told us, "I go to the park nearby to take a break from my
house." . . .

I.H.: And that is what makes a big difference. One is a space that you decide
how you want it, and the other is a space imposed on you. These are
spaces occupied illegally, and the other are spaces assigned to you.
People do not want to live in this Infonavit way, like URBI, GEO . . .
because it isn't healthy to live like that, not at all.

On the one hand, Tijuana is very arid, and housing here is extremely
expensive, because the demand for housing is always larger than the
supply. Tijuana is growing five times faster than San Diego. Tijuana
can't satisfy the demand for housing, because the demand is constantly growing. And besides, the people who come here don't have the
money to make the payments on a GEO or URBI house. A lot of people
just take over a piece of land, build their house, steal electricity and
water from the government, and that's it. In the neighborhood where I
take pictures, there is a ranch on one side that has a gigantic trans-
former which everyone depends on for electricity, and the owner of
that land and the neighborhood have an agreement. There are light
poles which are increasingly better made—before there was just a
stick holding up a lot of wires or they were all strewn on the ground.
Now the people have come together and painted the light poles yellow
and they put all the wires on it. It's a little more organized now.

F.M.: Which photos are the most representative of your work? For example, I
am thinking of the picture of a house made out of trash that says: private property.

I.H.: That is a house made completely out of wooden boards or scraps of
wood; it has a staircase made out of tires and the front door has a huge
lock and a sign that says: Private property. No entry. It's very representative. The photo of the diablitos is another one: all those wires connected

to a light pole they are robbing their electricity from. Another photo that can sum up Tijuana is a house made out of televisions, completely made out of the back parts of televisions. I'm saying that this image could characterize Tijuana because it brings everything together; it is very emblematic of Tijuana: use and reuse, and not only of materials, but also of culture.

F.M.: Moving on to another topic—very present in Tijuana today and in your recent work—do you think that there has been more violence in the last three years?

I.H.: The violence here is related to drugs and kidnappings. Tijuana is broken, devastated by crystal meth and heroin. But most of all, crystal meth is what is distributed the most and what affects the neighborhoods the most. In Nueva Esperanza, it is getting worse every day, just like the rest of the city. When I started working in the neighborhood, people didn't complain about robbery very much, but now, on the other hand, they are constantly saying, "I can't leave my house because they'll break in as soon as I walk away."

But in terms of the violence that we are dealing with today in Tijuana, the most dangerous on a day-to-day basis are the kidnappings and the assaults. Look, let me explain: Even seven or eight years ago, like in 1999 or even in 2000, you'd hear about murders, dead bodies abandoned in blankets on the outskirts of the city, but everyone knew that it had to be someone that was in some way involved with the local mafia. They were very cruel deaths; there were even codes that were associated with the mafia. For example, there were killings that had a whole ritual process before taking place. The newspapers at the end of the 1980s and the beginning of the 1990s talked about all of this: the narcojuniors, the middle-class teenagers, coming from "good families," who were getting into drug trafficking; the Tijuana cartel versus another cartel. In Tijuana, the profitable businesses were prostitution, human smuggling (organized by a network of people called polleros), drug trafficking, but lately kidnapping was added to the list. As time has passed, the mafia businesses have diversified: for example, now the same drug mafias are switching and focusing on kidnapping. Kidnapping is the most lucrative business except for drugs; besides, the police are totally in on these deals, so the violence has gone up considerably in the last four years, including gun battles between kidnappers and police officers that have lasted for hours without stopping. And at first, before kidnapping became so popular in the city, if you heard about them kidnapping someone, it was someone like a friend of a cousin or a neighbor, someone distant. But now, kidnapping has become so popular that is "normal" to have a relative or even more common a friend who has been a victim. Before, at the beginning of the nineties, you'd hear they'd kidnapped someone and it was almost like in a Hollywood movie, huge rewards, anonymous phone calls, and exorbitant amounts of money asked as ransom to get the victim back. Now they'll kidnap you in Tijuana for only 10,000 pesos, like $1,000. And even worse: there have been people who were kidnapped, paid their ransom, and afterward the kidnappers keep coming by every week for more money just to keep blackmailing them without letting the person go. When they take the families of a kidnapping victim to make a report at the anti-kidnapping office—a very hidden place from which, if you don't leave, no one finds out what happened to you—to get more information, you already know that the information is going straight to the kidnappers, or more like you realize that it is actually the same people. Kidnapping is something everyone knows about, something scary that you see every day on TV, in the papers, you hear about it on the street and with your friends, and when it happens to you, it changes your life. There are thousands of stories like this now. They are things that have become very common: it's "normal." Also, recently, because of the mafia's diversification into new illegal activities, there are a lot of robberies from ATM machines. But they are robberies in which they have even tied an ATM to a car to take it and all the money. So now in the news, every day they steal at least one ATM. Since the new president of Mexico took over, a lot of soldiers were sent here to reestablish "order." Today, there is a military presence all over Tijuana. They came and set up their camps and to wait for the president to give them their orders. And you see them like that all over the city, passing by in the war tanks. Just imagine, the level of breakdown in the police is so bad that the military ran an ad on TV that said that to really resolve a kidnapping, you should call them and not the police — they are also part of the government but they belong to another branch.

   This is how we are living now in Tijuana: on one side the helicopters of the U.S. army protecting the borders alongside the Border Patrol cars, and on the other side, the police officers running around in cars with no license plates, chasing after who knows who. And finally, the soldiers passing by in their tanks, looking for I-don't-know-what, or rather, showing off their ability to respond to any problem. In the middle of all this, the population and the drug dealers who share a space of constant violence.

F.M.: What is the connection between your interest in material culture and these episodes of violence, the people who commit them, and their victims? It seems to me that now you are moving to a new type of research: one tied to objects that are perhaps less intimate, objects that are not found in a house—like posters that identify individuals being sought by the government (the most wanted)—but also more "emotional" ones, that provoke a different kind of emotions, emotions more tied to fear, defensiveness, aggression. Could that be the case?

I.H.: I have always been interested in the city, public space, and everything that happens in it. That is to say, I am interested in observing the dynamics and the relationships that we are building within these spaces in a certain historical moment. In the case of my photographs which show aspects of the violence in Tijuana, what interests me is to speak about the issue once again using objects as starting points. For example, the photo of the public poster that says "Se Busca" or "Missing." That simple image reminds you of a whole problematic situation that involves the city, that is affecting it. And yes, as you say, it is more about objects found in less intimate space, public spaces, but that in the end are connected to emotional aspects, more intimate aspects of people's daily lives surrounded by violence.

The photographs on pages 255 to 263 are (unless noted otherwise) from the collection of Ingrid Hernández.

San Ysidro Immigration Checkpoint, Tijuana, 2005. Digital photography, 76 × 50 cm.

Pharmacy on Avenida Revolución, Tijuana, 2006. Pharmacies have played an important role in Tijuana's economy due to the fact that thousands of people cross the border each year to purchase medications without a prescription at low prices—pharmaceutical tourism. The legendary Avenida Revolución, once known for its plentiful clubs and bars, is now recognized for its plethora of gigantic pharmacies. Digital photography, 28 × 36 cm.

Casa de cambio, Tijuana, 2007. Digital photography, 28 × 36 cm.

Summer in Playas de Tijuana, behind the border wall dividing Mexico from the United States, Tijuana, 2008. Digital photography, 76 × 50 cm.

View of the eastern part of the city from Colonia Sánchez Taboada, Tijuana, 2007. Digital photography, 76 × 50 cm.

Illegal electricity connections hung from a light pole of the Federal Electricity Commission in Colonia Margarita Morán, Tijuana, 2010. Analog photography, variable dimensions.

House Entryway, Tijuana, 2004. Part of the Outdoor Project. Digital photography, 110 × 140 cm. Private collection.

House Made of Green Pallets, Tijuana, 2004. From the Project Tijuana Comprimida. Digital photography, 76 × 50 cm.

House Made of Television Backings, Tijuana, 2004. From the Project Tijuana Comprimida. Digital photography, 76 × 50 cm.

Tangled Diablitos (illegal electricity connections), Tijuana, 2004. From the Project Tijuana Comprimida. Digital photography, 76 × 50 cm.

Triptych No. 3, Tijuana, 2005. From the Project
Irregular. Digital photography, variable dimensions.

anta Fe: Suburb between the cities of Tijuana and Rosarito, Tijuana, 2007. Digital photography, variable
mensions.

Secured Property, Tijuana, 2008. A property secured by the Specialized Investigative Unit on Kidnapping (Unidad Especializada en Investigación de Secuestros, SIEDO) in Tijuana, used as a safe house by the Arellano Félix cartel. On this lot on January 17, 2008, a member of the Arellano Félix cartel clashed with the municipal police, state agencies, and the Mexican army. The gun battle lasted more than three hours. In the House of Stone—as this property was called—six men were gagged. Digital photography, 40 × 60 cm.

Shot Marks, Tijuana, 2008. These shot marks show the caliber of the weapons used during the armed confrontation between hired gunmen and agents from all three levels of the Mexican government on Thursday, January 17, 2008. Digital photography, 40 × 60 cm.

Missing Person Sign, Tijuana, 2008. As a result of the violence in Tijuana, the number of missing people has increased, and, in some cases, family members of the disappeared have organized to look for their relatives. Digital photography, 28 × 36 cm.

The Bloodiest Year, Tijuana, 2008. Eight columns from one of the most widely circulated newspapers in Tijuana during what was declared to be the bloodiest year the city had ever seen. Digital photography, 40 × 60 cm.

FOURTEEN

Jesse Lerner

Borderline Archaeology

Surrounded by emptied *caguamas* of Tecate beer and a pair of tele-vision monitors showing giant, shifty eyeballs, the renowned seventh-century ruler Lord Pacal—Mayan noble of the ancient city of Palenque—has taken the form of a blonde child bedecked in green feather boas and has crossed the U.S.-Mexico border in a pre-Columbian lunar module. Alongside this Olmec moon unit—a co-lossal head perched on golden-trimmed low-rider landing gear—the fearsome Aztec goddess Coatlicue dons her space suit and, like a Mesoamerican Neil Armstrong, salutes the U.S. flag. One highly ine-briated eagle has landed.

This hallucinatory scene, a vision of Chicano science fiction wor-thy of Sesshue Foster's *Atomik Aztex*, is a futuristic fantasy of a post-NAFTA North American space program presented in the mixed media installation by the brothers Einar and Jamex de la Torre. The pair moved from conservative, hyper-Catholic Guadalajara to beach-side Orange County while still in elementary school. They grew up there in the 1970s, surfing, partying, reading speculative accounts of pre-Conquest space travel such as the immensely popular *Chariots of the Gods* by Erich von Däniken, and watching pseudo-documentaries on ersatz archaeology, like *In Search of Ancient Astronauts*, Harald Reinl's adaptation of von Däniken's book. Today the two divide their time between San Diego and Baja's Ensenada. Their over-the-top installa-tion, created for *Mixed Feelings*, an exhibition about the border me-tropolis at the University of Southern California's Fisher Gallery, in-troduces us to the strange transformations that occur when Mexico's pre-Cortesian cultural heritage reaches that country's northern bor-der, in this case, that most delirious zone at the border's western ex-treme, a region where San Diego's military bases and million-dollar ocean-view homes rub up against Tijuana's postapocalyptic land-scape wasted by neoliberalism and drug wars, a space where the hy-brid and the syncretic are the norm, and where mutations, no doubt

14.1. Rubén Ortiz Torres, *Paisaje Romántico con Estacionamiento Maya* / Romantic Landscape with Maya Parking Lot, Tijuana, salt print, 2003.

induced by the tons of toxins dumped recklessly by the area's many maquila-doras, proliferate madly.

The contemporary replicas of Mesoamerican archaeological objects found throughout the greater Tijuana area are the products from a variety of differ-ent practices and motivations, ranging from commercial impulses to com-missioned, high-profile exercises in site-specific "high art" installation. Per-haps the most readily visible examples are simply money-making ventures, like thousands of plaster miniatures of the Aztec "calendar stone" airbrushed in "inauthentic" colors, the Chac Mol bookends and other kandy-colored tangerine-flake pre-Columbian tourist art that abound at the stalls peddling souvenirs. If it is true, as Josiah Wedgwood claimed, that copies of ancient objects "most effectively prevent the Return of Ignorant and barbarous Ages,"[1] then Tijuana is surely at the forefront of the struggle against igno-rance. But beyond the mass-produced plaster of Paris merchandise for tour-ists, Tijuana has state-sponsored replicas and a Mayan-themed nightclub, a monumental stylized Cuauhtémoc mounted atop a pedestal in a traffic circle and an ambitious rooftop complex of models that includes miniature ver-sions of the best-known pre-Columbian sites of Mexico. What is at stake with

14.2.
Postcard of an Aztec calendar stone in
a market of Tijuana, 1970s.

all of these multiples and doppelgängers? Why are so many of them here, of
all places? The replicas of the Chac Mol that adorn hotels in Mérida and Pisté
announce a local icon, but what do we make of a T-shirt adorned with an
image of Chichén's Chac Mol and the caption "Tijuana"? How useful are the
readings of the display of the Mesoamerican past offered in seminal texts of
Octavio Paz or Jorge Ibargüengoitia, or more contemporary deconstructions
by Quetzil Casteñeda and Sherry Errington, when these displays are transported to the context of the border regions?[2]

Prior to Spanish colonization, the territory that is today the northwestern
Mexican state of Baja California Norte was inhabited by Tipai, Paipai, Kiliwa,
and Nakipa Indians. Their nomadic lifestyle and modest form of social organization are reasons that their visual culture favored petroglyphs and cave paintings, nothing like the monumental pre-Columbian ruins that bring millions of
tourists to Mexico's central valley and to the southeastern (Mayan) peninsula.

Erle Stanley Gardner promoted Baja's pre-Conquest murals and petroglyphs as tourist attractions,[3] but most international travelers come looking for an essential, "deep" Mexico, and this means pyramids and colossal Mesoamerican sculptures, not traces of rock carvings in the desert. Irrespective of their beauty, the glyphs and paintings that the region's earlier inhabitants left behind in places like El Palmerito and San Fernando Velicata do not hold the same drawing power as do massive structures associated with stories about human sacrifices and ritual perforations of the flesh, capable of conjuring up sadistic visions fueled by Mel Gibson's lurid, gory epic. As if to compensate for this lack of monumental ruins, we find constructions of a much more recent epoch: the numerous examples in fiberglass, plaster, or plastic replicas modeled after objects from the Totonac, Maya, Zapotec, and other ancient Mesoamerican cultures, a wide range of artifacts scattered throughout Baja's largest city, Tijuana, and beyond. In their northward migration these ersatz ruins undergo every kind of transformation, suggesting a virtual taxonomy of possible strategies of the miniature and the replica, the revision and the copy. All of them struggle collectively to assert the place of national mythology and history in a landscape where these are always in danger of receding, while addressing diverse audiences and satisfying disparate needs.

Every such instance of the public display of pre-Columbian replicas in the border city of Tijuana is Janus-faced, looking simultaneously northward with anxiety and anticipation to the free-spending tourists, luring them on even as they ward off the encroaching cultural menace they represent, and southward to Mexico City, the gravitation center of nationalist narratives. For the tourists from North America and elsewhere, these objects function as signposts of alterity, highly visible markers of Mexico's otherness, indicators that the traveler has left the U.S. behind. They proclaim that Mexico is heir to a long and impressive cultural heritage, and that the "zonkeys" (a Tijuana burro painted with zebra stripes to pose for the characteristic tourist photo) and the all-the-tequila-you-can-drink specials that are clustered around the southern side of the border crossing are not the sum total of Mexican culture. Certain pre-Columbian replicas, by virtue of their placement and their English-language signage, seem principally to have this function. This is the case, for example, of the Olmec, Teotihuacano, and Mayan replicas that line Avenida Revolución, the city's most touristic thoroughfare, a boulevard cluttered with themed bars (Red Square, the inevitable Hard Rock Café) offering plentiful alcohol at all hours, souvenir shops, "Aztec massage" parlors and gentlemen's clubs, all catering to visitors. The same is true for the replica of an Atlas of Tula that formerly marked the Tourist Information Bureau's offices, also on Avenida

Revolución. Here the replica takes on a didactic function, taking the content of the archaeological museum out of doors and substituting durable fiberglass replicas for authentic pieces. These displays bring basic information and faithful likenesses about ancient Mesoamerica to a public that is more diverse than that which frequents most of the museums housing the originals, a public that generally speaking has not come to Tijuana in pursuit of a lesson in archaeology.

For the Mexican these objects have functions different than those of the originals in Mexico City; their presence in the cityscape reconnects the nation's center with Tijuana, a city whose place at the furthest margin of Latin America, closest to the United States, most distant from the interior of the nation and its centralist myths and identity, is problematic for nationalists. Like ancient Rome and its far-flung empire, Mexico City and the rest of the republic (condescendingly referred to as la provincia, the provinces) exist in a highly asymmetrical relation of power, one that must be continuously reasserted and renegotiated. Residents of the capital fear that the border breeds a dangerous drift of identity, subject to the nearly irresistible pull of the larger northern neighbor. Residents of the border, they like to say, speak Spanglish, Pocho, or Caló rather than proper Spanish, and embrace too readily other markers of a North American (U.S.) identity. It is tempting to read these Chilango criticisms as a reflection of their own anxieties about the erosion of national traits in an era of globalization. Ironically, like the bigoted rants of the Minutemen and xenophobic AM radio "shock jocks," it is a critique that blindly places all of the emphasis on one-half of what is a reciprocal dynamic, ignoring the complexities of the two-way process of interpenetration in favor of nationalistic posturing. In this context a statue like the six-ton bronze of the last Aztec emperor, Cuauhtémoc, perched atop a column on the Paseo de los Héroes, an update of the more neoclassical Cuauhtémoc on the Porfiriato's showplace, the Paseo de la Reforma in Mexico City, anchors Tijuana within national narratives. If Porfirio Díaz's appropriation of the pre-Cortesian past answered Europe with a similar claim on a noble past, Tijuana's Cuauhtémoc turns his back (quite literally) on the colossus of the north. Even as these objects function as ties binding the Mexican republic's most distant urban outpost to the metropolitan center, they reveal those gaps that separate the precarious border realities from those of the interior.

The art world produces multiples as well. Seated on a row of steel stepstools attached to the fence that demarcates the international boundary are 111 identical plaster figurines representing Tlazoltéotl, the Aztec goddess of filth and putrefaction, grimacing in the pain of childbirth. These replicas

14.3 Postcard of the Tijuana tourist information booth with monumental Toltec replica on Avenida Revolución, 1970.

form a part of *La mitad del camino*, a site-specific installation by the interdisciplinary artist Silvia Gruner created for the international arts showcase called InSITE '94. The setting for the installation was Tijuana's working-class Colonia Libertad, a neighborhood abutting the international line and, at the time, an area frequently used by undocumented immigrants as an embarkation point for the dangerous crossing northward.[4] Suspended eternally in the pain of childbirth, Tlazoltéotl squats and grimaces, as her child's head and arms emerge from her vaginal opening. She is a liminal figure, forever between pregnancy and motherhood. In pre-Cortesian times, Tlazoltéotl was associated with fertility as well as sexual excess and perversion, with both male and female forms.[5] Gruner's project installs this deity within a politically charged, liminal space, the threshold between the United States and Mexico, between the first world and the third, between north and south. For the migrants passing through the area, this dangerous crossing point marks the space between home and exile, citizenship and "alien" status.

The original jade upon which Gruner's figurine is modeled is itself a border crosser. Purportedly from Central Mexico (though for a time the American Museum of Natural History's Gordon Ekholm considered it a fake),[6] the object was brought by an officer of the defeated Emperor Maximilian to Paris, where a description of it was first published.[7] Subsequently the diplomat and art collector Robert Woods Bliss acquired the sculpture and brought it to the United States. It is currently exhibited with the rest of the Woods Bliss collection in the exquisite pre-Columbian gallery designed by Philip Johnson, part of Harvard's Dumbarton Oaks in Georgetown, Virginia. Before Gruner exhibited her multiples, it served as the prototype for the gold-colored figurine snatched from the Peruvian jungles in the opening sequence of the first entry in the Indiana Jones franchise, *Raiders of the Lost Ark* (1981). Gruner's repatriation of the figurine, or at least of its likeness, as the prototype for multiple plaster replicas perched on the fence in Tijuana completes a circuitous migration that corresponds to successive (and competing) imperial claims on Latin America, first by the Old World, then by the Yanquis. Multiplied over and over, the Tlazoltéotl figure returns to Mexico not as a repatriated replica of (quite possibly forged) cultural heritage, but as a signpost for the migrant, an incongruous aberration on the very visible marker of the international line that is the border fence.

Erica Segre reads Gruner's installation insightfully, acknowledging the references to Frida Kahlo's iconic paintings *Autoretrato de pie en la frontera entre México y los Estados Unidos* (1932) and *Mi nacimiento* (1932). Segre contrasts Gruner's use of the pre-Cortesian with both the militant reclaiming of identity through Mesoamerican imagery in an early generation of Chicano artists and the ironic recapitulations of the neo-Mexicanistas,[8] and proposes instead that we understand Gruner's image as a catalyst, "inviting but not prescribing an imaginary reconstruction."[9] The reconstruction is neither of a mythic Aztlan nor of an essentialized and authentic deep Mexico, but rather, given both the dubious authenticity and the thematic content of the prototype, perhaps one of an invented, emergent identity, like Frida's self-invention depicted in her *Autoretrato de pie en la frontera entre México y los Estados Unidos*.

West of Colonia Libertad, in a tourist development called the Pueblo Amigo, a replica of Palenque housing a discotheque towers over the stucco facades referencing colonial adobe. Pueblo Amigo is a conglomerate of buildings-assign, architecture that has learned as much from Las Vegas as it has from the Maya. The Mayan disco is covered with synthetic materials that approximate the appearance of hewn stone. Feathered serpents copied from Teotihuacan (enhanced with water spouts emerging from their mouths, absent from the originals), a bamboo banister straight out of a tiki bar, a waterfall cascading down the building's facade and the inexplicable stand of papyrus (perhaps symptomatic of a von Dänikenesque inability to distinguish Middle America and the Middle Kingdom?) all reveal an eclectic sensibility, reminiscent of the

Mexican structure at Epcot Center or one of the delirious pastiches of Robert Stacy-Judd.

Though the clientele is mostly Mexican, the Pueblo Amigo's ersatz Palenque introduces to Tijuana a pre-Cortesian theme park architecture more characteristic of Cancun and the newer developments along Quintana Roo's so-called Maya Riviera. Rubén Ortiz Torres's memorable photograph of the site parodies Frederick Catherwood's pioneering depictions of Mayan ruins, the first modern images of the Mayan ruins that circulated widely.[10] Like Catherwood's representations of himself and his traveling companion, John Lloyd Stephens, illustrating the latter's account of their travels, Incidents of Travel in Central America, Chiapas and Yucatan and Incidents of Travel in Yucatan, and in the twenty-six hand-colored plates titled Views of Ancient Monuments in Central America, Chiapas and Yucatan, the ruins here are juxtaposed with a human figure, which serves as a reference for scale and as a compositional element. Catherwood's images implicitly contrast the energetic behavior of the two explorers, measuring and mapping the ruined edifices, directing the clearing of brush, with the indolent natives, slouching or sleeping amid the deteriorating traces of an earlier civilization's monumental ambition. In Ortiz Torres's paraphrase, the intrepid Anglo explorer arrives to find the dense undergrowth of the jungles of Chiapas replaced with a parking lot. Like Catherwood before him, he arrives with the technology necessary for objective, enlightened registration of the surviving vestiges, a view camera and a tripod. In contrast to Catherwood's views, however, the "natives" are nowhere in sight. They have parked their cars and walked across the border to shop at the outlet malls of San Ysidro.

Another kilometer or so further west from the Pueblo Amigo's Palenque and we arrive at the site of the failed theme park Mexitlán, the most ambitious attempt to bring ancient Mesoamerica to Tijuana. Mexitlán's Palenque is infinitely more faithful to the original than the Pueblo Amigo's. These doublings of Palenque's tower in such close proximity suggest a general law that explains why a high-modernist architecture is bound to fail in Tijuana: this is a place where less is never more. Tijuana could not, it seems, settle for just one Palenque. Nashville, Tennessee, has only one Parthenon, after all, and Slobozia, Romania, has only one Eiffel Tower (and one replica of the Southfork Ranch, as invented for television's hit show Dallas, 1978–91). In contrast, Tijuana is a city where a pared-down modernism gets lost in the chaos. Here, in an inversion of Mies van der Rohe's famous dictum, more is never quite enough.

Nowhere in Mexico is the nation's archaeological and architectural heritage miniaturized and synthesized on a scale comparable to that of Mexitlán, Pedro

Ramírez Vázquez's enormous rooftop celebration of Mexico's national patrimony just a few blocks from the busiest international border crossing in the world. Of all the postmodern pyramids, plaster pre-Columbian figurines, replicas, degraded copies, and striking likenesses found in Tijuana, those that were exhibited at Mexitlán distinguished themselves as the most serious in purpose, the most ambitious in scale, and the most meticulously crafted. I would dispute the characterization of one respected scholar of the border landscape, who has characterized Mexitlán as "Mexico's brush with Disneyland";[11] the tourist developments around Xel Ha, with their "Indiana Jones Tours" of "real" Mayan villages, have a better claim to that title. Mexitlán is less comparable to the flagship enterprise of Anaheim than to other, more successful (at least in business terms) attempts to miniaturize and synthesize an entire nation's architecture into a single site, such as those found in the Netherlands' Madurodam, Élancourt's France Miniature, East Jakarta's Taman Mini Indonesia Indáh, Latrun's Mini Israel, and Shenzhen's Splendid China (Jinxiu Zhonghua). These places contrast with those attempts to render the highlights of the entire world's architecture heritage in miniature, as is the case of Splendid China's companion park, Window of the World, Austria's Minimundus, Japan's Tobu World Square, or Beijing's World Park (Shijie Gongyuán). Mexitlán's project is emphatically a national and nationalistic one, as its name suggests: to reduce the nation to a scale at which its entirety can be surveyed in a single glance.[12] Disregarding chronological or geographical principles of organization, Mexitlán displays southern and central Mexico, colonial, modern, nineteenth-century, and pre-Cortesian architecture side by side.

Not one to be guilty of false modesty, Ramírez Vázquez includes several of his own buildings from Mexico City among the scaled-down survey of the nation's architectural highlights; these include the Basilica of the Virgin of Guadalupe, the National Anthropology Museum, the Azteca Stadium from the National University campus, the former home of the Secretaria de Relaciones Exteriores at Tlatelolco, and the complex's tallest structure, the Mexicana de Aviación tower. If there is a teleological element that is nearly inevitable in all such displays, here this takes on an egomaniacal edge. The line of development of a national architecture begins with the Castillo at Chichén Itzá, the pyramids of Teotihuacán and the Templo Mayor of pre-Conquest Tenochtitlán, passes through an assortment of colonial splendors, and culminates in the work of Ramírez Vázquez. Conspicuously absent from the survey is any local reference. None of the architecture of Baja California merits inclusion, while the central valley of Mexico is proportionately overrepresented. In the absence of what is deemed "important" architecture locally, the miniatures compensate for a cultural deficit of the north. This contrasts with other parks of architectural miniatures in which local landmarks stand side by side with distant ones. The miniaturized segment of the Great Wall of China reproduced at Beijing's World Park (only an hour's drive from that other, even greater, wall, the "real" one) functions to assert that China's cultural heritage holds its own among those of the other great nations of the world. But for the visitor to Mexitlán, the message is that the "real" heritage of Mexico is elsewhere, further south, and that Tijuana ought to look in that direction to better appreciate the national heritage. The oversized signage for a multinational chain store looming just over and beyond the rooftop park, the gargantuan Smart and Final sign above the diminutive version of Teotihuacán's Pyramid of the Moon, insistently reminds the visitor of border realities: instead of UNESCO-designated World Heritage sites, Tijuana abounds in big-box stores and transnational commerce.

Though unquestionably impressive on the levels of esthetics and ambition, shameless in its nationalist and self-congratulatory agenda, Mexitlán has not been successful as a business proposition. It's not hard to imagine why this might be. It is at once too educational to function as a theme park, not educational enough to be a museum, not fun enough to be an amusement park, not meaningful to most tourists (who are generally unfamiliar with the original structures referenced), and too expensive for most tijuanenses. Disassembling Mexitlán was a piecemeal affair. First to go was a three-dimensional map of Mexico with figurines in regional costumes reminiscent of the cultural geographic murals done by Miguel Covarrubias and his brother Luis.[13] After the initial public response proved disappointing, the owners removed this model, placed closest to the stage, and began to book local punk bands to perform there on weekends. They found they had to install temporary chain-link fences to prevent slam dancers from stage diving onto the miniature National Palace of Fine Arts, or pogo dancing onto the diminutive Monument to the Revolution. Even this desperate effort to bring in crowds was not enough to make Mexitlán financially viable. Today the park is used for concerts; all the architectural models have been removed and are stored unceremoniously on their sides in the structure's parking garage. Only the street-level replica of the Atlante of Tula by the front entrance, one of only two artifacts rendered life-size, remains. The weather-worn sign and a giant, decaying plastic piñata now mark the site of this once-fabulous exercise in replication, still used as a venue for concerts.

The inclusion of a Covarrubias-style ethnological map and a scale model of the National Anthropology Museum, itself a treasure house of painstakingly rendered models, suggest Mexitlán's links not only to scaled-down national architectural digests along the lines of Madurodam and Splendid China, but also to other familiar monuments from the era of the PRI's long monopoly on power that function as metonyms of the Mexican nation. The substitution of dolls in regional costumes for the caricatures of Covarrubias's panorama of folklore (in the style of Miguel's El arte popular mexicano, 1951, housed in the former Museo Nacional de Artes e Industrias Populares in Mexico City) carries unfortunate associations. The indigenous population is infantilized and rendered as playthings for the amusement of the much larger, adult visitor. The Indians are children; we (Spanish speakers) are adults. While the human figures within the 1:25 scale architectural models are miniscule, reminiscent of people viewed from an airplane just after takeoff or of the point of view of the narrator of Bernardo de Balbuena's colonial celebration Grandeza mexicana, the dolls of the ethnological map are not to scale, but rather are children's toys, towering over the national geography. In lieu of the sweeping, syncretic vision of Covarrubias or Balbuena's New World replica of an imported European ideal, the inevitable association is with—yes, Disneyland's—"It's a Small World after All" (originally the Pepsi Pavilion at the 1964 World's Fair in New York City) that infantilized the native population and enlists us all in a nationalist fallacy.

The juxtaposition of Ramírez Vázquez's high-modernist vision with the kitsch display of dolls undoes Clement Greenberg's binary of avant-garde and kitsch, and offers instead opposition, an uncomfortable vision of their cohabitation. While Mexitlán itself offers a grand, national sweep of progress, the ethnographic map is static and ahistorical. The archaeological and architectural miniatures are specific and accurate; the ethnographic types are generalized, even stereotypical. There's a similar juxtaposition in Oscar Niemeyer's Memorial da America Latina. Inside one of the pared-down, modernist structures, visitors to that tribute to the shared heritage and experience of Latin Americans can stroll across a glass-covered map of the continent populated once again by dolls in regional folkloric costumes. The ideological message of Niemeyer's park, pan-Latin and explicitly leftist, is quite different from Mexitlán; it is one of continental solidarity, based on a shared history and subaltern status. Towering in the middle of the central plaza of the complex, a monumental cement hand reaches skyward as it bleeds from a gash in its wrist. The blood dripping from the wound congeals to form the outline of Latin America, literally illustrating Eduardo Galeano's venas abiertas. The collision of the pared-down modernism with the kitsch populism of the small

Latino world is disconcerting, as if belying the architects' faith in the popular appeal of their own aesthetic vision.

Mexitlán's miniature Palenque is more faithful than the Pueblo Amigo's, and complete; it includes not only the palace with its exceptional tower but also a scale model of the Temple of the Inscriptions, where the mortal remains of Lord Pacal (and the relief carvings that inspired the de la Torre brothers) were found. In that temple, in distant Chiapas, in the far south of Mexico, the Mexican archaeologist Alberto Ruz discovered in 1952 that the stone slabs of the floor concealed a staircase leading down into the structure's interior, descending to a large, corbeled chamber containing the king's sarcophagus. The lid depicts the ruler in ecstasy, curled in a fetal position and reclining backward. While many archaeologists understand the relief as representing the king's rapturous entry into the underworld upon death, more fanciful viewers have interpreted this as proof of pre-Columbian space travel, noting the similarity with the characteristic position assumed by astronauts in flight. Crash landing over the delirious landscape of Tijuana like the exploding shuttle, scattering chunks of detritus hither and yon, these ersatz pre-Columbian artifacts are true mutant landmarks within a heady border geography.

Notes

1 Quoted in David Lowenthal, *The Past Is a Foreign Country* (Cambridge: Cambridge University Press, 1985), p. 306.
2 I am referring to the readings of the National Anthropology Museum in Octavio Paz's *The Other Mexico: Critique of the Pyramid*, trans. by Lysander Kemp (New York: Grove, 1972), especially pages 108–12; and in Shelly Errington, "Nationalizing the Pre-Columbian Past in Mexico and the United States," in *The Death of Authentic Primitive Art and Other Tales of Progress* (Berkeley: University of California Press, 1998), pp. 161–87. See also Quetzil E. Casteñeda, *In the Museum of Maya Culture: Touring Chichén Itzá* (Minneapolis: University of Minnesota Press, 1996).
3 See Gardner, *The Hidden Heart of Baja* (New York: William Morrow, 1962). Perhaps predictably, anthropologists gave a cool reception to the archaeological adventures of Perry Mason's creator. One described it as "naïve to the point of being pitiable": William C. Massey, "Book review," *American Anthropologist*, New Series, vol. 66, no. 4, part 1 (Aug. 1964): p. 954.
4 Subsequently the reinforcement of the border fence, part of a continuing militarization of the international border, has forced this illicit migration further eastward.
5 See Juan de Torquemada, *Monarquía India* (Mexico: Editorial Salvador Chávez Hayhoe, 1943), vol. 2, p. 62.

6   Elizabeth P. Benson, "The Robert Woods Bliss Collection of Pre-Columbian Art: A Memoir," in *Collecting the Pre-Columbian Past*, edited by Elizabeth Hill Boone (Washington, DC: Dumbarton Oaks, 1993), pp. 21–22.

7   E. T. Hamy, "Note sur une statuette méxicaine," *Journal de la Société des Américanistes*, vol. 3, no. 1 (1906): pp. 1–5.

8   Erica Segre, *Intersected Identities: Strategies of Visualization in Nineteenth- and Twentieth-Century Mexican Culture* (New York: Berghahn Books, 2007), pp. 265–69.

9   Ibid., p. 254.

10 This comment is not meant to discredit the proto-archaeological efforts at Palenque by writers and illustrators such as José Antonio Calderón (1784), Antonio Bernasconi (1785), Antonio del Río (1787), Guillermo Dupaix and José Luciano Castañeda (1805–7), and Baron Jean-Frédéric Maximilien de Waldeck (1834–36); these earlier depictions, however, circulated only in very limited fashion. In contrast, Stephens and Catherwood's best seller captured the popular imagination; *Incidents of Travel in Central America* went through twelve printings in the first three months following publication. See Victor Wolfgang Van Hagen, *Maya Explorer: John Lloyd Stephens and the Lost Cities of Central America and Yucatán* (Norman: University of Oklahoma Press, 1947), p. 197.

11 Lawrence A. Herzog, *From Aztec to High Tech: Architecture and Landscape across the Mexico-United States Border* (Baltimore: Johns Hopkins University Press, 1999), p. 160. Herzog summarizes arguments that Mexitlán's goals were didactic, unlike Disneyland's commercial and entertainment goals, as well as similarities between the two manufactured landscapes.

12 The Splendid China theme park in Citrus Ridge, Florida (1993–2003), sister park to that of Shenzhen, represents a unique attempt to transport this sort of miniaturization of national heritage beyond the nation's borders.

13 I am thinking of Luis Covarrubias's mural for the National Anthropology Museum, and Miguel Covarrubias's mural for the former FONART building. These are illustrated in Sylvia Navarrete, *Miguel Covarrubias: Artist y pintor* (Mexico City: Consejo Nacional para la Cultura y las Artes, 1993), pp. 102–3; and Alfonso de Neuvillate, *Arte Contemporaneo en el Museo Nacional de Antropologia* (Mexico City: Du Pont, 1985), 44–47.

Filmography

Chariots of the Gods (Erinnerungen an die Zukunft) (Harald Reinl, 1970)
In Search of Ancient Astronauts (Harald Reinl, 1973)
Miracles of the Gods (Botschaft der Götter) (Harald Reinl and Charles Romine, 1976)
Raiders of the Lost Ark (Steven Spielberg, 1981)
En medio del camino (Sarah Minter, 1994)
Apocalypto (Mel Gibson, 2006)

Redefining Sodom

A Latter-Day Vision of Tijuana

Sprawled along the western portion of the border between the United States and Mexico, Tijuana has long been treated with enormous disdain by both countries. In the United States, it is regarded as a city of sin, a playground of rowdy sailors notable only for wild strip bars and a violent drug trade. In Mexico, on the other hand, the northern frontier is considered a leaky portion of the national dam, a site of insufficient patriotism where Anglo-American culture and language seeps in and contaminates the country. Faced by sneers on either side, buffeted by the winds of Prohibition, the Second World War, and national currency crises, the city drifted haphazardly for almost a century.

In recent years, however, Tijuana has begun to talk. A small but viable publishing industry allows local writers to challenge accepted ideas about the border region, providing a forum for the reevaluation of the city and its inhabitants. Whereas earlier generations of intellectuals left the area in order to practice their various crafts, authors such as Roberto Castillo, Rosina Conde, Luis Humberto Crosthwaite, Fran Ilich, and Regina Swain write from and about the border, redefining this space as worthy of creative attention. In an effort to escape the essentialism that has generally marred descriptions of Tijuana, they focus on individual histories, locating the city's character within its diverse inhabitants rather than its tourist-oriented spectacles. Theirs is a Tijuana populated by teachers, construction workers, and secretaries as well as drug dealers, prostitutes, and cholos. Ignoring the scorn often heaped upon the northern dialect, furthermore, many of them write in the colorful, colloquial forms common to the streets of the border. Through valorization of the distinct lives and voices of Tijuana's inhabitants, these authors attempt to restore dignity to the urban environment of the area and agency to an otherwise objectified and ignored people.

Although many local authors deserve critical attention, this essay focuses on the works of Roberto Castillo and Luis Humberto Crosthwaite as representative articulations of a new vision of Tijuana. I begin by explaining the sources of border images common in the United States and Mexico, and then trace the historical and economic shifts that facilitated the rise of a new generation of local artists. After establishing this framework, I analyze the works of Castillo and Crosthwaite, discussing their conceptions of the Mexican-American border and their hopes for Tijuana in the new millennium.

"South of the Borderism"

The denigration of Tijuana by the United States is not a unique phenomenon, but simply one manifestation of the general scorn with which Anglo-Americans have long viewed Mexico. During the mid-nineteenth-century expansion of the United States into what is now the American Southwest, Anglos began to define a collective identity in contrast to the "other," the Mexican. In "Writing the Border: The Languages and Limits of Representation," Norma Klahn says: " 'South of the Borderism' is . . . the way that the United States and its peoples have come to terms with Mexico as they continuously invent an 'other' image and define and defend their own. In their writings, and in contrast to the ways they constructed or invented themselves (stereotypically, as morally superior, hardworking, and thrifty), Anglos portray Mexicans at best as mysterious, romantic, fun-loving, laid-back, and colorfully primitive; alternatively, Mexicans are seen as conniving, highly sexualized, disorderly, violent, and uncivilized" (Klahn 1997: 125).

This "othering" has taken many forms, but it initially focused on the idea that the mixed racial background of Mexicans (peninsular Spanish and indigenous) left them weak and inherently degraded. Anglo-Americans, descended from the hard-working Puritans, were conversely envisioned as racially pure and filled with the strength of the Protestant Ethic. This doctrine of difference gave imperialism the quality of a civilizing mission and allowed the United States to justify repeated attacks on Mexican sovereignty as part of "the mission Anglos assumed as civilizers of the hinterlands, with a need to control all that was seen as barbaric—sexuality, vice, nature, and people of color" (123).

Over a hundred years after the current international border was established, Anglo-Americans continue to view Mexicans primarily through the tropes of difference, inferiority, and barbarism. Recently, concerns about illegal migration have magnified this problem, producing images of Mexican hordes slipping across a porous line to steal jobs and abuse welfare programs. Within this atmosphere of disdain and fear, the border between the two countries has taken on significance beyond a simple political separation. Klahn argues, "As soon as a boundary is established, the other side becomes desirable, the threshold to cross into the unknown, the yet-unexplored landscape" (1997: 125). Marking the limit between the "civilized" but boring society of white North America and the teeming areas of the dark, mysterious South, the international line is both a threat and a lure to Anglo-Americans interested in proving their fortitude, breaking the rules, or running away. Because visitors approach the border with such a preconceived sensation of combined desire and trepidation, they tend to find exactly what they anticipated on the other side. In both fiction and nonfiction, Anglo-Americans describe crossing into Mexico as a kind of descent into hell. These writers, drawing on decades and centuries of racial prejudice, see nothing but barely hidden violence and uncontrolled sexuality in the dark faces of the locals.[1] Frightened but fascinated, they cross in droves in order to experience what they understand as a more primitive and intense world.

Tijuana, which claims to be the most-visited border city in the world, has become the object of more "South of the Border" ruminations than perhaps any other location.[2] According to popular U.S. discourse, the city is the ultimate symbol of Mexican lust, dishonesty, and darkness (Tabuenca Córdoba 1997: 191). The notion that Tijuana sin stems from a basic corruption in the Mexican character, however, is easily disproved by the fact that most of the vice industry on the border was established by and for Americans. María Socorro Tabuenca Córdoba discusses the origin of these images, stating, "The classic image of the border as brothel can be traced back to the Prohibition era in the United States" (191). During Prohibition, Anglo-American businessmen forced to shut down bars and brothels at home reopened them in Tijuana, developing the city into what David Arreola and James Curtis call an "extraterritorial American enclave" that allowed U.S. citizens to pursue their desires in a Mexican fantasy land free of the constraints of civilized society (Arreola and Curtis 1993: 102). As they point out, "In a nation gone dry and straight and in the absence of a Las Vegas, Tijuana emerged as a convenient yet foreign playground, tantalizingly beyond the prevailing morality and rule of law north of the border" (100). The Casino de Agua Caliente, perhaps the most famous symbol of Tijuana perdition, was controlled by Anglo-American businessmen and patronized almost entirely by the U.S. elite.

Despite the fact that the Tijuana vice industry developed in response to Anglo-American demand, visitors from the United States continue to interpret its presence as symptomatic of the lawlessness and immorality of Mexico as a whole. Indeed, one might argue that the continuation of this belief is necessary for the maintenance of the barbaric Mexican / innocent American dichotomy. Since the character of the United States is so strenuously defined against that of its southern neighbor, Tijuana must be seen as vastly different from the Anglo-American cities just over the border. In "Tijuana: la ciudad cinematográfica," Humberto Félix Berumen writes, "In the majority of cases, there is a clear tendency to emphasize moral corruption, misery, or the poverty of Tijuana's lower classes" (2001b: 4). Indeed: "In all of the cases, the same stereotypes are reaffirmed, the same stereotypes that have now become part of the Tijuana imaginary—the city of vice, of moral corruption, of drug trafficking, and indiscriminate violence" (5).

These images have lasted for so long because of their tremendous appeal to Anglo-American audiences. Emphasizing the dirt and sleaze of Tijuana, they produce a sense of self-satisfaction and entitlement with regard to the supposedly clean, pure environment of the United States. This lamentable tendency continues even in contemporary films with relatively sympathetic tijuanense characters such as Traffic (Soderbergh 2000). In this film, all of the Mexican scenes were shot in a dusty brown-and-white, creating a sharp contrast to the green grass and blue swimming pools of Traffic's San Diego. The "old West" style of photography encourages audiences to read into Tijuana common ideas about the nineteenth-century American West, such as gun battles in dusty streets, prostitutes in busy brothels, and other images of lawlessness and degradation. San Diego may be marching into the new millennium, but Tijuana seems to be stuck in the sepia-toned netherworld of Jesse James and Wyatt Earp. This distancing gives viewers of Traffic access to a collective fantasy about American progress and wealth and Mexican poverty and backwardness. Movies such as Traffic help to further refine our stereotype of the Mexican as the "other," propagating a vision of Tijuana as an uncontrolled conduit through which the danger of the south penetrates and pollutes the safety and security of the north.

"North of the Borderism"

Akin to the Anglo-American phenomenon of South of the Borderism is the deep disdain directed at Tijuana and the other border cities from the interior of Mexico. Tijuana, isolated from the central power structure of the country by more than a thousand miles, has been known to the rest of Mexico largely through films that emphasize the most sordid aspects of the city. These images depict Tijuana as a place of drug traffickers and trinket sellers lacking any real sense of national identity (Tabuenca Córdoba 1997: 189). The local popularity of opposition political groups and the presence of aspects of Anglo-American consumer culture in Tijuana have fueled this perception, leading Mexicans from the interior to believe that they are witnessing the slow secession of the northern border regions to the United States (Arreola and Curtis 1993: 104). Oscar Martínez observes, "It has long been traditional for Mexicans from the interior to criticize fronterizos for their alleged complacency concerning illegal practices that permeate the border dollar economy; their alacrity to learn the English language; and their tendency to adopt *norteamericano* consumption habits, customs, and dress styles" (1988: 119). The representations of Tijuana that reach the center of the country do not fit in with the vision of centralized and uniform Mexicanness propagated by the state, and border residents are consequently seen as "barbarous, lacking in national identity, and . . . their urban centers (Tijuana y Ciudad Juárez) as cities of sin" (Tabuenca Córdoba 1997: 2). Mexican prejudice against the border cities has been almost as pervasive as the "den of sin" idea of Tijuana common in the United States, and perhaps more damaging for the role it has played in preventing these areas from becoming nationally recognized urban centers.

The notion of Tijuana as a worthless city of sin and strife is a result of the reflexive centralism and defensive nationalism long present in Mexican political culture. Danny Anderson writes that the border is expected to function not only as a political divide, but furthermore as a "limit of the nation and national identity" (1995: 29). Sergio Gómez Montero agrees, arguing that the border is seen as "a limit that is always in danger . . . where the overbearing presence of the United States is Mexico's sword of Damocles" (1993: 93). From the perspective of Mexico City, Tijuana and the other border metropolises do little to block this sword, allowing Anglo-American culture to pollute Mexico on a daily basis. As Tabuenca Córdoba says, "The general belief is that the border is a place of easy penetration by language, customs, and lifestyle due to direct contact with the United States" (1997: 186). The routine contact that border residents have with Anglo-American culture is presumed to have weakened their Mexicanness, leaving them damaged citizens. This is particularly true in the area of language, where the presence of Anglicisms and other aberrations in the border lexicon is taken as evidence of diminished national pride (Bustamante 1982: 2).

A Border Renaissance

Though attacked on all sides by negative portrayals and blatant stereotyping, Tijuana has begun to fight back. In the past twenty years, the growth of maquiladora industry has made this previously backwater city into an economic powerhouse attracting enormous migration from other parts of Mexico. No longer is Tijuana simply a gateway for exodus into the United States; instead, people are staying. This fact is now widely known throughout Mexico and the world. In the January 26, 1998, *Los Angeles Times*, Anne-Marie O'Connor wrote that Tijuana's "fabled 1% unemployment rate attracts men and women looking to work hard and break free of the barriers to upward mobility that are found in many Mexican cities where land is scarce and those born poor are condemned to die with nothing." Monthly wages for professionals as well as factory workers are higher than elsewhere in Mexico, attracting immigrants from across the social spectrum ("Mexico" 1998). The city has grown rapidly in size as well as wealth, doubling in population every decade since the 1950s (Proffitt 1994: 153). As a result of the growing prosperity and prominence of Tijuana, even the central government has increasingly recognized "la actualización creciente de la frontera norte como región estratégica para México" (Gómez Montero 1993: 19).

With this realization, apparently, came a desire to reclaim and renationalize Tijuana. After years of inattention, the 1980s saw a sudden rush of federal investment in literary workshops, musical groups, art exhibitions, and other government programs along the border. New universities and research institutes were opened, and previously existing ones were given more money and more support.[3] This was truly groundbreaking, considering that the reality of Mexican centralism has long dictated that money for cultural activities remain in and around the capital. Even as late as 1994, Gómez Montero asserted that "80% of the allocation destined by the federal government for culture . . . [is] invested in the Federal District" (1994: 117). Since its inhabitants were generally considered barbaric and immoral, Tijuana received very little support even when compared to other northern cities such as Chihuahua (Tabuenca Córdoba 1995: 160).

Although programs aimed at increasing educational and cultural opportunities in the city were certainly appreciated, they were not perhaps entirely altruistic. Oscar Martínez believes that when "[b]order cities assumed high priority within the grand scheme of decentralized national development, [this] led to the creation of economic and cultural programs intended to improve the standard of life and to reinforce Mexican culture and customs"

(1988: 122). Rosina Conde argues that federal funding for cultural development was intended to "cultivate and nationalize the border states by revealing the essence of what it was to be Mexican" (Conde 1992, qtd. Tabuenca Córdoba 1995: 155). In her understanding, the sudden interest in border issues that developed during the 1980s resulted from Mexico City's desire to reassert the ties of national identity and prevent Tijuana from becoming too estranged from centralist culture. As Tijuana became richer and more important to the outside world, Mexico City finally began to take an interest in this long-ignored city of the northern frontier.

Mexico City may have intended to draw Tijuana into the national fold by means of cultural and educational funding, but this largess of support did not diminish the very regional focus of Tijuana art. Indeed, "the emergence of regional literary forms was clearly indicative of a tendency to reject the federal government in Mexico City and to affirm regional interests, as paradoxical as this may seem in light of support programs subsidized by the federal government" (Tabuenca Córdoba 1995: 156). A perfect example of this subversion lies in the gradual conversion of the Centro Cultural de Tijuana (CECUT) from a monument to the achievements of central Mexico to a space that showcases Tijuana writers, visual artists, and musicians whose messages frequently conflict with the national fantasies constructed in the capital. Although "considering the lack of autonomy of Mexican states, it would be naive to think that any artistic-cultural phenomena could be promoted without the previous blessing (or malediction) of the Mexican government," Tijuana artists have succeeded in establishing distinct visions that consistently reject centralism and embrace the hybridity of the northern border (156).

Even local academics funded almost entirely by the federal government have created new Tijuana narratives to counter those of uncertain nationality and cultural pollution. José Manuel Valenzuela Arce argues, "There has been much talk about the dangerous possibility of the 'selling out' of border residents; nevertheless, at the border there are a number of strong sociocultural movements of resistance that use symbols, images, and historical recuperation to analyze border identity in the face of the United States" (2000: 116). According to Jorge Bustamante, conclusions of diminished border nationalism have been drawn "because of subjective interpretations of select data, such as the use of English words given Spanish transformations in daily borderspeak" (2000: 176). In his analysis: "At the northern border, lo mexicano is whatever is not the U.S. Which is to say that the otherness of the U.S. helps the border define lo mexicano. Paradoxically, the proximity to the U.S. is what gives the border a window into its own ethnic identity, which does not happen in the interior, where the experience of otherness is not as direct and immédiate" (177). Accordingly, tijuanenses may incorporate signs and symbols from elsewhere without perceiving a contradiction between them and a fluid but strong sense of national, ethnic, and linguistic selfhood.

Whereas earlier intellectuals were forced to go to the Federal District for the resources necessary to pursue their careers, the beginning of national investment in Tijuana created the funding and support for a small but significant cultural community. The CECUT, providing a forum for all types of art, has had an enormous impact in the foundation and development of this resourceful group. As classical guitarist Alberto Ubach reports, the "1982 opening of the sprawling federally funded Cultural Center . . . was a watershed event for Tijuana, and instrumental in getting him to settle back in his native city" (San Diego Union Tribune 2001). Programs like the Orquesta de Baja California have brought classical clout to the region, while exhibits like the annual banners show bring entries from Tijuana and around the world. The CECUT also hosts book readings, literature discussion groups, and meet-the-author programs designed to publicize local writing.

Though the CECUT and other government organizations have served as the hub of the Tijuana cultural renaissance, growth has been sustained on a more grassroots level. An increasing number of coffeehouse performance/exhibition spaces have sprung up, providing support to developing artists. In recent years, area painters like Norma Michel and Tania Candiani have become well known on both sides of the border. Nortec, a local version of electronic music that combines techno, norteño, and contemporary Latin sounds, has made a big splash in the United States and Europe, as has the punk band Tijuana No!. Finally, a new generation of border writers, most of them born in the 1950s and 1960s, has risen up around the infrastructure provided by the CECUT and local universities like the Universidad Autónoma de Baja California.

These writers have put Tijuana on the literary map by using the city not only as their base of operations but also as the setting of their novels, short stories, and poems. The list of participants has grown enormous in recent years, and includes such diverse figures as the poet and essayist Heriberto Yépez, the science fiction and detective novelist Gabriel Trujillo Muñoz, and the playwrights Hugo Salcedo and Ursula Tania.[4] Of these authors, Roberto Castillo and Luis Humberto Crosthwaite have been particularly visible supporters of the border city aesthetic. Reflecting the newly revived local pride, these two writers attempt to reveal the city in all its complicated and diverse reality. Although at times mocking the official image-rehabilitation projects of Tijuana, they help the cause by quietly countering the many stereotypes that have for so long ruled the international vision of the city. Portraying Tijuana as a space in which domestic lives unfold instead of as an impersonal world of sin, Castillo and Crosthwaite bring the urban border and all its complicated and vibrant humanity to life.

Roberto Castillo Udiarte

Roberto Castillo, a border-born writer who was educated in Mexico City, plays with reader expectations about Tijuana through his attention to quotidian urban life. Although Castillo has written many works of fiction, poetry, and journalism, I focus in this essay on an early poem, "La última función del mago de los espejos," a recent poem, "Welcome Tu Tijuana," and on the Johnny Tecate vignette series that he continues to publish. Fifteen years and a great deal of literary production separate these works, but they seem to me to exemplify Castillo's ongoing relationship with the city of Tijuana. "La última función" gives readers a glimpse of the people who make up Tijuana through the words of a barker luring passersby into a show. Almost two decades later, "Welcome Tu Tijuana" is a more straightforward invitation to a world in which languages and cultures unite to form a new and exciting hybrid. Finally, the vignette series features the adventures of Johnny Tecate, a frontier resident bumbling through urban experiences ranging from rising taxes to car theft to the vagaries of the Border Patrol. By focusing on the daily joys and sorrows of the people of Tijuana, Castillo emphasizes the growing diversity and importance of a city that was until recently portrayed as a collection of anonymous prostitutes and trinket sellers.

Castillo makes notable use of the language of Tijuana, writing in a phoneticized version of the norteño dialect and frequently employing the Anglicized phrases common in the area. As he pushes the speech patterns of the border to the center of his work, Castillo firmly rejects the centralist doctrine dictating that this language is "un-Mexican" and uneducated. His style can be analyzed using the conventions for other types of oppositional discourse. For example, William Leap discusses the use of "queer language," arguing that the rehabilitation of words like "queer" and "faggot" by homosexuals actually functions to position the gay community within the "speaking" mainstream and straight listeners/readers in a "listening" margin which has to struggle to translate/understand queer language. In his analysis, " 'queer' is no longer a status of the 'other,' as defined by the conventions of the mainstream. Queer is now the starting point for the queer's own social critique, and the mainstream is now positioned, in spite of its objections, within the margin" (Leap 1996: 104).

Likewise, Castillo's use of the frequently mocked Tijuana dialect serves to reclaim this language, making it the voice of daily life rather than an easily dismissed object of ridicule. Readers who do not speak norteño are forced to translate, an action that in itself legitimates the importance of the language as a primary means of communication. In Castillo's writings, the recuperation of the border dialect is akin to the reimagining of the entire frontier milieu, as readers must personally rearrange the geography of power in order to understand this language and space as central and their own as marginal.

While observers and writers from the Federal District have disparaged from afar the "bastardized" and "unpatriotic" nature of border Spanish, Castillo presents this language as a vibrant blend that is nonetheless totally Mexican. Johnny Tecate goes "zapping entre canal y canal" (Castillo 2000a); residents of Tijuana drive "pickups" (2001d); people have "baby showers"; and the border becomes "el bordo" (2001b). During the Christmas season, the locals go out to see the "santocloses" (2001a). This hybrid language forms in the margins of two countries and language traditions: "damas y caballeros / welcome Tu Tijuana / el lugar más mítico del mundo / donde las lenguas se aman y se unen / en el aló, el oquei, el babai, y el verbo tu bi" (2001e). Even the title of this poem is a play on the mixed languages of Tijuana, for the use of the word *tu* is not just a misspelling but furthermore seems to indicate that the city itself is being welcomed to a new era: that is, "Welcome You Tijuana." Tijuana, a space of ambition and growth, is being introduced to the world, an idea perhaps symbolic of the city's literary emergence from the myth and stereotype of its past.

Castillo celebrates the remarkable hybridity of the frontier culture, but reality forces him to acknowledge the political and national structures that impede what might be considered a natural cross-border blending. In a pointed response to centralist concern over the diminished Mexicanness of border residents, Castillo shows the extent to which nationality in Tijuana is enforced and enacted on a daily basis:

> Con su español aprendido de los anuncios de Taco Bell y McDonald's, el agente [estadunidense] pregunta: "¿Ser tú Johnny Tecate?"
> El Johnny contesta: "¡Sí, yo soy!"
> "¿Tú vivir en Tijuana?"
> "¡Sí, yo vivir en Tijuana!"
> "Pesar a inspecshión sacundaria." (Castillo 2001c)[5]
> [In Spanish learned from Taco Bell and McDonald's ads, the agent asks, "¿Ser tú Johnny Tecate?"
> Johnny answers: "Yes, it is I!"

"¿Tú vivir en Tijuana?"
"Yes, I to live in Tijuana!"
"Pesar a inspecshión sacundaria."]

Constant harassment and discrimination from Anglo-Americans makes it impossible for Mexicans to forget national difference, limiting the level of potential hybridization and effectively disproving the myth of frontier-zone identity loss.

Castillo uses local arcana as well as dialect to draw the reader into his version of an insider's Tijuana. Since most of the Johnny Tecate series has been published by *Letras Libres*, a Mexico City–based culture journal, readers from the center of the country who have perhaps never before thought seriously about Tijuana now puzzle out stories which take for granted a baseline knowledge of the social and political history of the city. In vignettes like "Vía Santana," Johnny muses over such local issues as the possibility of renaming streets after famous tijuanenses instead of numbers, forgettable politicians, or faraway heroes: "Today, the Avenida Hipódromo will be renamed Avenida Los Tucanes de Tijuana . . . la Revu will be Rita Hayworth, Javier Batiz will be the new name of Segunda, Díaz Ordaz will now be known as Lupita D'alessio, and we are thinking of changing various streets to Gato Félix, Castillo Peraza, and Julieta Venegas" (Castillo 2000b).[6]

Although both the streets and the people named are quite famous within Tijuana, some are unlikely to be recognized by an audience outside the border region. Castillo, however, appears unconcerned by this fact, saying, "The references to local issues force the reader to enter the world of the border, emphasizing the importance and centrality of this region, especially compared to Mexico City." Even if outsiders don't know all of the names mentioned in this Johnny Tecate vignette, the very foreignness of some will remind them of the inadequacy of more commonly available depictions of Tijuana. Castillo proves the complexity of Tijuana by confusing his readers, forcing them to discard more simplistic understandings of border culture in order to enter into a city of intricate detail.

This "education of the outsider" theme is addressed more specifically in several vignettes in which visitors arrive in the city with a standard set of border expectations only to be confronted by more complicated local versions of Tijuana. In Castillo's recent vignettes, Johnny Tecate acts as both the "typical" tijuanense and as an ambassador for the city:

Johnny Tecate goes to the airport to get his friend Panchito Coyoacán. Pancho has never been to Tijuana, and his references only come from jokes, adventures, myths, legends, and what he sees on TV and reads in the press. . . . "Where are we going?" Pancho asks.

"To Playas."

"Tijuana has a beach?"

"Yes, even though if you're not from here you might not know it ; you only know about bars, knock-offs, the 'other side,' migrants, drug dealers, and other things." (Castillo 2001b)

A couple of friends from Chihuahua who came to visit Tijuana just 48 hours ago . . . talk about their first impressions of the border city: it's ugly, it's where Lomas Taurinas is, the climate is wonderful, that they didn't know there was a beach, that the lines to cross to San Diego are eternal, that Avenida Revolución is desolate, that we didn't know that Tijuana was so big, that the food is really good. (2001d)[7]

In these scenes, Castillo addresses national and international stereotypes of Tijuana, asking readers to understand that our own images of the city may not be complete or even accurate. Johnny, the author's alter ego, enlightens us as he muddles through the everyday joys and tragedies of Tijuana: worrying about crossing the border, contemplating local architecture, and dealing with apathetic government functionaries in an effort to recover his stolen car (2002, 2001c, 2000c). He experiences Tijuana for us, and through him we gain access to the people in buses and bookstores otherwise invisible to tourists. They are the heart of Roberto Castillo's Tijuana, and Johnny mirrors this world for his tourist friends as well as their reading counterparts.

The idea of mirrors is particularly important in Castillo's work, for Johnny Tecate and other characters are essentially present in order to reflect a more elusive protagonist: the city itself. In an introduction to a compilation of Castillo's poetry, Luis Humberto Crosthwaite remarks that Blues cola de lagarto was for Castillo the beginning of an ongoing "description of Tijuana, the context or wrapper within which the passions of its characters circulate" (Crosthwaite 1996: 10). "La última función del mago de los espejos," by far the most famous poem from Blues, introduces the characters that make up the city through the urgings of a barker. Although the barker is calling in passersby to look at a show, we realize in the end that the true interest lies in the people he addresses:

If you live in Happy Valley
    And exercise daily in your blue sweatsuit from JC Penney . . .
    If your husband is useless

And you are a rich housewife . . . if you are an executive
An office mannequin with a chemical smile
If you are a frustrated secretary . . . if you are a lonely man
Or a left woman . . . if you are a nocturnal policeman
Recent predator of young girls . . . if you are a prostitute in the Zona
   Norte
If you're a flower salesman
Window washer, newspaper vendor
Fire eater
Alms collector . . . Come on in, come on in
In a few minutes
The last show of the magician of mirrors will begin.

[Si usted vive en el valle de la felicidad
   y hace ejercicio diariamente con su traje azul de ieicipenis . . . .
   si su esposo es un inútil
   y usted es dama benefactora . . . . si usted es un ejecutivo
   un maniquí de oficina sonrisa de fluoruro . . . .
   si usted es una secretaria frustrada . . . . si usted es un hombre solo
   o una mujer quedada . . . . si usted es un policía nocturno
   resentido violador de cholitas . . . . si usted es una prostituta de la zona
      norte . . . . si usted es un venderamosderosas
   limpiaventanillas, periodiquero,
   tragafuego
   pordiosero que pide por dios . . . . pásele, pásele,
   dentro de unos minutos comenzará
   la última función del mago de los espejos.] (Castillo 1996)[8]

The magician of the mirrors will reflect this random selection of Tijuana inhabitants, showing them as a united group whose composite face is also the
face of the city. The characters may believe themselves separate individuals
with nothing in common and no obligation to one another, but the mirror will
demonstrate that they are irrevocably connected via the urban fabric of Tijuana.
By thus gathering these diverse human components in one tableau, as Gabriel
Trujillo Muñoz points out, Castillo "synthesizes the inherent contradictions
within the genetic progress of a border city like Tijuana" (1989: 144). Castillo
simultaneously satirizes the Tijuana stereotype of barkers calling people into
strip shows and suggests that the scene on the street may be far more interesting than the artificial spectacle of the sex club, drawing readers away from
prefabricated visions of the city and toward a more personal interpretation.

Luis Humberto Crosthwaite

Luis Humberto Crosthwaite is equally concerned with Tijuana, but his treatment of the city differs from Castillo's. Whereas Castillo focuses on the daily problems and joys of the city, Crosthwaite's oeuvre is a less immediately critical love song to Tijuana past and present. As such, his novels and short stories are filled with memories of a Tijuana gone by and celebrations of local culture. In this essay, I focus on several of his works, namely the short stories "Marcela y el rey: al fin juntos en el paseo costero," "Tijuana," "Si por equis razón Federico Campbell se hubiera quedado en Tijuana," "El gran preténder," and "Todos los barcos," and the novels *La luna siempre será un amor difícil* and *Idos de la mente*. In these works, Crosthwaite at once acknowledges the historical and contemporary problems of the border city and concludes that its ambition and opportunity can work to overcome all these handicaps. He praises the distinct culture of northern Mexico, even redeeming the much-maligned figure of the cholo as a symbol of local resistance. The Tijuana featured in the works of Luis Humberto Crosthwaite includes nostalgia, bitterness, and neglect, but it is above all a space of continuing innovation and enthusiasm. Crosthwaite rejoices in this world, asking readers to drop their stereotypes and enter with him into a city of local children and foreign tourists, norteño musicians and maquiladora workers.

Crosthwaite is less obviously focused on language than Castillo, but his use of postmodern writing techniques is a strategic means of invoking the linguistic dissonance of a colorful and confusing border city. As Humberto Félix Berumen writes, "Luis Humberto Crosthwaite has distinguished himself from the start through his vision of literature as a ludic space. His arrival on the literary scene was a breath of fresh air and brought humor to local storytelling" (2001a: 58). He does not employ phoneticized fronterizo dialect as frequently as Castillo, but his attention to "heteroglosia . . . the constant use of various kinds of languages" aids in his cheerful depiction of a carnivalesque world (60). In books such as *La luna*, literary forms as diverse as theatrical dialogue, personal letters, recipes, lists, school essays, and funny sketches share space and compete for mastery. Anglicisms merge with traditional Mexican Spanish, and the language formed in the interaction is that of a frontier constantly in motion. The colloquial, tough-guy accents of the cholos come through in "El gran preténder," a story in which the use of the barrio as a collective narrator emphasizes a view of Tijuana as the living, breathing sum of its inhabitants. Crosthwaite's language brings to life a city of enormous con-traditions and tremendous fun, in which rich narrative and character complexity emerges in a whirlwind of different viewpoints and voices.

In "El gran preténder" and *Idos*, Crosthwaite celebrates the unique and frequently disparaged norteño culture as well as its source in the barrios of the border cities. "El gran preténder," reprinted in the 2000 collection *Estrella de la calle sexta*, focuses on a group of 1970s-era cholos, members of a lower-class youth movement long cursed for lawlessness and a failure to uphold Mexican culture. These groups arose in the frontier cities, and their most common characteristics were generally described as disdain for authority and the law, the use of a distinct dialect, and the cultural appropriation of various symbols popular among Chicano youth in the United States. José Manuel Valenzuela Arce argues that *cholismo* is the "most popular movement among poor youth in Northern Mexico" (2000: 117). According to Carlos Monsiváis, "cholos are born from the experience of repression, not just from imitating their North American counterparts but from social oppression . . . without negating the transcultural dimensions, the cholo is, without a doubt, a genuine national product" (1985: 166). However, since the cholo represents "the great paradox of importing national symbols from the Chicano and Mexican barrios of the United States," they were frequently considered emblematic of a loss of national pride at the border and shunned as sources of bad press (Valenzuela Arce 2000: 117).

Crosthwaite legitimates this much-maligned figure, giving life and agency to the teenagers involved in the movement. After years of official denigration, "El gran preténder" rewrites the story of cholismo to acknowledge the widespread social repression largely responsible for the movement: " 'El Saico has a serious authority problem. That's what the teachers told his mom to scare her, so she would take him out of school and put him to work" (Crosthwaite 2000: 130). Like the author, the narrator/neighborhood is conscious of these external class and social forces: "It's the repression, damn repression that doesn't let you live" (110). Faced with disrespect and lack of support from the larger society, the kids of the poor neighborhoods turned to cholismo to give worth to their identities. This sense of empowerment is explicitly stated in the book: "In the Barrio there are no bosses. In the Barrio, we're carnales, homeboys, locals" (106). In a world in which there is "so much going against us, against cholos, against all the barrios," the embrace of cholo culture provided a positive subjectivity (145). Indeed, as Berumen says, "El gran preténder" allows for the "revindication of the barrio as a space of community and social identity for young people" (2001a: 59). Although the cholos have often been depicted as a point of shame for the northern border, Crosthwaite presents this lower-class youth community as a vibrant site of mutual support and struggle.

In a similar vein, *Idos de la mente* valorizes the distinct musical forms of the northern border as a legitimate and important vehicle of cultural expression. Whereas outsiders have long derided Tijuana as a cultural vacuum, Crosthwaite's novel celebrates the city as a space of norteño innovation. He flouts conventional mockery of the low-class beginnings of this genre, finding beauty even in the Zona Norte district of Tijuana, where prostitution is tolerated and fledgling norteño musicians try their luck in the bars and cantinas: "Tijuanenses come timidly to the Zona, without the drink that reminds them they are kings of the night. One by one, the cantinas open up the earth. And the norteño musicians begin their eternal journey, offering songs that lift the spirit and make the heart beat to the rhythm of a pasodoble, a polka, or a chotís" (Crosthwaite 2001: 36). In the border-town red-light district so often regarded with disgust and disdain, the musicians Ramón and Cornelio find "a familiar environment and continuous music": "Waiters, bartenders, escorts, pimps, all respect them. Even other musicians. There's always someone ready to accompany them on upright bass, accordion, or saxophone. And then another accordion shows up to accompany Los Relámpagos, a bajo sexto, some guitars. There's always a prostitute with a beautiful voice and a bartender who sing harmony. On sad days, the Zona is full of music and parties. A family party. A party where neither sorrow nor shame exists" (41).

Though much of the official rehabilitation of Tijuana has revolved around the social cleansing of characters like the ones introduced above, Crosthwaite shows how the independent and ambitious culture of the frontier unites and redeems even its most sordid streets. The sentimentality of these moments plays on the sentimental joy of the lyrics themselves, drawing us into a world in which judgment can wait for the morning and the artistic experience provides both solace and beauty.

Crosthwaite's enthusiasm with respect to the cultural heritage of Tijuana is all but infectious, but his attention to the problems of the city makes it clear that the border and its residents have suffered from mistreatment by both Anglo-Americans and other Mexicans. In particular, he is critical of the use of Tijuana by U.S. tourists as a place of release for lust and greed. In "Todos los barcos," Ken is dragged to a strip club by his brother Steve. While Steve and his friends fit the typical tourist stereotype of lewd, crude adolescents, Ken is far more interested in thinking about his ex-girlfriend than in the sleazy seductions of the burlesque: "How could he avoid it? He always thinks about her, since he met her. Okay? Since he was introduced to her in school and she smiled and said my name is Carol. Okay, okay. . . . Another woman starts dancing. Very different. Thin, short, brown. She dances slowly. Horizontal scar on her belly. Eyes that shine. Men get out of their seats and offer dollar bills, more and more bills. She eggs them on: they touch her breasts, ass, and crotch. But Carol noticed him. She really noticed him. She smiled, she let her hand be held" (Crosthwaite 2000: 72).

Unlike the prototypical Anglo-American tourist, Ken refuses to use Tijuana and its inhabitants to "blow off steam" and exercise desires forbidden at home. His brother is determined to introduce him to the prefabricated sexuality of the strip bar, but Ken cannot help noticing the artifice of this setting and longs for more meaningful connection with Carol. A tourist himself, he shies away in horror from the behavior of other tourists: "To Ken they seem stupid, they've always seemed stupid" (69). In "Todos los barcos," Crosthwaite's humanization of the often-anonymous figure of the tourist allows him to critique from within the standard visitor experience of Tijuana, forcing us to recognize its inherent abusiveness without drifting into generalized mockery of Anglo-Americans.

The relationship between Tijuana and the United States is further criticized in "Marcela y el rey: al fin juntos en el paseo costero," a very early short story that attacks Anglo-American cultural and political imperialism. In this story, the contrast between U.S. invasions of other nations and the country's own vigorously patrolled borders could not be more amusing. U.S. culture in all forms flows freely through Tijuana, even including a drunken and forgotten Elvis who wanders the beach and says things like, *"Oh let me be (oh let him be) your teddy bear"* (Crosthwaite 1989: 175). Nor are the political excursions of the United States insignificant, as random pedestrians discuss the fact that "the Americans are intervening in Central America, what fuckers" (175). Despite the Anglo-American colonization of other countries and regions, access to the United States is guarded jealously and without mercy: "HEY YOU. CAUTION! YOU ARE ENTERING THE UNITED STATES OF AMERICA, THE MOST POWERFUL COUNTRY IN THE WORLD. DON'T DO IT!" (175). The expensive weaponry of the Border Patrol is worthless against people who have nothing to lose, however. When Marcela and the King become desperate in their impotence against the power of the empire to the north, they ignore the signs and the men waving pistols and cross the border to their deaths: "Those fools never understood that neither they nor their guns existed for Marcela and the King, that they were, like the border, just small crosses on a map that's been been burning for a long time" (176). In "Marcela y el rey," Crosthwaite uses the figure of Elvis to address issues of citizenship, immigration, and selfhood, attacking outright the oppressive and exclusionary practices of the United States. He addresses the desperation and rage felt by those continually faced with the rejection of the border fence, pointing out that the overprotected frontier is little more than an arbitrarily drawn line in the sand.

The United States is not the only villain in this story, though, and Crosthwaite uses "Si por equis razón Federico Campbell se hubiera quedado en Tijuana" to critique a different version of discrimination against the border cities. Federico Campbell, a Mexican author born in Tijuana, became successful only after moving to Mexico City and establishing contact with the literary powers that be in the center of the country. In this short story, told in the form of a list, Crosthwaite imagines how Campbell's life would have differed had he remained in Tijuana. In Crosthwaite's scenario, Campbell publishes his first book at a young age after being tapped as a potential writer during his childhood. Unfortunately, "the Mexico City critics ignore his work" (1993: 35). His second book, photocopied and distributed by hand for lack of funding, is equally ignored. After being dismissed from his menial job at a University Extension for disseminating ideas "against our ideology" he goes to work at a "Curios Shop de la Avenida Revolución" and ignores his old friends when they stop by (36). Finally, after he dies, "the Mexico City critics speak well of him" (37). This is an amusing story, but it succinctly describes the difficulty of surviving as an author in a provincial city in an environment of tremendous centralism. More than most of his work, this story seems to speak of Crosthwaite's own life, showing the nervousness of a young author unsure of his ability to succeed while remaining in Tijuana. Perhaps in part because of its personal nature, "Si por equis razón" is a very effective indictment of the failures of centralism and of the dismissive attitude of Mexico City toward the culture of the border region.

Despite Crosthwaite's attention to the problems of Tijuana, the city that finally emerges from his works is a contradictory but vital center of ambition and enthusiasm. This prevailing sense of optimism is evident in *La luna siempre será un amor difícil*, a novel in which the protagonist reaches self-awareness and peace through the opportunities and freedom of the border experience. More than simply a migrant, Xóchitl/Florinda is a time traveler who, after meeting up with an amorous conquistador, is transported from her indigenous home in colonial "Mexicco-Tenochtitlan" to the modern city of Tijuana (Crosthwaite 1994: 13). Once her knight in shining armor takes off for the greener lands of the United States, though, she stagnates in the tightly constrained female sphere of his relatives' home. She mourns her own forced inactivity, and imagines that "if she was a man, she would put her hands in her pockets and walk along the beach. . . . The night. The lights. Other men walking with their hands in their pockets" (87). After she accepts her husband's absence as permanent and finds a job at a local maquiladora, however, Florinda begins to advance into the external world. She leaves the room where she watches television to pass the time, and strolls around "the shopping malls, goes to the movies, buys a pack of cigarettes and then throws them out because she doesn't know how to smoke" (141). This radical step into independence might be difficult elsewhere, but Tijuana is so perfect for Florinda's development that it even contains an apartment specifically for rent to "a single woman who wants to rebuild her life on her own because life and buildings both have the pure cadence of forgetting" (153). Florinda begins her journey in the submissive role of a woman waiting for her husband, but the diversity and liberty of the border metropolis allow even a transplanted sixteenth-century Indian to find a home. Despite its continuing problems, Crosthwaite's Tijuana is a space of promise in which the tragedy of the Conquest can be rewritten so that the Spaniard ends up a miserable illegal alien and the indigenous woman takes charge of her life and her finances. Far from the stereotypical den of sin envisioned by outsiders, Tijuana is a relatively egalitarian world where historical wrongs can be corrected and norteño music is the soundtrack to confusion and joy.

Conclusion

Roberto Castillo and Luis Humberto Crosthwaite attempt to reimagine the history and present of Tijuana, moving beyond traditional images of vice and grime into a new vision of a diverse and exciting city. In their novels, poems, short stories, and vignettes, they enter into the lives of otherwise anonymous people filtering through the border world, bringing them to life for an audience perhaps more accustomed to impersonal descriptions of frontier tourist spectacles. In "Tijuana," Crosthwaite discusses memories of the city in the 1960s and 1970s, sharing nostalgia for a personal landscape unavailable to a casual visitor:

> Life changes and the landscape is transformed: it's the result of progress. There's no other option than thinking about old times (which aren't even that old) as an old album of photographs: turn its pages and sigh. . . . The true trace doesn't reside in the shopping malls or in the Centro Cultural. Tijuana will always be the same, without any change—at least for me—in Boni's baseball hits, in being chased by the opposing team, in pistachio

ice cream, in the chamois and saladitos that they sold in the Botica Sher. (Crosthwaite 1993: 19)

This Tijuana rounds out contemporary ideas with the perspective that comes from many years spent in a city. It is not limited to strip clubs and drug dealers, but rather includes "Botica Sher's storefront full of candy" (18) and, when combined with Castillo's work, bookstores filled with "cookbooks of indigenous cuisine, self-help books, useless best sellers, good literature, histories of foreign countries, catastrophic prophecies, biographies of unknown people" (Castillo 2001f). Mocking the accounts that attempt to contain Tijuana within the easily available stereotype of border sin, Castillo and Crosthwaite show the diverse narratives that make up a city of over two million inhabitants. The Tijuana of Castillo and Crosthwaite is one open to innumerable interpretations, and it serves as the ultimate rebuttal of the essentialist judgments that have so long haunted this city of the frontier.

Notes

I would like to thank the Fulbright Commission for giving me the opportunity to study in Tijuana, and the Colegio de la Frontera Norte and particularly José Manuel Valenzuela Arce for providing me with invaluable support and encouragement in my research. I am also very grateful to all the authors and critics, especially Humberto Félix Berumen, Roberto Castillo, and Luis Humberto Crosthwaite, who helped me with ideas and resources in the course of working on this chapter.

1 See Jack Kerouac, "A Billowy Trip in the World"; Cormac McCarthy, All the Pretty Horses; Paul Theroux, The Old Patagonian Express: By Train through the Americas; and many other memoirs, short stories, novels, and films.

2 This is asserted in numerous tourist brochures for Tijuana, and goes uncontested in more rigorous literature. It is perhaps unproven that Tijuana is the most-visited border city in the world, but the numbers seem to speak for themselves. In 1994, 28,107,449 foreign nationals crossed the border into Baja California. Crossing points are limited to Tijuana (San Ysidro, Mesa de Otay), Tecate, Mexicali, and Andrade. Since Tecate and Andrade are very small towns attracting almost no tourism and Mexicali is also quite unpopular with U.S. tourists, it seems that the vast majority of these foreigners were heading into Tijuana. This idea is supported by U.S. Bureau of Transportation statistics for the same year. The numbers have only increased since then, according to informal accounts (data from "Baja California Indicadores Turísticos 1989–1995" and U.S. Department of Transportation 2001).

3 For example, the Colegio de la Frontera Norte, founded in 1982 as the Centro de Estudios Fronterizos del Norte de México. Name changed in 1986.

4 Other local writers of note include Rosina Conde, Fran Ilich, and Regina Swain (all mentioned earlier in this essay), Francisco Morales, Julieta González Irigoyen, Elizabeth Cazessús, Marco Antonio Samaniego, Eduardo Arellano, and many

more too numerous to name here. Humberto Félix Berumen is an important local literary and cultural critic who has edited a number of anthologies of regional literature.

5 At the San Diego–Tijuana border crossing, individuals that the U.S. Border Patrol finds suspicious are sent to secondary inspection for further investigation. This procedure can significantly lengthen the already painfully slow process of crossing into the United States from Mexico.

6 Los Tucanes: a norteño band based in Tijuana. "La Revu": local slang for Avenida Revolución, the famous tourist strip of Tijuana. Rita Hayworth: American actress "discovered" while performing in Tijuana. Javier Batiz: the "Godfather of Mexican rock" and a Tijuana native. Lupita D'alessio: Mexican singer and actress. Gato Félix: Hector "El Gato" Félix Miranda, a local investigative reporter assassinated by people with ties to the Arrellano-Félix drug cartel. Castillo Peraza: former president of the Partido Acción Nacional (PAN), a very popular political party in anti–Partido Revolucionario Institucional (PRI) Tijuana. Julieta Venegas: tijuanense rock musician who has developed a national and international reputation.

7 Lomas Taurinas: Tijuana neighborhood where a PRI politician, Luis Donaldo Colosio Murrieta, was assassinated in March 1994 while campaigning for president.

8 "Ieicipenis": the department store JC Penney rendered in border dialect. "Venderamosderosas": sidewalk rose vendors, i.e., "Vende ramos de rosas."

References

Anderson, Danny J. 1995. "La frontera norte y el discurso de la identidad en la narrativa mexicana del siglo XX." In *Nuevas ideas; viejas creencias*, ed. Margarita Alegría de la Colina, Carlos Gómez Carro, Elsa Muñiz García, Graciela Sánchez Guevera, and Tomás Bernal Alanis. Mexico City: Universidad Autónoma Metropolitana Azcapotzalco.

Arreola, David D., and James R. Curtis. 1993. *The Mexican Border Cities: Landscape Anatomy and Place Personality*. Tucson: University of Arizona Press.

"Baja California Indicadores Turísticos 1989–1995." 1995. *Semblanzas: Un recorrido turístico por el Estado de Baja California de 1989 a 1995*. N.p.: Baja California Poder Ejecutivo, Turismo.

Berumen, Humberto Félix. 2001a. *Narradores bajacalifornianos del siglo XX*. Mexicali: Fondo Editorial de Baja California.

———. 2001b. "Tijuana: la ciudad cinematográfica," *Tijuana Metro*, October.

Bustamante, Jorge. 2000. "Frontera México-Estados Unidos. Reflexiones para un marco Teórico." In *Decadencia y auge de las identidades: Cultura nacional, identidad cultural y modernización*, ed. José Manuel Valenzuela Arce. 2nd ed. Tijuana: Colegio de la Frontera Norte; Mexico City: Plaza y Valdés.

———. 1982. *Uso del idioma español e identidad nacional. Encuesta en siete ciudades: Acapulco, Cd. Juarez, Matamoros, México, D.F., Tijuana, Uruapan y Zacatecas*. Tijuana: Centro de Estudios Fronterizos del Norte de México.

Castillo Udiarte, Roberto. 2002. "De estatuas y monumentos," *Letras Libres*, January 6.

———. 2001a. "Una canción de Navidad," *Letras Libres*, December 25.

———. 2001b. "Welcome Tu Tijuana," *Letras Libres*, December 6.

———. 2001c. "Cruzar la frontera con finta de musulmán," *Letras Libres*, October 28.

———. 2001d. "César Vallejo come mariscos en Tijuana," *Letras Libres*, October 13.

———. 2001e. "Welcome Tu Tijuana (poem)," *Bitácora*, August 30.

———. 2001f. "La esquina del Johnny Tecate: En la librería del centro," *Bitácora*, May.

———. 2000a. "La esquina del Johnny Tecate: De cómo lo norteño ocupa un lugar en el espacio virtual," *Bitácora*, December.

———. 2000b. "La esquina del Johnny Tecate: El Johnny Tecate por la Vía Santana," *Bitácora*, October.

———. 2000c. "La esquina del Johnny Tecate: Al Johnny Tecate le robaron su carro," *Bitácora*, September.

———. 1996. "La última función del mago de los espejos." In *La pasión de Angélica según el Johnny Tecate*. Tijuana: Centro Cultural Tijuana. Originally published 1985 in *Blues cola de lagarto*. Mexicali: Gobierno del Estado de Baja California.

Conde, Rosina. 1992. "¿Donde está la frontera?" *El Acordón. Revista de Cultura* 7: 50–52. Quoted in María Socorro Tabuenca Córdoba. 1995. "Viewing the Border: Perspectives from the 'Open Wound.'" *Discourse* 18: 146–68.

Crosthwaite, Luis Humberto. 2001. *Idos de la mente: La increíble y (a veces) triste historia de Ramón y Cornelio*. Mexico City: Editorial Joaquín Mortiz.

———. 2000. *Estrella de la calle sexta*. Mexico City: Tusquets Editores.

———. 1996. "Literatura: historia de nuestra pasión," introduction to *La passion de Angélica según el Johnny Tecate*, by Roberto Castillo Udiarte. Tijuana: Centro Cultural Tijuana.

———. 1994. *La luna siempre será un amor difícil*. Mexico City: Editorial Eco.

———. 1993. *No quiero escribir no quiero*. Toluca, Mexico: Ediciones del H. Ayuntamiento de Toluca.

———. 1989. "Marcela y el rey: al fin juntos en el paseo costero." In *Tijuana en la literatura*, ed. Ramiro León Zavala. Tijuana: Instituto Tecnológico de Tijuana. Originally published 1988 in *Marcela y el rey al fin juntos*. Mexico City: J. Boldo i Clement; Zacatecas: Universidad Autónoma de Zacatecas; Centro de Estudios Literarios de la Dirección de Investigación.

Gómez Montero, Sergio. 1994. *The Border: The Future of Postmodernity*. Baja California Literature in Translation 3. Trans. Harry Polkinhorn and Sergio Gómez Montero. San Diego: San Diego State University Press.

———. 1993. *Sociedad y desierto: Literatura en la frontera norte*. Mexico City: Universidad Pedagógica Nacional.

Kerouac, Jack. 1960. "A Billowy Trip in the World." *Lonesome Traveler*. New York: McGraw-Hill.

Klahn, Norma. 1997. "Writing the Border: The Languages and Limits of Representation." In *Common Border, Uncommon Paths: Race, Culture, and National Identity in U.S.-Mexican Relations*, ed. Jaime E. Rodríguez O. and Kathryn Vincent. Wilmington, DE: Scholarly Resources.

Lcap, William L. 1996. *Gay Men's English*. Minneapolis: University of Minnesota Press.

Martínez, Oscar J. 1988. *Troublesome Border*. Tucson: University of Arizona Press.

McCarthy, Cormac. 1992. *All the Pretty Horses*. New York: Alfred A. Knopf.

"Mexico: Wages, Maquiladoras, NAFTA." 1998. *Migration News* 5, no. 2.

Monsiváis, Carlos. 1985. "Cholos y pachucos. Materialización de una estética." In *Reglas del juego y juego sin reglas en la vida fronteriza*, ed. Mario Miranda Pacheco and James W. Wilkie. Mexico City: Asociación Nacional de Universidades y Institutos de Enseñanza Superior.

O'Connor, Anne-Marie. 1998. "Mexico's City of Promise." *Los Angeles Times*, January 26.

Proffitt, T. D. 1994. *Tijuana: The History of a Mexican Metropolis*. San Diego: San Diego State University Press.

San Diego Union Tribune. 2001. "Cuidad de arte [City of Art]," November 4.

Soderbergh, Steven, dir. 2000. *Traffic*. Perf. Michael Douglas, Don Cheadle, Benicio Del Toro, Luis Guzmán, Dennis Quaid, Catherine Zeta-Jones. USA Films.

Tabuenca Córdoba, María Socorro. 1997. "La frontera textual y geográfica en dos narradoras de la frontera norte mexicana: Rosina Conde y Rosario San Miguel." PhD diss., State University of New York at Stony Brook.

———. 1995. "Viewing the Border: Perspectives from the 'Open Wound,' " trans. Michael Petras. *Discourse* 18: 146–68.

Theroux, Paul. 1979. *The Old Patagonian Express: By Train through the Americas*. Boston: Houghton Mifflin.

Trujillo Muñoz, Gabriel. 1989. "El mago de los espejos." In *Tijuana en la literatura*, ed. Ramiro León Zavala. Tijuana: Instituto Tecnológico de Tijuana.

U.S. Department of Transportation, Bureau of Transportation Statistics. 2001. "U.S.-Mexico Border Crossing Data 1994–2000." Washington, D.C.: U.S. Department of Transportation.

Valenzuela Arce, José Manuel. 2000. "Identidades culturales: Comunidades imaginarias y contigentes." In *Decadencia y auge de las identidades: Cultura nacional, identidad cultural y modernización*, ed. José Manuel Valenzuela Arce. 2nd ed. Tijuana: Colegio de la Frontera Norte; Mexico City: Plaza y Valdés.

Crossfader Playlist

Living (through) Tijuana

It happens again. I see it live and direct from the scene. Like all of Tijuana were a theme park and there were nothing else to do but sit back in the taxi and enjoy the ride, just stare through the window at our disaster of a city, this perfect example of no-holds-barred postmodernity.

Feeling (un)safe, check. The patrol cars massing in another commercial-school zone, the insistent ambulance sirens, dozens of armed, restless agents, nosy people making comments without knowing what's really going on. Seeing everything as some kind of blood-and-bullet show, without imagining that the illusion of it being *them vs. them* is rapidly disintegrating, the lie that the conflict doesn't affect us yet and won't invade our own comfort zones.

No one wants to even imagine that what we are living through (badly) is a gore movie, one of the ones they show on the weekend at 3 A.M., that it will shake much more than some middle-class fears and the social conformity that has been our companion for the last twenty years.

"The situation is completely intolerable now," we hear the host of a popular local radio show say. It's the same thing that a housewife is thinking, the dismayed housewife who, like the wife of Reverend Lovejoy on the Simpsons, asks *someone to think about the children* as she gets out of a taxi in one of the many fortified parts of the city. God help them, she manages to say to us.

Days later, on the way to a Thanksgiving dinner, a friend points at an empty corner around the corner from his parents' house, reporting like a TV correspondent: "That's where the narcos left three dead bodies wrapped in blankets."

Yeah, it's hard to accept: la city is a violent playground (Nitzer Ebb dixit).

This year I've seen the most unimaginable things in the media: obscene close-ups of a series of disgusting murders meant to satiate our morbid curiosity and leave us gasping for air, the sadism and cruelty of the posthuman tragedy, the unrelenting update of lives converted into mere statistics. A torrent of blood.

The press drops any pretense of ethics in pursuit of that segment of the market that devours crime news with savage nervousness. The way the media wallows in the violence and the spectacularization of civic fear seems to be covering up both a moralistic stench and a chart of economic salvation. Some day we, the people of Tijuana, we'll make them pay for their despicable contribution to the present psychosis.

Because of all this, blogs are a better option for finding out what places to avoid, tips for noticing the behavioral tics of the invisible enemy now lurking all over the place, the judicial system's anomalies, details the press covers up, the hidden realities of the impoverished masses whose ranks we've let swell. And then the blogs of the people who think "it's hard to stay quiet when it hits so close to you. Hard when it become a modus viviendi." *The ones who write for the people who aren't here anymore, for the ones who've dissapeared.*

Tijuana isn't Gotham City. There aren't any superheroes to respond to our calls or competent authorities to attend to our appeals. What can be done in a city that's devouring itself? Write a post-everything *j'accuse* fingering the criminal impunity, the police corruption, and a state overwhelmed by its inefficiency and the lack of strategies for attacking the first problem and controling the second? Analyze our debilitated value system and its impact on social breakdown, the ideals of the drug-dealing youths and their connection to consumerism and generalized disillusionment? Entrust Tijuana over to some supreme power (whichever one it might be)?

Will it help anything to walk through the various theories dealing with fear as a means of control, prayer chains, the importance of a life and honest work, political participation, solidarity marches, and occasional, well-directed protests? Or will we turn people from Sinaloa into the perfect target for attacks, letting them stand in for the misnamed narcoculture in the border imaginary? Tijuana wasn't like that before.

Two thousand eight will go down in history as a terrible year: the more than seven hundred dead and a series of excessively dramatic images (those kindergarten kids and the shootout that were transmitted around the world,

Aiko Enriquez Nishikawa's sad farewell letter to Tijuana, the stories heard during the marches for peace and safety, the riots in the Penitenciaría). Too many things, too many.

Terrible? Yes, but as our neighbors on the other side of the border say: *Life goes on.*

I'm part of a generation that grew up with the privileges of progress and that carefree feeling that the city has stood for since its beginnings. A generation that defends Tijuana nightlife tooth and nail as a way to escape-valve the implosion of violence that used to be selective but now is a kind of lottery of death.

Tijuana is our home, our border roots, our web of friends, our work, and our dreams. Like so many who head out every morning to face the uncertainty and turmoil of capitalism gone wild, I can say this: I'm not afraid, I don't want to be afraid, I refuse to be afraid.

One more thing: if we lose Tijuana, Mexico has no future.

The Tijuana We've Got Coming

Thursdays are like my Sundays. The days I don't go to work, when I can wake up as late as I want. I work twelve hours on Wednesdays. The only thing I want to do when I get home is tumble into bed and kick back. I've done just that the last two weeks. Rest is good for me.

Today was no exception. The sound of the phone woke me up. It was noon. My sister, telling me to turn on the TV, a shootout. I turned it on and, starting with that moment, that Thursday will forever be marked in my memory.

The images I see are like out of a movie. I remember on a local news show I heard a businessman famous for his cultural and media missteps say that Tijuana looked a lot like Pakistan. I remember a statement, from only a few days ago, by a police chief saying we were living through a war in Tijuana. I remember this entire week there hasn't been one day I've woken up without reading news of some murder, kidnapping, drive-by, etc.

I followed the news on three different channels. I turned on the computer to check the Web sites of the national newspapers to see if there were updates. Information wasn't flowing. I kept watching the same images on an endless loop. Zooms, pans, close-ups. There was something obscene in these images that, at that moment, I couldn't quite identify but I knew something about them bothered me.

I work close to where the shootout took place. A few blocks away. Sometimes I hail a taxi on the Boulevard. Several of my friends and students live over there. I talked to a few of them on the phone. They're fine . . . nervous, upset, worried, but fine. They can't leave their work / their house / their school.

I realize this is a new kind of experience when I see no one knows how to act, how to behave, how to react. On the TV News, the reporters look for the best image, the most dramatic one, the one that might work for I don't know what purpose. They've lost their way and aren't providing information, balance, control. And so I watch images on the TV that far from providing information, just strike the short match of our social psychosis, injecting fear, uncertainty, rage.

The media boasted about presenting the most complete information, the reporters said they felt like they were in a war zone, shamelessly interviewing kids and people on the edge of a breakdown, enthusiastically showing the same images over and over again. Qué vergüenza.

One of the local news shows comes on at 3 P.M. I sat down in front of the TV and watched the images again. I changed the channel and they had the same images (different shots, different angles, but still the same). Soundbites, threats transmitted on the radio dial, silence. Gunshots.

I went back to the news. In the overwhelming number of violent images, I made out the familiar faces of two much-loved friends of mine. Two girls sitting on the patio of their house, with the channel's microphone in one hand, both of them waiting perhaps for some question. Yeah, it's them: the byline identifies them by their first and last names. Their image was on the screen for a few, three, five seconds? I reacted when I saw the same images from the last few hours come back on. I decided to call them, several of their friends and family members were thinking the same thing and decided to contact them. At the end of the call, one of the girls said to me: *We lost her*, R. No, I answered. Not yet.

I know what she's talking about: mi city, nuestra city.

I had a few things I had to do today. The people in my house asked if I was going out. Yeah, I'm not going to be held hostage. If fear wins, we'll end up barricading ourselves in our homes like they did in Medellín. Our fight is for our freedom, for the power to move around this city, nuestra Tijuana, to not let them defeat us. Despite the fact criminals face no punishment and have no fear, we have to keep on doing even the smallest and most insignificant of our daily activities.

I went out.

I went to visit a friend. I walked a few blocks listening to Ciëlo on my headphones. When I got there, he had coffee and pizza waiting. He's upset, sad, all messed up by what happened. No one with a sensitive bone in their body or a little solidarity could feel removed from the tragedy of the situation. We know the fight is not between good guys and bad guys. We all participate in this. We're implicated by our silence, our indifference, our typical attitude of "I don't care as long as it doesn't affect me."

It's barely 6 PM and we can't take our eyes off the TV news. Once again the same images. Those images now starting to circulate around the world. We see them on the Internet. We'll see them tomorrow in the papers. We see them. Yes, they're obscene, terribly obscene. Will we remember them like the pictures from March 23rd? Will it be a defining moment for TJ? With these questions and a lot of other ones banging around in my head, I said goodbye to my friend.

Even though the media was telling everyone not to leave the house, I went to el Centro. It's calm. I passed by a few businesses with the TV on. News, of course. In the taxi, the people, none of whom knew each another, talked about what had happened. There are several versions out there. I've never believed rumors. The worst thing was seeing proof that scare tactics work.

When I got to the CECUT, I asked to be let off. It's an old refrain that culture is our only possible way out. What happened today is still the main topic. Everyone has something to say, something to express, something to feel. We all saw those images. We all reject them.

Just like me, there were several others who didn't pay any mind to the official recommendation. We go out that night to feel alive, to prove we're alive, to feel like our city's alive. Directors of cultural institutions, university professors, journalists that are sick of so much shooting, housewives, teenagers who kill time waiting to see Taurus do Brasil, people who put together university cultural programs, people who had the idea to visit the CECUT on a day like today. A lot of people, strange for January, surprising for this Thursday in particular.

Before heading home, I went with Boo, a very close friend, to the Starbucks at the beach. This might seem like an empty and ridiculous thing to do, in view of what had gone down. Even so, it was the best way to end a horrible day. We had a good time talking about the books friends have recommended we read, the little things that come up in the process of getting a master's, joking about future trips and group therapy techniques. There, sitting down, drinking a latté, watching a ton of people laughing and chatting with their friends, I understood that everything had not been lost.

Back to la realidad. I made it in time to see the national TV news. *Hechos* plays the same images again, the extended version. Like three or four minutes. I don't understand. Or I do understand: they're into anything morbid, into emotional blackmail, they're shameless and completely insensitive. Change the channel. Another news show, this time with their logo superimposed on the exclusive images. Sick to my stomach.

On the Internet, I found out more things, more reactions. I read about it in a few blog posts. All of them talk, locate the place where it happened, know people who live nearby, are indignant or moved by the images. Some of them say—openly or between the lines—what we all know and don't want to recognize: we are also guilty. The city's open, receptive nature makes it progressive and paradoxically makes its own survival all the more difficult.

It's almost twelve. I know that, despite not wanting to, these images will invade my dreams. Despite it all, have a good night, Tijuana.
PS: Yeah, I know. I'm a goddamn optimist.

Tijuana Makes Me Happy

The adjective good is used / to describe people / and things that in principle I dislike. / The adjective bad is used / to describe people / and things that in principle I like.
—JOSÉ MARÍA FONOLLOSA (*City of Man: New York*)

I have always said Tijuana is the center of the universe. —LUIS HUMBERTO CROSTHWAITE at the presentation of his book *Instructions for Crossing the Border*

Tijuana is not Tijuana. —FIAMMA MONTEZEMOLO

I Love Tijuana

La city is a virus, a meme that circulates with no restrictions, altering a reality that is more and more delocalized in particular ways. Tijuana is anywhere. Allá y aquí, pixilated in the unconscious collective of the new global dream. Primera advertencia: Don't be fooled by the myth and the legend (it's not Sin City and not the happiest place on Earth). We've left behind that rough-and-tumble city perpetuated in movies for overgrown adolescents or that illusion called the American Way of Life. Tijuana is much more than the clichés repeated by the people who come to try to decipher it, loaded down with all their prejudices. Just glancing briefly at these oft-recycled images is enough—the enormous naked lady, the industrial parks, la línea fronteriza, la calle principal—to understand they're tiny pieces of a minor simulacrum based on a charismatic reality in full-blown restructuring.

Romanticizing the border does no good (sorry, nothing's the same as it used to be). Some people decide to live it with all its dynamics, processes, and problems. Others don't; they invent different ways to live through it. Both are there, moving through the same urban space but in almost parallel worlds. That's why, if what we live are, as one of the new physics theories posits, multiple "nows" that proceed at the same time, this is something we can discover: the Tijuana that still believes in the miracles of Juan Soldado and that doesn't recognize the culture jamming of the story of Santa Olguita (the girl raped and killed in 1938 is promoted to the public in her recent adaptation into a holy saint card); Tijuana as a perpetual escape route, as a place without laws; the Tijuana of land invasions on the extreme edges of la city and their violent evictions later on; the welcoming Tijuana of the Argentinian pop singer Ricardo Ceratto; the Tijuana riled up by the latest designer drug; the Tijuana where los bachilleres with no future wait after school for the camioncito that'll take them straight to the night shift in the maquiladora; the Tijuana considered a new cultural mecca; the conservative Tijuana that doesn't know how to deal with the concept of alterity; the Tijuana of Avenida Revolución, calmly receiving the contingent of patriotic jarheads with their eyes popping out of their heads fighting for the attention of big-busted, steely-assed nymphs; the Tijuana of impunity and corruption at all levels; the Tijuana in the national press iotra vez!; the Tijuana of electronic and avant indie pop; the Tijuana that isn't known and that hides when they come to try to find it on a weekend; the Tijuana that laughs because it knows that, in the end, nothing/everything is the truth. Fission Tijuana, not fusion Tijuana.

Tijuana doesn't keep still, she moves, she's moving, that's why it's so hard to get a handle on her and why it's so easy to put labels on her post-Canclini that all end up saying the same thing, cracking a fascist morality that condemns what it doesn't comprehend and providing an undercover preview in real time of what's to come. That's why trying to define what is always mutating, besides being unproductive, is quite pretentious. You choose: Tijuana as a rollercoaster in free fall or the übertrip de tu vida. O las dos cosas at the same time. No big deal, really.

I love TJ, for thousands of reasons, for its crystal-iced vibe and the faribolesque spirit of its streets, for being creative in spite of its precariousness and for pushing on despite tremendous neglect, for its multifaceted character, polychromatic and metathematic, for its bar-hopping nights and its obvious social contradictions, for its incredible audacity and its obvious ingenuity dealing with everything foreign, for transcending a *leyenda negra* that is only brought up by those seeking to benefit from it, for being something more than that, because my home and a huge network of coconspirators are here, because I do and because why not and because who cares what they're talking (shit) about anyway.

Just Say Tijuana

As a border space where the reality of the developed world coexists with the reality of underdevelopment in Mexico, Tijuana attracts the gaze of people living through, observing, or following at a distance what happens in la city. This is why, for some years, the main concern of the authorities and business groups has been improving the city's image in the interior of the country and also abroad which helps, in some ways, to recover the competitive advantage of yesteryear, as far as it relates to cheap labor and foreign investment so essential to confronting the ferocious onslaught of the Chinese maquiladora industry.

Nevertheless, there's an awful lot going against the city. For example, on MTV Latino's program *Urban Myths*—in which they cleared up whether different rumors people spread were true or false—they asked the specific question: Are there problems south of the border? The response was an unconditional True. There are complaints that some police demand up to $100 to let go of partying tourists visiting the city. And although you might not believe it, a representative from the City Police shows up, saying "Some of our officers do it. Puede ser, puede ser." The corruption is like that, high-profile and brazen.

That's why it's not surprising a quick Google search turns up 441,000 links in response to the query "Tijuana's bad image." It's also no shocker that an endless stream of groups have appeared (Tijuana Renacimiento, Tijuana Trabaja, Tijuana Opina, Imagen Tijuana) whose goal is to expressly counteract that representation with another image more in line with what they think life is like here. This effort brings to light three very different visions of the local reality: one that pines for the past (reflected in the Agua Caliente Minaret), blaming all the bad things in the city on "those immigrants" who brought disorder with them, destroying the postprovincial calm, and dreaming of attaining San Diego's order and aseptic cleanliness; another vision held by those born in the late 1960s, the 1970s, and the beginning of the 1980s, brought up on Saturday cartoon shows, who had American alternative rock as their generation's soundtrack and who, when they were in elementary and middle school, celebrated both Halloween and Día de los Muertos like it was no big deal, who see San Diego as a natural extension of TJ; and the new Tijuana that since 1985 has received a growing number of people from all different parts of Mexico (according to data from INEGI, in 2000, only 39.73 percent of the people living in the city were born in Baja California), which is growing out east and whose residents have a different accent, almost never go to el Centro, don't have visas, and aren't interested in going to San Diego.

These three visions diverge in their view of the desired identity and image of la city, although the extremes have certain things in common: the new Tijuana looks more and more like the Tijuana yearned for by many with their moralistic views of its problems, while still reflecting huge differences in terms of strategies for survival. Among them, there is a metageneration of *tijuanenses* (made up of writers, musicians, academics, politicians, multidisciplinary artists, among others) who don't really care a lot about the whole leyenda negra issue; they know about it and they study it to use it in their artistic, academic, or media work. Nada más. Tijuana doesn't make them defend everyday events and realities that would be present in any city with similar characteristics. So sorry, Tijuana just isn't that unique.

Tijuana Kills Me!

At a stop sign, at the entrances to working-class colonias or to suburban developments advertising themselves as the perfect oasis, dodging the ever-present danger of being in the middle of a dirty *bulevar*, you can see the newspaper vendors hard at work selling the afternoon edition of *El Mexicano*, a sensationalist paper that, with headlines almost always in red, almost unintentionally maps out a bloody guidebook to the goings-on of Tijuana *profunda*. What they do best is spiraling violence: *encobijados*, *levantones*, clandestine graves, knife victims, a shootout at the door of a stylish club, rapes, or the increasingly easy turf killing. Life is hard and life is cheap, or, at least, that's what they tell us. How many more people have to die before we flee from la city? How many articles and news stories will we have to read before we really feel like we're living the catastrophe we see on TV?

My friend Sergio Brown, communicologist and visualist, tells me that when people ask me what life is like in Tijuana, I should answer by saying there's a lot of fear, that murders and violent acts are happening everywhere all the time. That I should tremble as I list everything that has happened recently, that my voice should be sad and upset, that I should ironically transmit the media's oft-repeated refrains. He says we should reclaim that image of a ciudad killer as our own, we should sell it, that we should give those morbid journalists the tour of their lives. Let them discover, shall we say, the savage side of la city at its worst possible moment (at its most real and unadulterated). Drop them off at three in the morning in the most hard-core parts of La Morita or El Grupo México. We should consider leaving them to their own devices in a brown-neck bar like El As Negro (now fallen out of favor since it's Manu Chao's favorite place in Tijuana) or El Grullense. We should take them to one of those seafood restaurants where just one look could alter their fate forever. Organize it so they run into a gangbanger from Calle XV3 in the middle of Avenida Revolución, one of those tattooed ones ready for anything so they can write "We can report that Barrio XV3 run deep in Baja" on their Web site. In the end, we want them to remember that ex–presidential candidate Colosio visited one day and he didn't make it out alive. That Tijuana, La Tijuana Killer, unfortunately is also mi city.

According to data from the PGJE, in 2003 there were 295 recorded homicides. By the first week of September 2004, that number had reached 214 (including a set of fourteen committed in the span of a week). In all media outlets, not just local ones, there are reports about a fight to the death between the Arellano Félix Cartel and "El Mayo" Zambada's group, ruthless rivals fighting to maintain and control the smuggling routes through the city. At the beginning of 2004, Víctor Clark Alfaro, director of the Binational Committee for Human Rights, told the Los Angeles paper La Opinión that "the violence has become something mundane. A daily pattern of deaths has been established that is related to the presence of organized crime." Nevertheless, in the majority of cases, said acts of violence do not claim the lives of innocent people, except in a few, unfortunate incidents.

Much has been said of the narcojunior connection, about how these young children of Tijuana's elite involved in the drug trade have gone from being a mere anecdote to permeating all strata of Tijuana society. The causes are multiple and varied: some say it's due to a lack of real opportunities or society and its consumerist imperative, family breakdown, the lack of values, or the fact it is an easy way to get hold of money and a relative positive of power. One of my classmates from middle school was one of the first to be executed in a cruel and exacting way. Other friends quickly tired of scrawling a cross in the yearbooks on the photos of their class members who had been killed or sought out by the DEA or other legal authorities. Despite all this, there are those in la city who bet, without even the slightest doubt, that the narcojuniors will make the comeback of the year in 2005, but remade into what's already being called "the new freak scene" (successful professionals living the good design life, elegant junkies, and super cuckoos).

Jesús Blancornelas, codirector of the Tijuana newspaper *Zeta* and an expert on the subject, exposed the city's clubs in his opinion column in the newspaper *Frontera*—he didn't say which ones—as hotbeds of de luxe cokeheads (well, he calls them *enviciados encumbrados* or "pompous miscreants" in his *arancherado* style). Anyway, he makes the statement there that the middle class and *los humildes* don't have the money to buy cocaine. Yeah, one of his young associates should bring him up to speed. The middle class prefers ecstasy or acid. Cocaine is out; *los humildes* (which sounds like a seventies group popular with the maquila crowd) prefer crystal and ice.

If one pays attention to what's happening on the street, it doesn't come as a surprise to find out that Tijuana still takes first place in drug consumption in the country, according to the statistics of the Subsecretaria del Sistema Estatal de Seguridad Publica. People take drugs (the cost of a dose can run from one to five dollars). Whatever drug and wherever (in El Bordo, in La Revu, in Plaza Fiesta, in Pueblo Amigo, in Zona Río, in La Coahuila and nearby areas, in the alto-standing developments and in the rough *barrios de la periferia*, at raves and concerts, everywhere). In Tijuana, you just have to go to a corner store, a *tiendita* (one selling food, not the other kind) and read the little sign that's always there "Focos Cinco Pesos" to know what's really going on or go to any weekend party to see the staff in a synthetic trance. The use of marihuana is so common that a lot of people don't even consider it an illegal drug anymore. As has been seen in other places, prohibition has never been a viable solution; neither has the so-called fly swatter approach. With all that in mind, Tijuana could be, this is true, the social laboratory of postmodernity that sociologists and communicologists talk about so much, as it seems to put into practice the words of the political analyst Federico Reyes Heroles, who made clear, on his last visit, that the only possible way to control the drug industry and its social impact was legalization. Tijuana experimental zone.

Furthermore, since 2002, the problems brought by alcohol consumption to the city have returned to the headlines (needless to say we have the highest consumption of beer per person in the country and one of the bars—Las Pulgas, sí señor—sells the most beer in all Latin America). Recently, an initiative by the PAN has sought to abolish, for purely economic reasons, the so-called Ley Seca, or Dry Law, in Baja California (which was implemented in 1915 and specifically prohibits the sale and consumption of alcohol on the day before and after an election) and in another instance, there is a bizarre proposal to eliminate the words "Lady's Night" on signs, neon and otherwise, in the bars. But this isn't all; in his zeal to end *barras libres*, a PRI party leader once said that the only thing these businesses accomplish with those kinds of promotions is to incite young people to drink alcohol endlessly for hardly any money and he added, "It's enough for a young person to have fun until one or two in the morning, and I don't see the need for extra or additional hours." None of them see alcoholism as a serious health problem in la city; rather all of them see it as a form of moral collapse that has to be ended. What they don't know is barras libres are out of style with the people who go out to have fun in the city. The bars with beer for a dollar rule.

Tijuana Dream

Callejeando. Everytime I walk these street something unique happens. There's always something different. A business that's closed, new cafés and drugstores offering the ultimate pill for losing weight, some homeless who took over the most weirdo nooks and crannies, tons of freaks, loads of lost tourists and cops hard at work. I walk and watch, listen and spy, sit down and then wander one more time down streets that, by force of habit, end up being just as familiar as the people we call family. For the last few years, I've gotten into the habit of carrying my digital camera to take pictures of what I see in my daily travels. I have a collection of photos of my favorite urban characters in their natural state (the Bob Marley clone cleaning car windows at the intersection of Calle Segunda, the Siete Culos hyper-drunkie poet in El Turístico, the scabby superstar Maguana hanging around the *mercados populares*, the karaoke family at the door of my favorite ATM, Señora Cajas and her cardboard house right in front of the entrance to the ex–Palacio Municipal). A few weeks back, one of my projects was to take pictures of the backs of people walking around el Centro. After the loud cries made public in the peace and safety marches held a few months back that you couldn't walk peacefully around la city anymore, my idea was to prove that this wasn't so true. I took almost a hundred photos in different places, high and low, safe and really scary. I figured out that none of the people I took pictures of were watching their backs. Each one of them was walking at their particular rhythm, flowing with a relative freedom around Tijuana.

In la city, that made-in-the-media fear that would keep us from going out and wandering around Tijuana hasn't won quite yet. Apparently, public spaces are under control, vice and pleasure locked away at home and, despite it all, you can wander around God's streets protected by police officers and video cameras with high-powered zoom, with the possibility that any night at the usual checkpoints they could surprise us with Breathalyzer tests. The American "No Loitering" made into rule of law. Everyone happy and safe at home. A return to decency, it seems. Sorry, Tijuana still has the party deep inside.

iDonde hay PAN se vive mejor! This slogan is still plastered in practically all the places I walk through to get to work, to go to school, or to head back home. Whether on a banner or a sign, it's the same message. Leaving aside the obvious religious connotation, we still have to notice the reductionist vision of whoever invented or recycled or appropriated it: our well-being is reduced to a matter of food (*pan* of course means bread in Spanish, as well as being the acronym for the Partido de Acción National). And the circus? What happened to the circus? The recent PRI victory in the race for mayor in Tijuana is a sign: the circus has now come to town, with its exotic animals and everything else. No importa, I was part of the 60 percent of people who didn't vote, but I don't feel guilty, since I know I've got a front-row ticket to this surreality show. The businessman Hank Rhon promised in a meeting with college students that Tijuana was going to be *bien curada* (super cool) beginning in December. Or at the very least, there will be a lot to comment on and analyze.

El weekly viaje a San Diego is one of our most deeply rooted border customs, one that just won't die despite the peso-dollar fluctuations. It's said that San Diego is the pretty side of Tijuana. A cliché about to go into bankruptcy, under stress from the misuse of pensions, corruption, and the baggage of being "The Finest City in America." My friends use the Sentri lane to cross the border quickly. And they smile as they say, "No more long line or bikes or domineering Immigration agents." I know, in ten or fifteen minutes, you're across and in the old empire. When I don't have time, I get on a $1.50 bus and in less than an hour, which I almost always spend reading a Baudrillard book or correcting my texts, it drops me off right in front of the Immigration agent. If I'm feeling really confident, I have an adventure and get in line Saturday morning right at the time when there's the most traffic. Since 9/11, crossing la línea has changed so much. There's more and more surveillance on the trip over and it's always congested. Crossing la línea is unpredictable. I can take a few minutes or hours to do it. At the front of the line, I hand over my visa and answer the agent's routine question with a moment's hesitation: *I don't bring nada de México.* I amble over to the trolley and buy an All Day Pass for five dollars first, making a mental plan of the spots I'll hit that day. Yeah, amo a San Diego as much as I love Tijuana. Like Richard Hell, that New York punk poet, my love comes in spurts.

It was the early eighties, I was headed over on a family trip to San Diego. I still remember it like it was a slow-motion video: the *pollos'* crazy break-for-it—*ilegales, compas* looking for better opportunities or however you want to call them—through the slew of cars in line and how we shouted euphorically when one of them was able to dodge the soldiers there to stop them from getting on the freeway. Or even more sad, from a window of the restaurant Coco's, when we saw them come out of some nearby storm drains scared, dirty, and wet. Things change in a decade, now it's normal to see, all of sudden, right before getting to the review checkpoint, a guy opens the door to his car and runs toward Mexico, leaving it behind in the middle of the line to cross. Everyone knows that, after they inspect the car, you'll see one, two, three, or even five people get out of the trunk. And even though you can't do anything about it, it's rough to see them emerge confused and all sweaty with their shoes, sneakers, or boots in their hands.

In Tijuana, there's another border too: the language one. Phrases, slang, inflections, tones, and accents. There they are, we hear them when we change the dial on the radio to listen to the morning shows with their *sonidito sina-loeanse,* when we cross la línea, in the cultural programs on the university stations, as we hang out talking at a café or in the typical weekend drunkfests, while we're chatting online or in normal coming and goings. The ones of us who live here, the ones who just got here and the ones on their way, we construct la city and la city constructs us as we get to know her. Every day, language is resemanticized, recontextualized; as the communicologist Ricardo Morales has explained it, it's reconstructed by all of us, artists, the public, advocates for fronterizo ways of communicating and fronterizo culture. In Tijuana, language has moved past the narrow alley of Spanglish, *lo pocho,* or *chicanismos* (too seventies, too radical, too religious). The Tijuana writer Heriberto Yépez has mentioned on his blog that one of the reasons behind the use of English on the border is what he calls "emotional detachment" and he argues everything is *más* light in English, full of overused clichés. He equates the use of English to an escape (from reality, from Mexicanness). I think English provides the simple gift of economy; when dealing with a more complex idea—Yépez is right about this—it moves the idea, and only the idea, to another context and although its usage often is reduced to media-friendly sound bites already charged with meanings, that doesn't mean the use of Tijuanero Spanglish is a condescending way of looking down on someone else or a submissive nod to the gringos. As an epilogue, it's worth adding an anecdote that Yépez has told about being at a literary *encuentro* in Guadalajara and receiving a compliment for speaking Spanish so well despite being from Tijuana. Yeah, we can speak Español too.

Culturosa City

In a recent talk at the CECUT, as part of a series of events bringing together the artistic community in the Tijuana–San Diego area, Norma Iglesias, a former researcher at the Colef, said, *en inglés*, that Tijuana was moving quicker than any of its artists. True. Despite that, its artists recognize its movement. La city, we already said it, is moving.

If its artists go slow, the media in general is even further behind. I can tell more than a hundred stories about all the people who've come in the last ten years to cover the Tijuana experience. Big names and unknown names, indies and official operators, with agendas and without them. I've talked with a huge number of journalists, writers, musicians, academics, and video and film makers trying to discover and then take away their own Personal TJ that boils down to what others have already said. That's why it's not strange they still haven't registered or understood a couple of phenomena on the wild *periferia* of la city or the anomalous Tijuana that is coming out of a permissive Centro. On the other hand, they've provided a sneak peek of what's to come. The ones who defend the periferia of la city point to hip-hop, a return to the cholo aesthetic, and wager their lives for the barrio; through break beats and hard rhymes they show what's going on: violence, police harassment, the influence of drugs, the legacy of neoliberal catastrophe, the poverty of la city. It's the seventies otra vez, graffiti without a critique, monosyllabic Spanglish de El Ei, poverty all riled up and concentrated in isolated groups of young folks who'll die young. That's why the old guard is scared that soon they'll see them blossoming in DVDs.

On the other side, el Centro and its allies. The Tijuana Bloguita Front (TJ.BF) is/was a swarm of more than a hundred blogueros (writers, musicians, designers, architects, fanzineros, academics, videographers, radio programmers, journalists, and more) who live in Tijuana, bringing together the experimental and the academic, the superficial with a hint of perdiction (*sic*), avant-preppies and the coolturoso, el underground and the mass media in a postreality show that spans la city. They take the party with them, they walk the talk and document it all in an infinite number of Weblogs. It's today's Tijuana, half space invaders (clubs, galleries, schools, institutions), half disaster waiting to happen; an open viral web that has no morals and is hard to satiate, with different information hubs and varied communication platforms. Theirs is an attempt to recreate la city, mix possible realities together, ironically comment on the construction of "lo tijuanense," shake up antiquated structures, and, in the process, make the most impossible places fashionable as objects of study for academics from various parts of the world. The TJ.BF is ON, close by here, dancing to a DJ spinning mixes semiotically, on the edge of la nada, with the tedium of everyday life in their faces, immersed in something that is barely known: postborder life, the joy of living en la city, the challenge of what seems impossible to interpret.

The War Is Over! TJ Won

In the words of Marc Auge, though he was referring to Paris: "As long as Tijuana keeps resisting Tijuana, Tijuana me gusta." Tijuana is un teenager who always wants to be up on the latest trend, be buten cool and megadiver; however, it needs no alibis: la city is rebellious and transgressive per se. Tijuana is a mix of styles and epochs; it's not static, it does a 360 on the establishment's rules and loses itself in the most devastating euphoria. Tijuana scratches, caresses, stimulates.

This is what there is: a future of great challenges and opportunities, with a 1950s main avenue under surveillance with technology from the twenty-first century, an economy based more and more on the dichotomy of cartels and police corruption, made of bleeps and scratch in lost bars, of flirting glances at the old new empire always on the lookout, the language play that will replace the Spanglish that so deeply bothers the defenders of a model that was never ours, a new morality that greatly resembles the old morality, glancing at brochures with detailed instructions on how to leave the border. Whatever, this is the way it is: today everything is border, fissure, the largest chunk of what previously was an idea of nation. In Tijuana, people stick around, euphoric or resigned, because, paraphrasing Fromm, in the end, they weren't headed anywhere anyway.

Or not. If you notice, there's a riot going on. Remember one thing: la city is NOT a utopia or a dystopia, it's the afterparty where you hear the last call. We'll keep on having fun while the next thing starts. ¿Qué? We don't know and don't care, here we're enjoying the time we have left to live. A few years back, the Borderhacker activists used the catchphrase "Delete the Border" in their v.3. We, all ironic, are still pushing a different version: "Delight the border." And come as you are (Nirvana dixit). All welcome, no problema. Come before it's gone and the party's moved on to someplace else. Come to witness the moment when TJ reinvents itself on pay per view.

Tijuana has no fear. Tijuana is (a) heroic (drug). Everything here happens at the same time, but we don't realize it; it's a white label for a beyondeada generation that rebels with electrobeats of a radiant future, right on the line dividing this from that, calculating the moment that'll decide the fate of all the parties in the future and of the other extraordinary actions or even the social uprising expected one of these days.

Second warning: Just like Juan Luis Curiel suggested at the end of the show he had in the seventies on the local channel 12, if you didn't like Tijuana, don't tell anyone.

BTW, Tijuana makes me happy, so happy.

in/out lines

En la línea fronteriza. A blazing sun and a line at least an hour and a half long. Whatever, it's what you have to go through to satiate the ridiculous desire to get the last copy of *Dazed and Confused* and flip through the used bins at a couple select music stores. As always, the time passes slowly, but, to my pleasant surprise, the line is moving pretty fast considering the hour and it being the weekend.

The conversations make the wait easier. Up ahead, Mexican Americans taking their weekly supply of Gamesa cookies to some San Diego suburb; further back, a group of Europeans switch between a heavily accented English and their native French. I inadvertently eavesdrop on some of the conversations. It's either that or make do with watching the cars go by, because this Saturday I decided to cross by myself.

We get to the point where the first American officer is standing. Instinctively, I check my wallet: I want to make sure I've got my passport. Yeah, I've got my visa, enclosed in the same protective envelope they gave me years ago. My breathing relaxes a little and I walk forward.

We're already in the installations of the USA. At least, the signs prohibiting loitering are better translated now (though they still translate *violators* as "violadores"—rapists). It's funny to see how people lower their voices, barely speaking, and move super slow like they're not trying to draw attention. Somehow, the line has a pacifying effect. No Cameras. No Photos. Every act, every movement, every conversation is being recorded. We know it. We're used to that invisible Big Brother, the one we know is always there. In this line under constant surveillance, we're all suspect. Standing in line, waiting, walking, crossing over isn't just a formality, wasting time in a kind of limbo / gray zone / dead space / a no place that still modifies the way we act before entering what they advertise as paradise.

Others don't make it. They're caught with fake passports, expired permits, mistakes on their papers, stolen identities. Sometimes, like today, we see them lined up in a different line, in the same space but in the opposite direction. They barely talk, walk slowly, as if they were trying not to draw our attention, those of us practically in front of them. A family with their hands secured behind their backs, one after the other. The parents at the head of the line, their teenage kids in the middle, and at the back, the littlest ones. All of them with their heads down, trying to hide their faces in the collar of their Nike jacket or their Gap sweatshirt, staring down (like a shoegazer from '85) at the laces on the sneakers they bought in some *mercadillo* in Tijuana.

At the front of the line, we all keep our mouths shut because we know we could be one of them. With my incredible ear, I make out one of the French guys tell another in his weird English: *The official gives back them to where they belong.*

Five minutes later, I'm buying a Trolley ticket, downtown San Diego awaits.

Tijuana Youth: Entre la Cultura y la Fiesta

Sometimes, the glare of the hype can be so deceptive. You can't live in the past and try to maintain long-lost glories or fight endlessly against *leyendas negras* there's really no purpose to revisit. You can't believe everything you see, hear, or feel (so sorry, more than skepticism, it's common sense). That's why, if a few years ago the well-known magazine *Newsweek* declared la city as one of the new centers of culture and vitality, it was, let's say, a tardy recognition of what's going on, a move to bestow validity in a market that insists on declaring new attractions and expanding the possibilities of business as usual. It's already been said that Tijuana moves faster than its artists and critics.

Nevertheless, contrary to that exoticizing, reductionist logic, Tijuana has never stopped being fashionable, in vogue, discovering trends, providing a preview of the immediate future just at the moment when it's about to happen. The people writing the recent history of la city are part of a metageneration of Tijuana artists, all of whom live life without hiding the truth, without holding back, without taking themselves all that seriously; they do all this as they watch the myths getting weaker and weaker (The main myth? The one that implied you had to leave Tijuana to be able to get any recognition or relative success), that are familiar with and circulate around the whole city, that flow through job networks and collaborate with anyone or any group, whether institutions, private initiatives, or following the Do-It-Yourself punk maxim. Tijuana open source.

Youth is just a word, as Bourdieu said, another category to contain a segment of the population, or as Rossana Reguilla notes, "a social agreement and a productive agent in the world." In la city, these youthful agents, whether incorporated or dissident (in regard to cultural consumption or the structures of the predominant culture), have shown their capacity for change and their brazen disregard for official discourse when they enter its traditional environs. Otherness is put on the table for discussion and the contradiction of meanings-results becomes part of the creative environment (a faribolesque postmodernism, the art of recycling, urban loops, porous borders, the feeling of always being in a self-representative vortex, the aesthetics of the ugly, the street). A new batch of young people who, faced with the contemporary situation in Tijuana, proposes culture as the antidote to barbarism (Sergio González dixit).

What moves them? What do they propose? Among their interests are the recuperation of the city, the rescue and mobility of spaces, the promise of the party and the pleasure that comes from living in a city as bizarre as ours, confronting a social reality that allows almost everything. Yes, but they go further than that, joining that lovey-dovey feeling with post-PC irony, academic criticism with the posture of a person who lives the street with an everyday naturalness, the search for new languages through appropriation and resemanticization of what's considered ordinary (what the majority sees as something unnecessary, superficial, and even vulgar). That's why, among many other reasons, their cultural products (books, music, design, installation art, video and visual art, among others) find homes in such diverse sites as international exhibitions or marginal supplements. Of course, they're all totally media savvy.

In her excellent book *The Reality Overload*, Annie Le Brun said that "if, despite the degrading adulation of it, youth can still possess some sort of beauty, then that beauty is that of despair, for it is youthful despair that is sometimes capable of rekindling those vital questions that the culture strives to reduce to ashes." I am thinking about the instrumental work of the Nortec Collective and their post-fronterizo, audiovisual hybrid; in the visual art exhibitions *Urban Diagnostics* and *Larva* (which provoked so many debates and diatribes because of the unevenness/ambiguity of their curatorial criteria); in the emergence of a new exciting pop scene that can be located—after the Nortec phenomenon—at the crest of the musical wave (the promise is to be found in groups like Shantelle, Ibi ego!, The Polardroids, Aeroplanos, Niña Cámara, among others); in the candid image of the city and its characters that appears on national channels via Bulbo's documentaries; in the B-side present in the audiovisual imaginary of Art Core; in the music and video workshops for teenagers organized by a group of collectives (Nortec, Bulbo, Yonke Art, Pragma) all setting out to build a new generation of artists; in those cult authors, the newest ones who just showed up or those who fill the pages of fanzines and books of poetry (Heriberto Yépez, Omar Pimienta, Paty Blake); visual artists who are starting to sell in regional markets (Julio Orozco, Tania Candiani, Jaime Otis); the generation of punk DJs bringing life to the Tijuana night; the neo-graffiti crews that insist on seeing la city as a huge canvas; the influential presence of theatre artists and independent dance groups in national shows and conferences; the explosion of street hip-hop, converted into cronistas of the periferia (Sociedad Anónima, Tijuas Steelo, Legión Marvel); the other record labels (Static, At-At, Discos Invisibles, Eklegein) that represent a more experimental and risk-taking underground; in the collision of design, music, and Internet that global radio was given rise to; in the new interactive media represented by the now almost five hundred active blogs documenting life in Tijuana from every possible angle. Perhaps some of those I've mentioned don't propose the vision that the mainstream and its acolytes would like, but (always the but) you have to recognize that, as Los Fresones Rebeldes would say, algo hay.

Those and other up-and-coming artists are looking to reflect, as the researcher Fiamma Montezemolo mentions in her text *Tijuana Isn't Tijuana*, not just one Tijuana, but rather thousands of Tijuanas, because they know la city is that "on-going game of diversities, of simulated truths" and in the end artists decide "not to lie about themselves, even though that doesn't mean they have to tell The Truth." Without a doubt, they know they are part of something that needs no leaders, that the real enemy is monolithic thinking and that, as the old bolero says, sólo se vive una vez. You only live once. BTW, we still think the fiesta tijuanera will keep on raging at full blast.

---➤

posted by rafa # July 10, 2005

The Counterculture in Mexico: Ese pedazo de onda

You never know who you're working for. We imagine other possible worlds for ourselves and they end up being the sets for the last Coke commercial.

Phrases become advertising slogans, clichés of the younger generation blasted into the void in a script by marketing experts and images by an avant-garde video artist. A bet lost (or won, depending on the particular case).

I was there—like James Murphy in that first Can concert in Cologne—witnessing our little big revolution, flipping the coin in the air, waiting for a change in our favor from that damned bitch named luck that betrayed us and ended up biting us. It still hurts.

I'm that guy who marched in that seminal protest, squaring off with a he-gemonic position, the one who yelled louder than everyone else, shouting slogans for the change that—what an irony—came late and only partially, the one who never ran away. I am the one who translated the lyrics of the songs they liked so much and then helped them build a scene we thought was progressive and liberatory; the one who wrote in magazines that did away with outdated patterns of language and information, which would open the door to so many debates in our huge (hypocritical) Mexican family. I'm the guy who sent out the invitation to trip and experiment with psychedelic substances and with a passion free of that Catholic guilt that prevented us for so long from connecting with our "inner deep." I'm the one who invented—by transgressing—a new language that was a starting point for new alliances and a more believable and intimate picture of what was to come. *Do you remember me?*

How to talk about a situation that develops in a concrete context and historical moment but which has real effects on our present? By making a summary judgment like Heath and Potter? Sublimating the idealist content and disregarding the naïveté? Pointing out the catastrophe hiding behind that deeply rooted positivism? Taking sides even after the defeat? Perpretrated under a new system of analysis that allows one to judge without a romanticism that spoils all critical positions? A hard choice.

Authenticity is, by definition, a threat to what is pompously called "the other," which is, of course, not our equal. The need to create a new culture (Gramsci dixit), an outburst of enthusiasm debated—individually and in groups—before the model of a gray existence, minimized and mimetic, with no opportunities, organized by the great invisible hand of the market and its speculators. The lack of authenticity is what, supposedly, has been imposed upon us. I'm not so sure about that.

Anticonformity is the typical rebuke of the system (the much-feared error in the matrix).

In his book on the counterculture in Mexico, José Agustín draws a line which unites and interrelates different youth tribes with diverse behaviors and activities—*pachucos*, rebels with a cause, *jipitecas*, punks—through specific moments in the second half of the twentieth century. The popular author is correct when he asserts that the history of the counterculture is a history of incomprehension and repression. What's even better is he narrates how and why this has happened in an informed, detailed way with a great sense of humor. José Agustín has given us the gift of an ideal book for all kinds of deep discussions: complicated, intellectual, heated, light, and generational, among many other types. He does this because he takes us to the heart of the matter, he shoots from the hip and polarizes: them or us. There is no middle ground. Some were/are based in that categorization, some are strong and idealist, and the others yuppies and conformists. And you, *¿de qué signo eres?*

In Mexico, the counterculture—this magic little word that could be stretched by followers and detractors to include everything unsaid—was/has always been taken as a protest and a reaction to a dominant culture, without ever establishing itself as a real productive counterweight. The result? A dialogue between people who don't listen to each other, a struggle between opposing forces with (almost always) flawed arguments on both sides, since they don't understand the actors and factors involved, a generalization that leads us—like everything—to a disastrous end, which, in this case, was still a bit positive.

What is our position on cultural expression—film, music, literature—in the face of the dominant system about drug consumption, the influence of religion, the sexual revolution, the right to pleasure or language itself? In his book, José Agustín throws out ideas about collective karmas, a boundless camaraderie, some likeable characters in a nonstop party deliriously chatting about mysticism and social struggle. The (temporary) triumph of the Dionysian.

How and how much has it changed? The answer can be found right now on thousands of Internet pages, in new fanzines, in no-longer-young groups that construct their lives outside of the traditional circuit and the market speculation on what's cool, alternative, authentic. Or maybe not, and maybe it's time we find out that, confirming what that Sonny Curtis song says, the system won despite armed uprisings, a fractured multiculturalism, global-phobic contingents on endless tour, separatist and isolationist postures, and vain attempts to give it the royal finger. Failure is unavoidable, but, *caray*, we sure did have fun.

Something to point out: if the jipitecas emerged in the sixties as a reaction to a system as repressive as the one in Mexico—which it was and still is—and faced with a reduction in the possibility for ensuring equity and justice in all arenas of daily life, it must not be forgotten that these serve as a bizarre counterpoint for the arrival of a new brood of reactive and meticulous young people (the Yunque Youth, for example) on the social scene. Honestly, a psychotic reaction.

In his book *The Elemental Particles*, the French writer Michel Houellebecq—who was abandoned by his hippie mother—wrote a frontal attack on the May 1968 generation in France in which he questions its liberatory meaning in order to, as the Americans say, *Take No Prisoners*. With a disillusioned nihilism typical of a good punk song, Houellebecq excoriates this, the epitome of a youth movement.

Does the issue of the counterculture in Mexico matter right now? Of course the answer is yes and no. The contemporary situation is impossible to decipher if one doesn't understand—and transcend, you could add—this particular juncture. Suspiciousness—this very Mexican trait—suggests to us an overbearing assimilation by a system which Greil Marcus, that great American critic, spoke to us about when he condemned the fact that there isn't a hint of rebelliousness that survives in the individual after the normalizing instinct of the great social machinery. In the end, we are all everything (Marcos, Atenco, Walmart, Sabritas, El Chavo del Ocho, a duopoly on the same).

Flipping a double-sided coin.

Nevertheless, something's left, something will remain.

Crazy Crazy Night

Yes, these have been extremely important days for la city. Tons of violence caused by the impunity of a few, the complicity of many, and years and years of corruption. Lots of sensationalist media commotion, never-ending loops of lifeless bodies are a clear sign of the violent times we're facing. Headlines betting on huge profits gained from the public's morbid fascination and leading straight to collective psychosis. Fear, *todos saben*, as a tactic for control.

Despite all this, la city is alive. It feels alive. It knows it's alive. A bunch of festivals happening at the same time, events all over the place, Tijuana overflowing in its euphoria to reclaim the street, asking for moments of fun and pleasure in the face of so much tragedy. Tragedy that's become normalcy.

The night is transformed. We get together despite everything we see on the TV news: the overflowing euphoria of engaging conversations and shared complicity makes us sweat in (almost) never-ending mornings. The rhythms, the overwhelming feeling of No Fear, the last call for la juventud bulletproof. Dance, dance, dance . . .

Waiting for friends who're at other bars, who send texts saying, "ya vamos, wait us" (*sic*). We wait, the party gets bigger, it grows like the wild Tijuana night (that cliché exploited so much in the *crónicas* that come out in the Sunday supplements). *Abrazos* and celebration, there's always someone here who's having a birthday, someone who's coming back or someone leaving (they're all reasons to go out and celebrate in a city that wants to see us locked away in our homes: they won't get their way). The next stop, a concert.

The place is completely full. I make it to the bar (and I don't leave). Interesting conversations with the artsy crew, then laughing and laughing like crazy with some amigas and their amigas. The girls are fighters, they don't let anyone off the hook for anything. (I'm happy listening to them, watching them laugh, trying to seduce one of them, knowing beforehand that nothing's going to happen that hasn't already happened . . .)

At four or five in the morning, I don't know what time it is anymore, we end up at Las Tortas Cubanas. The road to the Tijuana West Coast is just a few feet away, the day is ending without even noticing. We survived in the city of fear and impunity: Mission accomplished.

--➤

posted by rafa # September 27, 2008

A Party for Democracy

Today I was walking around near Calle Segunda and Constitución.
Closed to traffic.
A lot of people waiting for something, blue, white and orange balloons.
A girl alone on a platform sings *cumbias* (the second song was by Selena).
A group of women dance up front.

Someone passes by me holding up a P.A.N. flag.

The kids are having fun on a couple inflatable moonwalks.

Officers from a bunch of different police agencies monitor the scene.

I can't tell the difference between the police cadets and the thugs wandering around downtown.

They look almost exactly the same: same haircuts, same attitudes.

I walk around the street, recognize some prominent politicians.

Of course, local politicians.

Ex-classmate from school or ex-regulars of la noche TJ.

Extremely fat.

They say politics makes people fat.

They announce over the sound system that a caravan of more than 500 cars is about to get there.

"Viva la democracia," shouts the cumbia-singing girl.

Everything is so mixed up, everything is so absurd.

Democracy is just another buzzword, a cliché, a ruse, the voice of an ignorant majority.

The whole sad show is boring to me, and I decide to head home.

---➤

posted by rafa # Saturday, July 2, 2005

usei (rough mix)

YOU SAY

. . . I'm the next big thing to happen, a character lost in a bad sitcom, the spirit of California.

. . . Someone wants to change the dialect to say new things, misses the goal, supports the death penalty, always comes late, stirs up those núcleos de social instability, has un apetito por la destruction.

. . . I'm a retard, a misogynist, un Televisa Kid, a member of el Yunque Youth, a dummy when it comes to important things, a blind date fetishist, a dry style wanker, lo más.

. . . I'm a molesting child, the jail bait, a wife beater, a rapist, a non-English speaker, un extranwero, a little liar, ese pobre bastardo who fucked up his life one more time.

. . . Que Ron Jeremy, Charlie Rose, Joey Greco, Nick Kent, Seymour Stein, Todashi Yanai, or the goalie of el club de la esquina are all more important than I am.

YOU SAY

. . . She's a prime choice filete, a strangely geometric blindness, a pretty pub(l)ic disorder, something that only by being lazy finds serenity, a weird combination of apathy and complacency, an enigma whose solution is limited by a court decision.

. . . She's the girl who pops out of the cake, a victim of postpartum depression, the heart of the deal, someone who has to soak themselves in promises from God.

. . . She sabotages her own audition, swears time destroys (almost) everything, an imposition that declares herself our enemy, a home run or the threat of a fight hanging in the air.

. . . She's the picture of beauty, a street empty after the latest riots, the obstacle to our turn to the impossible, the possibility of a ménage à trois.

. . . She's a bitch, the love of our entire life, una saladera, someone that goes after a dream without thinking about collateral damage, the melody of those songs that have an implicit charge of sadness to them.

YOU SAY

. . . He's a gameboy, a Farfisa sound, a professional poser who'll end up a human ashtray, someone who'll have to beg for forgiveness for putting national security at risk.

. . . He's the guy that thinks about what his life has become as he sits on the corner of the bed, the memory of things past, a yoke to break, dead desire in some old boxers.

. . . He's the one who answers those questions asked by an absurd and bored old man. (What is freedom? Have you ever felt disappointed? When will all this end?)

About la Fama de la City

How many more dead bodies you think we need before la city shoots us out like bullets? (Pardon the expression.) How many more articles and reports do we have to read before we feel like we live in a permanent state of anxiety?

We're not leaving.

La city is ours, we're not going to leave it.

The street is ours, we're not going to stop going out.

And yeah, they can say we're the most violent place ever (we're not).

And yeah, they can say it's impossible to live here (the living is good, fuck you).

Y sí, la city es nuestra.

I Love Tijuana

I LOVE TIJUANA for being anarchic, resourceful, fun loving, bent on freedom, and nocturnal.

I LOVE TIJUANA because I've never cared about fighting against what's left of the leyendas negras a go-go or against the media's sensationalist opportunism, not even against the cold distance of those who see la city as San Diego's backyard. Tijuana just is.

I LOVE TIJUANA because I live it to the extreme, because you can't buy my tijuanidad on an estampita and it's not a product of ready-made poser (re) structuring, because it's inside of me and it's obvious every second. As I travel around la city every day, I (re)meet her in her constant state of change, catching the details and feeling the energy that lives in cities that one day will be sacred.

I LOVE TIJUANA, mi city.
July 11, 2009

October 20, 2006
the statement
the sentence

"Everything they tell me about Tijuana, I believe it all."
*Heard in Hermosillo, Sonora

January 20, 2006
the question
the question

Protests, checkpoints, curfews . . . aren't the solution to la city's problem of
    violence and impunity. Or are they? And when will the authorities press
    the "panic button"?

April 27, 2008
from twitter
rhetorical question

What's more important? Fifteen hired killers dead or 3000+ people fired
    from the maquila this week adding to the % of unemployed in TJ?

September 28, 2008
phrases for days like this

About the violence in TJ
"I demand that if this isn't going to stop, it should at least be more
interesting."
—Abraham

October 20, 2008
la city in blue

Out the window of a bus heading who-knows-where, I watch the city
disappear, the reality of the violence and the forgotten campaign
promises blurring it into oblivion.
Vaya prisa.
This is how we live.

Poetics of . . .

Poetics of forgetting and imperfect questions thought up on a Wednesday
afternoon.
Poetics of breaking away from the Judeo-Christian monopoly on feelings of
guilt.
Poetics of passwords and usernames.
Poetics of post-traumatic experience and shopping spree vertigo.
Poetics of intelligence brought on by the effectiveness of social networks
and the absence of real dialogue.
Poetics of street protests and productive value in free fall.
Poetics of the death of government bureaucrats and neoliberal
bulletproofing.
Poetics of what happens once in a lifetime and the stuff none of us can
recognize as their own.
Poetics of dyslexia and disappointment with the end of a surprisingly good
show on TV.
Poetics of 14×1.
Poetics of trips abroad and good wishes.
Poetics of people nominated and executed in a kind of ominous lottery.
Poetics to warm up and blow party streamers.
Poetics of unacceptable failures and those budgets focused on rebuilding a
country.

Poetics of teenage anthems and the unbearable days of that blind summer.

Poetics of the unilateral and the false celebrity honesty.

Poetics of pretty people and their favorite commercials.

Poetics of American school shootings and their repercussions in the suburbs.

Poetics of oversaturation and the loss of the unstoppable road to ruin.

Poetics of grammar and its actions.

Poetics of shame and the Puritan look of a teenager without MySpace.

Poetics of a noontime reading, of the loneliness of middle-aged people and the sales of shares in times of crisis.

Poetics of the uselessness of Twitter rank, of Firefox bugs and euphoria about Google video chat.

Poetics of the towns near Morelia and soulless karma.

Poetics of troubled retailers and crosses that crowd the frontline of the people's defiance.

Poetics of millionaires' fear and their significant losses.

Poetics of big mistakes and savagery.

Poetics of sadness as an everyday presence.

Counterculture, Rockers, Punks, New Romantics, and Mods in Tijuana

Beyond the common stereotypes associated with the city, beyond the logical reasoning of everyday life (the people who traverse, live in, and die in this city), at this point in time in the history of contemporary Mexican music, Tijuana represents a missing link between failure and genuine opportunity for transcendence. The city also represents dozens of stories that, over and over again, tell of the eccentric quest for an original musical voice in a region that was completely isolated from the rest of Mexico. This musical history is not easy to explain, and those who have been a part of the city's music "scene" at any point in its history probably have the ephemeral feeling that the concepts and the processes behind the music were more interesting than the end result. Rock 'n' roll never dies, but the spirits of its players—from generation to generation—these do.

We speak of rock 'n' roll as the most inadequate term to attempt to describe what has been brewing in Tijuana for more than four decades, at the national level, as an alternative metareality, as fantasy and omnipresence. We speak of "Rock Made in Tijuana" as an issue in itself and as a practical, immediate matter, due to the geographic location of the city, the bad habits of the Mexican record industry, and above all its immediate proximity to the first world via the United States.

This essay does not seek to be a recounting or a complete compendium of Tijuana's players and interpreters, but rather a brief biographical sketch in profile: the factors that underlie their achievements and failures, their principal motives the city's underrecognized contribution to the world of art, and its present context. One thing must be made clear: Mexico is a country of scarcities (that, we already know); and most of the population has basic needs to meet before "rocking."

Moreover, people generally prefer other styles of popular music. Nonetheless, beyond any doubt, thanks to those scarcities, Tijuana represents the best of creativity offering the best of Mexico in its wide-ranging musical scope.

Beginnings: The Myth and Reality of Tijuana Rock

Many people say that the point of departure for Tijuana Rock has to be the young Carlos Augusto Alves Santana strolling along Avenida Revolución, learning his first guitar chords on the stage of a strip joint from his mentor, Javier Bátiz, who, along with his band Los TJs, was already an icon of Tijuana nightlife in the late 1950s. Carlos Santana leaves for San Francisco to live with his family, puts his band together, plays at Woodstock, and becomes an international star, while Javier Bátiz stays in Mexico, goes off to establish himself in Mexico City, and is left in the hands of a less beneficent fate.

Javier Bátiz misses the chance to play at Avándaro (the Mexican Woodstock) in 1971, in Valle de Bravo, State of Mexico. He gets there late because, earlier that day, he plays in a Mexico City club where he worked on the weekends. After that and for the rest of the 1970s, he fights the Mexican authorities and the media, their blockade of anything that has to do with a national form of rock, unleashed by the images that Avándaro brought to Mexican TV. According to the authorities and the media, those images were an outrage against the proper morals of Mexico, in part thanks to the high-sounding words spoken halfway through the concert by the members of the band Peace and Love, who also came from Tijuana. The resulting repression that rock faced in Mexico over the next ten years is seen as an extension of the hard line adopted to conceal all things associated with the youth counterculture, a policy that began with the massacre of students at Tlatelolco on October 2, 1968. On that date, the government of President Gustavo Díaz Ordaz brutally repressed political and revolutionary student movements.

This myth that, depending on whom you ask, makes Javier Bátiz the hero/victim for staying in Mexico and makes Carlos Santana a sort of deserter/migrant champion of the American dream, illustrates in a way the difficulties faced by anyone from Tijuana, from that moment on and for the rest of their lives, when they tried to make a living from any type of rock.

The truth is that, although people may consider Carlos Santana a *tijuanense*, he was born in Autlán de Navarro, in the state of Jalisco, and learned to play the guitar with his father, the leader of a mariachi band, when he was eight years old. While his formative phase as a rock guitarist did take place in Tijuana nightclubs, his later progress corresponds more to the zeitgeist of late-1960s San Francisco than to his brief stay in Tijuana. Santana is perhaps the only Mexican rocker who has managed to transcend, artistically and commercially, not only borders but cultures as well.

For his part, Javier Bátiz, despite being considered by an enlightened group of fans as one of the archetypes of Mexican rock, found only frustration when he tried to present himself as an "artist," within the formulaic notion that Mexican media and transnational record companies had about rock. Although rock was an influential force in the pop culture of the 1960s, the model Bátiz followed—singing original songs, performing live, and developing an authentic rock sound influenced by African American blues—was not compatible with the culture of covering already well-known songs and performing with a prerecorded sound track, standards imposed by the media at that time.

Despite Javier Bátiz's efforts to introduce to Mexico the most authentic rock possible—without selling his soul to the whims of some A&R executive from such-and-such international record company—his discography of that era is almost unknown today, and his recent recordings are released by an independent label with limited distribution in the rest of Mexico. Today, Javier Bátiz lives in Tijuana and can be seen regularly in some of the city's venues; faithful to that original spirit he has never given up. Together with his sister, Baby Bátiz (the first female Mexican rocker, long before Alejandra Guzmán, Julieta Venegas, and Gloria Trevi), he undoubtedly represents a primordial epoch of originality, of the verve to innovate—or at least to introduce new musical forms in Mexico—something that has usually been received with hostility or disapproval by mainstream Mexican society.

Absent a landmark album representative of his career, without effective channels to distribute independent music, and with the country's inadequate infrastructure to support a rock culture, it is difficult to reach a verdict on Bátiz. Due to brutal conditions imposed by the media after Avándaro, it would be unfair to reduce his career to an anecdote or a cultural afterthought. Still, the association with Carlos Santana has to be at once the most fortunate and the least fortunate point of his career, since on this point weighs the judgment of "what might have been" if conditions in Mexico had been different or if Bátiz had followed his "student" Santana abroad. Nevertheless, the position he now occupies in the history of Tijuana rock, together with characters such as Lupillo Barajas (Tijuana Five) and Martín Mayo (El Ritual), is invaluable and undeniable.

The Resonant Comparative Advantage of Life on the Border

Living next to the most powerful nation on earth offers possibilities that, over time, represent a comparative advantage over other areas of Mexico. The ease with which one could move from one side of the border to the other to complete transactions, shop for clothes, technology, goods, and culture—in a Tijuana before the advent of cable television and the Internet—was a dream for many Mexicans, who finally came to stay in Tijuana. With only one Spanish-language channel available on local television, Tijuana seemed to be one of the cities most isolated from the Mexican capital, where the aberrant centralism of the country concentrated politics, media, and culture in Mexico City. Far from the reach of the media and what was considered Mexican culture, the city of Tijuana seemed in every sense to operate under its own rules and circum-stances. Still, with the government and media blackout of Mexican rock creat-ing a sort of black hole for an entire generation of rockers, the extent of the counterculture's resistance would not be visible to a new generation until the end of the 1970s.

While the rest of the country freed itself from recurrent economic crises at the height of an oil boom, the border region ended a totally dollar-based econ-omy and began its slow integration with the rest of Mexico. The generation born between 1967 and 1972 were members of a middle class with dozens of open options in a city that, during that decade, began a process of industrial-ization and welcomed with open arms hundreds of families who came to stay and take advantage of the new opportunities that the border city offered to new settlers.

The power of San Diego radio is essential to understanding its influence on a new generation that grew up in the 1970s. Just as Javier Bátiz was in-spired by the African American blues he heard over AM radio in his home, so the rock, disco, and jazz that tijuanenses listened to over FM radio in the 1970s, before the rest of Mexico heard it, had a globalizing effect on a new generation. Proximity with the United States offered a sort of front-row seat to the most important musical events of the era, while many of these musical trends did not reach the rest of Mexico until years later, if at all. This strange hybrid of a border Mexican, enlightened via San Diego by European and U.S. counterculture and pop music, is, without doubt, one of the most important elements in deciphering the artistic currents that emerged at the end of the twentieth century. These young Mexicans on the northern border, combined with the various socioeconomic problems of the region, especially migration and drug trafficking, have long made Tijuana a veritable spectacle for academics and visitors.

The strongest countercultural impact for a new generation of Tijuana residents occurred at the end of the 1970s, with the arrival of British and American punk and postpunk. Although punk was an underground movement, beyond doubt, it was on the border, in Tijuana, where the first punks were seen roaming the streets near Boulevard Fundadores, adjacent to downtown. Even if it seemed only a matter of imitating the aesthetics of the Los Angeles, New York, and London scenes, the genre managed to take root in Tijuana in the late 1980s, with bands such as Mercado Negro and Solución Mortal.

Doubtless, given the nation's cultural centralism, Tijuana's geographic location continued to be a disadvantage. As usual, the first rock bands from Tijuana had to try their luck in the nation's capital in order to be recognized and noticed by the media and international record companies such as BMG, EMI, or SONY (formerly Columbia).

Nonetheless, because of the latent fear the term "national rock" still evoked in some of the media, acceptance of the genre by the popular Mexican canon was still far away. This lag contrasted with other Latin American countries, for example, Argentina, where the government banned foreign rock, especially British, during the Falklands War, thus developing an entire national rock industry that is perhaps one of the most enduring and influential in the rest of Latin America.

By the late 1980s, the situation in Tijuana had improved greatly, and bands could set up concerts in bars and clubs. The notion of a house party had always been the ideal setting for a band to debut its music in a less-controlled environment. In the early 1980s, in a Tijuana so close to the entertainment venues of San Diego and Los Angeles, with the chance to see the greatest bands in the world, a new generation of Tijuana rockers was inspired, albeit in different ways, to present its own interpretation of the music.

From rock (La Cruz) to heavy metal (Armagedón), punk and reggae hybrids (Radio Chantaje, Chantaje, No!, and Tijuana No!), and electronic pop ensembles (Vandana, Synthesis, Artefakto, Laplace, and Ford Proco), the second half of the decade saw a large increase in these musical projects that managed to dominate the local scene. The main catalysts and influences were still radio stations from across the border, some of which, ironically, broadcast, as they still do, from Tijuana, using the city as a heaven-sent shelter from certain FCC laws and regulations in the United States. As a window to a world that was neither Mexican nor part of the United States, radio offered a perfect soundtrack for those fortunate ears that ended up receiving some musical education. And, as the national rock scene began to blossom, the possibilities were endless, especially when the new musical world emerging in Europe with New Wave and the New Romantic movement began to reach ears on the border through new radio formats that explored new trends, remote from more traditional rock. With the advent of MTV, Tijuana was one of the first Mexican cities to receive the feed through a local cable station, making the forms and intentions of modern rock and its variations easier to understand.

By the late 1980s, the new generation of youth that joined electronic music bands represented the first step toward what would become the Nortec Collective's projection to international fame in the late 1990s. Their music received a level of recognition outside of Mexico not seen since the triumph of Carlos Santana at Woodstock in 1969. Nortec's early efforts are vital to understanding their development as creators of electronic music. Although a recorded history of the time is limited and almost nonexistent, we can rely on the oral tradition and the personal experiences of its participants.

In the Space of Memory

The emergence of radio programs in the late 1980s (*Sintonía Pop*, *Noarte*, and *Expansiones del Rock*), broadcast from the cultural station of the Instituto Tecnológico de Tijuana, were the first efforts of any generation to relate the music that was being created in Tijuana with the musical movements evolving from the New Wave in Europe and the United States. This radio presence and the search for physical spaces, performance venues that allowed the live development of these bands, are key to understanding the underground nature of their scene. A small group of producers, supported by self-managed bands, were able to create a community that launched this small movement of musicians, along with artists and official cultural promoters, in the late 1980s.

The sudden growth of fanzines, also in the late 1980s, inspired by all those others that went hand in hand with punk and New Wave in London, Madrid, Los Angeles, and New York, was another means to define and connect the scenes in different countries of the Spanish-speaking world. Sadly, although many of the fanzines offer insight into events at that time, there is little or no musical record of the era.

Technology to record at home was still far away from becoming a reality, and the cost of recording in a professional studio was unattainable for high school students experimenting with synthesizers. Most of the surviving recordings of the time are more traditional forms of rock, but, no doubt, this reveals the lack of vision and the lost opportunities to have achieved at that time an adequate historical record of all those projects that, for the most part, exist only in memory, at a time when the cost of music production and recording were sky-high. Only the group Artefakto—with ex-members of some of the electronic bands of the late 1980s who would later become part of the Nortec Collective—managed to launch three independent records and even licensed one to the German industrial music label Zoth Ommog in the early 1990s.

To add fuel to the fire, and build on the myth that Tijuana has always been a center of attraction for rock, it is essential to mention the club Iguana's. Located in a commercial plaza a few steps from the border, even though managed by a San Diego agent and geared to the U.S. market, the club brought to Tijuana the most important musical acts of the late 1980s and early 1990s: from classic punk (Ramones, DRI, and Misfits) to postpunk (PIL and Tom Tom Club); from New Wave (Devo and OMD) to the nascent American grunge (Nirvana, Pearl Jam, Alice in Chains, and Jane's Addiction); from U.S. indie rock (Unrest, The Breeders, and Sonic Youth) to industrial goth (Nine Inch Nails and KMFDM); from heavy metal (Sepultura and Luzbel) to gothic rock (Creatures, Xymox, and The Mission UK); from the aftermath of danceable Manchester bands (Jesus Jones and Primal Scream) to the advent of the dance culture of the early nineties (Deee-Lite). All in all, the club offered a plethora of alternative music that bridged those two decades of musical high intensity. All this in our own backyard; an open window to a true and inspiring world.

Looking Again to Mexico City

By the mid-1990s, the lack of recording options continued to be a major drag on the new generation of bands. With the advent of digital technology, however, recording costs diminished considerably, so that bands like Nessie, Mexican Jumping Frijoles, Tijuana No!, Nona Delichas, Duende de Teatro, Ohtli, Bodhisattva, and Julieta Venegas were able to record high-quality demos and attempt to get signed by some important international label in Mexico City.

The challenge was still the same as in the days of Javier Bátiz: trying to compete with bands from Mexico City and cities closer to the capital—mainly Monterrey and Guadalajara. The bottom line was that the expense of transportation to and from these cities for executives from Sony, BMG, and EMI was more reasonable than traveling the enormous distance to and from Tijuana.

Even at a very favorable time for national rock, after the Rock in Your Language campaign in the late 1980s, which promoted mostly South American bands, mature and innovative Tijuana rock continued to be rejected in Mexico in favor of more accessible bands of lesser quality than what was happening musically in Tijuana.

Facing the challenge of trying to compete economically with bands from Mexico City, some Tijuana groups—such as Julieta Venegas and Tijuana No!—decided to try their luck in the capital. Over the last ten years, theirs are the only two projects from that era that have received the support of a "big" label. For everyone else, the only choice was self-management, the creation of independent record companies, and the difficult task of simultaneously being artist, promoter, agent, and label. Except for some modest propositions in the late 1990s, such as Nimboestatic and Swenga, both of which achieved limited national distribution, independent efforts did not find a solid base in Tijuana until the twenty-first century. Despite the efforts of distributors such as Opción Sónica, who reached a few hundred individuals, to speak of independent distribution was to speak of something nonexistent. Opción Sónica's great achievement, in spite of going bankrupt by 2001, was to tie together a series of independent projects from large cities in Mexico. The ideas coming out of Tijuana were always aesthetically and conceptually more interesting. Even a Mexico City–based magazine like La Mosca, the only national rock magazine at the time, recognized Nona Delichas as one of the best rock bands of 1997, ahead of some of the groups produced by international labels. The decade closed with an interesting book, Oye como va: Recuento del rock tijuanense (Oye como va: A History of Tijuana Rock), edited by José Manuel Valenzuela and Gloria González. With both its achievements and shortcomings, the book is the most reliable source for a detailed historical context of Tijuana rock from its origins to the end of the century.

From the Past, the New: The Nortec Revolution

In 1999, thanks to the persistence of independent promoters, writers, graphic designers, and a dedicated group of people who had been working in different aspects of the Tijuana music scene since the 1980s, the Nortec movement managed to take shape out of the emerging culture of Mexican electronic music. Through small parties in abandoned venues, boosted by the DJ culture with its creation of new electronic sounds at a rare, global level, the people behind Nortec had been advancing their technique and amassing experience for nearly ten years—passing through techno-pop, industrial, big beat, and techno.

The sounds of the large bands from the state of Sinaloa, ranchera music and other traditional popular music from northern Mexico, mixed with electronics, echoed the successful formula of the world music genre and combined it with first-world technology. The quality of Nortec's proposal, the certainty that this music represented all of the social dichotomies of a modern city like Tijuana, situated between the third and first worlds, represented what trumpeter Jon Hassel calls the potential for a fourth-world music.

For the first time in the musical history of Tijuana, the historical tapestry of its context was scrutinized and appropriated to invent a new, characteristically Mexican, musical genre. Given the healthy competition of its members— Bostich, Fusible, Terrestre, Panóptica, Hiperboreal, Plankton Man, and Clorofila—and their visual exploitation of all things "border," the Nortec Collective is one of the best musical offerings Mexico has given the world, along with mariachi and norteño music.

In a similar attempt to internationalize, albeit less splashy than Nortec's efforts, the work of Loopdrop and Murcof has generated, at least among the majority of specialized critics, a minor buzz for two *tijuanense* projects that were also mixed in Europe, released in Mexico, and, to paraphrase an advertisement of the current government, were up to date and avant-garde. All of the above-mentioned acts emerged before the world as first-rate international artists.

Musical Tijuana after 9/11

Tijuana finds itself at a historical crossroads in its relationship with the United States and the rest of Mexico—between a rock and a hard place. On the other hand, the changing and increasingly strict controls on access to the United States are a burden on the inhabitants of Tijuana and its musicians. On the everyday level, the relationship is not as smooth, nor as direct as it used to be. Tijuana is no longer a tourist destination for Anglo-Americans; for the most part, only Mexican Americans visit its streets and its tourist traps. The joke is now on us.

At the same time, all the media distinctions that made Tijuana a kind of geographic limbo have vanished almost completely. Tijuana has joined the rest of Mexico in every way, due to the growing migration from the south that goes on ceaselessly. Little by little, the city is recuperating its industrial economy; although there are constant threats that all its industry will move to China, where labor costs are lower. Despite the economic vicissitudes of a convulsing world, Tijuana is standing firm, if trembling a little. And thanks to the Internet, Tijuana has lost the privilege of being the first to know what is happening in the musical world outside of Mexico. Faced with other musical manifestations now emerging in other parts of the country, Tijuana no longer holds an exclusive advantage. Now, the playing field is even.

Even as the infrastructure of the international music industry collapses in Mexico due to rampant piracy and the "ills" brought on by the Internet, surprisingly, independent music distribution enjoys robust health at the national level, increasing its scope and field of action. The same Internet has also brought Tijuana closer to the rest of Mexico and succeeded in raising its best producers to the level of their counterparts in Montreal, Cologne, and New York.

Musical Tijuana is about to get started again, post-Nortec; it offers a new generation of musicians with a broad array of tools for self-promotion and a scope that was unthinkable three years ago. There is no doubt that the ease technology affords everything means that we face a new era—the revival of what Tijuana music will be in the second half of the first decade of the new century.

The foundations are already laid, with a new generation, though more traditional in its definition of what music ought to be, distancing itself from the Nortec boom and rethinking what it wants to be. I am still waiting for some Mexican Velvet Underground to appear, a band that would change and transform musical precepts around the world.

Although there is no internationally recognized rock tradition from Mexico, I have no doubt that, sometime, such a possibility might emerge. Perhaps it won't arise in the near future from Tijuana, as so many of us anticipated; but, for forty years, the city has set the bar very high for the rest of Mexico. All that came before has been, in truth, very easy. For Tijuana, the difficult part starts now: achieving permanence and continuity, within the context of what happens outside. This is what will finally define to the world the city's legacy in the musical history of Mexico.

Borderline Ghosts

From *Touch of Evil* to *Maquilapolis: City of Factories*

I assemble filters. I assemble electrical components. I assemble oxygen masks. I place rings in the machine. I tape electronic pieces. I assemble urinary bags. I assemble furniture. I package telephones. I inspect lenses. I package pantyhose. I assemble power cords, television parts, toys, oxygen sensors, intravenous tubes, batteries . . . —LOURDES (maquila worker in *Maquilapolis: City of Factories*)

The new emerges in the eventful moment of its return. —MICHEL FOUCAULT

From Border Representations of Tijuana to Borderline Screens

Much cultural and film studies ink has been spilt over the broad category of "border" cinema and moving-image media from the late 1980s on.[1] This literature includes writings on films, videos, and multimedia works dealing with issues of intercultural translation across diasporic and transnational communities, to autoethnographic strategies in personal documentaries, to tactical deployment of media by "minority" activists in multicultural political landscapes, to questions of self-representation associated with the emergence of the politicized category of indigenous media, to pioneering postcolonial critiques of classic auteur cinema's exotic fascination with the dangers and frissons of border crossing. Attributed to a multiplicity of liminal subjectivities discrepant with one another in the affective and political economies of late capitalism, "hybrid micro-cultures"[2] and their attendant intercultural forms of spectatorship and oppositional ethos (often overlapping but never fully coinciding with the larger category of Third Cinema) have been particularly prominent in anthropologically informed scholarship engaged with such intensely marked ethno-racialized modernities as Brazil or Mexico, or militarized geopolitical border zones and states of exception such as the ones between Morocco and Spain; Palestine, Lebanon, and Israel; and, for the purpose of this essay, between the United States and Mexico.

Tijuana can boast a rich and heterogeneous cross-genre repertoire that includes such films as Orson Welles's *Touch of Evil* (1958), Steven Soderbergh's *Traffic* (2000), Alejandro Gonzáles Iñárritu's *Babel* (2006), Jesse Lerner and Ruben Ortiz's experimental documentary *Frontierlandia* (1994), Chantal Ackerman's documentary and installation *From the Other Side* (2003), and the project commissioned by the binational public art event InSITE, El Miedo (Antonio Muntadas, 2005), that explores and interrogates, as the title suggests, the alleged affective economy of fear characteristic of border life. More recently, two untimely interventions, discussed below, can be added to the list: Sergio de la Torre and Vicky Funari's *Maquilapolis: City of Factories* (2006) and Sergio de la Torre's installation *Nuevo Dragon City* (2008). An important body of work, mainly in Spanish and seldom read,[3] has flourished over the past two decades that chronicles in exquisite detail representations of Tijuana on celluloid, both in silent films and talkies, from the 1920s on when the city served mainly as the backdrop and film set of Hollywood's culture industry, to the present that extends in new forms, but that nonetheless bears the trace of the foundational paradigm, of the immoral, lustful, and violent Tijuana of the Black Legend, or, in the words of *tijuanense* historian Humberto Berumen, of "Tijuana the horrible."[4] Speaking of the aesthetics of garbage that characterizes a certain tendency of certain national and/or Third Cinemas, Robert Stam enthusiastically observes: "Here I would like to focus on three related aspects of these aesthetics, namely: 1) their constitutive hybridity; 2) their chronotopic multiplicity; and 3) their common motif of the redemption of detritus."[5]

Stam's deployment of garbage heaps "as both metaphor and synecdoche" has also been a commonplace representational strategy that continues to inform perceptions of Tijuana.[6] TJ is the "horrific" and "horrible," mediated through the tropes of detritus and decomposition that would eventually come to dominate both critical and mainstream representations of Tijuana in Mexican and U.S. cinematic and political imaginaries. Thus Tijuana falls within the intercultural framework that assigns to it, by ways of reversal gestures, a cultural politics and film aesthetics that laments and celebrates at once—that is, politicizes—the "horrible" and abject against the backdrop of an alleged purity and authenticity characteristic not only of its northern neighbor but also of its constitutive rival, Mexico City. Still and moving images of the borderline separating Tijuana from San Diego invariably juxtapose, ad nauseam and via a strategy that has long lost the subversive shock appeal of surrealist/situationist antiaesthetics, the clash (rather than Laura Marks's more subtle "meeting"[7]) of two sensoria. The disorders of the South are set against the backdrop of immaculate and repressive grids of the North, ultimately endowing the disorderly[8] with political-oppositional and decolo-nizing capital.[9]

In light of this, one can safely say that Tijuana has the potential to undo, in the same gesture, both grand narratives of modernity and cross-cultural searches for alternative modernities, enabling us to move toward more com-plex engagement with contemporary intermedial forms of life, the disorderli-ness of which ought to be framed less and less in both ossified poststructural-ist gestures of reversal and in self-recursive actualizations of the differential force of modernity. Said differently, there is another mode of sensing the bor-der that continuously emerges long before two geopolitically and culturally distinct sensoria can be delineated. Emblematic of the cross/inter/transcul-tural and border crossing, "Tijuana the horrible" is also its impasse.

The literature I am questioning here zooms in on Tijuana as a convulsive (cinematic) city caught in an interstitial imaginary: on the one hand, at the margins of Mexico's postrevolutionary nationalist culture and on the other, as a hyperrepresented waiting zone resulting from exclusionary migration policies and a racially ghettoized political culture in the United States. This interstitial framework has generated a proliferation of academic and nonaca-demic approaches that tend to reduce the practice of film historiography to a history of representations of the city on celluloid.[10] Tijuana, the modernist cinematic city and urban experiment that emerged on the screen in the 1920s, is nonetheless often caught in such binaries as popular cinema and art film, fiction and documentary, cross-cultural and nationalist-nativist ways of see-ing. Consequently, histories of border representation accentuate these dichoto-mies by reducing the city to a binational geopolitical dynamic, to a mere mar-gin of the Mexican nationalist imaginary, and since the 1990s increasingly as a cosmopolitan haven for site-specific artists and curators. The beginning and the end of the nation, the before and after the border, Tijuana is seldom en-gaged as a screen assemblage, at once simultaneous and discrepant with the history of representations that guarantees its name and status as a border city.[11]

I would like to take here another approach, one that doesn't reduce the con-stitutive excess of moving images to confining strategies of representations, or that doesn't conflate the multipolar libidinal economy of Tijuana-based mov-ing images to the category "cross-border." My approach eschews a mode of at-tention that frames Tijuana as an incommensurable, radical urban and cultural alterity, as a form of desire for radical and ghostly otherness, projected onto a blank screen, only to be neutralized and consumed as a commodity or neat bi-national representation (i.e., internationalism or cosmopolitanism as a mere

All stills in this chapter are from *Maquilapolis: City of Factories* (de la Torre and Funari, 2006).

cross-cultural encounter between nationals or diasporic subjects). Images of Tijuana become either indelible entries in a site-specific cross-cultural archive (at best), a boudoir of both Hollywood productions and the films of the Golden Age of Mexican cinema, or merely an inexhaustible source of anecdotal information (e.g., the city that gave birth to Rita Hayworth).

Tijuana offers instead the possibility to rise above the nitty-gritty of at once academic disciplinary and geopolitical patroling and to inaugurate new forms of collaborative dialogues between academics, cultural producers, screen practices, media makers, journalists, and independent researchers moving alongside, within, and beyond the border of this decidedly intriguing city in the throes of political economic (maquila factories, outsourcing to Asian markets), affective (fear, violence), juridico-political (state of emergency and narco-war), and institutional (CECUT, the cultural center of TJ, has recently been under increasing pressure from official cultural policy at both national and state levels) convulsions. Tijuana is one of those complex cities that has suffered from being hailed as the postmodernist border city par excellence. And unlike how many writers, social scientists, artists, and curators would have it,[12] Tijuana's urban state of fragmentation and seeming cultural pastiche—its postpolyphonic state of affairs so to speak—does not make it an exceptional city and paragon of hybridism. It is at once more and less than that: a place haunted by

the phantasms of modernity and modernization, a place that gives a chance to ghosts and ur-phenomena to show up, even if fleetingly during the generous temporality of a screening session, in an eventful return. This makes Tijuana new, not exceptional, because it allows the eventful return of things that do not lend themselves easily to incorporation into either the fabric of its everyday life or into the academic category of border studies and its subterranean link to the Mexican postrevolutionary nationalist frameworks of *mestizaje*, or into the regimes of visibility characteristic of attempts at representing/crossing Tijuana as a binational border-crossing zone.[13] Tijuana is in this sense a profoundly modernist city in dire need of alternative models of transgression. For these to be actualized would require an alternate conceptual framework alongside both intercultural modes of spectatorship and so-called Post-Theory's critique of the Gaze. While the latter, as Žižek has noted, "relies on the commonsense notion of the spectator (the subject who perceives cinematic reality on the screen, equipped with emotional and cognitive predispositions),"[14] the former, unquestionably open to a radical politics of the unconscious, nevertheless is still unable to conceive of contemporary postcolonial encounters beyond the framework of national culture, its traces, its de/re-territorializations, its diasporic embodiments. The intercultural is in the end always hinged on a sense of in-between that succumbs, in the final instance, to the interpellative force of the national as it seeks to escape it. One can experience, however, this postcognitive and postnationalist site of reflection—that is, a site within and alongside normative perceptions and understandings of an irrevocably binational Tijuana—through a singular group of moving images that has recently emerged in two experimental moving-media practices. The moving images I now turn to enact the staging of phantasies that not only externalize cross-cultural and transnational, intersubjective encounters but also make tactile the shock of modernity and its attendant interplay of organisms, machines, and the ghostly life-forms that move in between.[15] These ghosts, the ghosts of modernity, cannot be visualized, but become, provisionally, actualized as "haptic visuality."[16] They are imperceptible to both gaze theory and its attendant epistemological reversals as well as to most intercultural frameworks and their attendant contamination by the iterations and performativity of the "national."

An Ur-Image: Tijuana Women Workers Leaving the Factory

The experimental documentary Maquilapolis: City of Factories (2006) is a provocative collaboration between the Bay Area filmmaker Vicki Funari and the artist Sergio de la Torre. The vivid color documentary, shot in both 16 mm and digital video, is a powerful mixture of observational documentary, experimental ethnographic film, and carefully crafted mise-en-scènes. It explores the daily lives of women who work in Tijuana's maquilas (assembly plants located in so-called free-trade zones) through poignant interviews, and reflects on the state of the factory economy and culture in contemporary Tijuana. A city that has been labeled the Factory City—as the subtitle of the film reminds us—Tijuana continues to be a major transit zone for migrant workers, the majority of which are women. As further restructuring of the global political economy proceeds, indeed as factories relocate toward Asia, China in particular, the futures of Tijuana remain uncertain. Maquilapolis evaluates these futures in the form of a contemporary meditation, collective and personal at once. That it manages to do that, and act as a much-needed breath of fresh air in contemporary documentary film practice, is one of the several achievements of this intriguing piece of experimental documentary filmmaking.

The film focuses on two women, Carmen Duran and Lourdes Lujan, who detail their own specific economic hardships and their chronicle of a hyper-medicalized everyday life, ranging from being exposed to toxic fumes in the workplace to seeing their neighborhood-qua-ghetto being flooded by industrial sewage from the factories. As the women mobilize to protest one particular waste site, an abandoned battery recycling factory that has been leaching tons of cadium, arsenic, and lead into the soil, maquiladora promoters—site owners, developers, trade officials—still boast the benefits of this trade arrangement. Meanwhile, a representative of Tijuana's Secretary of Industrial Development boasts about the higher wages and standard of living enjoyed by maquila workers compared to workers living in the rest of Mexico. But for employees in this informal economy, who migrate from all over the country and from Central America for work, these jobs are far from a dream come true.

As one of Carmen's coworkers says: "I make objects, a replaceable part of a production process. . . . I don't want to be an object. I want to be a person. I want to realize my dreams." While one may infer from this comment a naive deployment of the Enlightenment distinction between person (subjectivity) and object, the annihilation of subaltern subjectivity by a ruthless capitalist mode of production, Carmen's statement is more of an affirmative form of resistance through an invocation of modernity's foundational distinction between mechanism and organicism that continues to haunt our internationalist encounters. And in this sense there is perhaps more than codirector Vicky Funari's claim and motivation to undertake the *Maquilapolis* project: "The factory workers who appear in *Maquilapolis* were involved in every stage of production. We wanted to embrace subjectivity—their subjectivity—as a value, and to merge our filmmaking with their voices."[17] This statement is intimately related to another dimension: the question of technologically mediated self-representation as a form of counternarrative and redemption of desubjectivized and disembodied selves. Reparative theories of subjectivity are indeed a powerful conceptual paradigm to think and transform limit-experiences that complicate our contemporary ontologies of life and death, subject and object, elite and subaltern, observer and observed, North and South geopolitics. This is not to say, however, that Funari's comment repeats the antimachine attitude at the core of many theories of subjectivity, nor does she embrace the technocultural fabulations of cyborg theory that would no doubt be appropriate in this context given the fact that *Maquilapolis* could lend itself to an aesthetics of the prosthetic or more classical phenomenological theories of embodiment. On the contrary, Funari's passionate observation points to the very fragility of our conceptual weapons when dealing with ghostly limit-experiences such as those of Carmen and her coworkers.

Indeed, to watch maquila women workers, uniformly dressed in dark blue blouses, leaving Sanyo and Mitsubishi factories in Tijuana is to think of the ghostly quality of the contested ur-image of cinema, cinema's symptomatic image. Like a flash, another eventful cinematic intervention comes to mind,

Harun Farocki's found-footage film project documenting twentieth-century images of workers leaving the factory:

> The film *Workers Leaving the Lumière Factory in Lyon* (*La Sortie des Usines Lumière à Lyon*, 1895) by the brothers Louis and Auguste Lumière is 45 seconds long and shows the, approximately, 100 workers at a factory for photographic goods in Lyon-Montplaisir leaving through two gates and exiting the frame to both sides. Over the past 12 months, I set myself the task of tracking down the theme of this film—workers leaving the workplace—in as many variants as possible. Examples were found in documentaries, industrial and propaganda films, newsreels, and features. I left out TV archives which offer an immeasurable number of references for any given keyword as well as the archives of cinema and television advertising in which industrial work hardly ever occurs as a motif—commercial film's dread of factory work is second only to that of death.[18]

Maquilapolis can be located within recent debates in documentary film studies in general, and specifically in relation to the category of the "performative documentary" introduced by Bill Nichols. This emerging mode of documentary filmmaking not only enables innovative uses of the now-conventional gesture of handing the camera to film subjects to allow them a measure of self-representation, but also stages scenes of a more conceptual character that allow for a blurring of the ontological divide between the fictional and the factual that has always haunted documentary film studies. One such scene shows maquila workers standing on a dusty plain—one of the many hills in Tijuana that have been flattened to accommodate industrial parks—miming and enacting in mechanistic fashion their daily movements on the assembly lines. In another scene, the camera zooms in on women's faces as they recite the name of their employers, which appear on the screen as they are spoken: Samsung, Panasonic, Sanyo, Sony, and dozens more, until the screen is filled.

Such a highly stylized scene presents a "distinct disturbance to ethno-graphic and documentary film, and clearly embodies a paradox: it generates a distinct tension between performance and document. It uses historical referentiality less as a subject of interrogation."[19] Rather than acting in the realist documentary mode that pits social facts against reflexive and concep-tual labor, *Maquilapolis* directs its message elsewhere where political life, in-deed the life of the political, and experimentation with film form coexist productively. The choreographed scenes reveal a creative way of sensing, be-yond visual visuality, contemporary forms of living labor, the remaking of industrial machine-human interfaces through gendered forms of resistance, while also inviting viewers, us, to confront our agency as consumers in the context of a biopolitical order of things. Moreover, the spectral quality of these scenes sets in motion the return not only of the Gaze that reveals the *dispositif* of power-knowledge-vision that structures the rapport between ob-server and observed in classic/colonial ethnographic film,[20] but also of the very substance of the image movement that gives it its ghostly, uncanny qual-ity in the first place. For these reasons, and tensions that haunt the produc-tion process itself, of filmmaking, of object-making and self-fashioning, *Ma-quilapolis* allows something ambiguous to emerge, something paradoxical that requires us to rethink and to tone down current celebrations of the so-called postindustrial age and its attendant immaterial forms of labor. It re-minds us of the persistence of industrial cultures in the midst of postindus-trial political economies, in the midst of outsourcing and factory relocation from powerful centers to developing political economies. It certainly puts in trouble recent exalted claims of a porous and interstitial so-called postborder condition that would have us think that Tijuana is the site-specific paragon of a city that harbors a hybrid model of cultural identity.

Rare are the occasions when are we fortunate enough to view contempo-rary films and videos that provocatively and intelligently blur the founda-tional and constitutive distinctions between fiction and nonfiction film, mainstream and experimental cinema, autoethnography and observational documentary, cinema verité and mise-en-scène. Even less frequently are we presented with the chance to encounter a piece of filmmaking that gives that perverse pleasure we derive from repetition of uncanny images, images at the limit point of collapse of the strange and the familiar, and when we witness a singular, although always partial, recapitulation of the history of early moving images. But what is even more rare is when the combination of these formal and aesthetic gestures in the liminal space of a movie theater transforms the collective and personal act of viewing into both an ethical and political one. It is perhaps for that reason that those fleeting moments experienced in the midst of our disenchanted late modernity can be referred to as events. It is always an uncanny sensation to have a glimpse of the spectral quality of cinema's ur-images of workers leaving the factory, to have a glimpse of their afterlife. It will come as no surprise, at least to those whose relationship to images is a vocation, that coincidence and resilience sometimes produce eventful moments where the history of moving images and political economy reconnect in "productive" ways.

For this and other reasons *Maquilapolis* is a complex audiovisual experiment and collaborative process (between artist and filmmaker; among artist, filmmaker, and local factory workers/activists) that not only takes for granted the obvious hybridity and porosity of any given cultural and political context, but also tackles the most difficult issue of visualizing and gendering labor processes and life histories at the point of contact where the "industrial" and "postindustrial" meet, and are resisted via multiple strategies, including filmmaking. Tijuana's ghosts had already appropriated and possessed the names of ominous film titles: Orson Welles's *Touch of Evil* (spirit gone awry through its encounter with the frisson-generating cultural and illicit Other), Chantal Akerman's *From the Other Side* (death drive), *Maquilapolis* (ghosts in the machine). This spectrality too operates in Sergio de la Torre's recent installation *Nuevo Dragon City*: a mise-en-scène of ten third-generation young Chinese Mexicans from Tijuana locked in and instructed to perform a sensation of confinement through repetitive movements, pacing back and forth across the rooms that make up one of the city's many decrepit and abandoned spaces in which they were thrown as material for a site-specific installation. This action, documented and looped as a video piece, somewhere between film and contemporary art, operates a ghostly return of constitutive outsides that comes back to haunt the nation, at its imagined extremity, Tijuana, and if one digs a bit deeper one will find that *Nuevo Dragon City* unmakes the very fabric of mestizaje that subtends both Mexican nationalism and cultural identity among the Mexican American/Chicano diasporas. By zooming in on Chinese Mexican subjects that do not fall within the constitutive exclusion of indigenous groups that would culminate in theories of mestizaje from 1920 on, de la Torre's installation opens the possibility for a nonindigenous media practice and alternate historiography of migrancy in Mexico and, indeed, the United States. Postcolonial theory's key signature, that of performing historiographic revisions through the blind spots of national culture, is here expanded and inscribed onto the phenomenology of the loop at work in the installation. In addition to indigenous groups and media, both *Maquilapolis* and *Nuevo Dragon City* open the possibility for a renewed history of workers and nonindigenous groups.

And one cannot but be possessed by these two screen experiments and conjure up how one's encounter with Tijuana itself brings back, in unexpected forms, the ghosts of modernism and modernist film theory[21]—the spectral quality of ghosts and machines characteristic of early avant-garde city symphonies and the ur-scene of women workers leaving the factory in the Lumiere brothers' actualities—that have been spirited away by hasty claims of a porous and interstitial "post-border condition"[22] stretching from south of the border to Los Angeles. The ghosts are effects of the violence of the "post" itself, and welcoming them back generates the possibility of a para-ethics of research, conviviality, spectatorship, and sensorial pedagogy that requires much more than cross-cultural forms of spectatorship and research strategies. Both *Maquilapolis* and *Nuevo Dragon City*, the experimental documentary and the site-specific installation project, enable a spectral approach to the cinematic imaginary of Tijuana that condenses both larger political economic processes marked by the diacritic INDUSTRIAL and the nationalist-cosmopolitan tensions of Tijuana. Almost like companions to one other, these two films incarnate the spirits that return to haunt binational border life in Tijuana and, by extension, ongoing efforts to perform a geopolitically situated haptic criticism at the border between film/media studies and contemporary anthropology. As concretely and elegantly put by Avery Gordon, this would require that we not only give up some of our romantic inclinations by relating to "those who live in the most dire of circumstances as possessing a complex and often contradictory humanity and subjectivity that is never adequately glimpsed by viewing them as victims, or on the other hand, as superhuman agents,"[23] but also by engaging life, border life, and its ghostly forms through the design of equally complex interdisciplinary frameworks that seem to invent new object-subject relations.

And so the borderline ghost asks, between bare and impersonal life: how can you, living in the context of the cruel economy of attention and distraction characteristic of industrial and postindustrial capitalism, living in our

border city where maquila factories have become totems of political and cultural life (representations), fail to sense these moving images as looped returns that exceed the hybridity and interculturality of all border life?

Notes

1   This includes not only the watershed work of Gloria Anzaldúa and the scholarship specifically addressing questions of binational or minority media and film representation at the U.S.-Mexico border (Maciel, Fregoso, Lerner, Noriega, Fusco, Gómez-Peña), but also the more general cross-cultural reflections on borderland cinema and media arts in the work of Faye D. Ginsburg, Lila Abu-Lughod, and Brian Larkin; A. Guneratne; Hamid Naficy; Lucy Lippard; Michael Renov; and Ella Shohat and Robert Stam.

2   See especially Laura Marks, The Skin of Film.

3   See the sharp literary criticism and novels of tijuanense writer Heriberto Yépez, especially his recent Al Otro Lado / On the Other Side (Planeta, 2008) and its attendant critique of the "hybrid." Noteworthy here are also the writings of leading chronicler of Tijuana Humberto Berumen, and the encyclopedic three-volume book on representations of Mexico in world cinema in film historian Emilio Garcia Riera's México Visto por el cine extranjero.

4   See also the hard-boiled fictions of the Mexico-U.S. border from Gabriel Trujillo Muñoz's recently translated Tijuana City Blues to James Ellroy's classic Tijuana, Mon Amour.

5 Robert Stam, "Hybridity and the Aesthetics of Garbage: The Case of Brasil," in *Estudios Interdiscplinarios de America Latina y del Caribe*.

6 See Anthony Guneratne, *Rethinking Third Cinema*, p. 29.

7 Laura Marks defines intercultural spectatorship as "the meeting of two different sensoria, which may or may not intersect . . . an act of sensory translation of cultural knowledge." *The Skin of Film*, p. 153.

8 It should be obvious that I am arguing contra this specific vision of the disorderly while searching for other forms of disorderly resistance that do not conflate intercultural spectatorship to clearly defined binational/cultural sensorial-scapes. Rather than a contrast between moving images on each side of the Wall separating Tijuana from San Diego (juridico-political dimension) or Tijuana from Mexico City (national-ideological), either by taming through militarization, or overflow through border crossing, or resentfully performing TJ as cosmopolitan versus nationalist Mexico City, without being dismissive of the productivity of symbolic and physical boundaries, the disorderly I have in mind would have affinity to Benjamin's "blasting open" of historicist accounts that frame the transcultural as neatly distributed between geopolitically overdetermined sensorial categories such as North/South and center/periphery.

9 That the disorderly interrupts the continuous flow and order of things is not inherently a decolonizing political-ontological horizon, nor is saying the latter a wishful return to the certainty of the grid. Approaches hinged on ontologies of purity and garbage are important steps, but they always seem to rely on gestures of reversal. It might be more useful to view this ever-changing and always already hybrid disorderly as any other singularity, neither derivative of nor constituted by contrast to something ontologically different allegedly lacking chaos in the first place. Tijuana is a "whatever" disorderly City, in the sense of Gilles Deleuze. The more we understand our border worlds as always already polyphonic, the less we will conceptually invoke hybridity, and its attendant purity/contamination ontological underpinnings, and the more we will attempt to theorize the Whatever as a more radical category of the political.

10 This history of representation is, for instance, carried out in the work of Norma Iglesias. See her valuable "Border Representations: Border Cinema and Independent Video" in *The Post-Border City: Cultural Spaces of Bajalta California*, pp. 183–213. Although her contribution and encyclopedic knowledge of the region is not questioned here, her mode of historiographic approach leaves very little room for further theoretical elaboration for thinking an extratextual taxonomy of moving image of the region.

11 It should be noted that I adopt here the concept of assemblage from Gilles Deleuze, in particular in his implicit reevaluation of the concept in his *Essays Critical and Clinical* and in *Dialogues* with Claire Parnet. Tijuana, the name, exceeds the regional geographic, urban, and binational location that fixes it. Approached as an assemblage, "Tijuana" becomes a syndrome of sorts, a convergence of symptoms grouped, dissociated, and regrouped in new forms so that it is made to exceed Tijuana's repeated denomination as a border city. Alongside its history of representations, Tijuana becomes freed from itself.

12 See the work of Norma Iglesias and especially the curatorial statement and intro-duction essay by curator Rachel Tigael to the exhibit *Strange New World* held at the Contemporary Art Museum, San Diego. For an incisive critique of *Strange New World* (in particular) and curatorial visions of Tijuana (in general), see especially Fiamma Montezemolo: "Eco, Narciso, y Los Procesos Fronterizos" (*Letras Libres*, 2005) and "Bio-Cartography of Tijuana's Art Scene," *InSite* 2005.

13 I have in mind here the pioneering performances and writings of Guillermo Gómez-Peña and his transgressive "border brujo" projects that rely on reverse anthropology that once had powerful political-decolonizing purchase. I suggest here an attitude of transgression that is less spectacular and sovereign, less bound to classic ethnographic categories and more attuned to contemporary an-thropology, in the end an attitude or ethos that complicates the lines between outside and inside from a more vulnerable and less heroic position.

14 See Slavoj Žižek, *The Fright of Real Tears: Krzysztof Kieślowski between Theory and Post-Theory* (British Film Institute, 2001), p. 34.

15 See Akira Lippit's (2007) reflection on the fake documentaries and found-footage films of Waleed Raad and Jay Rosenblatt. "Staged and performed, phantasies can be seen as psychic film projections," p. 180.

16 See Laura Marks's concept of haptic criticism in *Framework* (2004).

17 Interview with PBS, 2007.

18 See Farocki in *Senses of Cinema* (online journal).

19 See Bill Nichols, *Blurred Boundaries*, p. 63. It goes without saying that Nichols's heuristic modal taxonomy allows for interconnections between participatory, reflexive, and performative modes of documentary filmmaking.

20 See especially, Fatimah Tobing Rony's discussion of Felix Regnault's protoethno-graphic film apparatus in *Third Eye*, in particular chapters 1 and 2. Although a gesture that has now become familiar to those of us who are passionate about experimental cinema, *Maquilapolis* exemplifies Tom Gunning's now-famous the-ory, on which Rony and others like Catherine Russell rely, that this main feature of the "cinema of attraction" has gone underground only to reappear in avant-garde and experimental film, among other minor genres. For an incisive use of the Deleuzian concept of the minor, see in particular Akira Lippit, "The Only Other Apparatus of Film," pp. 177–79.

21 Malcolm Turvey's article "Vertov: Between Machine and Organism" is a symptom of our fascination with both modernist film theory and city symphonies, and the complex intersections between historiography, theory, and screen practices. These returns to Vertov, for instance, are more than mere cinephilic dispositions: they are the effect of the spectrology that guides the hand writing this essay on *Maquilapolis*.

22 Michael Dear and Gustavo Leclerc (eds.), *The Post-Border City: Cultural Spaces of Ba-jalta California*.

23 Avery Gordon, *Ghostly Matters: Haunting and the Sociological Imagination* (University of Minnesota Press, 2008), 2.

References

Anzaldúa, Gloria (1987), *Borderlands/La Frontera: The New Mestiza*. San Francisco: Aunt Lute Books.

Berumen, Humberto Félix (2003), *Tijuana La Horrible: Entre la Historia y el Mito*. Tijuana: Colegio de la Frontera Norte.

Cusset, François (2008), *French Theory: How Foucault, Deleuze, Derrida, and Co. Transformed the Intellectual Life of the United States*. Minneapolis: University of Minnesota Press.

de la Torre, Sergio, & Funari, Vicky (2006), *Maquilapolis: City of Factories*. Video. Mexico and United States, 70 mins.

Farocki, Harun (2001), "Workers Leaving the Factory," in *Senses of Cinema*. http://archive.sensesofcinema.com/contents/02/21/farocki_workers.html.

Fregoso, Rosa Linda (1993), *The Bronze Screen: Chicana and Chicano Film Culture*. Minneapolis: University of Minnesota Press.

Fusco, Coco (2002), *Corpus Delecti: Performance Art of the Americas*. London: Routledge.

García Canclini, Néstor (1995), *Hybrid Cultures: Strategies for Entering and Leaving Modernity*. Minneapolis: University of Minnesota Press.

Ginsburg, Faye D., Lila Abu-Lughod, and Brian Larkin (eds.) (2002), *Media Worlds: Anthropology on New Terrain*. Berkeley: University of California Press, 2002.

Gómez-Peña, Guillermo (2000), *Dangerous Border Crossers: The Artist Talks Back*. London: Routledge.

Guneratne, Anthony, & Dissanayake, Wimal (eds.) (2003), *Rethinking Third Cinema*. London: Routledge.

Herzog, Lawrence A. (2003), "Global Tijuana: The Seven Ecologies of the Border," in *The Post-Border City: Cultural Spaces of Bajalta California*. Ed. Michael Dear and Gustavo Leclerc. London: Routledge, 119–42.

Iglesias, Norma (2003), "Border Representations: Border Cinema and Independent Video," in *The Post-Border City: Cultural Spaces of Bajalta California*. Ed. Michael Dear and Gustavo Leclerc. London: Routledge, 183–213.

Lerner, Jesse (2005), "Arqueologia Fronteriza." *Replicante* no. 2: 24.

Lerner, Jesse, and Rubén Ortiz Torres (1995), *Frontierland/Frontierlandia*. Chicano Studies Research Center Cinema and Media Art Series.

Lippard, L. (1990), *Mixed Blessings: New Art in a Multicultural America*. New York: Pantheon.

Lippit, Akira Mizuta (2007), "The Only Other Apparatus of Film," in *Derrida, Deleuze and Psychoanalysis*. Ed. Gabriele Schwab. New York: Columbia University Press.

Maciel, David R. (1990), *El Norte: The U.S.-Mexican Border in Contemporary Cinema*. San Diego: Institute for Regional Studies of the Californias / San Diego State University (Border Series).

Marks, Laura (2004), "Haptic Visuality: Touching with the Eyes," in *Framework: The Finnish Art Review* no. 2 (2004): 79–82.

———— (1999), *The Skin of Film: Intercultural Cinema, Embodiment and the Senses*. Durham, NC: Duke University Press.

Montezemolo, Fiamma (2006), "Bio-Cartography of Tijuana's Art Scene," in *Situational Public: InSite 2005*, pp. 314–18.

—— (2005), "Eco, Narciso, y Los Procesos Fronterizos," in *Letras Libres*, 53.

Naficy, Hamid (2001), *An Accented Cinema: Exilic and Diasporic Filmmaking*. Princteon, NJ: Princeton University Press.

Nichols, Bill (1994), *Blurred Boundaries: Questions of Meaning in Contemporary Culture*. Bloomington: Indiana University Press.

Noriega, Chon (1992), *Chicanos and Film: Representation and Resistance*. Minneapolis: University of Minnesota Press.

Renov, Michael (1995), "New Subjectivities: Documentary and Self-representation in the Post-Verité Age," in *Documentary Box* 7: 1–8.

Riera, Emilio Garcia (1988), *México Visto por el Cine Extranjero*. Universidad de Guadalajara.

Shohat, Ella (1994), *Unthinking Eurocentrism: Multiculturalism and the Media*. London: Routledge.

Shohat, Ella, & Robert Stam (eds.) (2003), *Multiculturalism, Postcoloniality and Transnational Media*. Piscataway, NJ: Rutgers University Press.

Stam, Robert (1998), "Hybridity and the Aesthetics of Garbage: The Case of Brasil," in *Estudios Interdiscplinarios de America Latina y del Caribe* 9, no. 1. http://www.tau.ac.il /eial/IX_1/stam.html.

Tigael, Rachel (2006), *Strange New World: Art and Design from Tijuana*. San Diego: Museum of Contemporary Art.

Tobing Rony, Fatimah (1996), *Third Eye: Race and Ethnographic Spectacle*. Durham, NC: Duke University Press.

Trujillo Muñoz, Gabriel (2009), *Tijuana City Blues*. France: Les Allusifs.

Turvey, Malcolm (2007), "Vertov: Between the Organism and the Machine," in *October* no. 121: 5–18.

Yépez, Heriberto (2008), *Al Otro Lado / On the Other Side*. Mexico City: Planeta.

—— (n.d.), "On 'Hybrid.' " http://heriberto-yepez.blogspot.com/.

The Kidnapped City

The finger arrived in the mail next to the gas bill and the grocery store coupons, bubble-wrapped in a sealed envelope with no return address. By then, Luis had already been gone for two months of his thirty-four years. His severed finger—they didn't even put it on ice; they just let the blood dry, the skin purple, the smell swell—was proof that he was alive, that he existed, that the rest of his body was somewhere, still warm, still beating. The finger meant they wanted more money. If he was still alive enough to lose a finger, then there was still money to be made. They took him from right in front of his house, in front of his wife, his three young children inside, in plain view in the middle of the day on his quiet street in Playas de Tijuana—a tranquil coastal neighborhood known for its remove from the chaos of downtown where the only big news of late was the opening of a Starbucks. They asked for directions and Luis walked over to the car to help out. They pulled him inside. They were not wearing masks. As soon as my wife heard that, she knew things would be bad for her cousin. In the logic of kidnapping, the mask is a chance for survival; if the kidnappers cannot be identified, they might consider releasing their hostage. No mask and the release is harder to imagine. Luis must have known that too; he knew his fate as soon as he hit the backseat. He was never coming home.

My in-laws were active in raising money. There was a breakfast—the whole extended family brought checks, whatever you could afford. Every dollar counted. They wanted $2 million. We raised $100,000. We don't know when they killed Luis, if he was even alive when the money was being gathered. We do know that they drove out of town to dump his body alongside the highway to Tecate. He was picked up and brought to the city morgue as a John Doe and only weeks later did a family friend who works in forensics recognize his face in a photo search.

The memorial was wrenching. There were people everywhere. The men stood on the steps by the entrance, as if they were guards or escorts, trying to look tough and proud and strong but their faces gave them away—they were outside because they couldn't bear to go in. Especially Luis's father. I had met him just a few months earlier. It was my father-in-law's birthday and we took over the concrete backyard of one of his niece's homes in Playas. There were family photos on the folding tables and balloons tied to chairs. A man with perfectly gelled hair was singing boleros and pop ballads into a portable PA system. A woman with a face of sweating stone was chopping meat and pressing corn into tortillas, and all of the nieces and aunts and grandmothers took their turn on the piñata. Candy fell. The little ones scurried.

I couldn't keep my eyes off Luis's father. He's tall and thick with the muscles of hard work. He had his jeans up high on his boxy waist, belted tight; he had his cotton long-sleeve Oxford unbuttoned midway down a chest full of furry gray ringlets of hair. He kept his big arms crossed, his face unmoving, stern, serious. He crushed my hand when he shook it. His fingers were hardened sausages, their skin rough from building things, fixing motors. He looked like El Indio Fernández, the classic Mexican film star who protects the village on horseback, who stays alive squinting into the setting sun. One thing he wasn't though was a man who cried. So when I saw him on the stairs of the memorial hall, it rocked me to the core. The shirt was still unbuttoned, the jeans still high, but his son was dead and now his face was red and pickled; his eyes were pools of salt. It was as if his body never expected to know what it was now knowing, as if his muscles and joints had never fathomed that something as intangible and immaterial as death or loss could break them down.

Upstairs in the chapel, deep silence was sporadically punctured by spasms of grief, anguished cries quickly muffled by the sweaters and shawls of comforting shoulders. In his prayers for Luis, the priest told us not to grieve, but to use his loss as an inspiration to keep living our lives to the fullest—plenamente, plenamente he repeated—to leave the service focused squarely on the here and now. He prayed for the family, for Luis's kids, for his poor, poor wife. And then he prayed for the city. He begged God to have mercy on Tijuana, to take its streets back into his loving arms. I put my arm around my sister-in-law and asked what she was feeling. "Sadness," she said. "And a lot of anger."

Anger is the right word. Luis was thirty-four. He had just opened a little store to sell glass for windows. Sure he liked a new car now and again and sure he liked to pick up the check and be all macho and valiente once in a while and sure he liked to take his wife to Saverios and not even read the prices on the wine list. But he was solidly working-class gone middle-class TJ and he was not a criminal or a drug dealer or a money launderer or a CEO or a corporate scion or a politician. He was taken just so he could be used to get some money for someone who had even less. He was taken because he could be taken. He was taken because he could die and it didn't matter to his killers, because his life, like their lives, didn't matter. This is no city, no country, no world, no time, no era to get precious and high and mighty about the value of human life. Our blood—all of our blood—runs cheap. We mean nothing to anyone. We are as good as what we are worth—to factories, to smugglers, to bosses, to marketing companies, to kidnappers. Discardable. Dumpable. Interchangeable.

It used to be that the kidnapped almost somehow—if we were to perversely confess it—deserved it. They were shady or their parents were shady. There was always a connection. Nobody gets rich without shortchanging good at least once. Even when they took the pop star Thalia's sister, people joked that it was her fault for having a sister who not only made bad pop music but who married Tommy Mottola. But even she was returned.

At the end of the memorial, I met an old friend of my father-in-law, El Manitas, or "Little Hands" (his were anything but). "I hear you write about Tijuana up there," he said. "Did you see the letter in the paper today?" he asked me. I hadn't. "It's about the kidnappings, all this horrible mess. You need to read it. Then you need to write about it. It's important for people in the U.S. to learn about what's happening here. Mexico needs to be criticized. It's the only way things will change."

The letter was written by Aiko Enríquez Nishikawa. Her brother Celso had suffered a fate similar to Luis's. Like Luis, Celso came from a hard-working family who came to Tijuana to pursue the opportunities the city promised to offer—first during the industrialization boom of the 1960s and 1970s and then during the global boom of the 1990s. He was a father and a husband. He was clean. After he was kidnapped, money was given, phone calls were made, threats were issued. When proof of life stopped, the family stopped giving money. The kidnappers surrounded the house with cars and opened fire, ready and willing to kill anyone they could for more money, or just ready and willing to create more fear. Because that's what is happening here too—to create fear is to have power. As the father of a dead narcojunior once told Jesús Blancornelas, "I gave my son everything—the best home, the best car, the best family name. I now realize that I could never give him what he wanted most—power."

Aiko's family called the city police, then the federal police, then the military police. Nobody came to help them.

Celso was surely dead and they had endured all that they could. So they packed up their house and, like so many, left the city to live in San Ysidro or Chula Vista or National City or San Diego.

This is how she ended the letter:

> This letter represents the pain, the anguish and the anger that we feel. It's a desperate cry for an answer, an explanation, a hope, a demand of our rights, the ones we never had while living this hell that we don't wish on anybody. More so when we couldn't get help from the people who are paid to protect and serve, combat and take care of, guard the safety of citizens. But unfortunately they are the ones who protect and help the criminals get what they want.
>
> When are you going to take action? When are you going to clean the municipal, state and federal institutions in a real and forceful way? When will there be real laws that punish kidnappers and the bad behavior of corrupt agencies, with sentences that serve as en example so that this doesn't keep happening?
>
> What will happen to our country with its good people? When will we stop living so cowardly and start fighting for a better future for the sons and daughters of Mexico?
>
> I love Mexico and Tijuana, it's the place where I was born, my country. But it's impossible to live here.
>
> Goodbye Tijuana.

In 2001, the Tijuana critic Leobardo Sarabia published an essay about the impact of narco culture on Tijuana life. "Violence in Tijuana," he wrote, "is limited to those who have something to fear, who work in the dirty business. . . . Tijuana is no Beirut, no Medellin. . . . Tijuana violence is selective, pragmatic, at the service of the defense and amplification of territory acquisition and the settling of scores."

Yet seven years later, a week after Aiko published her letter, a week after Luis died, he had changed his tune. Violence in Tijuana, Sarabia admitted, was no longer selective or pragmatic or part of the strategies of organized narco crime. Narco violence joined with increasing poverty and desperation equals a new culture of violence—one that unloads its clips in a wild, unfocused spray. Now entire restaurants are held up at once. Now taxi drivers are kidnappers. Now ATM machines get plucked from vestibules within seconds. Now violence is not selective—now everyone has something to fear.

"Violence creates a new reality," he wrote in Eme Equis. "Another atmosphere. It transforms the familiar city into an ominous one—nocturnal, uninhabitable."

Everyone in cities like Tijuana and Juárez and Culiácan knows someone: who has been kidnapped, whose family is in a witness protection program, who is dead. The hottest cars on the used car lots come with bulletproof windows. People are putting up new fences around their homes, new bars on their windows; the newest real estate trends in Tijuana are luxury high-rises that advertise, above all else, high-tech security and surveillance systems. When the phone rings at the office and the voice on the other end gets the name slightly wrong or asks about schedules or asks too many questions, you know to hang up. When the phone rings at home and the voice on the other end tells you that it's your aunt calling and all your aunts are dead, you know to hang up. When a car sits for too long outside your home or office, you know to keep watch, to leave through the back. When you go out for a drink with friends you know to call each other as soon as you get home. When the calls come every day, when the cars wait every day, you know to change your schedule, to not keep a routine. You know to sell your car and get a different one every few months. You know that in Mexico—like in Johannesburg, like in Beirut, like in São Paulo—this fear is your life.

As the Tijuana police chief Alberto Capella said after he survived an attack of two hundred gunshots, "It's as if criminals have corrupted us all." On the night of the shooting, the book on his nightstand was the policy anthology *Transnational Crime and Public Security*. It was left full of bullet holes.

I came home from the memorial mad—there was anger for Luis's killers, but more anger for the cops who let it happen, for the cops who let the cops let it happen, for the military troops who let the cops let the cops let it happen, for the mayor and the governor and all the lawyers who look the other way. I was angry at globalization. I was angry at free trade. I was angry at capitalism. I was angry at anyone who made money saying the world is flat. I was angry with my colleagues for romanticizing the border, for refusing to admit that it's a violent place, a criminal place, that horrible things do happen there. I was angry with friends who wrote off narco violence as U.S. media myths. I was angry at myself for agreeing with them.

More than Luis, I was mourning our world order. I was mourning the fatal character of the global economy, its "perennial gale of creative destruction," to borrow the famous words of Joseph Schumpeter. The kidnapping of Luis and the kidnapping of Celso have left indelible marks on their families, but they should also leave indelible marks on all of us. Mexico has been kidnapped, abducted and tortured, and held hostage by the corruptions of capitalist striving and economic inequality.

As Schumpeter wrote back in 1947, "Capitalism creates a critical frame of mind which after having destroyed the moral authority of so many other institutions, in the end turns against its own."

To think, as I did, that the tragedy of Luis's death was that he played by the rules, that he was one of the "good guys," was naive, myopic, and arrogant. The tragedy is the political and social economy those rules belong to, an economy based on depletion and exhaustion and endless exploitation—of workers, of ideals, of morals, of resources, of bodies. I am not suggesting that blame be taken from individuals whose actions produce fatal consequences. Individuals kidnapped Luis, individuals extorted his family, individuals cut off his finger, and individuals dumped his body. But we are all motivated, in part, by the systems and beliefs and values we inherit as true; "the traditions of all the dead generations weigh like a nightmare on the brain of the living," as Marx saw it. And Luis's kidnappers, like so many in any country where poverty and social disintegration are the prevailing order, acted within a context that any of us who too quickly judge them are also a part of—the glaring and extreme inequities of globalization. So I'll say what many others—from Rabbi Jonathan Sacks to George Soros to Rebecca Solnit—have already said: there needs to be an ethics of globalization, an ethics of capitalism, a morality of modernity. The men who killed Luis—who exist on a continuum of corruption and murder that extends all the way to Washington—are murderers and criminals and they blatantly and unforgivably flaunted and rebuked and ignored those codes that must from now on be held precious to the stability of a human future.

If I sound like I am doing a bad Hannah Arendt impression, I apologize, but ever since that memorial, I have had her writings on the Eichmann trial bumping around in my head, hearing echoes of her infamous "banality of evil" charge in the way I've been thinking about drug lords and *mafiosos*—what is globalization's "banality of evil"? What kind of moral shifts, ethical abysses, does the relentless pursuit of free-trade profiteering and imperial accumulation and national security privatization engender in everyday citizens who are not invited into the executive lounges and board rooms of global bling? What Mexico is currently living out is just one headline-grabbing, too close to the U.S. for comfort, example of the dark side of the global economic promise: extreme inequity that produces extreme behavior that results in extreme casualties. Indeed, Tijuana has been a central setting for this unfolding story, whether it was the opening of the border to foreign maquiladora manufacturing plants in the late 1960s—establishing a dependence on export-processing factories for jobs, establishing a pattern of wage labor abuses, of feverish migration and overpopulation and ecological devastation that continues to this day—or the blow dealt in 1994 by the passage of NAFTA, opening the border to the transit of imports and exports but closing it, violently, militarily, to the transit of the people who make and consume those imports and exports.

The cumulative result has been a border metropolis of over two million people where poverty grows daily on hillsides made of recycled cardboard, where the glimmering steel-and-glass bounty of San Diego venture capital and international banking is in perfect, unblocked, plain view of an Indian from Michoacán who walks stairs made of tires and drinks water tainted with toxic runoff. If there are, indeed, "social costs" of the border's industrialization—as a 2002 research team decided at the Center for U.S.-Mexican Studies at UCSD—then those social costs, those costs shifted away from the money makers and onto communities and citizens, must also include the kidnapping industry and the drug economy, must also include the death of Luis and Celso.

For Luis's kidnappers and the drug cartel bosses and their kowtowing hit men, evil is banal; death and killing carry no moral rebuke, no ethical doubt, no human problem. If Eichmann was the perverted extreme of the modern bureaucrat, then how could we not, if even for a moment, consider kidnappers and cartel hit men as the perverted extremes of the global capitalist? Kidnappings and drug sales are, at their core, market operations, economies like any other, fueled by maximization of profits, drugs just one more product shipped from Mexico's export-processing zone so beloved by the United States and Asia, and the biggest export at that—making more money for Mexico than oil or tourism. It's a multibillion-dollar economy that works—dirty money ending up clean in real estate deals and private businesses. It also just so happens to be a deadly economy.

Marx, ever underestimated for his ability to turn a phrase, put it best: "One capitalist always kills many."

Here are some numbers to consider:

- In 2007, there were 2,500–3,000 drug-related executions in Mexico, three hundred of which were cops.
- In 2008, between May 1 and May 9, nine high-ranking police officers were killed, leading some of the remaining officers in similar positions to ask the United States for political asylum, leading the U.S. government to enter yet another word into the lexicon of homeland security and legislative zenophobia—*narcoterrorism.*
- In 2008, more than 1,350 people were murdered in drug trafficking–related crimes. Those murdered include police, judges, doctors, lawyers, soldiers, reporters, politicians, and innocent victims. The killings have been private and public, individual and mass.

- Between 2000 and 2005, cocaine shipments from South America to Mexico doubled and meth seizures quintupled.
- In 2007, the cross-border drug trade was worth over $25 billion. Ten billion of that came south across the border into Mexico as bulk cash.
- In 2008, a Tijuana battle between rival factions within the Arellano Félix cartel left fourteen dead on a Sunday morning. Another shooting went down next to a kindergarten. Seven people were killed in thirty-six hours the first weekend in June.
- A week later, a bundle of marijuana valued at $2.2 million was found in jalapeño pepper crates at the Otay crossing.
- Forty doctors were kidnapped in 2008 alone.

When Felipe Calderón took office in 2006, one of his principal vows was to clean up Mexican drug corruption. He continues to order federal police and military police to the country's most battle-worn regions and in late 2007, he worked with President Bush to write up the Merida Initiative, designed to deliver U.S. $1.4 billion to the Mexican government over three years to fight the war. The ironies of the initiative are twofold: those billions would be spent to fight a war against the interests of U.S. consumers—the United States is less than 5 percent of the world's population and accounts for over half of the world's drug consumption. Most of what is consumed comes through Mexico. Second, 90 percent of all the guns used to kill all of the people who keep dying in Mexico come from shipments bought and sold in the United States. One of the narco favorites has long been the Colt 38 Super—as American as Bob Seger. As Mexican attorney general Eduardo Medina Mora recently told Portfolio magazine, "US consumers are already financing this war, only it's on the wrong side."

There is no such thing as the Mexican drug war. There is only the Mexico-U.S. drug war. This is a transnational game, as much L.A. as Sinaloa, as much about the Sonoran Desert as Interstate 5. Just look at the most famous narcocorridos of all time, "Contrabando y Traición," which starts with a car full of marijuana in Baja but ends in an alley in Hollywood. It's a lesson that Orson Welles tried to teach us many years ago when he made Touch of Evil, the last great noir film that put the onus of corruption, of evil itself, on the United States (its Tijuana-esque border town was actually Venice Beach). The moral of the story was radical then and it's radical now: the touch of evil is not Mexico, it's the United States. In his film, the most innocent man was Mexican. The most corrupt man was a white American cop. There was Mexican crime and vice, but it existed through the joint efforts of Mexican and American lawmakers.

"All border towns bring out the worst in a country," Charlton Heston's Mexican cop character, Mike Vargas, says in the film, but it's never clear just what country he is talking about.

-->

Isaiah, chapter 1, verses 17–23: "Your rulers are rebels, companions of thieves; they all love bribes and chase after gifts."

Jesús Blancornelas, the late founder of Tijuana weekly paper *Zeta* and once Mexico's prime chronicler of narco culture, began his 2002 account of the rise of the Tijuana-Sinaloa cartel helmed by the Arellano Félix brothers with a curious, and potent, claim: "Drug traffic in Mexico and the US owes more to government circumstances and less to opportunist and permanent *mafiosos*." If we blame the individuals, we are not just barking up the wrong tree, we're in the wrong forest to begin with. The critique lies with the state, for it is the state that not only generates and regulates the laws that create and control the flows of illegal substances and illegal money, but it is the state that then allows those flows to happen all while feigning to criminalize it. The state creates criminals that the state protects.

Or as Mexican writer Carlos Monsivais put it: "The emergence of the narco is the most serious episode of neo-liberal criminality. If that is where the big business is, the victims are the profits. And with them comes the protection of the mafias by power itself." The narcos themselves know this all too well. In his 1997 DEA testimony, Alejandro Hodoyan Palacios, aka El Lobo, one of the Arellano Félix cartel's key hit men, said, "In Tijuana nobody kills for free. Every death has a reason, even though nobody is allowed to know what it is."

Two instances from Blancornelas's narco chronicle El *Cártel*—still yet to be published in English—bear this out dramatically. First, the Mexican ambassador to France wrote to Blancornelas in 1994 accusing the office of the governor of Baja California of being wittingly responsible for allowing drug violence to surge in the early 1990s and take over the political and economic life of Baja. In his words: "The state is responsible for the protection of drug traffickers and for the wave of violence it produces." After reading the letter in *Zeta*, the governor of Baja himself, Ernesto Ruffo Appel, wrote a response in which he admitted that, indeed, his government lost control; narco culture had too easily, too overwhelmingly, entered the realm of politics and security. A narco state was born. "It is getting hard to tell which you are in, drugs or politics," Ruffo said. "Things are heading in a dangerous direction." Indeed, in 1993, Blancornelas published a list of all of the members of the PGR (Mexico's federal justice agency) who had been on narco payrolls. The list is three pages long. It does not include the names of all the cops at every level of Mexican enforcement, including those who in the nineties were busted for stealing cars in San Diego; who worked as bodyguards for the mafiosos; who moonlighted as members of el peloton, the firing squad of the Arellano Félix cartel; nor does it include the names of the twenty-eight customs officers found in the mid-nineties to be tied to mafiosos or to the five Border Patrol agents who did the same. As more than one Tijuana critic has noted, in Tijuana, there is more than one drug cartel. There is the Arellano Félix cartel, but there are also the PRG, the Mexican army, and the federal police.

The collusion between traffickers and cops and government officials is not a remarkable fact. It is the great transparency of Mexican politics. Even the corrido singers sing about it. In their song about the narco wars, "La Frontera Roja," Los Tucanes de Tijuana do the usual cuernos de chiva talk, bigging up the narcos, but they quickly talk about how the guns are used by mafiosos just like they are by the police—there is yerba and coke and killing for territory, but the protagonists are mafiosos and politicians: "The mafia has power, the TV said. But how are the police not seen as the bigger fish?" They sing, "The mafia does not have an end—the law cooperates with them. . . . Red border they call it, for all of the blood runs through it."

In May 2008, the chief of Mexican police was killed in a hit ordered by the Sinaloa cartel and carried out by a federal officer. In the nineties, Mexico's antidrug czar was famously found to be working for the cartels. In Baja, General Sergio Aponte led antidrug offensives and in April named names of corrupt officials on the pages of Frontera. He also noted that Baja's antikidnapping squad was actually a kidnapping squad—police work as cartel bodyguards; federal agents help coordinate air shipments.

But why here? Why the border?

Borderlines are by their very nature fertile for what security analysts call "crimogenic" conditions. Because they divide markets and restrict the exchange of goods and people, creating differentials and asymmetries in cost and incentive and profit, criminal enterprises usually take advantage of these conditions and exploit the asymmetries: auto theft, money laundering, trafficking, black markets, smuggling, prostitution. Sarabia has called this "fatal geography as Mexican destiny." The border between the United States and Mexico is the only border in the world that separates a developing nation from the world's richest country, the only border that separates consumers who spend five times more a year from their southern neighbors. It is also the most-crossed border in the world, and ever since NAFTA, crossing has intensified, making illegal trafficking easier and more active. As the anthropologist Carolyn Nordstrom reminds us, there is no such thing as legal routes of traffic as distinct from illegal routes of traffic—all routes of trade and traffic are markets; the legal flows alongside the illegal. The reality of the contemporary world is that what we call the economy is always legal and illegal together. Where legal products move, so do illegal products, often in the same trucks, in the same boxes, in the same cans of jalapeños.

This blurring began to take shape in the 1970s when the United States initiated its crackdown on the cocaine trade based in Colombia and Miami, causing the trade to shift to the Mexican state of Sinaloa. Soon Mexican mafias were responsible for 70 percent of the cocaine consumed annually in the United States, leading to an estimated $30 billion a year in drug profits. The destination was the United States and Tijuana was simply in the way, perfectly positioned as a gateway. The Arellano Félix brothers came to TJ in 1984. They rose in power because the government allowed them to. As the eighties became the nineties, the stage was increasingly fixed and everyone knew the score: all drug murders went unsolved because police were gangsters, politicians were investors, lawyers were on the books, and justice was paid for. After DEA agent Kike Camarena was tortured and killed in 1985, the suspected killers were protected by the then-governor of Jalisco, who never brought charges. When Carlos Salinas became the president of Mexico years later, the same governor was soon his attorney general. The Salinas reign was the epitome of the narco state eating itself alive. In 1993, Arellano Félix hit men executed the highest-ranking church official in Mexico—Cardinal Ocampo. They did it in Guadalajara while an Aeromexico flight waited for them, then took off, only to land in Tijuana where federal agents let them escape. Then came the 1994 triple threat: a shootout between state and federal police that left five dead, the murder of PRI presidential candidate Luis Donaldo Colosio by an unstable factory worker who was believed to be on the payroll of both drug kingpin El Chapo Guzmán and Salinas himself, then the murder of the chief of police. And yet nobody did a thing—how could they?

How could we? Nineteen ninety-four was the year of NAFTA, the year that free trade would be asked to change the world, when modern Mexico was to join postmodern America in a quest for global economic reform. So what if the Arellano Félix hit men were from San Diego gangs, so what if the drugs all flowed north—the United States was innocent, Mexico was innocent—the drug war was kept under the radar and off the political stage and the audience was asked to believe that the drama they were watching wasn't actually happening.

The binational choice to turn a blind eye opened the floodgates for blood and bullets and money. In 1999, the Arellano Félix gang was responsible for four hundred deaths we know of. They were brutal in the nineties, unimaginably cruel and savage, killing anyone for looking at them the wrong way—spilling a drink, crashing a party. As one of their hit men put it, "Killing is a lark for them—a diversion. They laugh after a death, they go eat lobster in Rosarito. That's how it is."

Ramon Arellano was killed in 2002 and Benjamin was put in jail for life. But the cartel's grip on Mexican politics continued to be maintained, most obviously in 2005 with the election to the Tijuana mayoral office of Hank Rhon—a billionaire criminal with ties to the Arellano Félix brothers and ties to a few assassinations of his own. When he became the leader of Tijuana, the growth of the local narco state had reached its peak. Now mafiosos hadn't just bought off political leaders; the political leaders were the mafiosos. And worse for Tijuana, this particular mafioso wasn't just into gold and fur coats and women the way Ramon and Benjamin were—he was narco excess converted into state power: a zoo of over 333 endangered species, a hairless rat in a cage behind his desk, eighteen children from multiple wives, a proud drinker of tequila spiked with bull testicles, Cirque du Soleil flown in for his birthday celebration, and most famously, an addiction to collecting rare white tigers.

When Hank left office, some thought Tijuana had hope, that something could shift. The years after he left office were more quiet than usual. Then this year had to come along and everyone had to see those kindergartners running for their lives beneath a flurry of bullets, over and over again.

--➤

But what is there to do?

After the January shootings next to the kindergarten, Rafa Saavedra, a Tijuana fiction writer and critic, weighed in on his blog:

> If fear wins, we will end up prisoners in our homes like they did in Medellín. Our fight is for liberty, for the ability to move freely through this city that is OUR Tijuana, to keep fighting so that more punishment will be rough to the criminals. . . . Some say what we all know and we don't want to recognize—the fault is also our own, the open and receptive character of our city that has made it known as a progressive place, a place where change can happen, is also the characteristic that is now working against its survival.

As the violence reached its peak, one of Rafa's friends called to tell him, "We've lost her." We've lost Tijuana. Rafa refuses to agree. He refuses to give up on the city he loves.

His sentiment reminds me of another call for Tijuana's salvation, issued during an earlier era of drug traffic and political corruption—the 1950s, when the Korean War gave Tijuana military tourism a much-needed shot in the arm. It involved the journalist Manuel Acosta Meza, editor of *El Imparcial*, who broke story after story about a crime syndicate running Tijuana life. When the cartel was found to be using schoolchildren to move weed, Acosta Meza began a daily attack in the press, exposing the cartel's links to prostitution rings and local politicians. When the cartel went after Meza, he ran headlines like, "Here we are you vultures" and "I accuse you." In 1956, he was executed right in front of his house.

In a rare case of responsible Hollywood filmmaking about border life, Columbia Pictures released *The Tijuana Story* in response that very same year. Granted, it dubbed TJ the "frankest, gaudiest, sin town in the world," but its true focus was the story of Acosta Meza, played by Rafael Acosta, and his battle with the "vice lords," the struggle "to get Tijuana cleaned up," and the death of the free press. They threw in James Darren for some teen-beat star power and pot-smoking tourist subplots and shirtless beach scenes, but even he ends up dead, running from the cops into the Pacific before washing up limp on the rocks. The film's plot stays focused on a city at war. Its final scene is Acosta Meza's funeral, which is interrupted by his former publisher, who offers some final words:

> Knowing Manuel as I did, I can tell you what would have satisfied him today, not our tears or our guilt but the knowledge that he did not die in vain, that the bullets that crashed in his body infuriated us into action, gave us the indignation and courage to resolve that we have had enough of terrorism and gangsterism, that living under the syndicate without pride is intolerable. Manuel was right: there is no power in the world stronger than us—together we can clean up Tijuana—all it takes is the will.

Infuriate us into action. Enough of terrorism and gangsterism. No power in the world stronger than us. As Rabbi Abraham Joshua Heschel once wrote: "Few are guilty but all are responsible. If we admit that the individual is in some measure conditioned or affected by the spirit of society, an individual's crime discloses society's corruption."

And so in Tijuana, citizens march. In Tijuana, a banner now flies on a city overpass that reads, "We've had enough—death penalty to all kidnappers."

While on the surface it is important and valuable for President Calderón to be declaring war against corruption and drugs, while it is important and valuable for the United States to pour billions into the Merida Initiative, both moves will be—ultimately—futile. Both moves miss the bigger picture. The situation we find ourselves in has lasted over a century, a situation born of imperial conquest and nineteenth-century land grabs and attempts to use the expansion of territory as a way of securing markets in the name of civilizing democracy. It is a situation that has been inherited, one that has structured every fiber, every cell, of Mexico's relationship with the United States. Drugs and violence are a Mexican crisis, but they are also a U.S. crisis. They are a crisis of the global moment, nourished by economic and social asymmetries of such false equalizers as free trade and globalization.

Drug wars and the endemic poverty of resources that fuel them—what Bill McKibben has called "the mathematics of inequality"—can be healed, but only as part of a larger culture of healing and structural economic change. If Immanuel Wallerstein is right that the demise of neoliberal globalization has begun, if Peter Barnes is right that this capitalism will soon undergo a massive upgrade of its operating system into capitalism 3.0, if a long, incremental revolution of structural transformation of lifeways, social ethics, and attitudes toward the responsibilities we all bear as stakeholders in the greater commons is upon us, as impossible to ignore as a carbon cloud or a dried oil well or a fallow field of a Mexican farm, then the U.S.-Mexico drug crisis might just have what nobody has assumed could be possible: an end in sight.

--➤

I want to call up the request line and make a special request to the border DJ. I know you've got the new one from El Potro de Sinaloa to play, or the new ones from El Tigrillo Palma, Voz de Mando, and Larry Hernández, or classics from Los Invasores or the Los Toucanes tune about Ramón Arellano. But how about tonight we hear some stuff off the playlist, some tunes that have yet to be written: instead of corridos about the mafiosos, instead of corridos about the women who dress up as nuns to smuggle cocaine, instead of the simulated AK-47 gunshot blasts, instead of Los Razos holding rifles next to young girls in bikinis and cowboy hats, how about we hear a corrido for the missing, a corrido for the dead, a corrido for mourners, a corrido for a lost country, a corrido for inequality. I know, I know, they're hard to find. You won't hear them bumping out of Suburbans or Ram Chargers or Tahoes. They don't sell them at swap meets or MixUp. But you'll hear them in living rooms and churches and community centers, melodies shaped in sighs and sobs, choruses sculpted by cries.

You know how everyone always says that corridos tell the truth about Mexico—well these corridos tell the truth too, but in ways we haven't heard yet. So put one on if you don't mind, Mr. DJ, and play it loud so that all of Sonora can hear it, all of Baja, all of Sinaloa and Jalisco and Los Angeles and Washington, D.C. Let it bounce off the boulders into the poppy fields and every plaza that's ever been controlled. Let it break the glass of tinted windows and cocaine mirrors, let it rattle through Los Pinos and the White House and through every Blackwater training station and every Border Patrol ammo locker. I can't guarantee it will be a hit, but it will be heard. Play it loud so that someday, maybe, we won't ever have to hear it again.

Note

This chapter was originally a lecture delivered at Zócalo Public Square on July 14, 2008.

TWENTY

The Line

I'm in line, in line, I'm in line so I can leave this country. It's something natural, an everyday thing. To my left, a family in a Nissan wagon, to my right, a gringo wearing sunglasses in a Mitsubishi sports car. Through my rearview mirror I see a young girl in a Volkswagen. In front of me, a Toyota. We are leaving the country and it's something natural, an everyday thing.

I would like to move forward, but this line of cars is in no hurry. Not even with this heat that squeezes us and forces us to sweat. The heat is like a fat relative, effusive and impertinent.

How much time has gone by? Someone, somewhere, has the guts to honk and the sound is short and timid, afraid of the consequences. The young girl, the gringo, the family, we look back and try to find him. All around us there are Ford cars, Plymouth vans, Chevrolet trucks.

The line doesn't move.

Some people get out of their cars and look toward the gate. The landscape evaporates. Who is holding us back? Far away, nothing answers our question, only the heat hugs and burns us.

Time leaves. It leaves us alone in the middle of this lagoon, castaways, forgotten. The family in the Nissan is the first to show symptoms of desperation. A girl cries inconsolably inside the Volkswagen. Her brothers and her parents try to calm her down. The gringo turns his radio on and demonstrates the power of his stereo. The young girl closes her window. Volkswagens don't usually have AC. She sweats and sweats and sweats.

All of a sudden, to all of the drivers' and passengers' surprise, the gringo's line moves a few centimeters. That wakes us up, gives us energy, fills us with hope. It seems like the gate is not a distant object, it seems like someone could stretch out his arm and touch it.

It doesn't move.

The Toyota in front of me is the second one to show signs of anguish. Tries to leave our line and invade the gringo's. It's a crazy act that is met by the anger of other cars. I step on the gas to move forward to a point that will prevent her from backing up. The gringo doesn't know mercy and blocks her access. The Toyota becomes an island. It's driven by a woman. It looks like she doesn't understand. Doesn't know what to do. She tries to move back; she can't. Our line goes its way. I'm not sure: I think she deserves it for trying to abandon the line. I'm not sure: I think her action was treasonous and deserves punishment. I'm not sure.

We move. The woman stays behind in the middle of the sea. She begs every driver and gets nothing in return.

Now, in front of me, there's a Ram pickup truck, tall, with big tires. Behind the wheel, a man with a Texan hat. Behind me, the young girl brushes her hair, fixes her makeup that starts to melt. Sweat covers my face. The gringo's music is insistent and stabbing.

I'm trying to remember why I'm here, leaving my country. Another far-away horn. I can see around me that some lines have started to move. The girl is still crying inconsolably. Her family ignores her.

In the beginning there were vendors. I'm trying to remember. They walked next to the cars, offering magazines and newspapers. In the beginning they were offering us serapes and statues made of plaster. In the beginning, that was in the beginning. Now we are alone. I see cars, cars, colored cars whose roofs shine under the sun.

The man with the hat gets out of his enormous pickup truck and walks toward the gate. What if the line starts moving forward and another car invades us? What is this man trying to do? Is he crazy? The young girl looks worried, scared. Her face asks for help, she asks me for help. I want to step on the gas, step on it all of the way, finish this long wait. I look out my window and I can't see the man. Where is he? All of a sudden I'm overwhelmed by a feeling of courage and trigger what becomes an extensive honking of horns, then another, then another. The sound mixes with the heat, mixes with other lines, the other cars, the other drivers. The man comes back to his pickup truck and I'm sure he hates me.

The girl stops crying when her mom hits her in the face.

See my hands? They are wet, they slip from the steering wheel. I don't hear the gringo's music anymore, lost, at the front, lost at the front. Before us, the man in the hat discovers that our line isn't a real one, that it doesn't go all the way to the gate. It's a branch trying to seduce other lines. The man begs to be let in, takes off his hat, asks nicely. The young girl does the same. I'm disappointed by their cowardice. I was expecting solidarity, them sinking with the ship, that we would continue until the end. Idiots. The young girl rehearses a splendid smile with every motorist. I'm disgusted by her attitude. The family gets lost in the front, in front, in front. The man with the Texan hat has gotten tired of being nice and moves forward without mercy. The pickup truck hits the bumper of the gringo's car. It's a mild but powerful bump. There's confusion. There's expectation. The young girl's smile finally captivates a driver. I see them, disgusting, through my rearview mirror. What are they promising with their looks? Idiots. The driver lets her in but he didn't notice I was watching them, measuring their steps, calculating. A precise movement of the steering wheel and I win the space from the young girl in the other line. She tries to follow me. Her admirer moves forward and doesn't let her through. There was only one available space. I'm sorry, idiot. Then other cars, other cars, others. She hates me, I know. Do you think I care? The gringo confronts the man with the hat. They throw words at each other that cut, rip, they grapple. I see them stay behind, they deserve it. In front of me, an old woman in a Mercedes. Behind me, a huge fat guy in a small Renault.

It doesn't move.

Who is at the threshold? I imagine a guard with a blue uniform, saying who is virtuous, who is malignant, who enters his country, who goes back. I can't see him yet, however, his close presence floods the environment while the heat, the heat.

Three lines to the left, some women fight, they pull their hair, they hit each other. People laugh, encourage them to continue with the fight. A kid barks from one woman's car. Barks like he's crazy, like a kid, like a dog, he barks. It's funny, very funny and my hands don't stop sweating. My hands become water. I can see how they melt, their lines vanish, the nails fall off. Then I understand that without lines on my hand I have no destiny, I don't have life or death, nothing to hold me, just this line, this desire to go to the border, cross, leave this nation, enter another.

Here's my passport.

From an unidentified place you can hear a scream, a scream that inspires neither fear nor compassion, a scream. The gate is close, I feel it close, my whole body feels it, my body melting, my body becoming liquid. Am I here? I get out of the car, I want to know with certainty where I am. Honks-honks. Where's the gate? Honks-honks. Where is the judge who will deliver my sentence. I want to know, I want to know now. Honk-honk-noise. A person comes close, I feel their hand on my arm. Fury-noise-disorder. Hit it is the only thing I can do, kick it, overpower it until it falls to the ground. The line moves. I go back to my car and unleash the fury of my engine so that the woman moves and lets me go. She does it in a hurry and limps when she feels that my car is almost on top of her.

I imagine the guard looking at my passport, examining it against the light, looking for any reason to not let me in, any insignificant reason to turn me back. I am here, my heart feels it and accelerates its rhythm. The longing, the longing. How much longer?

An unknown man approaches my car and lashes against the door with his fists. He tries to hold me back. Idiot. There is no way. He can't, he won't do it. A metal object close to my hand hits his face, it sinks in his face.

Four more left, three more left. I'm almost there. Where is my passport? My passport. I lost it? Through my rearview mirror, the fat guy in the Renault seems to be showing it to me with sarcasm. Look at him, look at him. He has it in his hand. I see him light a match, I see the fire, he laughs, uncontrollably, he laughs. Two left, one left. The heat is on top of us. A long silence covers us. A car, another car. The silence is eternal, excessive. I look around me, I look up, down. My passport is on the floor. Here is my passport.

The guard is blond and has green eyes.

Where are you going?—He asks me.

Wait
Look at the guard's eyes
Take a peek
There you will find a dawn without noise, and a house next to the sea
Do you see it?
If you get close, through a window you will see the inside of the house
Look closely
Can you see me?
I'm waking up
I get up from the bed, go to the kitchen and have a cup of coffee
I inhale the aroma
I look out the window and stare at the sea; the waves moving in / moving out
    on the sand

I'm going to take a walk on the beach, I will let the foamy water touch my
   feet
I'll smile
I will sit and the breeze will cover my body
—*What are you bringing from Mexico?*—The guard asks me—*Can you hear me?*
Far away I see a woman that loves me
Here she comes, on the beach
She's beautiful, isn't she?
She gets closer, sits down next to me
Look, look at her hands on my hair, her hands on my face
She says that everything will be OK: calm down, calm down, everything will
   be fine
I have no words
Only silence
A long and pleasant silence
We look at the waves for a while
Then we get up from the sand and go back home.

TITO ALEGRÍA received a doctorate in urban development and planning from the University of Southern California, Los Angeles; a master's degree in urban development from El Colegio de Mexico, Mexico City; and a degree in architecture from the Universidad Nacional de Ingeniería, Lima, Peru. Since 1987 he has been a professor of planning, urban economics, and urban sociology in the Department of Urban and Environmental Studies at El Colegio de la Frontera Norte, Tijuana, Mexico, and he is a member of the Mexican National System of Researchers (SNI). His research work covers several aspects of the cities, but focuses particularly on urban development in the Mexico-U.S. border, cross-border employment, urban land use, intraurban subcenters, socioresidential segregation, land regularization, and the urban integration of foreigners. On these topics he has published three books and diverse academic articles in nine countries; his most recent book is *Metrópolis Transfronteriza: Revisión de la hipótesis y evidencias de Tijuana, México y San Diego, Estados Unidos* (Transborder Metropolis). He has been a visiting scholar at the University of California in San Diego; Universidad Autónoma de Nuevo León, Mexico; and Iuav University, Venice, Italy. He has done consultant work for local governments in Mexico and for the UN Habitat program.

HUMBERTO FÉLIX BERUMEN is a Zacatecas-born writer residing in Tijuana since 1964. He is the author of *Tijuana la Horrible* (Colef-El Día 2004) and *De cierto modo: La literatura de Baja California* (UABC-Tijuana 1998) and the editor of a compilation titled *El cuento contemporáneo en Baja California* (UABC-Tijuana, Instituto de Cultura de Baja California, 1997). Félix Berumen is head librarian at El Colegio de la Frontera Norte and currently teaches at Universidad Autónoma de Baja California.

ROBERTO CASTILLO, AKA JOHNNY TECATE, or el róber de playas, writes whatever his heart demands, translates poetry he likes, loves dearly his women, drinks regional red wines and enjoys music and family reunions, hates violence and intellectual interpretations of life, and, sometimes, he likes to dance to sauvecito by malo.

IAIN CHAMBERS is Professor of Cultural and Postcolonial Studies at the Università degli Studi di Napoli, "l'Orientale," Italy. He has recently transmuted his interdisciplinary work on modernity and metropolitan cultures into a series of postcolonial analyses of the formation of the modern Mediterranean. His most recent publication is *Mediterranean Crossings: The Politics of an Interrupted Modernity* (2008). He is also editor with Lidia Curti of *The Post-colonial Question: Common Skies, Divided Horizons* (1996), and the editor of the volume *Esercizi di Potere. Gramsci, Said e il postcoloniale* (2006).

LUIS HUMBERTO CROSTHWAITE is a Mexican writer and editor, born in Tijuana in 1962. He is currently a columnist for *Milenio Diario*, in Mexico City, and *Enlace*, the Spanish-language section of the San Diego Union-Tribune, San Diego, California. He has published *Puro border: Dispatches, Snapshots and Graffiti from La Frontera*, *Idos de la mente*, *Estrella de la Calle Sexta*, *Lo que estará en mi corazón (Ña'a ta'ka ani'mai)*, *The Moon Will Forever Be a Distant Love*, *No quiero escribir no quiero*, *El gran PRETENDER*, *mujeres en traje de baño caminan solitarias por las calles de su llanto*, and *Marcela y el rey al fin juntos*. His editorial and literary work has received various prizes in Mexico. He won a grant from the National Fund for Culture and the Arts in the Young Creators category in 1990, and from the State Fund for Culture and the Arts in the category of Established Writers in 1995. He is now a member of the National System of Creators.

TEDDY CRUZ has been recognized internationally for his urban research on the Tijuana–San Diego border. After obtaining a master's degree in design studies from Harvard University, he received the first James Stirling Memorial Lecture on the City Prize from the Canadian Center of Architecture and the London School of Economics. Most recently, his work represented the United States in the 2008 Venice Architecture Biennial and was included in the *Small Scale, Big Change* exhibition at the Museum of Modern Art in New York. He is a professor of public culture in the Visual Arts Department at the University of California, San Diego, where he cofounded the Center for Urban Ecologies.

EJIVAL, writer and DJ, has been an active citizen of the cultural scene in Tijuana and a tireless promoter of it since the late 1980s. His independent work as a producer and his intense passion for music and frontier life have led him to write about these topics in various media around the world. His approach and work with leading artists from Tijuana, including Nortec Collective, Murcof, and Torolab, have placed him as a witness to the artistic dynamism of the border. This enthusiasm led him to establish the electronic music label Static Discos in 2002 alongside Fax and Murcof, two of the most visible electronic artists of the region. This effort has been recognized in the foreign media, such as the BBC, as one of the definitive independent labels in Mexico.

TAREK ELHAIK is an anthropologist, moving-image curator, and an assistant professor in the Cinema Department at San Francisco State University. He is interested in articulations between so-called national-peripheral anthropological traditions, the historical avant-gardes, and contemporary art worlds. Straddling the conceptual, sensorial, and disciplinary borders of the anthropology of art, film studies, visual studies, and art history, he is currently working on a manuscript titled *Curatorial Work: Ensouling, Assembling, Installing*. With the etymological registers of the term *curare* in mind, he explores linkages between the history of clinical concepts, theories of montage and assemblage, and the disorders of contemporary (post)secular visual cultures. He draws his reflections, specifically, from both his two-year ethnography of curatorial laboratories in Mexico City and previous work as a curator of Middle Eastern and North African experimental media.

GUILLERMO FADANELLI, born in Mexico City, is the founder and director of *MOHO* magazine. He is a video maker and has written for several magazines and newspapers in Mexico, Spain, Germany, and Chile. His books include El *día que la vea la voy a matar* (Grijalbo, 1992); *Terlenka* (Moho, 1995); *No hacemos nada malo* (pseudonym Peggy López, Moho, 1996); *Barracuda* (Moho, 1997); *La otra cara de Rock Hudson* (novel, Plaza y Janés, 1997); *Regimiento Lolita* (urban chronicles, Times, 1998); *Clarisa ya tiene un muerto* (novel, Mondadori, 2000); *Lodo* (novel, Debate, 2002); *La otra cara de Rock Hudson* (novel, Anagrama, 2004); *Compraré un rifle: Group of Tales* (Anagrama, 2004); and *Hotel DF* (Random House, Mondadori, 2010). He received the IMPAC prize for *La otra cara de Rock Hudson* for the best published novel in 1997. Guillermo received the Colima National Prize in Mexico in 2002. Some of his work has been translated into German, Italian, French, and other languages.

INGRID HERNÁNDEZ, born in 1974 in Tijuana, lives and works in Tijuana. For over ten years, she has been a teacher, researcher, and workshop instructor in educational institutes as well as for independent associations in Mexico and Bogotá. Hernández's work is widely exhibited in museums, art spaces, and galleries including Galerie Michel Rein, Paris, France; National Center for Contemporary Art, Moscow, Russia; La Raza Gallery, Los Angeles,

California; Museo de Arte Moderno, Mexico; and Museo de Arte Carrillo Gil, Mexico. Residencies include ISCP in New York and FONCA-MinCultura, in Bogotá, Colombia. In 2008 the Mexican National Council for Culture and Arts (CONACULTA) published *Irregular*, a monograph presenting Hernández's body of work.

JENNIFER INSLEY-PRUITT is an associate in the litigation department of Debevoise and Plimpton LLP. She holds MAS in Spanish and English from the University of Pennsylvania and a JD from New York University School of Law, where she was the editor in chief of the *Journal of International Law and Politics*. She is the author of several articles on contemporary border culture, including "Border Criminals, Border Crime: Hard-Boiled Fiction on the Mexican-American Frontier," *Confluencia: Revista Hispánica de Cultura y Literatura* 19 (2004).

KATHRYN KOPINAK holds a doctorate in sociology from York University and is currently professor of sociology in London, Canada, and a senior fellow at the Center for Comparative Immigration Studies at the University of California, San Diego. Her main areas of research are international migration, globalization, political sociology, urban sociology, sociology of the environment, gender and development, sociology of work and occupations, Mexico, and U.S.-Mexican borderland studies.

JESSE LERNER is a documentary film and video maker based in Los Angeles. He has curated film and photography exhibitions for the Robert Flaherty Seminar, the Guggenheim Museums in New York and Bilbao, and the National Palace of Fine Arts in Mexico City. His books include *F Is for Phony: Fake Documentary and Truth's Undoing* (with Alex Juhasz), *The Shock of Modernity*, and *The Maya of Modernism*.

RENÉ PERALTA, born in Tijuana in 1968, was educated at the New School of Architecture in San Diego and at the Architectural Association in London. He is currently director of the Master's of Science in Architecture with Emphasis in Landscape Urbanism program at Woodbury University, San Diego. His research work includes *Worldview Cities Tijuana*, a Web-based report on urbanism for the Architectural League of New York; and he is coauthor of the book *Here Is Tijuana!* (Black Dog Publishing, London, 2006).

RAFA SAAVEDRA is a writer and freelance journalist. His work has been published in magazines and culture supplements in Mexico. He has been editor and coeditor of several fanzines and independent publications. He is the author of the books *This Is Not an Exit: Postcards of Leisure and Hate* (The Spine, 1996); *Buten Smileys* (Yoremito, 1997); *Away from Noise* (Moho, 2003); and *Crossfader 2.0* (Nortestación, 2011). In 2010 he won the State Prize for Literature in Cultural Journalism awarded by the Institute of Culture of Baja California. Since 2001 he has been the producer and host of the *Selector de Frecuencias* radio show.

LUCÍA SANROMÁN is an independent curator and writer. She formerly served as associate curator at the Museum of Contemporary Art, San Diego, where she most recently curated *Jennifer Steinkamp: Madame Curie* (2011), *Viva la Revolución: A Dialogue with the Urban Landscape* (cocurated with Pedro Alonzo in 2010), and *Here Not There: San Diego Art Now* (2010). She also curated a large-scale site-specific installation by Los Angeles–based artist Ruben Ochoa (2010) as well as monographic exhibitions by James Drake, Yvonne Venegas, Brian Ulrich, Hector Zamora, Peter Simensky, Joshua Mosley, and Nina Katchadourian, among others. In 2008, Sanromán cocurated, with Ruth Estévez, the group exhibition *Proyecto cívico / Civic Project*, the inaugural exhibition for El Cubo, at Centro Cultural Tijuana. She has worked on *Proyecto Coyote* for Encuentro Medellín 2011, and a 2012 exhibition for the University of California, San Diego, on the intersection of science and art. Recent published articles include "Between a Rock and a Hard Place: From Radical Art to Radical Optimism" on the work of Andrea Bowers and Daniel Joseph Martinez.

MICHELLE TÉLLEZ is an assistant professor in the Women's Studies Program at Arizona State University. She is currently on leave and is a Chancellor's Postdoctoral Fellow in the Latina/o Studies Program at the University of Illinois, Urbana-Champaign. Her areas of interest include transnational feminism, globalization studies, social movements, and border studies.

SANTIAGO VAQUERA-VÁSQUEZ is an assistant professor in the Department of Spanish and Portuguese at the University of Iowa, specializing in Chicano/a and Mexican literatures and cultures. His current research focuses on cultural production from the U.S.-Mexico borderlands. Aside from his academic work, he is also a writer and has published stories in international literary journals as well as in major anthologies on contemporary literature in the Americas.

HERIBERTO YÉPEZ is the author of more than a dozen books of fiction, poetry, and nonfiction in Spanish, dealing with American and Mexican literature and culture in general. He teaches in the arts program at the Universidad

Autónoma de Baja California in Tijuana. He has received several national awards for his books in Spanish. His titles in English include *Here Is Tijuana!* (Black Dog, 2006) and *Wars. Threesomes. Drafts. And Mothers* (Factory School, 2008). He lives in Tijuana, where he's currently working on a project on post-Mexican poetics.

JOSH KUN is a professor in the Annenberg School for Communication and Journalism and the Department of American Studies and Ethnicity at USC, where he also directs the Popular Music Project at the Norman Lear Center. He is the author of *Audiotopia: Music, Race, and America* (2005) and coauthor of *And You Shall Know Us by the Trail of Our Vinyl: The Jewish Past as Told through the Records We Have Loved and Lost* (2008). He is the editor of *The Song Is Not the Same: Jews and American Popular Music* (2011) and coeditor of *Sound Clash: Listening to American Studies* (2012). He is a series editor for Refiguring American Music.

FIAMMA MONTEZEMOLO is an anthropologist and artist teaching in the Department of Art Practice at the University of California, Berkeley. She is the author of *La mia storia non la tua: La dinamica della costruzione dell'identità Chicana tra etero e autorappresentazioni* (2004) and *Senza volto: L'etnicità e il genere nel movimento Zapatista* (1999). She is the coauthor of *Here Is Tijuana!* (2006) with Heriberto Yépez and René Peralta.

Library of Congress Cataloging-in-Publication Data

Tijuana dreaming : life and art at the global border /
edited by Josh Kun and Fiamma Montezemolo ; with a foreword by Iain Chambers.
p. cm.
Includes bibliographical references and index.
ISBN 978-0-8223-5281-5 (cloth : alk. paper)
ISBN 978-0-8223-5290-7 (pbk. : alk. paper)
1. Arts and society—Mexico—Tijuana (Baja California).
2. Tijuana (Baja California, Mexico)—Intellectual life.
3. Tijuana (Baja California, Mexico)—Economic conditions.
4. Mexican-American Border Region—Emigration and immigration—
Social aspects.
I. Kun, Josh.
II. Montezemolo, Fiamma.
F1391.T36T455 2012
972'.2—dc23   2012011595